THE TRUSTED LEADER
BUILDING THE RELATIONSHIPS
THAT MAKE GOVERNMENT WORK

SECOND EDITION

Terry Newell
Leadership for a Responsible Society

Grant Reeher
Maxwell School of Citizenship and Public Affairs, Syracuse University

Peter Ronayne
Federal Executive Institute

Los Angeles | London | New Delhi
Singapore | Washington DC

CQ Press
2300 N Street, NW, Suite 800
Washington, DC 20037

Phone: 202-729-1900; toll-free, 1-866-4CQ-PRESS (1-866-427-7737)

Web: www.cqpress.com

Cover design: Paula Goldstein, Blue Bungalow Design
Composition: C&M Digitals (P) Ltd.

⊚ The paper used in this publication exceeds the requirements of the American National Standard for Information Sciences—Permanence of Paper for Printed Library Materials, ANSI Z39.48-1992.

Printed and bound in the United States of America

15   14   13   12   11   1   2   3   4   5

Library of Congress cataloging-in-publication data

The trusted leader : building the relationships that make government work / [edited by] Terry Newell, Grant Reeher, Peter Ronayne. — 2nd ed.
      p. cm.
   Includes bibliographical references and index.
      ISBN 978-1-60871-276-2 (pbk.: alk. paper) 1. Government executives—Professional relationships—United States. 2. Interagency coordination—United States. 3. Administrative agencies—United States—Management. 4. Executive departments—United States—Management. 5. Organizational effectiveness—United States. 6. Political leadership—United States. I. Newell, Terry. II. Reeher, Grant. III. Ronayne, Peter, IV. Title.

JK421.T88 2011
352.3—dc22

                                                                    2011012054

Contents

Contributors   vii

Preface   xv

Section I. Relationships: The missing link in government performance

Introduction: The context for leading democracy   1
Terry Newell, Grant Reeher, and Peter Ronayne

Chapter 1:   Values-based leadership for a democratic society   21
Terry Newell

Section II. Building relationships within government organizations

Chapter 2:   Self-awareness and leadership success   53
Beverly R. Fletcher and Alfred L. Cooke

Chapter 3:   Effective conversations: The genetic code of relationships   82
Len Kill Kelley and Debra Robinson

Chapter 4:   Coaching: A leadership imperative for the twenty-first century   112
Ron Redmon

Chapter 5:   Leading for team success   137
Gail Funke

Chapter 6:   Building high-performance organizations   170
John W. Pickering and Gerald S. Brokaw

Section III. Building relationships across organizational boundaries

Chapter 7:   The diversity opportunity   201
              Tom Gordon, Allison Linney, Kristina Energia Naranjo-
              Rivera, and Michael Rawlings

Chapter 8:   Collaborating across organizational boundaries   239
              Russ Linden

Chapter 9:   Career-political relationships: Going beyond a
              government of strangers   265
              Robert Maranto

Chapter 10:   Working with Congress: Building relationships
              across the constitutional divide   293
              Grace Cummings

Chapter 11:   Engineering experiences that build trust in
              government   318
              Lou Carbone

Chapter 12:   From e-government to e-governance: Harnessing
              technology to strengthen democracy   340
              George E. Mitchell and Grant Reeher

Chapter 13:   Global leadership: Strengthening a skeptical
              world's trust in America   371
              Peter Ronayne

Conclusion: What, then, is the job of the government leader?   395
              Dan Fenn Jr.

References   415

Index   433

Contributors

Gerald S. Brokaw (BS, psychology and chemistry) is a principal in the Commonwealth Centers for High-Performance Organizations, a management and organizational development consulting network working with executive teams in the public, nonprofit, and private sectors to improve organizational performance and manage large-scale organizational change. He was a managing associate in Coopers & Lybrand's Organizational Change Management Group and the executive director of the Management Technology Corporation. In these capacities he led major improvement initiatives for divisions of General Electric, General Motors, International Paper, Continental Telephone, Honeywell, and the Department of the Navy as well as a variety of other Fortune 100 and Public Sector organizations. Gerry can be reached at GBrokaw@highperformanceorg.com.

Lou Carbone (BA, political science) is the founder, president, and chief experience officer of Experience Engineering, a Minneapolis-based experience management firm. He has spent more than two decades in the development of experience value management theory and practice in a broad range of industries, including travel, health care, retail, technology, financial services, manufacturing, and education. He is the author of *Clued In: How to Keep Customers Coming Back Again and Again.*

Alfred L. Cooke (PhD, counseling) was most recently the director of the Federal Executive Institute's Center for Organizational Performance. He has been an organization development and human resources specialist for twenty years and focuses on leadership development, organizational consulting, strategic planning, human resources development, learning organizations, corporate university development, training, and program development. He was previously dean of graduate studies and later dean of education at Marygrove College in Detroit, Michigan, where he developed new master's degree programs in educational leadership and social justice. Prior to that, he was assistant director of human resources and chief learning officer at Detroit Edison Company. He has also held the position of director of the American University/National Training Laboratory

(AU/NTL) master's degree program in organization development and has taught at the university and secondary levels. He recently edited a reference book on human relations training and group facilitation, *Reading Book for Human Relations Training,* 8th edition for the NTL Institute for Applied Behavioral Science. Al can be reached at alynwood1@aol.com.

Grace Cummings (BA, international relations) is the founder of Working with Congress, a company that designs and conducts seminars to help people understand and effectively participate in the legislative process. Since 1995 she has pursued her passion for teaching as an adjunct faculty member at the Federal Executive Institute. She has also served as executive director of the Faith & Politics Institute, chief of staff to Reps. James O. McCrery of Louisiana and John H. Kingston of Georgia, and a consultant and staffer on a variety of political campaigns and public relations efforts. Grace may be reached at grace@workingwithcongress.com.

Dan Fenn Jr. (AM, government and international relations) is adjunct lecturer in executive programs at the Kennedy School of Government and former director of the John F. Kennedy Library in Boston, which is part of the National Archives and Records Administration. He was most recently special assistant to the chancellor, University of Massachusetts, Boston. His earlier government experience includes service as a staff assistant to President John F. Kennedy, commissioner and vice chairman of the U.S. Tariff Commission, and special assistant to Sen. Benjamin A. Smith of Massachusetts. He served two terms as a selectman in his hometown of Lexington, Massachusetts, and is the author or editor of numerous books and articles. Dan can be reached at fenndh@aol.com.

Beverly R. Fletcher (EdD, organization development) is a member of the senior faculty at the Federal Executive Institute. Her work focuses on organization development, transformation concepts and applications, and justice issues. Fletcher is the author of several books, one of which— *Organization Transformation Theorists and Practitioners: Profiles and Themes—* deals with how organizations are facing dynamic forces in the social environment that require them to either transform or cease to exist. Before coming to the institute, Fletcher served as an independent consultant to national and international organizations in leadership, strategic planning, conflict management, team development, executive coaching, and large-scale change. Her graduate-level teaching includes the human relations program at the University of Oklahoma, the management program at the University of Maryland University College, and the business administration and public administration programs at American University in Washington, D.C. Beverly can be reached at brfletcher@aol.com.

Gail Funke (PhD, economics) is an executive coach, organization consultant, and specialist in the development and implementation of leadership development programs. Her focus is helping organizations and individuals become maximally effective, particularly in the area of emerging leaders. She conducts teambuilding, delivery of short programs on preferences, decision-making, conflict management, and other sessions. She consults to individuals and organizations on outcome and performance-based issues, including resource allocation under constraint, strategic planning, and organizational change. Gail was senior faculty and dean for program and faculty development at the Federal Executive Institute for twelve years, where she also conducted the first government-wide international federal executive program, partnering with Johns Hopkins University and Tsinghua University in Beijing, China. In the policy analysis realm, she has worked internationally and in public sector agencies in over 40 states, examining the system and economic implications of policy decisions. Gail can be reached at gailfunke@gmail.com.

Thomas A. Gordon (PhD, developmental psychology) is a licensed psychologist, leadership coach, and organizational effectiveness consultant. He directs TAGA Consulting, a leadership solutions and change strategy firm that delivers systemic assessment, training, executive teaming, conflict resolution, process innovation, and diversity integration services nationwide. He helps clients to anticipate and respond decisively to complex, paradigm and process challenges, design high performance goals, develop the accountabilities to achieve them, and establish the systems to track and reinforce their progress. His faculty affiliations have included the University of Michigan, Temple University, Thomas Jefferson University Hospital, Antioch College, Goddard College, Medical University of South Carolina, Federal Executive Institute, and University of Pennsylvania. He embraces cross-cultural collaboration, travel, and exchange; speaks Spanish and Swahili; has coached youth basketball; plays tenor saxophone; and mentors rising social science and business professionals. Tom can be reached at tgordon@tagaconsulting.com.

Len Kill Kelley (MA, political science and public administration) is an adjunct faculty member of the Federal Executive Institute. He has held leadership, management, and policy development positions in the Federal government and was a member of the Senior Executive Service. His responsibilities have included assignments with the Department of the Navy, the Defense Logistics Agency, the U.S. General Accountability Office, the Department of Health and Human Services, the U.S. Office of Personnel Management, and the National Security Council. Len can be reached at seajayfarm@gmail.com.

Russ Linden (PhD, organizational leadership) is a management educator and author who specializes in organizational change and performance issues in the public and nonprofit sectors. He has his own consulting firm and is an adjunct faculty member at the Federal Executive Institute and the University of Virginia, where he teaches leadership classes to government executives. His research and teaching interests include collaborating across organizational boundaries, creating customer-focused organizations, and managing relationships in the workplace. His most recent book is *Working Across Boundaries*. Russ can be reached at russlinden@earthlink.net.

Allison Linney (MBA, general management) is the president of Allison Partners, an organizational development consultancy in Charlottesville, VA founded on the belief that people are at the core of an organization's success, and has served as an adjunct faculty member at the Federal Executive Institute. As a consultant and professional coach, she serves individual, corporate, non-profit and government clients seeking to integrate human performance theory and business strategy. Her expertise spans communication strategy and implementation, leadership development, organizational structure, group facilitation, training design, project management, change management, and process engineering. In addition, she has significant field experience in diversity and has developed strategies and conducted training programs to help foster diversity within teams and organizations. Allison can be reached at asl@allisonpartners.com.

Robert Maranto (PhD, political science) is the 21st Century Chair in Leadership at the Department of Education Reform at the University of Arkansas and previously taught at numerous institutions including Villanova University and the Federal Executive Institute. In concert with others he has written or edited ten scholarly books, including *Beyond a Government of*

Strangers. Bob recently coedited two books about groupthink, *The Politically Correct University*, which appeals to conservatives, and *Judging Bush* (2009), which appeals to liberals. Bob serves under April Gresham Maranto, Tony Maranto (b. 1999), and Maya Maranto (b. 2004). Bob can be reached at rmaranto@uark.edu.

George Mitchell (MA, economic and political science) is a PhD candidate in political science at the Maxwell School of Citizenship and Public Affairs at Syracuse University, where he is also a research assistant with the Transnational NGO Initiative in the Moynihan Institute of Global Affairs. He has been a research analyst in Dubai, UAE, a consultant in Washington, D.C., and a teaching associate, research assistant and Goekjain scholar in Syracuse, NY. His current research, based on data from the Transnational NGO Interview Project, combines exploratory statistics and computer-aided qualitative analysis to understand how transnational NGO leaders conceptualize their organizations' roles in world affairs. George may be reached at gemitche@maxwell.syr.edu.

Kristina Energia Naranjo-Rivera (MPA and MAIR) is a graduate research assistant at the Program for the Advancement of Research on Conflict and Collaboration (PARCC) at Syracuse University's Maxwell School of Citizenship and Public Affairs and S. I. Newhouse School of Public Communications. She has held leadership positions in the Coalition of Multicultural Public Affairs Students, Women's Caucus, and International Relations Students Association. In addition, she has worked with organizations including the Harlem Children's Zone, Inwood House, Human Rights Watch, Amnesty International, and the Foundation for Human Rights Initiative. She has authored and coauthored several articles; many draw on experiences studying or working in Brazil, Cuba, Mexico, Portugal, Spain, Uganda and the UK. Energia can be reached at klnaranj@syr.edu.

Terry Newell (EdD, educational administration) is president of his own firm, Leadership for a Responsible Society, and an adjunct faculty member at the Federal Executive Institute and the University of Virginia. He previously served as dean of faculty at the institute and in that capacity was responsible for its four-week, interagency Leadership for a Democratic Society program for senior federal government officials. In his twenty years at the U.S. Department of Education, he worked on educational innovation in elementary and secondary schools and higher education; he also served as director of training. His most recent work has focused on ethics and values-based leadership. Newell's publications have addressed values and ethics in leadership, organizational change, the future and its implications for leadership, and diversity and its effects on organizations and leaders. Terry can be reached at ResponsibleLeadr@aol.com.

John W. Pickering (PhD, American government and public administration) is a principal in the Commonwealth Centers for High-Performance Organizations, a management and organizational development consulting network working with executive teams in the public, nonprofit, and private sectors to improve organizational performance and manage large-scale organizational change. He served as deputy director and a senior faculty member of the Federal Executive Institute; was an executive with the U.S. Department of Housing and Urban Development; and taught political science and public administration at Lamar University, Florida State University, and Memphis State University. He is also an adjunct faculty member at the Federal Executive Institute and the University of Virginia's Weldon Cooper Center for Public Service. John may be reached at JPickering@ highperformanceorg.com.

Michael Rawlings (JD) is a senior faculty member at the Federal Executive Institute where he directs the institute's Center for Global Leadership and teaches conflict management and collaborative problem solving, American cultural studies, diversity and leadership, and international affairs. His federal career has included service at the Department of Homeland Security, the Interior Department, and Captain, U.S. Army JAG Corps at NATO headquarters. He has taught at the University of Richmond and the European Business School. A member of the Virginia Bar since 1986, he holds certifications at all levels of mediation practice with the Supreme Court of Virginia's Office of Dispute Resolution. He is a graduate of the University of Richmond, the U.S. Army Judge Advocate General school, and The College of William & Mary where he is on the Board of Directors of Swem Library and was formerly a Board member of the Gay and Lesbian Alumni association. He has published widely in the field of conflict competence, and as an Accredited Genealogist® he has assisted the U.S. Army and U.S. Air Force in locating next of kin and mitochondrial DNA matches for more than 500 KIAs from 20th century wars. Michael can be reached at RawlingsM@aol.com.

Ron Redmon (MA, public administration) has had a highly successful private practice as a leadership coach and consultant for the past fifteen years, following his career as a federal executive. His clients have included cabinet secretaries in the federal government and corporate chief executives. He serves on the adjunct faculty of the Federal Executive Institute, where he has taught coaching to approximately 1,000 government leaders. In addition, he has designed and delivered some of the institute's most well-regarded customized leadership development programs. Previously, he served for six years as the senior leadership coach for the Excellence in Government Fellows program of the Council for Excellence in Government in Washington, D.C. His training and development as a coach have been with most of the premier contributors to the field, supplemented by continuous learning in the fields of dialogue, general semantics, human dynamics, and systems theory. Ron can be reached at Redmon17@aol.com.

Grant Reeher (PhD, political science) is director of the Campbell Public Affairs Institute at Syracuse University's Maxwell School of Citizenship and Public Affairs, where he is also a professor of political science. He is on the adjunct faculty at the Federal Executive Institute. He is the author, coauthor, or coeditor of numerous books, including *First Person Political: Legislative Life and the Meaning of Public Service* and coauthor of *Click on Democracy: The Internet's Power to Change Political Apathy into Civic Action*. He has also published many editorial essays on various political topics, including pieces in the *New York Times, Chicago Tribune, Newsday, Philadelphia Inquirer, Ottawa Citizen,* and regularly in the *Syracuse Post-Standard*. In addition, he is host of a regional NPR public affairs show, "The Campbell Conversations," on the WRVO stations, and publisher of the public affairs blog, ReeherWindow. Grant can be reached at gdreeher@maxwell.syr.edu.

Debra Robinson (MA, applied management) has been a senior faculty member at the Federal Executive Institute. She was formerly the director of executive programs at FEI, directing the operations and design of the Leadership for a Democratic Society and short open enrollment programs. Debra came to FEI from the U.S. Department of Health and Human Services, Office of Inspector General where she served in a variety of senior leadership positions during her 25 year tenure. Debra specializes in individual and organizational assessments and frequently runs workshops for intact teams. She is currently in the process of earning her coaching certification from The Newfield Network. Debra graduated summa cum laude from Clemson University with a BA degree in English. She earned her masters from the University of Maryland. Debra can be reached at itsdebrarobins@yahoo.com.

Peter Ronayne, (PhD, international relations) is a senior faculty member at the Federal Executive Institute. He formerly directed FEI's flagship Leadership for a Democratic Society program, cofounded FEI's Center for Global Leadership, and launched FEI's Leadership Horizons Series for the Senior Executive Service. He joined FEI after studying, teaching, and researching at the University of Virginia. Pete is a leading voice in the public sector on generational and demographic issues and their impact on leadership and organizations. He also writes, researches, and speaks widely on issues of global leadership, neuroscience and leadership, and the future of public service and governance. A former presidential management fellow, Pete is an adjunct professor at the University of Virginia where he teaches undergraduate courses in world politics, diplomatic history, and leadership. Pete can be reached at pronayne@gmail.com.

Preface

We know from our personal lives that relationships are central to our well-being. This fact is no less true in government. Viewed from the outside, government is a complex set of structures, regulations, and programs. On the inside, it takes good relationships fostered by the people working there for government to function well. And even though good relationships alone cannot restore the trust in government that has been lost in recent years, they are essential to its revival. Strengthening those relationships is the subject of this book.

Because this volume is about relationships, we seek to have a productive one with you, the reader, and we employ several devices toward this end. First, the chapters are designed to stand on their own, so you may read them in any order you wish. Second, a "headnote" has been added to each chapter to assist you in understanding its focus and contents. Third, the chapters conclude with sections providing useful tips for leadership success and resources for further learning. Fourth, because the best relationships are reciprocal, we invite you to contact us—using our e-mail addresses below—with your own stories about the importance of building relationships in government, the tips and techniques you have learned from your own practice, and ideas about what additional questions we should address in this book in the future. Every book on this topic is a single snapshot of best thinking and practice. With your help (and some luck in sales) we can make future editions even better through our relationship with you.

Max De Pree, former CEO of Herman Miller, a popular office furniture company also noted for its dedication to ecodesign and building a high-commitment work culture, once said, "The first responsibility of a leader is to define reality. The last is to say thank you. In between the two, the leader must become a servant and a debtor." To the extent we have defined reality in this book, we owe thanks and are indebted to many who made it possible. This book would not exist without the contributions of the chapter authors, and so we thank them first. Second, we thank the thousands of public leaders, at all levels of government, who not only have taught our authors the lessons contained in these pages but also serve as successful daily reminders of how, at its best, government works for the

American people. These dedicated civil servants have earned our trust, our respect, and our great admiration.

We thank the faculty and staff of the U.S. Office of Personnel Management's Federal Executive Institute (FEI), whose behavior toward each other and the career government leaders they educate has, for forty-two years, built trust and relationships and supplied the inspiration for this book.

Charisse Kiino at CQ Press has been a splendid editor, supportive and directive in turn and in combination, as the situation demanded. The quality of the book was greatly enhanced by the excellent editorial work of Belinda Josey, Nancy Loh, and Jon Preimesberger, as well as by the marketing assistance of Chris O'Brien. Laura Webb's expert proofreading and Scott Smiley's comprehensive indexing further strengthened the quality of this work. We also thank Matthew Guardino for helping to proofread the manuscript. We thank the two reviewers of our proposal for this second edition, Kurt Fenske, Northern Arizona University-Yuma Branch Campus and Margaret Hopkins, University of Toledo. We thank the Campbell Institute for access to its polling data on American views of federal civil servants.

Finally, each of us thanks the other two for their dedication and their bonhomie, and each of us also has a special thank you to offer:

To Carol, my teacher and role model on how to build relationships and trust—and who has shown me the power of both to foster success in life and work;

To the memory of David Reeher, modeler of quiet and trusted leadership;

To Vincent and Claire Ronayne, who lived and taught a lifetime's worth of trust and service.

Terry Newell
ResponsibleLeadr@aol.com

Grant Reeher
gdreeher@maxwell.syr.edu

Peter Ronayne
pronayne@gmail.com

*I*ntroduction

The context for leading democracy

TERRY NEWELL, PRESIDENT, LEADERSHIP FOR A RESPONSIBLE SOCIETY
GRANT REEHER, DIRECTOR, CAMPBELL PUBLIC AFFAIRS INSTITUTE, MAXWELL
SCHOOL OF CITIZENSHIP AND PUBLIC AFFAIRS, SYRACUSE UNIVERSITY
PETER RONAYNE, SENIOR FACULTY, FEDERAL EXECUTIVE INSTITUTE*

The success of government depends on competence and trust. American government has grown dramatically in the past seventy-five years, and evidence indicates that it has accomplished much. Yet despite its achievements, many Americans distrust government, and that distrust threatens the nation's future success and the social capital that underlies its democratic institutions. Efforts to build trust, especially in the career, institutional leadership of government, are essential. Most strategies to improve government, however, have focused on macro-level changes, such as strategic planning, organizational structure, systems, oversight, and measurement. These changes work only if attention is paid to micro-level changes: building personal relationships. This chapter outlines the development, current status, and core issues surrounding trust in government, and it also outlines the plan of the book.

DURING THE PAST DECADE, the United States has been faced with at least four crises of historic and widespread impact. While the terrorist attack of September 11, 2001, Hurricane Katrina's direct hit on New Orleans in 2005, the financial collapse of 2008, and the massive Gulf oil spill of 2010 were not caused by government, the American public looked to government at all levels to respond with speed, effectiveness, and compassion. And the public has not always liked the response it saw.

Given the tax dollars invested in national defense, homeland security, regulatory mechanisms aimed at preventing irresponsible risk, and disaster

---

*The views expressed here are the author's and do not necessarily reflect those of the Federal Executive Institute or the U.S. Office of Personnel Management.

response, angry Americans have questioned whether they can trust the government. In each of these cases, mechanisms were in place that could have ameliorated what took place (or in some cases even prevented it), yet government did not always perform to expectations. It did not "connect the dots" to prevent 9/11; it did not collaborate across agencies and levels of government in the aftermath of Katrina; and it did not carry out its regulatory enforcement in a coordinated and effective way on Wall Street or on off-shore oil drilling rigs.

We contend in this book that poor working relationships within and across government agencies, and in their interactions with other levels of government, the legislature, a range of private and not-for-profit groups, and the public itself, are a core problem threatening effective government. Poor relationships lead to poor performance, and both breed distrust.

By way of contrast, government's response to the 2009 swine flu pandemic has generally been seen as much better (though, admittedly, the public and the press usually have less to say when government gets it right). Pandemic plans were in place; resources were targeted to emerging needs; and coordination and communication across agencies and among federal, state, and local levels went relatively smoothly. Government can succeed. It can build trust. Effective relationships make a major difference—but they take work. The work of relationship building is the task of this book.

The growth and performance of government

Counterterrorism, disaster response, mechanisms for the protection of financial markets and the assets of ordinary citizens, and public health represent just a few of the areas in which government action has grown dramatically in the past century. Since 1953 the number of cabinet-level federal agencies has doubled. In constant dollars, per capita federal government spending increased from $1,334 to $12,044 between 1950 and 2010, and state and local government combined per capita spending grew from $1,660 to $10,733 during the same period.[1] The size of the federal government (2.7 million civil servants) has not changed significantly since the mid-1950s, but there has been considerable growth in the federal government's contractor workforce, and between 1946 and 2009, state and local government employment grew from 3.3 million to 19.7 million, far outpacing the rate of growth in population as a whole.

The eight cabinet agencies created at the federal level since the end of World War II testify to the fact that citizens expect more from government.

In areas as diverse as space exploration, disease control and prevention, social services, environmental protection, transportation, and homeland security, citizens' expectations of the federal government far exceed those in earlier times and would no doubt shock the architects of our constitutional structure. This growth has occurred under Democrats and Republicans alike. The reason? The issues that public leaders now face are more numerous, more complex, more international in scope, and they require more systemic solutions.

In the midst of rising demand and public investment, how has government performed? Any tendered response is open to debate, but a careful study led by Derek Bok of Harvard University, using seventy-two indicators in various policy fields (such as economic prosperity, quality of life, opportunities, personal security, and values) suggests that government made considerable progress from the 1960s to the 1990s. The improvement was not uniform, but the outcome was far better than the prevailing image of government implies.[2] Nevertheless, an American Progress survey in 2010 found that only 33 percent of Americans had a lot or some "confidence in the federal government to solve problems," the lowest figure since that poll question was asked beginning in 1994.[3] Similarly, a Pew Research Center poll in early 2010 found that 54 percent of the public holds a negative view of federal agencies and departments, compared to only 31 percent with a positive view. Fully 74 percent said that the federal government does "only fair" or a "poor" job of running programs. Yet some federal agencies were rated higher than others. Of fifteen separate federal agencies asked about in the poll, six received a combined job rating of "excellent/good" above 50 percent, with the military the highest at 80 percent, followed by the U.S. Postal Service (70 percent), National Aeronautics and Space Administration (NASA), Centers for Disease Control (CDC), Defense Department, and Federal Bureau of Investigation (FBI). In contrast, only 33 percent gave the Department of Education an "excellent/good" rating, the lowest in the poll.[4]

Trust in politics and the political leaders of government

While the quality of government performance may be mixed, public perceptions about government's trustworthiness are not—and they are not good. As Figure I.1 shows, the percentage of Americans who "trust the government in Washington to do what is right" most of the time or just about always declined from a high of 76 percent in 1964 to a low of 21 percent in

1994. It rebounded slightly after 9/11 but has now dropped back to the point where fewer than one of four Americans (22 percent) trust the government in Washington. That distrust is increasingly turning into anger. Between 1997 and 2010, the percentage of Americans who say they are "angry" with the federal government rose from 12 to 21 percent.[5]

According to an October 2010 Gallup poll, 59 percent of Americans believe the federal government has "too much power," and 46 percent think it poses "an immediate threat to the rights and freedoms of ordinary citizens"—both percentages representing the highest reported in the period 2003–2010. Only 26 percent have a positive view of the federal government, a percentage equal to the standing of the banking industry and only above the oil and gas industry.[6]

On average, according to a 2010 *Washington Post*–ABC News poll, the public estimates that 53 cents of every tax dollar is wasted.[7] The proportion reporting they do not have a "say in what government does" increased from 28 percent in 1958 to 43 percent in 2004. The proportion reporting that "government is run for the benefit of all" declined from 64 percent in 1964 to 40 percent in 2004.[8] These are all dismal statistics.

Lack of trust is especially pronounced for elected leaders. When asked in 2006, "Would you generally trust each of the following types of people to tell the truth, or not?" just 48 percent trusted the president, and a mere 35 percent trusted unidentified members of Congress.[9] In 2009 a Gallup poll found that only 5 percent of respondents said they had a "great deal" of trust in the "men and women in political life in this country who either hold or are running for public office."[10]

The supposed causes of declining trust in government are a source of both consternation and disagreement.[11] Some link the downward trend in trust to dissatisfaction with the president and Congress.[12] Others suggest that the root of the problem is dissatisfaction with politicians, political parties, and government policies more generally.[13] Some have noted that trust in government tends to rise and fall with consumer sentiment and the state of the economy.[14] Still others say that skepticism about government was sown in Americans beginning with the colonial era and that the fertile ground of our innate suspicion has been watered not only by contemporary social values questioning all authority but also by the conviction that the political process lacks fairness and integrity.[15] On the other hand, Americans' unrealistically high expectations for government also likely play a role. The growing tendency of the media to paint a negative picture of government no doubt contributes.[16] In addition, sharper partisanship,

Figure I.1   Trust in the federal government

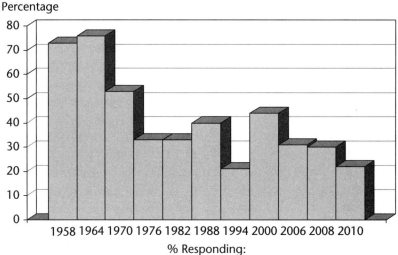

Percentage

% Responding:
"Most of the time/just about always"

Source: American National Election Studies, the Council for Excellence in Government, and the Pew Center.

denunciation of "big government" by Tea Party–backed candidates, and more negative political advertising by all parties have added to the problem.[17] And the list of probable suspects goes on.

Trust in the institutions and career leaders of government

Much of the distrust in national polls may be linked to short-term elected leaders, their actions, and our views about them. Career civil servants, however, are the enduring public face of government and comprise its inner institutional structure. Career civil servants carry a special responsibility for fostering trust. On them depends not only the delivery of more than $3.7 trillion in federal programs and services,[18] but also the ability of citizens to trust the specific instruments of government even if they do not trust political leaders and political institutions. Distrust of elected leaders may deplete the political capital with which they can govern, but distrust of career leaders can erode the broader social capital on which rests the long-term confidence in American democracy.

Perceptions of the trustworthiness of civil servants appear to be mixed but declining. In a 2006 Harris poll, only 62 percent of Americans reported that they would trust civil servants to tell the truth—higher than the figures for political leaders, but down from the 70 percent reporting trust in 1998.[19] A Hart poll for the Council for Excellence in Government in 2006 found that only 44 percent of Americans reported having "quite a lot" or "a great deal of confidence" in civil servants (17 percent reported "very little confidence").[20]

Recent data suggest that the 2007–2009 financial collapse and recession, anger at the federal government for its response to the crisis, a vocal conservative backlash against the policies of the Obama administration, and growing concerns about the national debt, have worsened the view about federal workers, even if they had little to do with what caused these events.[21] In a *Washington Post* poll conducted in late September 2010 (at the height of the congressional midterm election campaigns), 36 percent responded that "the quality of employees in the federal government is generally lower than the quality of employees who work in the private sector." Only 15 percent felt the quality of federal workers was higher. In the same poll, 49 percent said federal employees "work less hard than employees with similar jobs in private business."[22] A ForeSee Results/Nextgov study of government transparency, conducted in October 2010, asked respondents to rate federal agencies and departments on four measures that play a role in trust, and the scores were quite low. On a scale where 100 is the highest, citizens rated accountability at 35, competence at 39, goodwill at 33, and integrity at 33. Not surprisingly, trust was rated at 32.[23]

On the other hand, some studies have found that although Americans dislike and distrust government as a whole, they respond more positively when asked about their specific interactions with government officials in a particular program or agency—in the same fashion that citizens dislike Congress as an institution, but like their own representative.[24] Even in the above-referenced *Washington Post* poll, three of four who have actually interacted with a federal agency report that the experience was positive. Similarly, in the above-referenced government transparency study, when respondents actually interacted with agency websites, they gave them a transparency rating that averaged 75.8 and a trust score of 76, compared to their more generic response to agencies overall.

Data from the American Customer Satisfaction Index, for example, suggest that government programs are on the whole viewed by their "customers" as performing nearly as well as firms in the private sector, indeed in some cases much better—though admittedly some agency services are rated lower.[25]

Findings from two polls taken in recent years through Syracuse University's Alan K. Campbell Public Affairs Institute and the Maxwell School of Citizenship show this same pattern of mixed but declining results for trust in civil servants overall. On the eve of the 2006 mid-term elections, the 2006 Maxwell Poll on Civic Engagement and Inequality found that only 35 percent of respondents agreed with the statement that "you can generally trust public officials to try to do the right thing." And 52 percent agreed that "people like me don't have much say about what government does."[26]

But when asked more specifically about federal employees, 56 percent agreed with the statement that "the people working for the federal government are competent," and 65 percent said that in their interactions with federal government workers, they had "been treated with respect." Yet, by 2010, even these "positive" findings about federal civil servants had turned negative. A Campbell Institute poll repeated the same questions, and found that only 21 percent now agreed that "the people working for the federal government are competent," and only 37 percent agreed that in their interactions with federal workers, they had "been treated with respect."[27] In this same study, only 22 percent said that they could "trust federal civil servants to do what's right" most of the time.

Regardless of the exact degree of trust in the civil service and career civil service leaders, that trust is clearly under stress. General dissatisfaction with American institutions, public and private, seems to be working its way down past the political level and into the civil service. As value conflicts in society intensify, they are brought into the administration of government programs. Career leaders in government receive broadly worded and sometimes contradictory legislative mandates as lawmakers pass on or gloss over unresolved issues. Civil servants confront polarized citizens and groups as they seek to implement the (sometimes unclear) will of Congress and the administration. Perceived—and in some cases real—failure of government agencies to accomplish highly public missions or to address persistent problems is almost inevitable. Ultimately, trust in career government leaders and institutions suffers.

The danger to democracy

> A government ill executed, whatever it may be in theory, must be, in practice, a bad government.
>
> —*Alexander Hamilton*, Federalist Paper, *No. 70*

If citizens perceive that government is "ill executed," even if some of the reasons are unavoidable, democratic governance is called into question. If, for example, a deadly pandemic virus arrives, a public that does not trust government will ignore its pleas for quarantine and the targeted distribution of flu vaccines to health care workers and those most at risk. This result could quickly lead to panic and the failure of government in a self-fulfilling prophecy.

Lack of trust in the civil service operates at many levels. It creates skepticism among constituency groups and members of Congress, threatening the level of financial resources and political capital civil servants enjoy. Distrust can also decrease the voluntary compliance with laws and regulations, on which so many government programs depend. All this leads to greater congressional oversight and micromanagement of agency operations. As Figure I.2 illustrates, these consequences, in addition to the lower morale sure to infect government employees beset by mostly negative messages, can form a spiral of worsening distrust and performance.

As we have argued, distrust is not just a problem within the public. It also takes a toll among agencies, many of which must collaborate with each other to achieve public purposes. Consider the need for the Departments of Defense, Justice, and State and the U.S. Agency for International Development to work together to fix or prevent the failure of states abroad because such breakdowns pose a growing risk to the United States. If career leaders in and across these agencies and their subcomponent organizations cannot build effective relationships based on mutual trust and relationships that

Figure I.2 When trust declines

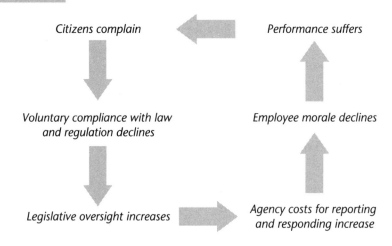

Citizens complain

Performance suffers

Voluntary compliance with law and regulation declines

Employee morale declines

Legislative oversight increases

Agency costs for reporting and responding increase

enable coordinated planning, training, and execution, their joint mission will prove unworkable.

Lack of trust among career civil servants also has an impact inside agencies. Distrust across functional boundaries within agencies, for example, restricts the free flow of information and personnel essential to solving complex problems requiring collaboration across organizational structures. The resulting poor performance and negative publicity can also make recruitment and retention of talented civil servants more difficult, even while many government employees are approaching retirement age and need to be replaced.

These effects also come at a time when trust in government by government employees themselves is under threat. Although government employees generally like their jobs, the trust they report in their immediate leadership chain of command receives mixed reviews, as Table I.1 shows. When employees lack trust in their superiors, organizations lose the creativity and commitment essential to high performance.

This problem is also reflected in the extent to which employees feel engaged in the work of their agencies. A 2008 study by the Merit Systems Protection Board found that only 35 percent of employees are actively engaged at work, where "engagement" includes such measures as feeling that they are respected, that their work is meaningful, that it makes good use of their skills and abilities, and that their opinions count. In contrast, 47 percent of federal workers are only "somewhat engaged" and 18 percent are "not engaged." When the "most engaged" agencies are compared with

Table I.1 **Trust within the federal government**

Question	*%*
"I have trust and confidence in my supervisor."	*Strongly agree: 31.9%* *Agree: 34.6%*
"I have a high level of respect for my organization's senior leaders."	*Strongly agree: 20.3%* *Agree: 35.4%*
"My organization's leaders maintain high standards of honesty and integrity."	*Strongly agree: 16.4%* *Agree: 39.3%*
"How satisfied are you with the policies and practices of your senior leaders?"	*Very satisfied: 10.6%* *Satisfied: 34.4%*
"Promotions in my work unit are based on merit."	*Strongly agree: 8.0%* *Agree: 27.4%*

Source: Federal Employee Viewpoint Survey, U.S. Office of Personnel Management, 2010.

the "least engaged" agencies, the former have higher performance scores on cross-government ratings, and their workers take considerably less sick leave, have fewer accidents, and file fewer discrimination complaints.[28]

The central role of career leadership in building institutional trust

> Nowhere in the Constitution of the United States, or the Declaration of Independence, or the Bill of Rights, or the Emancipation Proclamation, or the Old Testament, or the New Testament, do you find the words "economy" or "efficiency." Not that these words are unimportant. But you discover other words like honesty, integrity, fairness, liberty, justice, patriotism, compassion, love—and many others which describe what human beings ought to be. These are the same words which describe what a government of human beings ought to be.
>
> —*Jimmy Carter,* Why Not the Best? *1976*

As a candidate for president, Jimmy Carter noted that economy and efficiency are necessary but insufficient to build effective government. Honesty, integrity, compassion, love, and justice are important too—for these qualities build the relationships and trust that make economy and efficiency possible.

Because of their short tenure and public exposure, political leaders find it difficult to build trust. But career civil servants can have more success. And while generating political trust is largely outside the control of career civil servants, building institutional trust is not.

By fostering institutional trust, career civil service leaders can enhance both performance and the perceptions of their agencies. As Steven Van de Walle and Geert Bouckaert suggest in Figure I.3, public perceptions of agencies have an indirect but significant effect on public perceptions of government as a whole.[29] Although what happens inside and across agencies is not solely responsible for what the public thinks of government, it does make a difference.

For career civil servants, the core question is this: How can they strengthen relationships and instill trust inside and outside their organizations so as to foster agency success and positive public perceptions? Agencies that can do this reap the benefits of improved trust in their agencies,

Figure I.3 Multiple influences on trust in government

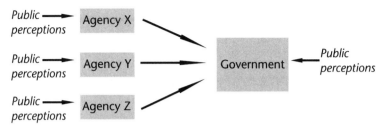

Source: Steven Van de Walle and Geert Bouckaert (2003), "Public Service Performance and Trust in Government," *International Journal of Public Administration,* 26, 8/9 (2003): 891–913 at www.informaworld.com.

even if overall trust in "the government" does not rise. The American Customer Satisfaction Index has documented this, as shown in Figure I.4. As citizen satisfaction (measured by a group of indices including, among others, the perceived quality and the courtesy and professionalism of government service delivery) rises, so does citizen trust in the agency, although overall trust in government seems little affected.

This book addresses the central role played by career civil service leaders in building trust in themselves and their organizations. Our thesis is that trust matters and that it can be created. Our focus is on the development of trust through building effective relationships among career civil service leaders, their employees, people in other organizations in the executive branch, the legislature, and the citizenry. We devote considerable attention to the federal government, but the arguments and insights apply equally at the state and local level. Relationships and the trust they engender or thwart were as important when Alexander Hamilton speculated about bureaucracy as they were 200 years later when Jimmy Carter reminded us that caring about those you serve is an essential measure of success, and they are equally important in this century of even greater complexity and the ever wider reach of government.

This argument rests on looking inside the "black box" of each of the agencies in Figure I.3. Figure I.5 suggests that, inside that box, agency performance and therefore public perceptions rest on both macro-level and micro-level factors.

Most efforts to improve government have focused on macro-level changes. Efforts as diverse as the Government Performance and Results Act (GPRA) (strategy and measures); the creation of chief financial officers,

Figure I.4 Strong link between satisfaction and trust

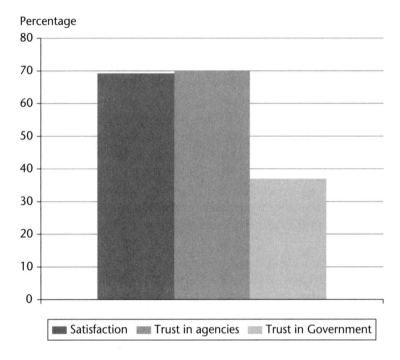

Percentage

Source: American Customer Satisfaction Index, 2007 Data.

chief information officers, and chief human capital officers (systems); performance management and pay banding (measures and systems); outsourcing (systems); the Office of Management and Budget's Program Assessment and Rating Tool (PART) (measures); and frequent reorganizations (structure) all have had a common goal: to alter the performance of agencies so as to meet public purposes and foster positive public perceptions.

The argument we make is that comparable emphasis on micro-level change efforts to build shared values, effective relationships, and therefore enhanced trust, has been lacking. The Obama administration's Open Government Directive to enhance transparency, participation, and collaboration, as well as its effort to build labor-management councils, is a case in point. While both of these macro-level system and process changes would no doubt enhance trust in government if successful, they are not likely to succeed without a complementary effort aimed at building trust though shared values and effective relationships. At best, the designers of

Figure I.5 Macro- and micro-level change levers in organizations

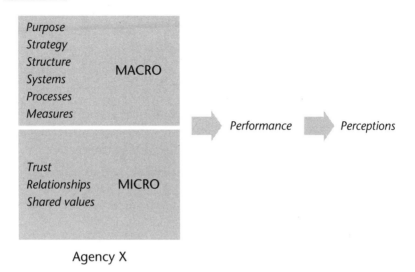

Agency X

macro-level changes have taken for granted the presence of shared values, sound relationships, and trust—they are assumed to exist. At worst, they have been ignored or viewed as the "touchy-feely" side of governing that requires neither attention nor action.

Trust and relationships: The critical connection

Building shared values, effective relationships, and trust is the "hard stuff" and can neither be assumed nor ignored in fostering high performance in government.

For the purposes of this book, we define trust as a foundational confidence among citizens, including government workers themselves, that government agencies and the people who work in them will act in a reasonably consistent way to promote their shared values and interests and respond to their long-term needs and wants. Like trust in other realms, trust in government is ultimately anchored in perceptions of integrity, inclusion, reciprocity, fairness, competence, and reliability—and it both depends on and fosters excellent working relationships.

In *The Trusted Leader*, we have chosen to focus on the leadership of career civil servants because we believe they have powerful leverage over the culture within their organizations. Using that power effectively may not guarantee institutions that earn the trust of the American people, but using that power ineffectively surely guarantees that such trust is lost.

Our definition of trust leads to several closely connected observations that are essential to the argument of this book.

First, as Figure I.5 and Box I.1 suggests, trust is foundational. It underlies and affects all work done within and across agencies. Without it, little of value can be accomplished.

Second, trust proceeds from the inside out. Interpersonal trust is essential to building team and organizational trust, which is essential to building trust with other agencies and among members of the public.

Third, lack of trust at any point in this chain has negative effects downstream. Lack of trust among intelligence agencies in sharing data, for example, can have a deadly effect on a military operation, even if trust and performance among military personnel is exceptional.

Fourth, trust is anchored in a relationship. We cannot speak of trust unless we speak at some level of trusting *someone*. Therefore, to build trust, we must build relationships.

We do not mean to belittle the importance of macro-level mechanisms for enhancing individual and organizational performance, nor do we mean to diminish the importance of performance itself in building trust. Rather, we argue that effective relationships and trust, anchored in shared values, make other government improvement efforts possible. Poor relationships and distrust between Congress and the agencies, for example, lead the latter to offer easy GPRA targets that they are sure will be met, or to disguise data when real results are not as promised. Poor relationships and distrust undermine efforts at personnel reform, as unions and management seek ways to protect themselves from the damage each assumes the other intends

---

Box I.1 Trust within the federal government

Trust is a foundational confidence among citizens, including government workers themselves, that both government agencies and the people who work in them will act in a reasonably consistent way to promote their shared values and interests and respond to their long-term needs and wants. Like trust in other realms, trust in government is ultimately anchored in perceptions of integrity, inclusion, reciprocity, fairness, competence, and reliability—and it both depends upon and fosters excellent working relationships.

to inflict. Similarly, the power of information technology to enhance government productivity and citizen involvement in government exists only in theory until those who are to use such technology trust each other enough to communicate with honest information—or to communicate at all.

Trust, relationships, and social capital

The importance of effective relationships seems intuitive, but talk of relationships often produces criticism that this "soft stuff" is neither useful nor learnable. The research record does not support such criticism.

The terminology used to talk about trusting relationships in the research literature often focuses on the term *social capital*.[30] High-quality relationships in which trust and positive regard are maximized represent positive social capital. Social capital, it turns out, is critical to organizational success. In a wide-ranging survey of the research and theory of social capital formation in organizations, Janine Nahapiet and Sumantra Ghoshal concluded: "Social capital facilitates the development of intellectual capital by affecting the conditions necessary for exchange and combination to occur. . . . One of the important barriers to the transfer of best practice within organizations is the existence of arduous relations between the source and recipient. Where relationships are high in trust, people are more willing to engage in social exchange in general, and cooperative interaction in particular."[31]

In another survey of the research, Gareth Jones and Jennifer George concluded that "shared values and expressions of positive affect typically result in individuals wanting to cooperate and to do whatever they can for the common good; hence, they will define their roles broadly to include whatever acts they are capable of performing that contribute to common goals and raise performance and competitive advantage."[32] And, speaking even more directly to the link between social capital and organizational success, Mark Bolino, William Turnley, and James Bloodgood argue: "Individuals in a group are more comfortable with uncertainty and less resistant to change when they like one another . . . workgroups in which members like one another may be more flexible, better able to adapt to a changing environment, and higher performing."[33]

Evidence from research on emotional and social intelligence demonstrates that building effective relationships that enhance trust and thereby create social capital requires a set of skills that can be learned. Daniel Goleman and the Consortium for Research on Emotional Intelligence place these skills (Box I.2) into four clusters.[34] These clusters and their associated skills

Box I.2 Emotional intelligence skills

Self-awareness	Emotional self-awareness	
	Accurate self-assessment	
	Self-confidence	
Self-management	Emotional self-control	Achievement
	Transparency	Initiative
	Adaptability	Optimism
Social awareness	Empathy	
	Organizational awareness	
	Service orientation	
Relationship management	Development of others	Influence
	Inspirational leadership	Conflict management
	Change catalyst	Teamwork and collaboration

Source: Adapted from *Emotional Competence Inventory (ECI) Technical Manual,* June 2006, 3–4; www.eiconsortium.org/research/ECI_2.0_Technical_Manual_v2.pdf.

have distinct and important interconnections. Self-awareness is necessary for self-management, and social awareness skills are critical for managing relationships. Further, if you cannot manage yourself, it is unlikely you will be good at managing relationships. Goleman's work also demonstrates that emotionally intelligent leaders—in our terms, leaders who can build relationships and trust—are more successful at creating organizational climates that foster the flexibility essential to innovation, commitment to a common purpose, a sense of responsibility, clarity around mission and values, high standards of performance, and the linking of performance to rewards.[35]

The plan for the book

> Trust is a social good to be protected just as much as the air we breathe or the water we drink. When it is damaged, the community as a whole suffers; and, when it is destroyed, societies falter and collapse. . . . Trust and integrity are precious resources, easily squandered, hard to regain.
>
> —*Sissela Bok,* Lying: Moral Choice in Public and Private Life, *1978*

Governing is a social act, and effective governance therefore requires social competence. Career leaders in government who can build relationships that produce trust have met a necessary, if not sufficient, condition for leading democracy. Philosopher Sissela Bok is correct to argue that trust once lost is hard to regain. This book is aimed at showing government leaders how to build effective relationships that foster the "social good" she so rightly prizes.

This is not a book of theory, although theory underlies every chapter. It is instead a book of practice. We emphasize lessons learned on the front lines of leading government organizations and the perspectives, skills, and tools that the most effective leaders have mastered.

To set the overall context for the book, Chapter 1 completes Section I with a focus on values in the context of government leadership. Terry Newell addresses the importance of being a values-based leader in building sound relationships and trust.

Section II looks at how government leaders must act to build effective relationships and trust *within* their organizations. In Chapter 2, Beverly Fletcher and Alfred Cooke argue that understanding, changing, and leading yourself is a precursor to building relationships with and leading others. Chapter 3, written by Debra Robinson and Len Kill Kelley, builds on the importance of self-awareness by focusing on the need, as a leader, to craft effective one-on-one conversations with others. Chapter 4, by Ron Redmon, broadens this even further by suggesting that leaders build trust as well by serving as masterful coaches to develop the self-awareness and self-leadership needed in those who work with them. Together, Chapters 2, 3, and 4 enable the government leader to forge the central molecular structure on which all else depends—the productive interpersonal relationship.

In Chapter 5, Gail Funke helps leaders build the first of the more complex structures essential to leading democracy: effective teams. Section II concludes with a focus on the broader organization. John Pickering and Gerry Brokaw pick up where the focus on teams leaves off: how to bring about large-scale organizational change that produces high-performing government agencies.

High-performing organizations, under the guiding hand of leaders who have built strong relationships and trust, cannot of course succeed alone. Other organizations with other agendas must be considered. Section III is based on the belief that career civil servants must lead in a broader context than the team or organization—they must lead *outside* the organization as well as inside it. Government leaders must find ways to collaborate with those in other organizations. Readers will not be surprised to find that building relationships and trust are essential here as well.

In Chapter 7, Michael Rawlings, Tom Gordon, Allison Linney, and Kristina Energia Naranjo-Rivera speak to the importance of being able to lead amidst the increasing diversity that characterizes our organizations and our society and how embracing the opportunities that diversity brings is a source of leadership. Russ Linden follows in Chapter 8 by addressing how to foster collaboration across organizational boundaries. Given the increasing need for cross-organizational work to meet complex public problems, the capacity to collaborate is a critical leadership skill.

In Chapter 9, Robert Maranto addresses one of the most delicate types of collaboration that leading democracy entails—how to work across the career-political divide. Why do career employees have such negative views of their political leaders, and why do political appointees come in with such guarded views of career leaders—and what can be done to ameliorate this destructive distrust?

Through the wisdom of the Founders, the nation has three branches of government, and little happens when they fail to work together for the common good. Grace Cummings, in Chapter 10, focuses on how career leaders in government can build productive relationships with the Congress.

In Chapter 11, Lou Carbone reminds us that, in the end, we build trust among citizens when they have a good experience with government. Drawing on research from psychology, sociology, and marketing, he maintains that the citizen's experience can be "engineered" so that it meets not just the rational but also the emotional needs that the public has in any service encounter.

The Preamble to the Constitution reminds us that career leaders in government are here for a reason, six of them to be exact: "form a more perfect union . . . establish justice, ensure domestic tranquility, provide for the common defense, promote the general welfare, and ensure the blessings of liberty. . . ." Sound relationships and strong bonds of trust within the branches and organizations of government are necessary to achieve the Preamble's promise, but they are not sufficient. As Abraham Lincoln reminded us at Gettysburg, government must be "by the people" as well as "for the people." This means trusting the people as well as asking for trust from them. *Washington Post* columnist Jim Hoagland captured this well when he observed that "demanding trust from the public without extending it invites great skepticism. Correcting this is one of modern history's great challenges."[36]

In Chapter 12, George Mitchell and Grant Reeher suggest that one of the best ways to trust the people—and improve government as a result—is to engage the public in governance. They explore how electronic communications technology offers a unique opportunity to involve citizens in new and productive ways.

Chapter 13, the last in Section III, reminds us that there is almost no issue or program in government that does not also have an international dimension or that is not affected by global events. Peter Ronayne argues, therefore, that building relationships and trust across national borders is also important in leading democracy.

The book concludes with Dan Fenn's passionate and poignant reminder that the Founders did not set out to make the civil service leader's job easy. Unlike the private sector, the public sector was consciously designed to frustrate anyone who attempts to exercise leadership. Career leaders in government, he suggests, bear a special responsibility to help the public understand why government works as it does. Americans owe their public servants a debt of thanks, he adds. They'll rarely receive it, but they have to earn it nonetheless.

Notes

1. These figures are based on U.S. government figures. See www.usgovernmentspending.com/US_per_capita_spending.html.

2. Bok (1997). See also Light (2002).

3. Better, Not Smaller: What Americans Want from Their Federal Government, July 2010, at www.americanprogress.org/issues/2010/07/what_americans_want.html.

4. *The People and Their Government: Distrust, Discontent, Anger and Partisan Rancor,* The Pew Research Center for the People and the Press, April 19, 2010, at http://people-press.org/report/606/trust-in-government.

5. Ibid., 3.

6. See "Dealing with the Federal Government's Image Problem," Friday, October 15, 2010, at http://pollingmatters.gallup.com/.

7. "Poll finds most Americans are unhappy with government," *Washington Post,* February 11, 2010, A03.

8. American National Election Studies at www.electionstudies.org.

9. Harris Poll, July 7–10, 2006, as reported at www.pollingreport.com/values.htm.

10. *Gallup Poll,* August 31–September 2, 2009.

11. See, for example, Barnes and Gill (2000). The authors sought to replicate the Derek Bok study in New Zealand, with strikingly similar results.

12. Luks (2001).

13. Van de Walle et al. (2002).

14. *The People and Their Government: Distrust, Discontent, Anger and Partisan Rancor,* The Pew Research Center for the People and the Press, April 19, 2010.

15. Nye, Zelikow, and King (1997).

16. Paterson (2000).

17. Nye, Zelikow, and King (1997).

18. Budget of the United States, 2011, at www.gpoaccess.gov/usbudget/fy11/pdf/budget
.pdf.

19. Harris Poll, July 7–10, 2006.

20. Hart (2006).

21. Anger at the financial complex reflected at least two strands of public distrust—that government did not exercise its regulatory responsibility to prevent the crisis and that it did not respond well when the crisis came (too tepid or too strong a response, depending on one's point of view).

22. "Federal workers criticized in poll," *Washington Post,* October 18, 2010, A1, A4.

23. ForeSee Results/Nextgov Government Transparency Study, October 20, 2010, at www.foreseeresults.com/research-white-papers/_downloads/foresee-results-nextgov-government-transparency-study-q3–2010.pdf.

24. Goodsell (2003).

25. Operated by the University of Michigan, the American Customer Satisfaction Index rates participating organizations/programs using a sophisticated telephone survey and methodology. At the end of 2009, the average score for all federal agencies on a scale of 0–100 was 68.7, compared to 75.9 for the private sector. Within government, scores varied from as low as 55 for individual paper filers at the IRS to 88 for retirees served by the Pension Benefit Guaranty Corporation. See www.theacsi.org.

26. The Maxwell Poll is a nationally representative poll of adults. For more on the poll contact the Campbell Public Affairs Institute at Syracuse University, at www.maxwell.syr
.edu/campbell.aspx.

27. Grant Reeher, *Cooperative Congressional Election Study,* 2010, Campbell Public Affairs Institute, Syracuse, NY, March 2011, at http://projects.iq.harvard.edu/cces/book/cces-2010–.

28. The Power of Federal Employee Engagement, U.S. Merit Systems Protection Board, September 2008, at www.mspb.gov/netsearch/viewdocs.aspx?docnumber=379024&version=379721&application=ACROBAT.

29. Van de Walle and Bouckaert (2003).

30. See Fukuyama (1995) for an extended treatment of trust and social capital in the performance of societies.

31. Nahapiet and Ghoshal (1998). Although this study focuses on building social capital in organizations, Fukuyama (1995) provides evidence that social capital formation in societies depends similarly on trusting relationships.

32. Jones and George (1998).

33. Bolino, Turnley, and Bloodgood (2002).

34. Goleman (2000a) presents the research case, and the emotional competence inventory (ECI) is the primary research tool that measures the four skill clusters. For information on the ECI, visit the website of the Consortium for Research on Emotional Intelligence at www.eiconsortium.org.

35. Goleman (2000b).

36. Hoagland (2006).

1 Values-based leadership for a democratic society

TERRY NEWELL, PRESIDENT, LEADERSHIP FOR A RESPONSIBLE SOCIETY

Building trust requires being a values-based leader. This chapter first argues that values-based leadership matters for multiple reasons. We are a nation founded on core values we share and care about. We aim to be a "city upon a hill," so that failure to live up to our values means we fall short of what we expect of ourselves. Leaders who violate core values cannot expect people inside or outside their organizations to follow. Failure to lead through core values means a failure to engender trust.

But public service leaders face conflicting value demands. How do they navigate among constitutional, citizen, organizational, professional, and personal values that often conflict? They need at least five skills to do so: they must act with integrity, listen, tolerate dissent, involve others, and make moral decisions. These skills must be put into practice in three arenas: in their personal leadership, in their organizations, and on the public stage.

For we must consider that we shall be as a city upon on a hill. The eyes of all people are upon us.

—Gov. John Winthrop, aboard the Arbella, *1630*

AS THE *ARBELLA* APPROACHED BOSTON HARBOR, Gov. John Winthrop, one of the first government leaders in their new land, reminded his followers that a life based on high moral values would not only ensure their survival and success but also was essential because of the public nature of their undertaking. Winthrop's exhortation was anchored in religious experience, but secular officials throughout American history have used his words to remind us that our nation—and our government—is still a "city upon a hill."[1] As leaders of government, we are expected to live and lead by high moral values. Values-based leadership builds relationships and trust. This statement is more than a nice sentiment. In a democracy, values-based leadership is essential.[2]

Ursula Henderson led by high moral values. As director of a veterans service center in the Department of Veterans Affairs, she faced the daunting challenge of managing veterans' claims with speed and compassion in an office where employees processed one file after another in a seemingly endless stream of boring bureaucratic work. Rather than remind them of their job descriptions and performance standards, she chose to remind them of Abraham Lincoln's Second Inaugural Address, that their job was "to care for he who has borne the battle, for his widow and his orphan," the same words carved in granite on their headquarters in Washington, D.C. She chose to draw on her passion for helping veterans and tell them a story from a movie about a severely disabled World War I veteran (*Johnny Got His Gun*). In the movie, the vet is bandaged from head to toe and can communicate only by blinking his eyes in Morse code. She wanted her staff to see that, in her words, "each file has a face." In short, she chose to lead by reminding them of the core values at the heart of their own lives and enshrined in the history of their agency. She lifted them to an ennobling public purpose. She demonstrated values-based leadership.[3]

Why does values-based leadership matter in government?

Ursula is not alone. Values-based leadership in government—the practice of leading individuals and organizations from a set of shared core moral values embodied in the leader's behavior and the organization's processes, products, and services—is widespread. But it is neither easy nor inevitable. Bureaucracy, the way we structure and run government agencies, does not automatically produce values-based leadership. The reliance on hierarchy—objective, rule-based, and loyal action—is not inherently moral. Faithful bureaucrats throughout history have done immoral acts. The Tuskegee Syphilis Study, conducted by the U.S. Public Health Service from 1932 to 1972, demonstrated that what Hannah Arendt called the "banality of evil" was not limited to Nazis.[4] But if not easy or inevitable, values-based leadership in government is still necessary. It builds trust, fosters effective relationships, and helps the bureaucracy to promote democracy.

Values-based leadership matters because core moral values underlie our commitment to each other as members of this nation. The Declaration of Independence enshrines "Life, Liberty and the pursuit of Happiness" as natural rights that precede government and whose protection is the only legitimate basis on which some may govern others. The "consent of the governed" rests on honoring voters' core moral values, and when those values are dishonored, consent is withdrawn.

The Constitution promises that our Union will only be "more perfect" if it will establish "Justice . . . and secure the blessings of Liberty." It proclaims a set of moral ends. It also prescribes a set of moral means by which we govern, including the need to respect majority rule, minority rights, and due process.

Values-based leadership matters because it instills trust in the citizens of the United States. As Robert Greenleaf argues in *Servant Leadership*, trust comes when people have confidence in the leader's values and competence.[5] Skill in the mechanics of governing is necessary but not sufficient to earn the public trust. Leaders need the power that comes from principle, not just the technique that comes from talent. Without trust, the constitutional compact does not work.

Values-based leadership matters because we want our nation to be that "city upon a hill." To the extent government executives lead by and demonstrate core moral values, they help build what Joseph Nye, former dean of Harvard's John F. Kennedy School of Government, calls "soft power."[6] American values and culture can build support for U.S. foreign policy and U.S. goals in the world if our values gain the admiration of people in other nations. In this sense, the "soft power" of values and culture complements the "hard power" that technology, military might, and economic prowess seek to provide. As other civilizations have learned, hard power may be necessary, but it is never sufficient for long-term leadership on the world stage. Other countries have to admire what a nation lives by as well as what it lives with. When values-based leadership falters, as it did so strikingly at Iraq's Abu Ghraib prison in 2003, for example, soft power suffers. We cease to live up to our aim to be that "city upon a hill."

Although Nye was primarily concerned with the international influence wielded by soft power, the importance of values-based leadership matters domestically as well. It is not hard to see why so few Americans trust the federal government to deal with pressing domestic issues when more than 80 percent in a February 2010 CNN/Opinion Research poll said that elected officials in Washington can be described as "heavily influenced by special interests (87 percent), "mainly concerned about getting reelected" (86 percent), and "out of touch with the average person" (81 percent). Only

22 percent described elected officials in Washington as "honest." Clearly, the pubic sees a wide gulf between its values and those it believes drive people in our national capitol.[7]

Values-based leadership matters because significant academic research shows that it is the most effective leadership approach over the long run. James McGregor Burns, in his classic, *Leadership*, contrasted three ways to lead.[8] Coercive or raw power works only until it is overthrown from within or from the outside. Transactional leadership, in which people follow because they are promised practical returns, such as a certain standard of living, can last a while longer. Eventually, however, the governed decide that the promises at the heart of the transaction are no longer met or no longer attractive. Only transformational leadership, where people are drawn together by core values they share, can be sustained over the long term. People want to see their values take root. Transformational—values-based—leadership works because it appeals to followers' most deeply felt values and in so doing empowers them to become leaders in their own right to sustain these values over time.

Values-based leadership matters because we are in a knowledge economy, especially in government. In a knowledge economy, success comes to those with the best ideas. Survival as a nation depends on thinking not only better but faster than those who would do us harm. How do we get the best thinking from not just our employees but citizens in general? It has to be freely given. We cannot compel knowledge contributions. People are more likely to share their creative thinking when they see it is in service to what they value. Values-based leadership releases this energy of innovation.

Finally, values-based leadership matters because it sustains organizations even as the people in them move on. In *Built to Last*, Jim Collins and Jerry Porras show that organizations lasting for generations have very few things in common. They differ in their size, structure, systems, skills, and strategies. But one thing they share is that they are all driven by a set of unchanging core values. Their leaders embed these values in the organization's culture.[9] Collins and Porras draw their examples from the private sector, such as Johnson & Johnson, whose core value around the safety of its consumer products led it in 1982 to pull every capsule of Tylenol from store shelves when a deranged man spiked a few with cyanide. Johnson & Johnson's point applies equally well to public organizations. The Marine Corps (see Box 1.1) is values-based and rightly viewed as a leader in this regard even by private-sector firms who visit its headquarters in Quantico, VA, to learn its values-based leadership approach.

Box 1.1   Core values of the U.S. Marines

HONOR: The bedrock of our character. The quality that guides Marines to exemplify the ultimate in ethical and moral behavior; never to lie, cheat, or steal; to abide by an uncompromising code of integrity; to respect human dignity; to have respect and concern for each other. The quality of maturity, dedication, trust, and dependability that commits Marines to act responsibly; to be accountable for actions; to fulfill obligations; and to hold others accountable for their actions.

COURAGE: The heart of our Core Values, courage is the mental, moral, and physical strength ingrained in Marines to carry them through the challenges of combat and the mastery of fear; to do what is right; to adhere to a higher standard of personal conduct; to lead by example, and to make tough decisions under stress and pressure. It is the inner strength that enables a Marine to take that extra step.

COMMITMENT: The spirit of determination and dedication within members of a force of arms that leads to professionalism and mastery of the art of war. It leads to the highest order of discipline for unit and self; it is the ingredient that enables 24-hour a day dedication to Corps and Country; pride; concern for others; and an unrelenting determination to achieve a standard of excellence in every endeavor. Commitment is the value that establishes the Marine as the warrior and citizen others strive to emulate.

Reaffirm these Core Values and ensure they guide your performance, behavior, and conduct every minute of every day.

Source: Marine Corps Values: A User's Guide For Discussion Leaders, 2–7; can be found at www.tecom.usmc.mil/utm/6-11B.pdf.

Why do career leaders in government need to be values-based leaders?

Values-based leadership matters in our democracy, but does it necessarily follow that bureaucrats themselves must practice it? Isn't the job of career leaders in government just to administer the laws? Can't we leave value-based decisions and leading by values to elected officials who, after all, are the only ones the people directly entrust with leading?

As the Introduction demonstrated, democracy is not that simple. About 2,000 political leaders are responsible for the overall direction of the executive branch, but it is the daily actions of more than 6,500 career senior executives, 50,000 managers and supervisors, and 2.7 million executive branch employees that translate that direction into action. At the state and local government level, nearly 20 million civil servants dwarf the size of the political leadership. Programs, policies, and behavior that are either faithful or not to our shared core values as a nation are the result. Unless career civil servants are also values-based leaders, the chain of constitutional leadership has a fatal, weak link.

George Washington sensed this intuitively in his first administration when he said that "In every nomination to office I have endeavored . . . to make fitness of character my primary objective." Abigail Adams stated it even more clearly when writing to her son, John Quincy Adams, himself destined for a life of public service: "Great Learning and superior abilities, should you ever possess them, will be of little value and small Estimation unless Virtue, Honor, Truth and Integrity are added to them."

Washington and Adams may have been principally concerned with elected or appointed leaders, but their words apply just as forcefully to civil service leaders. Federal employees, for example, take a solemn oath of office to "bear true faith and allegiance" to the Constitution and to "well and faithfully" discharge their duties. The definition of faithful is to be "steadfast in affection . . . firm in adherence to promises . . . and true to the facts or a standard"—moral values in service of a moral obligation.[10]

The U.S. Congress recognized the importance of leading by core moral values for all civil servants when, in the Code of Ethics for Government Service enacted in 1958, it stated as the first item: "Put loyalty to the highest moral principles above loyalty to persons, party, or Government department."

What values guide values-based leaders?

On the surface, values-based leadership seems simple and direct. Who would argue that leaders should not have strong moral values they exemplify in their daily work? Below the surface, however, people get nervous. Don't we want our civil servants to keep their values to themselves? What values are we talking about, and aren't moral values the purview of religious faith rather than secular government? In a democracy, people inevitably have value conflicts. Do we want unelected government executives choosing among competing values?

These questions have lasted as long as our republic, and they have no easy answers. But that does not mean they are unanswerable. Although we may never agree as a nation on a full set of moral values we all share, that does not mean we don't share many. Nor does it mean that we relieve our leaders of the requirement to identify and lead by moral values. Consider the alternative. If we do not want our public servants to adopt and lead by a set of core moral values, we risk relieving them of the need to think about and be accountable for morally acceptable action. So the question is not *whether* but by *which* moral values we want them to lead.

There are at least four ways to answer this question. Our Constitution offers the first and most important response. It encompasses a set of moral ends, established largely by the Preamble. It also encompasses a set of values-based means that we are held to "support and defend" (see Box 1.2). Values-based leaders must ask themselves if their actions adhere to these values.

A second guide is a set of core personal values. The popular notion that "everything is relative" is in fact not the case. Research by the Institute for Global Ethics finds that a small number of moral values are shared across the world. The institute's research includes surveys, contextual analysis, interviews and workshops, all of which ask the same basic question: What values count the most for you in living your daily life?

Figure 1.1 presents the results of a study conducted of 272 attendees at the State of the World Forum in 1996, a group that represented forty countries and fifty different faith groups. The data represent the frequency count

Box 1.2   Core values of the U.S. Constitution

Moral Ends

"We the People of the United States, in Order to form a more perfect Union, establish Justice, insure domestic Tranquility, provide for the common defence, promote the general Welfare, and secure the Blessings of Liberty to ourselves and our Posterity, do ordain and establish this Constitution for the United States of America."

Values-based means

Representative, elective government
Subordination of military to civil authority
Free exercise of religion, press, speech, assembly, and petition
Security against unreasonable search/seizure
Trial by jury
Divided powers/checks and balances
Majority rule/minority rights
Due process of law

Figure 1.1 Core values worldwide

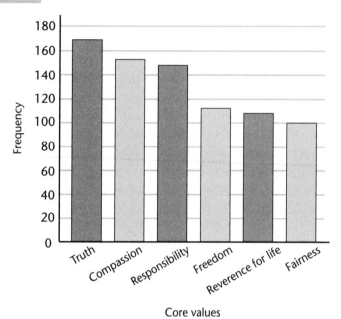

Source: Adapted from Rushworth Kidder, *Moral Courage* (New York: William Morrow, 2005).

when people selected their top five values from a list of fifteen. The same core values turn up at the top of the list in every other study the institute has conducted. These values speak to the importance of respecting the worth of each human being. Whether adherence to these values is anchored in one's religious faith or not, who would want a world—or a public official—for whom these values did not guide action?

Although the most-often-mentioned values may not represent the full set of core personal values that should guide public servants, they demonstrate that those values are, at least, not "up for grabs." They are a small, not an infinite number.[11] Still further, if citizens feel that government policies ignore their values, discontent and distrust grow. A 2010 study by the Center for American Progress found that only 39 percent of respondents agreed that the federal government "has policies that reflect my values," while 56 percent disagreed.[12]

A third guide is a set of professional values that emerges from two centuries of public service excellence—and failure. This group incorporates constitutional and personal core values and moves them into the realm of administrative behavior. They are captured best in codes of ethics crafted by those entrusted with furthering the profession of public administration and the behavior of public administrators. The ethical code of the American Society for Public Administration presents an excellent exampl of a powerful statement of professional values that must guide government executive action (see Box 1.3).

Yet another set of values that has some claim on career leaders are those inherent in and often formally established by their technical professions. These values should be consistent with constitutional and public administration values—and must be given secondary place if they are not. The values of the professions (for example, law, engineering, psychology, medicine) offer another set of standards that career civil servants in particular professions can use to guide their actions.

Even beyond constitutional, personal, public service, and professional values lay the additional value realms of organization, family, community, and religion. The question for career leaders in government quickly becomes not "are there values that must guide my actions?" but "how do I choose among the value claims upon me?" Answering that question demands mastery of a set of skills essential to values-based leadership.

Box 1.3 American Society for Public Administration code of ethics

1. **Serve the public interest:** Serve the public beyond serving oneself.
2. **Respect the Constitution and the law:** Respect, support, and study government constitutions and laws that define responsibilities of public agencies, employees, and all citizens.
3. **Demonstrate personal integrity:** Demonstrate the highest standards in all activities to inspire public confidence and trust in public service.
4. **Promote ethical organizations:** Strengthen organizational capabilities to apply ethics, efficiency, and effectiveness in serving the public.
5. **Strive for professional excellence:** Strengthen individual capabilities and encourage the professional development of others.

Source: American Society for Public Administration, www.aspanet.org. Each of these five broad areas contains four to eight behavioral statements that define expected actions of public administrators.

What skills do values-based leaders in government need?

If government executives want to be values-based leaders, they need a set of skills with which to approach their work. Values without skills are like engines without fuel—they are all potential energy. Skills move values into action. Any of the wide range of competencies in leadership skill lists might be called upon in a given instance by a values-based civil servant, but some will *always* be called upon. We suggest at least the following five:

1. Acting with integrity.
2. Listening.
3. Tolerating dissent.
4. Involving others.
5. Moral decision making.

Acting with integrity

Values-based leaders must be honest. In its simplest expression, this means they must not lie. Although one might "have to lie" at some point in a career to protect those in imminent physical danger—for example, an intelligence agent whose truthfulness would put his or others' lives in jeopardy—these instances are more rare than we might believe or wish to think.[13]

> Deception . . . strikes at the very heart and essence of democratic government. It allows those in power to override or nullify the right vested in the people to cast an informed vote. . . . Deceiving the people for the sake of the people is a self-contradictory notion in a democracy, unless it can be shown that there has been genuine consent to deceit.
>
> —*Sissela Bok,* Lying: Moral Choice in Public and Private Life, *1978*

"Telling the truth" seems like a straightforward principle. Asked if a report has been prepared to meet a congressional mandate, the path to truthfulness is an honest "yes" or "no." Leaders in government are faced with many situations, however, in which they may convince themselves that there are alternatives that are not exactly lies. For example, is withholding negative data about the performance of the organization a lie, if the request did not specify this type of information? What about suppressing a dissenting view on the meaning of intelligence data? Does a report that includes only statistics that buttress the organization's position represent a lie?

As Box 1.4 suggests, the territory between "the truth, the whole truth and nothing but the truth" and "an outright, known falsehood" contains a number of choices, which test moral principles. Failing to think carefully about these choices can ease the leader's way onto the slippery slope that makes future errors in truthfulness both easier to make and harder to see.

Truth-telling is more than not lying, however. It involves telling difficult truths, including to the public as well as one's superiors. In his Second Inaugural Address, as the Civil War was finally nearing its end, Lincoln told the nation—North as well as South—that the war was God's punishment for the sin of slavery. While his supporters were clearly ready to blame the South for the war, many saw no reason to blame themselves. Lincoln did—because the nation had allowed slavery to continue and supported a Constitution that allowed it as well. Writing to a friend, Thurlow Weed, on March 15, 1865, Lincoln explained his speech by saying that "It is a truth which I

Box 1.4   The path between truth and falsehood

The truth, the whole truth, and nothing but the truth

> Evading the subject
> Partial truth
> Withholding information
> Distorting data
> Manipulating statistics
> Being vague
> Presenting only one side of the argument
> Suppressing dissenting views
> Leaking selected information
> Using a false analogy
> Saying nothing
> Spinning the story
> Plausible deniability
> Bluffing

An outright, known falsehood

Note: The list of actions above, between the whole truth and an outright falsehood, is not meant to suggest any rank order.

---

thought needed to be told."[14] At a deeper level, then, integrity means "firm adherence to a code of . . . moral values."[15] One's behavior must be integral—in other words, consistent with professed moral values. In this sense, telling the truth is necessary but not sufficient for acting with integrity, which can also be defined as "the quality or state of being complete or undivided." To be a leader within this definition of integrity, moral words must match moral deeds. When a government executive has this kind of integrity, no one need worry if the lofty rhetoric he or she hears is somehow divorced from the actions seen. It is this kind of leadership that builds trust.

Listening

No one can be a values-based leader without the ability to listen. This means wanting to hear what others say and understanding the values behind their deeply held beliefs as much as it means having a set of skills that enable listening (for example, active attention, paraphrasing what we hear, and probing for understanding). It means having empathy for another even when we do not agree. To have empathy, the leader must work at getting inside another's thoughts and feelings—a task that is as important to attempt as it is impossible to fully achieve. Listening also means spending time on the other person or group's agenda as well as on our own, and it means understanding ourselves well enough to know when our own values, motives, and assumptions may be blocking the message others are trying to send. (Chapter 3 on effective conversations covers this skill in much greater depth.)

Tolerating dissent

This "skill" rarely shows up on a list of leadership competencies, but government executives who cannot "well and faithfully discharge" their duties as well as "support and defend" the Constitution. The Framers believed that dissent was not only inevitable but necessary in a republican form of government. James Madison counted on vigorous opposition among contending factions to preserve liberty.[16] And, as Thomas Jefferson often noted, "error of opinion may be tolerated where reason is left free to combat it."[17] But reason must be allowed to speak. Values-based leaders accept this requirement not only in the public arena but also inside their own organizations. Research is clear that government leaders who cannot tolerate dissent in their own ranks make bad, even disastrous decisions. For example, the National Aeronautics and Space Administration (NASA) *Challenger* and *Columbia* accident investigations both concluded that the inability to promote and hear dissenting views contributed directly to these tragedies. As the Columbia Accident Investigation Board noted in its report, commenting on both *Challenger* and *Columbia*: "The organizational structure and hierarchy blocked effective communication of technical problems. Signals were overlooked, people were silenced, and useful information and dissenting views on technical issues did not surface at higher levels. What was communicated to parts of the organization was that O-ring erosion and foam debris were not problems."[18] In both cases, the highest moral value of the preservation of life was somehow subordinated to lesser values.

A related characteristic of values-based leaders is their ability to tolerate ambiguity. A leader must hold off from closure—at least long enough to hear and consider dissenting views. Leaders must accept that they have neither all the data nor all the answers and that uncertainty accompanies tough decisions. Leaders who *have* to decide before they need to decide often rue the decisions they make.

Involving others

Values-based leaders in government seek to include people in the decisions that affect their lives. As noted, our Madisonian system demands multiple voices to protect liberty and relies on the belief that hearing different views contributes to better decision making. Social science research also shows that people commit to those values and actions they have a hand in shaping.[19] People resist change when they are frozen out of it. They are more likely to embrace it when they see it as their change—something that acknowledges and incorporates their values. Even though values-based leaders know that the final decision on both values and actions will rarely accept every input they receive, they aim to have people feel they have had a chance to be heard. (Chapter 12 focuses on the power of technology to involve citizens in governance.)

Moral decision making

Values-based leaders are more likely than other leaders to make sound, moral decisions. Being honest, listening, tolerating dissent, and including others are necessary but not sufficient skills to help leaders do the right thing. When faced with many alternatives and counterpressures, civil service leaders need the ability to think through the problems they face. This skill is not only a matter of using decision tools but also a matter of using moral imagination. If leaders don't know the questions to ask, and if they don't ask enough questions, their decisions will be shortsighted at best and destructive of core values at worst. To be human is to be limited by one's own "mental models," the way one makes sense of the world. Values-based leaders find ways to transcend the limits of their own thinking—to imagine the values conflicts they face from multiple perspectives and to see multiple moral choices about moving ahead.[20]

The questions in Box 1.5 can help leaders take a systematic look at making decisions with an eye to the value-based points of view at stake.[21]

Box 1.5 Exercising moral imagination: Questions to ask

Get the facts

1. What is the values dilemma as you see it? What values seem at issue as you define the problem?
2. Who are the stakeholders and how do they see the issue? What values matter for them?
3. What is at stake for you? What are your motives?
4. What are the relevant facts?
5. What values are in conflict now that you have a deeper understanding of the problem?
6. What assumptions are you and others making that might need to be tested?

Identify options

7. Who has responsibility to resolve this dilemma?
8. What results would define success for you? For other stakeholders?
9. What are all of the possible options?
10. What are the positive and negative consequences of the most promising options?

Make and implement a decision

11. What option best satisfies your core values while acknowledging and faithfully considering the values that matter to others?
12. How will you implement the chosen option and mitigate negative impacts?

What is the stage on which values-based government leaders act?

Values and skills come together in action. "All the world's a stage," Shakespeare reminded us. Government leaders know full well that they are always on stage. Their on-stage actions deliver or deny the promise of democracy. Their actions demonstrate or deny their understanding of the values that matter to those they serve. The three stages for values-based leadership action are: the public, the organizational, and the personal. These stages almost always overlap in practice.

The public stage

Anyone whose agency or action has received negative press on the front page of a major newspaper knows that leadership contrary to core moral values is the easiest way to invite public scorn. Those who break the law, violate regulations, or engage in ethically abhorrent behavior usually get the sanction they deserve. The simplest rule for values-based leaders: don't do wrong.

Unfortunately, avoiding wrong is not necessarily doing right. Values-based leaders in government must also:

Keep the public purpose in mind. Everything government does has a public purpose. That purpose enshrines core values in an organization's legislation, mission, and vision. Values-based leaders can always explain how their actions are faithful to that core purpose—and their employees can explain it, too. People say that Sen. Herman Talmadge, while visiting Cape Canaveral in the early 1960s, asked a janitor what his job was. The janitor's reply—"My job is help us get a man to the moon"—led Talmadge to become a fervent supporter of NASA, which until that time had struggled to get sufficient funding. Talmadge reasoned correctly that if a janitor knew that his job was contributing to a grand public purpose, so did everyone else. The story may be apocryphal, but it demonstrates that NASA's core purpose served as an ennobling statement for its workforce as well as the rest of America. NASA has had tough times to be sure, but core values and a core purpose see one through—and give government leaders something to draw upon when their agencies are confronted with adversity (see Box 1.6).[22]

Encourage the expression of differing interests. As discussed above, values-based leaders encourage—or at least support—the expression of different points of view and the values that underlie them in the belief that better policies and programs will emerge from a conversation in the light

Box 1.6 The power of public purpose

The mission statements of government agencies provide soaring rhetoric and meaningful substance that help keep the public purpose in the minds of agency employees (and communicate to the public how the agency is obligated to serve them).

Environmental Protection Agency (EPA) Mission

The mission of EPA is to protect human health and to safeguard the natural environment—air, water, and land—upon which life depends.

Federal Aviation Administration (FAA) Mission

Our continuing mission is to provide the safest, most efficient aerospace system in the world.

Department of Education Mission

The mission of the Department of Education is to promote student achievement and preparation for global competitiveness by fostering educational excellence and ensuring equal access.

than from one hidden in shadow. Their belief is anchored in considerable research on decision making, much of which argues for the value of disagreement.[23] On the public stage, values-based leaders are adept at using a range of methods to encourage healthy dialogue, including, for example, town-hall meetings, focus groups, surveys, websites, and personal conversations with main stakeholders. They also incorporate the spirit as well as the letter of the Administrative Procedures Act (APA) in their work. Originally passed to ensure that the expansion of government ushered in by the New Deal did not mean a distancing of government from public accountability, the APA has been expanded and refined. It provides multiple ways to encourage and listen to differing views. Requiring agencies to keep the public informed about their organization, procedures, and rules; providing for public participation in the rulemaking process; and establishing uniform standards for the conduct of formal rulemaking—all features of the APA—are important mechanisms that leaders who seek to build trust among the public they serve will use to open their decision making to a range of views.

Educate the public about the governing process. Encouraging differing views is most productive when there is a broad public understanding of how government works. Without an appreciation that we are a society that depends on collaboration and compromise, differing views can easily become shrill demands. Some Americans lack sufficient civic knowledge, and the result is that they act more like customers than citizens. As customers, they see paying taxes as the only obligation they bear. They don't have to participate in learning and thinking about public issues. They don't have to accept any responsibility for participating in public discourse and crafting solutions. They don't have to like paying for anything that may benefit others. In short, they don't have to have much civic-mindedness. They have only to vote and complain. They see their relationship to the nation as a contract not a covenant. This way of thinking can easily lead to distrust when the "deliverables" of the contract are, in their view, not forthcoming. By reaching out to citizens, explaining the process of governing, and helping them play a useful role, career civil service leaders can do much not only to build good policy and good programs but also to enhance trust. Reaching out may be difficult and leave the civil service leader open to criticism (as our concluding chapter in this book demonstrates), but it is both the price we pay and the promise we make as those who govern.

Make tough decisions that involve value trade-offs. Public executives deal with issues that lack easy, widely acceptable answers. These tough decisions almost always involve trade-offs among competing values. Where do we safely store nuclear waste? How do we balance the need to fight terrorism with protecting personal privacy? How can we provide for the aging baby boomer population without unfairly burdening the younger generation? As Dwight Waldo (see Figure 1.2) noted years ago, values-based leaders know that they have obligations to many individuals and groups whose values pull in different directions.[24] As a result, they recognize that they will often make decisions that please no one fully. They make them anyway, secure in the knowledge that they have allowed differing values to be expressed and considered. And they can articulate how they have addressed concerns about differing values in the decision-making process.

Consider the implications of potential actions on affected communities and the future. Most decisions involve what to do *now* in the context of a specific situation and group of stakeholders. But the impact of these decisions can have profound ripple effects on wider audiences and future points in time. Shifting resources to increase police protection in a troubled area may be the most sensible and politically expedient thing to do when faced

Figure 1.2 Dwight Waldo's ethical obligations of a public servant

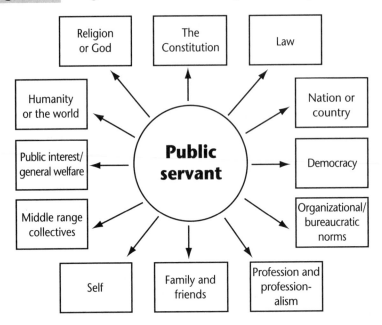

Source: Adapted from Rosemary O'Leary, *The Ethics of Dissent* (Washington, D.C.: CQ Press, 2006), 17.

with crime reports in the news, but the values-based leader will also ask additional questions before making this decision: How will this shift affect other parts of the community and their needs? Will increasing what we spend on police protection mean we have to decrease the budget in other areas and, if so, what effect will this have in the years ahead on preventive programs such as education, job training, and youth centers?

As Figure 1.3 shows, a government leader can set a wide or narrow limit on the scope of whose values to consider when facing the moral implications of prospective actions (the vertical axis). The leader can also consider the impact of potential decisions over a short time or longer span of time (the horizontal axis). At worst, public leaders cannot see beyond the immediate impact of a potential action on themselves and their immediate needs (the dotted box in Figure 1.3). But values-based leaders will set the horizon farther out in time and space. Although few decisions must consider the worldwide impact many years into the future (the dashed box), it is also true that few decisions are only a matter for one individual or one organization and their short-term interests.[25]

Figure 1.3 Moral horizons: Expanding the scope and timeframe of the leader's concerns

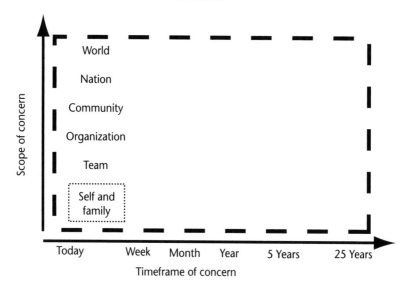

Stay in their constitutional role. Career government executives, who report to elected or appointed officials, are tasked with carrying out the policies and programs these officials direct—except where actions would be illegal, unethical, and/or unconstitutional. At times they must subordinate their personal values and professional beliefs, a very stressful role to play. A government executive may not agree with the policy to ban drug sale imports from Canada, fund a particular program, or ignore a pressing need out of political expediency, but that does not make those actions illegal or unethical. Nor do such actions give the leader the justification to refuse direction from above or to leak information to the media. Values-based leaders should express their views to their boss (see the section below on loyal dissent), but also remember that it is political not career leadership that has been elected and is answerable to the voters.[26]

The organization

Government executives are also on stage within their organizations. Creating a sense of trust and being effective outside in the public arena are rarely possible for leaders and their organizations unless values-based leadership also exists inside. Values-based leaders in government can take specific actions such as the following:

Foster a sense of public service. Just as Ursula Henderson did for her employees in the veterans service center, values-based government leaders demonstrate a passion for public service and instill it in their employees. They remind their workers of the core public purpose that created their organization. They also remind their employees of the core values behind that public purpose, values that come ultimately from the Constitution and the Declaration of Independence. Ben Scaggs at the Environmental Protection Agency (EPA) in Research Triangle Park, North Carolina, may not have told the public about Elliott, a nine-year-old asthmatic who could not play baseball when the air was unhealthy. But he told his EPA employees about him, because making the air cleaner for Elliott—and thousands like him—is what brought Ben to work each day. Even though his office and his staff were in support roles to those concerned with the Clean Air Act, he wanted his staff to know the importance of what they were supporting. And so, in the best traditions of values-based leaders, he exhorted his employees to find their own Elliott so that each of their days at work would be driven by the desire to serve.

Promote core values. Executives must articulate and reward behavior consistent with core values. For many employees, the biggest disconnect is between published values statements that hang on agency walls and their perception of how their leaders act. If the leader values integrity, he should publicly recognize the employee who has discovered a mistake and called attention to it. Even better, he should admit mistakes to employees.[27] The leader who acknowledges in a staff meeting, for example, that a decision he made did not work out creates an environment that allows employees to admit their mistakes and moves from the bureaucratic tendency to place blame to the moral tendency to forgive. If a leader values creativity, she should recognize the experiment that failed—and even embarrassed the agency in the process. If collaboration is a value, the leader should not give all the recognition and awards to solo performers.

> Ali Bahrami, a leader in the Transport Airplane Directorate of the Federal Aviation Administration made organizational values come alive every day. Several years ago, on a Friday at 3 p.m. he received a call of a "positive finding" on the vertical tail structure of an Airbus 300. Translated, that means the airworthiness of all similar planes was called into question. As Ali said, describing what happened next: "Some of us worked through the weekend to define a plan in order to assure the safety of the fleet. By Monday morning, we had a plan. On Wednesday, at about midnight, we prepared an airworthiness

directive which required certain actions. The same folks were at work the next day at 5:00 a.m. so that they could respond to potential inquiries." No one can doubt the values of service, safety, and commitment that permeate Ali Bahrami's organization, values he promoted in his own action and so clearly instilled in his employees.[28]

Promoting core values also implies identifying the small number that are both essential and on which there can be agreement. Organizations are most effective and efficient when their members agree on (and can easily recall) the core values that guide them.[29]

> I remember one of our first off-sites (at TSA). I asked around the table as to whether or not we had core values at TSA. They said, "Oh, sure." I said, "Well, how many do you have?" They said, "Oh, I think there might be like 10 or 11." I said, "Is anybody here able to recite those for me?" Of course, they could not, because they hadn't internalized them. We were at that point about three weeks old as an organization.
>
> —*James Loy, former administrator,*
> *Transportation Security Administration*

Ensure that employees do not confuse organizational means with constitutional ends. The reason for organizational policies, systems, and procedures is to achieve a public purpose. Many employees, forgetting the purpose, act as if the rules are the end not the means. They confuse organizational values with the constitutional values that must have primacy in their work. They deny a request for assistance because the forms have not been filled out perfectly rather than helping the applicant correct the problem. Admittedly, government agencies often have to struggle to appropriately balance organizational with constitutional values, but government executives lead that balancing act. It is not easy. Do employees bend the rules to respond to the needs of a citizen, or do they "treat everyone the same?" Values-based leaders in government do all they can to put public service above process. They encourage employees to challenge the rules and focus on the right.

Create an ethical culture and foster ethical conversations. People will confront ethical issues even (perhaps especially) in the best-led organizations. Should we adopt a policy that some in the public angrily protest? What do we do when asked to verify information publicly that we privately doubt is accurate? What should we say when asked to support a policy with which we personally disagree?

Figure 1.4 Elements of an ethical culture

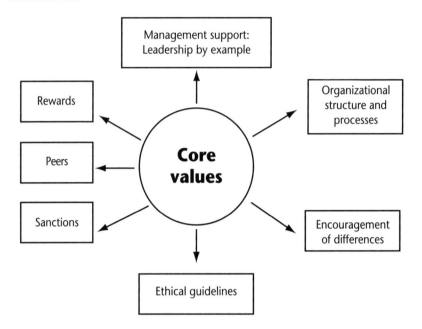

Values-based leaders expect such questions to come up. They engage employees in thinking them through. They use ethical issues as the basis of conversations in staff meetings, aimed at helping employees and the organization do the right thing. They create an ethical culture by ensuring that core values drive the organization. This task is one of leadership architecture in which they must ensure that all of the elements of such a culture exist, operate effectively, and support each other (see Figure 1.4).

When leaders foster an ethical culture, it makes a difference. A 2007 study of ethics in government by the Ethics Resource Center concluded that "[W]hen both a well-implemented ethics and compliance program and a strong ethical culture are in place within a government organization, misconduct drops by 60 percent, and reporting rises by 40 percent. Governments' risk of losing public trust can be mitigated."[30]

A central part of fostering this ethical culture is to remind employees of their constitutional oath of office. The Federal Executive Institute, for example, readministers the oath to all graduating government executives. The U.S. Air Force does so in a public ceremony to every officer receiving a promotion. In this action, its senior officers show, by the example of their behavior, that fidelity to the Constitution is essential to leadership.

The self

Career civil servants cannot be values-based leaders on the public stage or within the organization if they have not mastered the skills or lack the temperament to behave that way themselves. Leading from a values base means living from one. Government executives must do at least three things in their "always on stage" behavior, using the skills discussed above.

Model values-based leadership behavior. We are all faced with moral temptations—those decisions where we know that one choice is wrong—morally and often legally as well. These choices are easy for values-based leaders. They are covered by laws and formal ethical codes aimed at avoiding problems such as conflicts of interest and inadequate financial disclosure. Quite simply, faced with these choices, values-based leaders do the right thing. The tougher choices government leaders face are those between two or more courses of action all of which may be morally and legally right, and all of which may have some negative outcomes. Rushworth Kidder of the Institute for Global Ethics calls such situations ethical dilemmas.[31] They have no easy answers because a values-based case can be made for more than one choice. Does a leader give an employee a good recommendation for another job because he wants to move on and needs the promotion to support his family, even though he has not been a stellar performer? Or does the leader tell the whole truth when called for a reference? Values-based leaders have developed a way to think about such issues and make reasoned and reasonable decisions. Or to put it in the words of political scientist Louis Gawthrop, they can differentiate between what they can do and what they should do.[32] They do not confuse what is permissible with what is the best and most ethical course of action. They engage in self-reflection and model the way they want their followers to behave. They also often explain and engage their employees in discussion about value conflicts in their work. In this way, they also model the importance of dialogue in bringing diverse points of view to grappling with value dilemmas.

Engage in loyal dissent. Values-based leaders do more than encourage dissent from those who report to them—they practice dissent as well. They know how to take a stand when they disagree on a tough issue where core values might be violated—their own, organizational, and/or constitutional. As John Johns, former dean at the National Defense University and former faculty member at the Federal Executive Institute, reminds us, we have many ways to act in between the extremes of silence and whistle-blowing (see Box 1.7). Values-based government executives know how to practice

Box 1.7   Guidelines for loyal dissent in government*

1. Choose your issues carefully. Dissent tries the patience of superiors. Use your credits for dissent judiciously.

2. Do your homework and think it over. Do not shoot from the hip every time you disagree.

3. Clearly take ownership for your dissent.

4. Don't personalize the challenge; focus on the issue. Remember that reasonable people can honestly differ, sometimes with strong convictions, on issues.

5. Be objective and balanced in your analysis of the issue. Each of us is a product of our own unique experiences and we view the world based on those experiences. Try to put yourself in the shoes of the opposition, remembering that higher officials tend to view issues in a broader context.

6. Don't paint your superiors into a corner by challenging their judgment in public (or at a staff meeting unless the superior asks for a discussion of the issue), especially if they have taken a public stance.

7. Do not expect radical change in opposing views.

8. Know your boss. What are his/her central values and does the issue at hand relate to those central values? If so, change will be difficult.

9. Provide alternatives to the position you are challenging, i.e., don't be merely negative.

10. Choose your time to challenge. In general, try to get your oar in the water before a position has been announced.

11. Recognize when you have pushed the limit. Bosses differ in their tolerance of dissent, even when it is loyal.

12. Always remember that you may be wrong; you may even be ideologically biased.

13. Accept defeat graciously, i.e., don't pout. On the other hand, if you cannot live with the decision, from a moral standpoint, you have the option of going to higher authority, or ultimately resigning. (You may also feel justified in contacting Congress, interest groups, or the media. This **may** be loyal dissent in some instances, but it is often called "whistleblowing" and is judged by different criteria than loyal dissent.)

---

*This version is slightly abbreviated. For the full version, by John Johns, see *Constitutional Literacy Reader* (Charlottesville, VA: Federal Executive Institute).

Figure 1.5 Moral courage

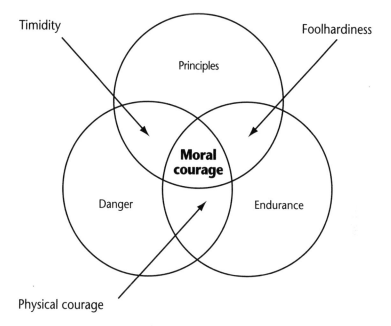

Source: "Moral Courage and Its Contraries," figure 8, from *Moral Courage* by Rushworth Kidder. Copyright © 2005 by Rushworth M. Kidder. Reprinted by permission of HarperCollins Publishers.

loyal dissent. They may ultimately have to blow the whistle, but that action, which often removes them from further significant influence in their organizations, is the last resort, not the first.

Act with moral courage. Acting ethically and engaging in loyal dissent where needed often require courage. Not everyone welcomes or applauds moral action. Physical bravery, the kind seen in battle, is what we usually think of when talking about courageous action, but most of the situations career leaders in government face will not call for that. Moral courage is what transforms ethical thinking into ethical action, and a government executive cannot be a values-based leader without it. Kidder argues persuasively that moral courage comes at the intersection of three circles of thinking, as illustrated in Figure 1.5.[33] The first is the sphere of principles. A leader cannot take moral action unless it is in service to moral values. The second is the sphere of danger. If the leader is going to exercise moral courage, he must consider the hardships: ostracism from social groups, personal loss of a job and benefits, and/or the anguish and ambiguity that come with not knowing what taking a stand will mean for the leader's organizational and personal life. The third is the sphere of endurance. Exercising moral courage often means a long, hard struggle against great odds with uncertain success. Note that Kidder argues that moral courage requires all three. Jumping into action on principle may be just foolhardy if the leader has not carefully evaluated the danger (hardships) being faced. Considering principles and danger but not engaging in enduring action is just timidity. Acting despite danger without thought as to the moral principles involved is physical courage and may be laudable in some situations, but it is not the same as moral courage.[34]

Conclusion

Values-based leadership in government is both essential and possible. It can be studied, understood, and learned. It can be instilled in others and enshrined in organizational practices. It builds trust, fosters productive relationships within and outside agencies and is essential to democratic governance. Values-based leaders—and organizations—are made, not born. They result when government executives see themselves in service to citizens. And service to citizens is what being a civil servant means, after all. It requires, among all else we have discussed, a large portion of humility.

It may seem odd to end this prescription for the behavior of values-based leaders in government with a paean to humility. Aren't leaders supposed to be charismatic, resolute, visible, and sure-footed? Was Washington humble? Lincoln? The short answer is yes, and they were charismatic, resolute, visible, and sure-footed, too. Humility is not a shrinking away from the world. It is an acceptance of one's ultimately small place in the grand scheme of things, of one's debt to so many others (whom we call followers and citizens), of one's human limits. It also indicates a stance of openness to what others have to contribute and to the values that matter to them.

This very finding has emerged in recent research on leadership. In *Good to Great*, Jim Collins asked what, if anything, was commonly shared among leaders who took well-performing organizations and turned them into great ones.[35] He found only two personal qualities. One was an intense will to succeed, and the other was great humility. Their humility created an atmosphere of trust and built powerful relationships that served them and their organizations well. Their humility helped them become values-based leaders.

George Washington spent forty years in public service. He led troops in the French and Indian War. He took command of the Continental Army and led it through eight years of hardship to ultimate victory. He served as president of the Constitutional Convention in 1787, and he served two terms as the first president of the United States created by that convention. At the end of his public service, Washington, who might well have been president for life if he wished, chose instead to relinquish power. In his Farewell Address in 1796, he spoke of his hopes for the country, his lessons for preserving the still fragile republic, and his personal gratitude for the honor of serving. Among his final words to a grateful nation was the recognition that a president too was human after all: "In the discharge of this trust," Washington said, "I will only say that I have, with good intentions, contributed towards the Organization and Administration of the government, the best exertions of which a very fallible judgment was capable."

This is values-based leadership at its very best.

Tips for leadership success

- Identify the core values that drive you in your life and work. These are the source of your power and passion, both of which are essential for leadership.
- Lead by attending to your core values. Recognize when your actions would violate these values and summon the moral courage to behave in a way that represents the best ethical traditions of government service.
- Be faithful to your oath of office and accept that you have taken an obligation that means subordinating your personal agenda to serving the public good.
- Approach your civil service leadership role with a sense of humility. Accept that there is much you do not know and perspectives you have not considered and find ways to learn and be open to alternative views.
- Build your skills in and exercise your ability to have integrity, listen, tolerate dissent, include others in decision making, and use moral imagination to consider a broad range of perspectives and options to act in a values-driven way.
- Build an organizational culture that supports keeping the public purpose in mind, expressing dissent, considering value trade-offs that accompany contested issues, and examining the long range implications of potential actions on all those affected by them.

Resources for further learning

Books

For a broad overview of values-based leadership and moral reflection in public life, consider reading the following books:

Terry Cooper, *The Responsible Administrator: An Approach to Ethics for the Administrative Role*, 4th ed. (1998). Cooper first presents a model for thinking about and addressing ethical questions and then tackles ethics at a practical level for the individual and the organization.

Janet Denhardt and Robert Denhardt, *The New Public Service: Serving, Not Steering* (2003). The authors suggest that the new public service sees the role of the civil servant as fostering democracy through active engagement of citizens in the creation and implementation of policy. The new public service requires the public administrator to think about what it means to create the good society and civic virtue.

Louis Gawthrop, *Public Service and Democracy: Ethical Imperatives for the 21st* Century (1998). Gawthrop argues that democracy can be preserved only when public officials imbue their thinking and action with three core moral values—faith, hope, and love. Effective pubic service, he maintains, requires a moral center not just following the law.

John Rohr, *Public Service, Ethics, and Constitutional Practice* (1998). Bureaucrats are not isolated from the policy process just because they are unelected. Rohr maintains that career civil servants can avoid abusing their power if they anchor their thinking in regime values—the constitutional values that shape society and should guide their thinking.

For focusing on specific issues and skills civil service leaders must address, consider reading the following:

Joseph Badaracco Jr., *Leading Quietly* (2002). Although the heroic, larger-than-life leader is sometimes needed in society, Badaraco argues that most situations are best addressed through the quiet leader, a person who does the right thing effectively but without fanfare. He identifies the eight tactics and three traits that characterize their actions.

Sissela Bok, *Lying: Moral Choice in Public and Private Life* (1978). Bok addresses under what conditions, if any, lying may be justified and the implications of lies on public trust.

Rushworth Kidder, *Moral Courage* (2005). The ability to think through ethical dilemmas is necessary but not sufficient to being an ethical person. The second ingredient needed is moral courage. It consists of deciding on the core principles and values that matter, understanding the dangers (to reputation, livelihood, and so forth) that may attend acting morally, and having the endurance to act and persist despite obstacles.

Patricia Werhane, *Moral Imagination and Management Decision Making* (1999). Why do good managers make unethical decisions? Werhane suggests that they may become locked into a particular conception of their role, a particular narrative of how the world works, a particular mental model that makes it almost impossible for them to see things from any other vantage point. Moral imagination, the ability to see a situation from different perspectives and to create and consider alternatives for appropriate action, is essential to managerial decision making that is both effective and moral.

For examples of ethical leadership and a strong culture in government, consider reading these books:

Donald Phillips and Admiral James M. Loy, *Character in Action: The U.S. Coast Guard on Leadership* (2003). During Hurricane Katrina, the U.S. Coast Guard was heralded for rescuing more than 30,000 people. The authors highlight the core values and leadership principles that made such success possible. The Coast Guard deliberately and passionately aims to develop character.

Jack Uldrich, *Soldier, Statesman, Peacemaker: Leadership Lessons from George C. Marshall* (2005). Credited with a major role in the allied victory in World War II as well as the Marshall Plan for the reconstruction of Europe, George C. Marshall is still one of the least well known of American generals and statesmen. This book explores his leadership principles and the role of selflessness, courage, candor, integrity, fairness, vision, preparation, and teaching others in ethical leadership.

Web Resources

Websites that are useful for exploring values-based leadership include the following:

Center for Ethics and the Professions, Harvard University, www.ethics. harvard.edu. The center encourages teaching and research about ethical issues in business, education, government, law, medicine, and public policy.

Ethics Resource Center, Washington, D.C., www.ethics.org. The center focuses on ethics research and education related to creating ethical individuals and organizations in the public and private sectors.

Government Accountability Project, Washington, D.C., www.whistleblower.org. This organization focuses on enhancing occupational free speech for government and private-sector workers. It has a large focus on supporting whistle-blower protections.

Institute for Global Ethics, Camden, Maine, www.globalethics.org. Started by Rush Kidder, the institute promotes ethical behavior in individuals, institutions, and nations through research, public discourse, training, and practical action.

Josephson Institute of Ethics, Marina del Rey, California, http://josephson-institute.org. The Josephson Institute conducts programs and workshops for leaders including legislators and mayors, high-ranking public executives, congressional staff, editors and reporters, senior corporate and nonprofit executives, judges and lawyers, and military and civilian police officers.

Office of Government Ethics, Washington, D.C., www.usoge.gov. This is the site of the federal government agency charged with overall management of ethics legislation and regulations enacted for political appointees and career civil servants who work for the federal government.

Notes

1. Winthrop (1630). More recent and high-level uses of the image of America as a "city upon a hill" include John F. Kennedy's speech in Boston on January 20, 1961, the day before his inauguration as president, and President Ronald Reagan's Farewell Address to the nation on January 11, 1989.

2. The notion of a "city upon a hill" is used here to reflect a view and an expectation that those who govern must demonstrate and build moral values in their roles as leaders and designers of organizations. Some who quote Winthrop use his passage to suggest that somehow America is special among nations, even selected by God to be a shining light to the world. That argument for American exceptionalism is antithetical to values-based leadership as it is used in this chapter because it assumes that Americans are better than the other peoples of the world. Such thinking runs directly contrary to the posture of humility toward and deep respect for others at the heart of values-based leadership.

3. Henderson attended the Federal Executive Institute (FEI) of the U.S. Office of Personnel Management in Class 247. This information is taken, with her permission, from the "leadership challenge" she prepared. The leadership challenge is an activity in which all program executives engage. It is their statement of how they wish to lead their organization into the future. Other examples taken from FEI executives in this chapter are also used with their permission.

4. Arendt (1963) offers a chilling study of what she refers to as the "banality of evil" as she traces the life and bureaucratic career of Adolph Eichmann, the civil servant perhaps most responsible for implementing Hitler's "Final Solution." In the Tuskegee Syphilis Study, physicians failed to provide penicillin to some African American patients even after its curative effects on the disease were known, just so researchers could study the progression of the disease in untreated patients. President Bill Clinton formally apologized for this moral breach on May 16, 1997.

5. Greenleaf (1977).

6. Nye (2004). See also Chapter 13 for a fuller treatment of the importance of values in international leadership.

7. CNN/Opinion Research Corporation poll, February 12–15, 2010. See www.polling report.com/institut.htm.

8. Burns (1978).

9. Collins and Porras (1994).

10. *Merriam-Webster's Collegiate Dictionary*, 11th ed. (Springfield, MA: Merriam-Webster, 2003), 450.

11. Using evidence from ninety-seven samples in forty-four countries, Shalom Schwartz (1994) demonstrates that the same values, clustered in very similar ways, show up in the cultures of a wide range of nations. Although certain value clusters may carry different weights in different cultures, there does appear to be a universal structure and content to the value set overall.

12. Molyneux and Teixeira (2010), 30. The relationship between "has policies that generally reflect my values" and confidence in government has the strongest correlation of six different questions asked (see p. 31).

13. Bok (1978) is a seminal work in this area. Bok offers a set of considerations for those in public and private life to use in determining if a lie is justified. The quote here is taken from the chapter, "Lies for the Public Good."

14. Letter to Thurlow Weed, March 15, 1865, at www.abrahamlincoln200.org/lincolns-life/words-and-speeches/default.aspx.

15. Merriam-Webster's, 450.

16. See *Federalist* No. 10, *The Federalist Papers*, at http://thomas.loc.gov/home/histdox/fed_10.html.

17. Jefferson (1801).

18. See Columbia Accident Investigation Board Final Report, chap. 8, 201, August 26, 2003.

19. The field of organizational development, pioneered in the 1960s and 1970s, draws heavily on research showing that participation breeds commitment as well as better solutions. For two more modern treatments of the same issue, see Heifetz (1994) and Kouzes and Posner (2002). Heifetz demonstrates that the significant problems facing public sector leaders lack technical ("one right answer") solutions and that only the involvement of others can lead to the adaptive solutions needed. Kouzes and Posner draw upon research showing the power of engagement to build a shared vision and a common commitment to act.

20. See Werhane (1999) for a cogent and thought-provoking discussion of the importance and elements of moral imagination.

21. Many writers have crafted ethical decision-making models and questions. An excellent book that lays out a number of approaches is Lewis (1991).

22. NASA's core purpose statement cited here was in place during the *Columbia* shuttle disaster. It has since been revised given NASA's new focus on manned lunar and Mars landings.

23. For example, see Janis (1989); Sunstein (2003); Surowiecki (2004); Roberto (2005).

24. Waldo (1988).

25. For a brief article on the concept of moral perimeters, see Kidder (2005b).

26. An excellent work on this topic is O'Leary (2005). Situations may arise in which a career civil service leader's personal or professional values are so much in the public interest that acting overtly or covertly against political leadership may be justified on ethical grounds. Such "guerrilla" action should be taken only after very careful deliberation, however, because civil disobedience is a practice that can seriously undermine democratic governance.

27. For example, the Veterans Health Administration has done pioneering work in reducing medical errors by creating a climate where people are encouraged to report rather than suppress them. See Longman (2010).

28. Quote is taken from the written description of Ali Bahrami's Leadership Challenge at the Federal Executive Institute. The document is undated.

29. See, for example, Jehn (2001). Quoted in Sunstein (2003), Jehn says: "For a team to be effective, members should have high information diversity and low value diversity. For a team to be efficient, members should have low value diversity. For a team to have high morale (higher satisfaction, intent to remain, and commitment) or to perceive itself as effective, it should be composed of participants with low value diversity."

30. "National Government Ethics Survey: A View of Public Sector Ethics," Ethics Resource Center, 2007, V.

31. Kidder (1995).

32. Gawthrop (1998).

33. Kidder (2005a).

34. Much of the physical courage shown in battle or by law enforcement officers or firefighters also includes moral courage. The two are not mutually exclusive. When a soldier risks her life to save her comrades, she has usually thought carefully about the values of accomplishing a critical mission and self-sacrifice for others before that moment arrives. This not only endows her physical courage with moral courage, it is often that moral courage that has made the physical courage possible.

35. Collins (2001).

Self-awareness and leadership success

BEVERLY R. FLETCHER, SENIOR FACULTY, FEDERAL EXECUTIVE INSTITUTE*
ALFRED L. COOKE, SENIOR FACULTY, FEDERAL EXECUTIVE INSTITUTE*

Self-awareness is essential for leaders. Without understanding themselves, leaders can neither draw on their strengths nor mitigate their weaknesses, and they undercut their efforts to build trust. Self-awareness requires self-knowledge and self-affirmation, gained through a lifelong process of discovery and change. To become self-aware, effective leaders use a variety of tools, such as exploring their values, examining their lives for lessons about what has shaped them and guides their current thinking, keeping a journal to reflect on ongoing leadership efforts, questioning the assumptions that underlie their behavior, and inviting feedback. This chapter describes these approaches and techniques that can be used to enhance self-awareness in each area. The chapter concludes with a brief discussion of the value of both mentors and coaches in the effort to enhance self-awareness.

What lies behind us and what lies before us are tiny matters compared to what lies within us.

—*Ralph Waldo Emerson*

You make your life your own by understanding it.

—*Warren Bennis*

TIM APPLIED FOR A POSITION within his agency that would have been a promotion for him. He successfully competed in a multiphased interview process and was told that he had been selected, but several months passed, and the

---

* The views expressed here are the authors' and do not necessarily reflect those of the Federal Executive Institute or the U.S. Office of Personnel Management.

selection was still not formalized. Tim was feeling doubt at this point. He was disappointed to learn indirectly that his current boss had communicated with the would-be new supervisor and asked that Tim not be given the new job because he was needed for his current program. None of this was communicated directly to Tim, even though he had informed both bosses that he would be pleased to work with them on transition plans.[1]

Tim faced a career-defining moment. How he responded would be guided by how well he understood himself. And his response would have a profound effect on his chances for the promotion, his career, and his relationships with both of these supervisors. In short, Tim could build trust in his relationships with his supervisors—or not—depending on what he did next. Although Tim was not in control of whether he got the position, he was in control of how he responded to the news.

According to Chris Musselwhite, "Although it is probably one of the least discussed leadership competencies, self-awareness is possibly one of the most valuable." Musselwhite further states that without self-awareness one cannot create trust in the organization.[2]

"Self-awareness is being conscious of what you're good at while acknowledging what you still have yet to learn."[3] The hard work of understanding oneself is not a destination where one arrives with complete and perfect self-awareness. Instead it is a lifelong journey in which one strives to become more self-aware at each milestone. The premise for this chapter was laid out in Chapter 1: becoming a values-based leader is not just a matter of picking values from a list; rather, it involves a lifetime of building self-awareness, engaging in authentic behavior, and being able to change.

Research suggests that if a leader is to be successful in building trust in the organization, self-awareness is ongoing internal work that is essential.[4] A basic assumption is that the process of becoming self-aware is a way of life. The focus therefore must be on developing leaders who are in a continual mode of self-learning.

Warren Bennis, a highly regarded pioneer in the field of organizational change and leadership, indicates that a leader cannot learn from someone else how to become fully self-aware. He notes important lessons to be learned in the self-discovery process:

> You are your own best teacher. . . . Accept responsibility. . . . Blame no one. . . . You can learn anything you want to learn. . . . True understanding comes from reflecting on your experience.[5]

Robert Tannenbaum, UCLA professor emeritus of the Anderson School of Management and one of the originators of the field of organization development, comes to a similar conclusion when he writes that leadership effectiveness relies on having an integrated knowledge of one's leadership behaviors, but, more important, effectiveness depends on developing an *internalized knowledge of self.*[6]

A model of leadership success

Figure 2.1 displays two major components of successful leadership: self-awareness and other awareness. Leadership success depends on gaining self-awareness through self-examination and change while also gaining willing followers through other awareness and adeptly influencing people to follow.

This chapter primarily focuses on the top portion of Figure 2.1—the self-awareness limb. Self-awareness involves self-reflection, values exploration, engaging in authentic behavior, and being able and willing to change. Although we explore the top half of the figure in more depth, it is important to keep in mind that the bottom half implies that trust develops only by understanding oneself and simultaneously understanding others.

Figure 2.1   Components of leadership success

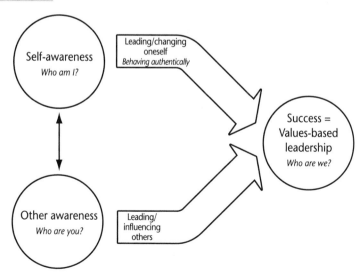

The matrix of the relationship between self and others is activated when answering the question, "Who are we?" The process of defining who we are together and successfully establishing that relationship is the basis for building trust. Values-based leadership therefore is the practical outcome of successfully understanding and managing oneself while developing trusting and mutually influencing relationships.

In our model, leadership success is measured in terms of the achievement of values-based leadership. Another way to look at this is to think of success as the achievement of a state in which the individual makes appropriate self- and other-affirming choices. Self-efficacy is a proactive process in which the individual is able to make self-affirming choices based on fundamental self-knowledge and esteem.[7] A simple formula describes this process:

Self-awareness = Self-knowledge + Self-affirmation ➡ *Self-efficacy*

As a senior executive at a government agency, Mary faces a critical meeting in which the agency's new director plans on discussing a change in the organization. Mary is concerned about one of the proposals that she believes fundamentally alters the agency's mission. Furthermore, this aspect of the agency's mission is the primary reason why Mary became a public servant fifteen years ago, and it continually provides her with the motivation to do her challenging job. Most of the other senior managers in the agency favor the proposed new direction. Prior to the meeting, Mary wonders whether she should go along with the change or voice her concerns. At some point, she asks herself, "Who am I?" She comes to the difficult conclusion that she must voice her concerns in an authentic way based on her core values and self-awareness. Mary engages in a process of reflecting on and becoming more aware of herself that ultimately leads to self-efficacy; as a result, she performs an important service to her organization.

Similarly, when you need to influence others and make decisions affecting others, the following formula has implications for successful leadership:

Other awareness = Other knowledge + Other affirmation ➡ *Other efficacy*

Although the focus of this chapter is on the first of these two formulas (self-awareness) the second formula has far-reaching implications for leaders. To be effective in her dialogue with the organization, Mary must be able to suspend her judgments about the motivations of the other managers. She must understand their underlying assumptions and interests and affirm them as individuals in order to develop creative ways collaboratively that address both their interests and hers and build trust. The implications for other efficacy[8] should be kept in mind as it comes into play in Chapters 3 through 5 on effective conversations, coaching and team building.

Self-awareness: "Who am I?"

Knowing others is wisdom, knowing yourself is enlightenment.

—Lao-Tzu

Knowledge of the self is the mother of all knowledge.

—Kahlil Gibran, The Philosophy of Logic

Self-knowledge is cognitive information we have about various fundamental aspects of our character. It is the information we gather through observing and reflecting on our past experiences and behaviors. It comes as a result of self-exploration such as, "I am proficient at ____." "I am not good at ____." "I have a preference for____." "Given a choice between ____ and ____, I tend to choose ____." "I am recognized for my ability to ____." "I most often see myself as ____." The list goes on.

The Myers-Briggs Type Indicator (MBTI) personality preferences; interest preferences in the Strong Vocational Interest Blank; personal sketches from a multitude of leadership profile instruments, and knowledge gained from multirater feedback—from those who supervise, report to, and are organizational peers—are all formalized means of gaining self-knowledge. Less formal, and perhaps equally as valuable, is observing one's own choices, behaviors, personal preferences, and habits, which are often overlooked indicators of self.

An instructor at a residential education center, Julie, is scheduled to meet with her boss, Stan, to go over the faculty schedule for the upcoming year. Last year, program coordination work, which involved being the "up-front" visible presence for a large class, was divided equally among five instructors. Although Julie completed her coordination tasks competently, she did not enjoy this part of her job. As an introvert, she experienced a high level of stress and found that coordination tasks significantly drained her energy and reduced her effectiveness in other areas. Because the organization in the current year is short two instructors, it is more important than ever for everyone to do their fair share of coordinating to make it all work. Julie wonders, however, if a simple division of labor is truly the best way to use the various talents that are available. Susan and Greg, two of her colleagues, are gregarious extroverts who thoroughly enjoy the "onstage" processes of coordinating large programs and do so with ease and grace. Both have expressed a preference for coordinating programs over most of the other instructor duties. Julie, however, is a whiz with program design and truly enjoys the more intimate setting of the small classroom and feels most effective there. She decides to bring up her concerns when she meets with Stan.

Knowing one's preferences is important self-knowledge that allows one to make effective choices about when to assume responsibility and when to seek to delegate to others.

Self-affirmation is the affective component of self-awareness. It represents what we like or esteem about who we are. Self-affirmation is highlighted by how we answer questions such as: "I value ____ about myself." "I like that I am ____." "It is important that others respect my ____." "I like myself because ____." "I try to let others know that ____ is important to me." Such responses get at the nature of what one appreciates about oneself. They reflect the affective and emotional responses that we need as human beings to validate who we are. For Julie, it is important to focus her attention on the strengths that she brings to the team rather than on what she may perceive to be her shortcomings as an introvert. By focusing on what she likes and values about herself, Julie is effective in talking with Stan, who agrees to her suggestion that those who have the greatest strength in doing coordination work be assigned more of it.

Self-efficacy is conscious and affirming choice-making.[9] The formulaic rule suggests that if you have a clear understanding of yourself and affirm the goodness and value that is in you, you will be able to make effective self-affirming choices. Efficacy also suggests that if you have knowledge of others and affirm their value, you will make "other affirming" choices as well. Efficacy is values-based. One's values are at the core of choice-making whether one makes choices about self or others.

Harvard professor Howard Gardner sums up the need for doing the hard work of developing self-awareness:

> I want my children to understand the world, but not because the world is fascinating and the human mind is curious. I want them to understand it so that they will be positioned to make it a better place. Knowledge is not the same as morality, but we need to understand if we are to avoid past mistakes and move in productive directions. An important part of that understanding is knowing who we are and what we can do.[10]

Tools for building self-awareness

> Look well into thyself; there is a source of strength which will always spring up if thou wilt always look there.
>
> —*Marcus Aurelius*

Over time we tend to develop patterns and ways of doing things that blind us to new possibilities and prevent us from seeking new knowledge that might change the way we see the world and therefore the choices we make. Gardner might well have spoken directly to us as leaders. What he suggests is that the goal of leadership is to make the best choices grounded in the knowledge of oneself and affirming who we are.[11] Among the many accepted ways to enhance self-awareness are:

- Knowing what is important—values exploration.
- Doing your autobiography.
- Keeping a journal.
- Examining your behavior through the "ladder of inference."
- Inviting feedback.
- Receiving mentoring and executive coaching.

Knowing what is important—values exploration

Values are emotionally charged and powerful mechanisms for ordering our existence. Our values play themselves out every day and in every area of our lives. They identify what is important to us in every aspect of ourselves. Many of us act out of values that we have never consciously considered. Successful leadership requires that we understand our values and what motivates us to make the choices we do. Furthermore, it is important to recognize that as leaders we act out of at least two sets of values: organizational and personal. These sets of values can be congruent and give us the potential for dynamic leadership; or they might be conflicting causing tension in our leadership, organizational relationships, and ultimately our ability to build and maintain trust in the organization. When we have not consciously explored our values, we can find ourselves in trouble without knowing that it is the result of conflicting values. Similarly, when we have not defined our values, we do not have a firm basis for identifying and comparing our options and making effective decisions.

Values exploration can be as simple as asking "What do I value?" "What do you value?" and "What values do we have in common?" Discovering answers to these questions can help both individuals and the organization to find ways to work together successfully.

Furthermore, as you explore your values, certain questions can guide the inquiry: Do your answers come from a spiritual or religious practice? Are they based in a cognitive and rational orientation? Are they from rules of behavior and guidelines learned in your childhood?

A simple values exploration exercise such as the one in Box 2.1 is a useful way to start individually exploring your values and also identifying possible conflicting values. You are asked to select your "top five" values from a longer list of possibilities. The act of choosing from a longer list helps clarify what values are most central and which may operate

---

Box 2.1   Values exploration exercise

What are your top five personal values and your top five organizational values? Having selected the top five, now place them in priority order revealing which are most important to you. Do they complement each other or come into conflict? What problems, if any, do conflicts (for example, valuing truth but also loyalty) create for you as a leader? Feel free to add other values to the list before you begin.

Personal values
(these matter most to me)
(*examples*)
- truth
- trust
- openness
- love
- family
- justice
- mercy
- freedom
- community
- economic security
- learning
- achievement
- harmony

Organizational values
(these matter most to my organization)
(*examples*)
- accountability
- responsibility
- creativity
- quality
- productivity
- teamwork
- integrity
- loyalty
- timeliness
- customer focus
- diversity
- effectiveness
- efficiency

more at the periphery of your life. Values can be added to the list as you gain insights.

Once individuals have completed important values exploration work, the organization can work together as a unit to explore mutually held values and discover how those values relate to their common oath of office; their shared commitment to the mission; and a new vision for the organization.

Tim, with whom we began this chapter, realized that his organizational desire to be loyal and a team player conflicted with some of his core personal values, especially his belief in justice (he had applied for and been selected for the job) and desire for achievement (he truly wanted the promotion). He struggled to find a way to honor both sets of values and decided to raise his concern with his current boss in a direct but nonconfrontational way. Although it was a difficult conversation, in the end they resolved the problem: he would report to his new job in another month, during which time he would train his successor. Being self-aware helped Tim deal with his sense of betrayal—and far more successfully than if he had just demanded satisfaction from his boss.

Similarly, in the case of Alex and Greg (see Box 2.2), their organization, ABA, is headed for trouble if they cannot find a way to see how their personal and organizational values are shaping their approach to the job and each other. The coming train wreck at ABA does not need to happen, but it will without more self- and other awareness around core values.

Writing your autobiography

A full or partial autobiography or memoir is a useful tool for exploring one's values, how they developed, and what effect they have had. Even the straightforward process of examining significant events in one's life and trying to discern what impact they had can be a powerful way to better understand one's values.

The basic premise of any autobiographical technique is that one goes back as far as one can remember and identifies significant events at the different stages of growth and development. Once events are identified, the questions of who was involved and why each event was important can lead to understanding how values developed and what in fact those values may be. It is useful to approach the exercise by finding a quiet place to do this work without interruption. Quieting one's judgmental voice and accepting

Box 2.2 The new boss and the train wreck*

Alex looked up at the lettering on the building as she entered for the first time, around 4:30 p.m.: Agency for Building America (ABA). She felt a chill of excitement. She had played no small part in the election of the new president, and at thirty-five, was known as the "go-to and get-it-done" person. This was her dream job. Raised by second-generation immigrants, she understood the determination and difficulties of small entrepreneurs.

She had about a year and a half, the average tenure of a political appointee, to make dramatic changes. She had studied the ABA and felt she knew the opportunities and threats. As the head of the micro enterprise directorate, she knew what the administration promised: "entrepreneurial enterprises: the heart of America." Yet the ABA had seemed not sure whether its mandate was to benefit small and minority businesses or serve as an appendage to larger corporations. Alex was here to make that all clear. "Small is good," she said to herself.

"Hi, I'm Alex Smith," she said to the woman at the desk. "I'm your new Executive Director."

"I'm Cecily Gordon and we've been expecting you." As Cecily came out from around her desk, Alex noticed that she was wearing jeans. "Casual Monday?" she asked. Cecily blushed. "No, we're just real informal around here," she said. Alex made a mental note to look into *that* policy right away.

"Cecily," she called, "I'd like to see the files for the last six months' activities of the directorate. How do I access them on my computer?"

"Oh," said Cecily, "They are not automated, and we haven't brought them up from storage yet. We figured you'd like to get comfortable first and then ease into everything."

"Well, I wish I had that kind of time," said Alex, "but I need the files immediately."

Alex was shocked by the antiquated paper-driven system. Her determination to support small business people increased as she observed all this. If not me, who, she pondered.

I need to shake them off their duffs, she thought. "Cecily, can you set up a meeting for me with my direct reports for 9 a.m. tomorrow morning, please? Alex thought she detected just a light head shake as Cecily left.

I'll change policies and figure out how to reduce the restrictions on grants and loans. I need to have my plans in place before I meet with my "reports," Alex thought. I sure hope they "get it" and don't fight it.

Greg Sheldon, deputy director for regional operations at ABA was on his way to the elevator when he learned about the morning meeting with his new boss. He thought about going into the director's office to introduce himself, but, based on Cecily's ominous words when she set up the meeting, he decided to wait. On his way out of the building he grumbled "this does not bode well for us."

On the metro, Greg thought about his long career, thirty-five years of which he spent working his way up from the smallest southern regional ABA office. Another cycle of politicos, he thought . . . . God save us from eighteen-month wonders! He thought about putting together a briefing to the new director for the morning meeting, highlighting the great work of the current leadership team. Although Greg saw himself as a role model and staunch supporter of work-life balance—he stopped people from taking work home and he even sent some home early when possible—tonight is an important exception, he concluded.

- What personal and organizational values drive Alex and Greg?
- What value conflicts are looming for the 9 a.m. meeting?
- How can either Alex or Greg avoid an ABA "train wreck"?

---

*This case is abbreviated. For the full version, see Gail Funke, Beverly Fletcher, and Alfred Cooke, "We Be Here: Change at the ABA" (Charlottesville, VA: Federal Executive Institute).

what is revealed as useful information for self-discovery (not as criticism of one's life) is important.

The example in Figure 2.2 is a Lifeline Exercise done by a federal executive. In completing this exercise, Jim discovered a number of connections he had not previously seen that helped him to understand his reactions to major decisions made in his agency. By listing the critical events in his life that stimulated significant emotional responses, Jim was able to go beyond his immediate reactions to recent similar events and make several important decisions for both his agency and himself.

Jim realized that the military values so prevalent in his background, recently reinforced when he moved his father's grave to Arlington National Cemetery, had made him overly dependent on a leadership style that assumed—and expected—strict adherence to a chain of command. This value cut against the more collegial culture in his agency, especially with the newer and younger employees he supervised. He struggled to find a way to honor his core values while acknowledging that they need not be firmly applied in all cases in his relationships with direct reports.

Figure 2.2 A lifeline exercise

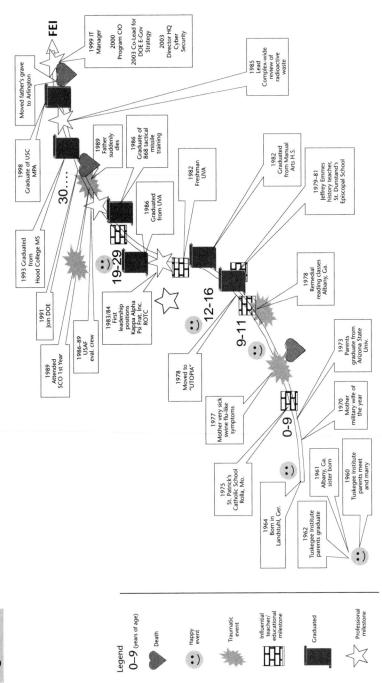

Legend

0–9 (years of age)

Death

Happy event

Traumatic event

Influential teacher/ educational milestone

Graduated

Professional milestone

Keeping a journal

The journal is an ongoing repository of experiences, thoughts, actions, and beliefs. It is a way of capturing internal thought processes and emotional responses so that they can be more systematically explored for meanings, underlying assumptions, and patterns. Keeping a journal can be formal in that one can set guidelines for what one will capture; or it can be random, exploratory, unstructured, and impromptu. Deciding how to go about keeping a journal and analyzing the results are often difficult tasks for novice journal writers. Perhaps the best way to get started is to find a quiet time and place each day and just start writing about experiences without judgment or attention to sentence structure, spelling, and grammar. The act of simply writing down information is often a sufficient stimulus for making greater sense of an experience. The writings will eventually provide enough data to look more systematically for trends, meanings, conclusions, inferences, and residual learning.

Margaret James Neill is a well-known teacher of how to keep a journal. She points to several good reasons for this approach, such as experimenting with new behavior; developing an internal feedback system that clarifies and reminds you of "what, how, and where" categories of information; freely expressing and exploring your feelings; learning more about your personal patterns and history and your current status; and enhancing your capacity to be aware of the inner dynamics of your life.[12]

Leadership development consultant Lawrence Porter proposes guidelines for keeping a journal to enhance self-awareness. He writes:

> Keeping a journal is one way of organizing and reviewing one's experiences. One way to do this uses a three-step process. First, describe the experience, i.e. "what happened"? Second, write your reactions to the experience, what you thought, felt, wanted, and did. Finally, write what you learned from what happened.[13]

Paul is a new federal executive from the private sector, who is now a supervisor of a small subgroup in his new agency. Box 2.3 is an excerpt from his journal. However you use it, the journal lends itself to self-exploration and awareness. Leaders who allow themselves to reflect upon their experiences find fertile ground in which they can grow and change.

Because life is complex and experiences rarely repeat themselves exactly, do not just think in terms of what you would do in the exact same

Box 2.3   An excerpt from Paul's journal

(date)

What happened?

Today I met with Margaret to go over her performance appraisal. My appraisal of her work was in my opinion extremely positive. It was my intention to use most of the time allotted to talk with her about my expectations of her and the staff in implementing my vision for the future of our group. However, she reacted to the appraisal with anger and accused me of belittling her. Her exact words were "I have never had a poor performance appraisal in my life. How dare you propose to assess my work and give me a negative appraisal when you have been here for only five months!"

My reactions

I was taken aback by her strong emotional reaction and my first impulse was to refute her accusations using strong language. I felt that her response was inappropriately aggressive and I was extremely disappointed as I had expected better from her. I found it very challenging to withhold voicing my automatic response to her outburst.

I am proud that instead of an automatic rebuttal, I observed my own anger at the exchange and formulated two responses: "Tell me more about how this appraisal impacts you." And "How would you like to word the appraisal so that it more accurately reflects your perceptions of your performance?"

By holding off on my emotional response and engaging her in a conversation, I was able to get her perspective and begin to develop an understanding of where she was coming from. I left the session with her agreeing to reword the appraisal. We will get together tomorrow to discuss it.

What I learned

This incident has brought home to me the need to be sensitive not only to the cultural expectations I have, but those of others in this new situation. I will have to be careful to clarify my intentions and expectations in ways that are different from my previous position. I need to be more sensitive to the paradigm differences that exist here and weigh my responses based on a careful self-review.

situation. Think about what can be taken from the experience and applied to other related and even unrelated situations. The journal is a good place to engage in this type of broad thinking. Go back to previous journal entries and look for generalizations, patterns, tendencies, and underlying principles. When we think more broadly, we make our reflection time significantly more beneficial.

As a general rule it is appropriate for leaders to think systemically about their own behavior just as they do about the organizations in which they operate. Systems thinking requires attention to relationships that sometimes have effects that are not obvious.

Examining your behavior through the "ladder of inference"

Cynthia was confused by the reactions she was getting from Tom, one of the executive assistants who worked for her. Every interaction they had was fraught with what Cynthia believed was aggressive and dismissive language from Tom. He had also begun to ignore her in ways that she felt were rude. After several "slights" from Tom, Cynthia decided to give him the same "cold shoulder." She made a decision to interact with him on a very limited basis and only when necessary to complete vital work.

Tom took Cynthia's response to him as confirmation of his initial negative response to her. Cynthia then saw Tom's "escalated rude behavior" as evidence that she should continue to avoid Tom as much as possible. Over time the situation with Cynthia and Tom deteriorated because they both failed to recognize the assumptions they were making about each other's behavior.

Before you can effectively challenge your assumptions, you must first become aware of when you are making them. The ladder of inference is a concept that helps to explain how humans very naturally go about making assumptions.[14] An inference is a conclusion derived from beliefs regarding what are thought to be facts. According to the ladder of inference (see Figure 2.3), we tend to assume that our beliefs and actions are objectively based on observable data in the "real world," and we are surprised when others do not see the "truth" as clearly as we do.

Chris Argyris, professor emeritus at Harvard Business School, says that data by which we make sense out of the world of events and experiences are all around us in infinite quantities. To keep from becoming overwhelmed by these vast amounts of information, we have developed the important ability to select limited amounts of data and make inferences from them based on assumptions that come from our values, beliefs, and previous experiences.

Our actions in turn are based on the assumptions that we make, which then leads us to narrowly select data in future experiences that are

Figure 2.3 The ladder of inference

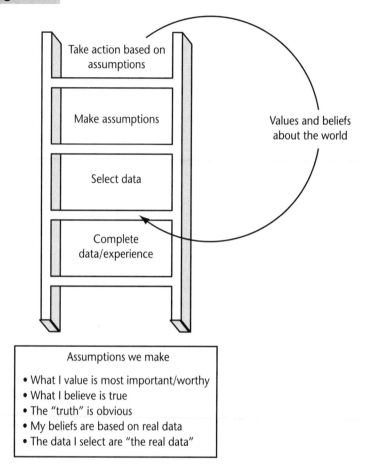

Take action based on
assumptions

Make assumptions

Select data

Complete
data/experience

Values and beliefs
about the world

Assumptions we make

• What I value is most important/worthy
• What I believe is true
• The "truth" is obvious
• My beliefs are based on real data
• The data I select are "the real data"

Source: Adapted from the work of Chris Argyris. See Peter M. Senge, *The Fifth Discipline* (New York: Doubleday, 1994).

similar. We do this to the extent of ultimately not even seeing the other data—especially those that contradict our assumptions. The irony is that without this ability to "narrowly select data," it would take an inordinate amount of time to understand our world of experiences. Consequently, making decisions would be time-consuming, costly, and even dangerous to us in many ways.

Therefore, our ability to make inferences is a good thing; it is useful in that it helps us to quickly understand what is happening and to make timely decisions. Paradoxically, this ability also poses an obvious danger—one that can lead us into taking faulty actions. If we are not aware that we are making an inference based on incomplete data, we will believe that the assumptions we make are indeed "the facts," that what we believe about the situation is most important and most worthy of attention, that what we know is absolutely "the truth," that the truth is obvious; and that our actions are based on "real data" because, naturally, the data we select are the real data.

By using the understanding gained from the ladder of inference, we can improve our self-understanding, communication with others, and leadership by exercising:

- Self-reflection: Becoming more aware of our own assumptions and beliefs and the data they are based on; and
- Self-disclosure (authentic self-presentation): Making our assumptions and beliefs and the data they are based on more visible to others through a process of dialogue.

According to Terry Newell:

> If we acknowledge that our actions may be based on selecting only certain data, meanings we assign to data (based on cultural and personal experiences and biases), assumptions we make, and/or our beliefs about the world, then we must also acknowledge that other people, with other ways of looking at the same hard data, may have different points of view worth considering. We can then offer our meanings, assumptions, and beliefs as hypotheses, subject to examination and change.[15]

The ladder of inference helped Cynthia and Tom. During a confrontation session initiated by Cynthia, they were able to clarify their inaccurate inferences and challenge their assumptions about each other. They each became more aware of the words they were using and how those words could be misinterpreted. They came to see that they were each making assumptions based on paying attention to only some of their actions and statements—in other words, selecting data to confirm their suspicions of each other—and entirely missing the supportive actions and messages each was trying to send. After their talk, Cynthia and Tom were able to reconcile their working relationship before it deteriorated beyond repair.

Inviting feedback

In our quest for self-knowledge, we may tend to think more highly of ourselves than we ought or, conversely, we may in our minds exaggerate our weaknesses and look down upon ourselves. We need a realistic view of our strengths and weaknesses if we are to know our true selves. How we see ourselves may be clouded by messages we received early in life or by faulty or outdated assumptions that we have nurtured over the years.

Paradoxically, we need other people to help us see ourselves more clearly, even though others have played a part in our skewed view of ourselves. We may not be prepared to face ourselves as viewed through others' eyes, but it is unlikely that anyone can totally avoid feedback: it comes at us in every moment that we live and take action. To deny feedback is to make a decision to isolate oneself from others and from life. Feedback is the way we learn about ourselves, others, the world around us, and the consequences of our behaviors.

To get a better understanding of who you really are, you must be prepared to receive feedback about yourself from others (see Figure 2.4). Joseph Luft and Harry Ingham, two well-known psychologists, created the Johari Window, a concept that helps us better understand the intersections

Figure 2.4 Feedback is self-awareness in relationship with others

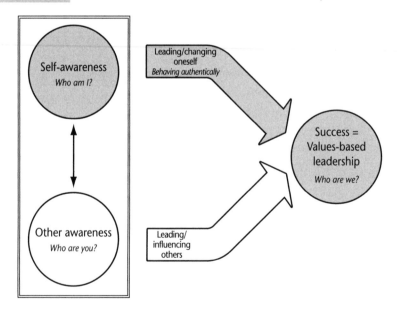

Figure 2.5 The Johari Window

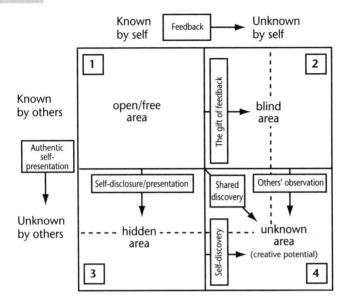

Source: Adapted from Alan Chapman, The Johari Window, 2003 online presentation at http://unpan1.un.org/intradoc/groups/public/documents/UNSSC/UNPAN022136 .pdf. Based on Joseph Luft and Harry Ingham, *The Johari Window: A Graphic Model for Interpersonal Relations* (Los Angeles: University of California, Western Training Lab, 1955).

between what others know about us and what we know about ourselves. This two-by-two matrix (see Figure 2.5) provides a visual metaphor for seeing into oneself.[16]

There are things we and others know about us and things that we and others do not know about us. When we know something about ourselves that corresponds with what others know about us, those things are in the upper left quadrant (Window 1)—the open, free, public, or known area.

Those things about ourselves known only to ourselves and hidden from others are in the hidden or private area (Window 3). Some people also refer to this area as the *mask*, the *façade*, or the *idealized self*. This area is accessible only by you and is in the area where you can work on self-disclosure or authentic self-presentation. Whenever you act authentically in congruence with who you truly are, you reduce the size of the hidden area, which becomes part of Window 1—the open area. It is this area that Cynthia and Tom opened up by sharing more about themselves as they made use of the ladder of inference.

One of the most difficult parts of this model for us to accept is the fact that we all have blind spots, and, unfortunately, others have a clearer view of them than we do ourselves. The blind area (Window 2) contains those things that other people know about you that you cannot see about yourself. This is where feedback is particularly useful. If the feedback you receive is about one of your blind spots, it is a most amazing gift—one that takes courage for the other person to give and may not always be appreciated by the recipient. It is a gift from someone else to you of a part of yourself. Cynthia and Tom also fruitfully explored this area when they finally sat down and, through conversation, realized that they were each blind to the assumptions they were making about the other—such assumptions often go unchecked.

According to noted sports psychologist and consultant Linda Bunker, blind spots (Window 2) and masks (Window 3) can also be "derailers" for a leader.[17] For example, if some mannerism, habit, or eccentricity I have is irritating to others but I don't see it in myself, it may stand in the way of effective communication. Or if I continue to "hide" or shield important personal information from others (perhaps thinking it is demonstrating my courage or strength), it may inadvertently send a message to colleagues that it is not okay to share their personal concerns or challenges.

Perhaps the most profoundly inspiring area of the model is in the lower right quadrant—the unknown or to be discovered area (Window 4). These are the things that neither you nor others know about you. It is the area of greatest creative potential and deep self-discovery—we truly do not know the limits of our potential. The important question to ask about this area is "How do I tap my unknown potential?" The answer to that question may seem simple—through utilizing a combination of authentic self-presentation (which opens up the known area and reduces the hidden area) and feedback (which also opens up the known area and reduces the blind area). These two things—authentic self-presentation and receiving feedback—can change your life in positive ways.

If you tell others that you want feedback, you must really mean it and allocate time for it. If not, you will do more harm than good to the level of trust in the relationship. People may be understandably reluctant to give you feedback because doing so is risky for the giver. When someone declares his inner thoughts about you, he is in fact self-disclosing and making himself vulnerable to you, and must then contend with your reactions. If the giver is unsure of your intentions, open invitations will be nonproductive. People will watch your body language and pay attention to your responses to test if you really mean it. If negative comments raise your personal defenses, people will soon conclude that you only want positive comments and will censor their remarks accordingly.

To avoid these problems, start small by asking only individuals you trust and who know you well. Ask for feedback about specific behaviors. For example, "When I did/said ____, how did you interpret my intentions? What did you feel? What did you think? What were your reactions?" Receive their comments nondefensively without rebuttal: "Yes, but ____" is interpreted as being nonreceptive to the feedback. Also remember to thank them and acknowledge their gift. As you gain more skill at asking for and receiving feedback nondefensively, continue asking others for the feedback you need.

A useful way to get feedback and test your assumptions at the same time is to clearly state the conclusions you arrived at about an experience and then ask selected individuals what conclusions they drew from that same experience. Compare notes with others as a way of engaging in a dialogue about the different perceptions. Avoid debating about who is right or wrong; one can learn much from simply attempting to understand different perceptions.

Another valuable tool for receiving feedback is a 360 degree (or multi-rater) assessment instrument. Such tools were developed because of the complex nature of asking for and receiving honest feedback from a number of different groups of people (peers, direct reports, and bosses) and should not be used as a replacement for interpersonal face-to-face feedback needed from individuals. When used appropriately and skillfully, 360 degree feedback can open doors to powerful follow-up conversations. In the context of this discussion, 360 degree assessments are used as a development tool, not as a tool for appraising performance. Moreover, if the purpose for using a 360 degree assessment is something other than developing one's interpersonal and leadership skills, it does not fall into the category of feedback discussed in this chapter. The value of 360 degree feedback is directly linked to the integrity of the process, and the integrity of the process is measured in terms of its purpose, administration, and the usefulness of its analyses. Characteristics of an effective 360 degree assessment tool are:

- The focus: to enhance self-awareness
- The goal: interpersonal and leadership development

- The method: instruments completed anonymously by direct reports and peers (the exceptions to anonymity is the direct supervisor, and of course the self report)
- The outcome: analyses provided in recognized, tested, and quantifiable categories (for example, the federal executive core qualifications/competencies)[18]

Feedback can provide learning opportunities for us if we can use the observations and reactions of others to become more aware of ourselves and the consequences of our behaviors. Comparing one's view of self (that is, one's scores on the 360) to the views of others is invaluable. The 360 degree assessment can help us become more aware of what we do, how we do it, and how it affects others—which can help us modify behaviors and become more effective in our interactions and communication. Asking for and receiving feedback requires courage, skill, understanding, and respect for self and others.

Receiving mentoring and executive coaching

> To thine own self be true; and it must follow as the night the day, thou can'st not then be false to any man.
>
> —*Shakespeare,* Hamlet

As career government executives with busy schedules and multiple pressures, it is not surprising that we have difficulty finding time to think about who we are, our strengths and weaknesses, our drives and personalities, our habits and values. In turn, a low level of self-awareness makes it almost impossible to be consistent ("true") in our words and actions. Congruence between who you are, your words, and your actions demonstrates the deeper meaning of the word *integrity*. How can you demonstrate integrity if the self is unknown? According to writer and artist Jennifer Hautman, without self-awareness, we continue to get "caught up" in our own internal dramas and unknown beliefs and values, allowing unclear thought processes to determine our feelings and actions.

> If you think about it, not understanding why you do what you do and feel what you feel is like going through your life with a stranger's mind. How do you make wise decisions and choices if you

don't understand why you want what you want? It's a difficult and chaotic way to live never knowing what this stranger is going to do next.[19]

Mentoring and coaching are two effective "tools" in the quest for consistency, authenticity, integrity, and trust.

WHAT IS MENTORING? A successful leader must be able to make good choices and produce effective action. Using a mentor is a process that aids decision making and effective action. A mentor is a veteran of the organization who focuses on transferring organizational knowledge to his or her protégé. The knowledge transfer is most often about critical processes, contacts, and interpersonal relationships that are unwritten and without which one cannot effectively perform in the organization.[20] A mentor helps the executive to expand his or her contacts and networks; focuses the executive's attention on critical assignments and activities; provides words of wisdom from his or her own experience; and gives support and encouragement. A mentor enhances self-awareness through giving feedback, encouraging self-reflection, and asking good questions that challenge the executive to examine his or her assumptions. A mentor, by sharpening the protégé's awareness of the organizational context, can also help the developing leader understand data and go down the ladder of inference before making a serious organizational mistake. Mentors are invaluable, and it is difficult to succeed in any complex organization without one.

WHAT IS EXECUTIVE COACHING? Executive coaching is a partnership between an individual executive and a trained coach to enhance the executive's current and future effectiveness in his or her organization. An executive coach works with an individual executive to identify the executive's developmental goals and pursue a plan for achieving those goals. Coaches draw from a broad knowledge base and an extensive repertoire of assessment and learning tools. Coaching assists the executive to increase self-awareness, understand the implications and consequences of his/her behaviors, and develop new skills and competencies designed to achieve the executive's particular goals. Executive coaching is voluntary, confidential, and tailored to the expectations and schedules of the individual executive.[21] Successful coaching involves the development of a trusting relationship and requires a good fit between the executive and the coach. Unlike mentoring, the executive coach need not have an understanding of the organization to be effective.

George has experienced difficulty communicating with Frank, his peer, and one of two directors in the agency. Frank did not attend meetings that George regularly scheduled, but George made an effort to show up at Frank's meetings. Frank seldom sought George's input when he needed to collaborate, and he avoided eye contact with George whenever the two were in meetings together. Frank seemed to consistently find ways to oppose suggestions from George. When asked to respond to George's requests, Frank usually gave short, curt answers. George was concerned about the ill effects his poor relationship with Frank had on the organization and he decided to get help by seeking the services of an executive coach. The coach helped George see his own behavior and how it might be affecting the relationship. George agreed to do the following:

- Write a letter to Frank identifying his concerns in nondefensive and nonaccusing language.
- In the letter request a meeting in "neutral territory" and suggest the possibility of a third party to facilitate the meeting if Frank so desired.
- In the meeting lay out the issues (again using nondefensive and nonaccusing language) and talk about their underlying common interests and the importance of improving their relationship for the good of the organization.
- Role play with the coach to practice choosing words to use and those to avoid in attempting to reach a mutually satisfactory outcome with Frank.

George wrote the letter. Frank agreed to meet but did not want a third party involved. Although George and Frank will probably never be best friends, others in the organization have seen a notable improvement in their working relationship and a marked improvement in the collaboration between their groups.

The importance of changing—finding the time

> There was that law of life, so cruel and so just, that one must grow or else pay more for remaining the same.
>
> —*Norman Mailer*

> People often say that this or that person has not yet found him or herself. But the self is not something that one finds, it is something one creates.

> *— Thomas Szasz*

One of the main reasons leaders give for not doing the work that enhances self-awareness and change is "I'm too busy—I don't have enough time." Making the time necessary to do this work is essential. Leaders find the time in various ways and places. You do not need hours at a stretch; even a few minutes a few times a day can make a powerful difference. You have time regardless of how busy your schedule is—you just have to carve it out.

- Reflect in the shower.
- Reflect on the commute to and from work.
- Reflect in the moments before you go to bed.
- Reflect with your family or significant other, either one-on-one or in a small group conversation, over meals.
- Convert some of your television or other recreational time into reflection time.
- When you set up your schedule each day, week, month, or quarter, schedule in reflection time.

Finding the time will help you discover who you are. When you know who you are, you may have a need or desire to change, and changing demands an emotional transition, a lot of effort, and a considerable amount of courage. Being self-aware will help you move closer to living your values and enable you to make more suitable choices that enrich your life and the lives of others in the organization. Being self-aware will help build your self-confidence as you become more true to yourself and authentic in every action. The ultimate benefits are improving your organizational relationships and gaining trust.

Tips for leadership success

In summary, the following practices may be helpful as public-sector leaders seek to increase their level of self-awareness:

- Increase your knowledge of what you value through values exploration.
- Write your memoirs or your autobiography.

- Write in your journal daily.
- Examine your behavior through the ladder of inference.
- Invite feedback from others.
- Find an organizational mentor.
- Get an executive coach.

Resources for further learning

Additional resources on self-awareness and related topics include the following:

Books and Articles

Richard Boyatzis and Annie McKee, *Resonant Leadership: Renewing Yourself and Connecting with Others Through Mindfulness, Hope, and Compassion* (2005). This book expands on the concepts of emotional intelligence by describing the highly stressful conditions in which leaders operate today and explains how leaders fall into what they call "dissonance" due to burnout. The authors primarily focus on how leaders might achieve ongoing, enduring "resonance" or qualities that allow them to be effective today, but also maintain their edge into tomorrow.

Alfred Cooke et al., *Reading Book on Human Relations Training*, 8th ed. (1999). A resource for anyone who wants to understand the dynamics of human interaction, this comprehensive collection of essays is for human resource professionals, leaders, managers, consultants, trainers, and students. The collection is divided into major skill-building areas, all necessary for improving professional effectiveness: communications, diversity, conflict, reentry (after the training experience), history and background of laboratory education, self-awareness, support systems, experiential learning, and group dynamics.

Howard Gardner, *Frames of Mind: The Theory of Multiple Intelligences* (1983). Gardner started a national debate with the theory of multiple intelligences, which holds that a unitary measure of intelligence does not take into account a variety of intelligences possessed by humans including mathematics, logic, music, language, and psychological perception. This seminal work outlined his theory, which started with seven intelligences and has grown to eight.

Spencer Johnson, *Who Moved My Cheese?* (1999). Johnson, a physician, created this "story" to help him deal with a difficult change in his life. It showed him how to take his changing situation seriously but not take himself so seriously.

Annie McKee, Richard Boyatzis, and Fran Johnson, *Becoming a Resonant Leader* (2008). In this book the authors share real-life, vivid stories that illustrate how people can develop emotional intelligence, renew themselves, and build resonance. The work uses twenty years of longitudinal research and practical wisdom in the development of experience-tested exercises and tools that help individuals to articulate their strengths and values and craft a plan for intentional change.

Matthew McKay and Patrick Fanning, *Self-Esteem: A Proven Program of Cognitive Techniques for Assessing, Improving and Maintaining Your Self-Esteem*, 3d ed. (2002). This work offers cognitive techniques for overcoming destructive emotions and provides a guide for challenging the inner critic. The authors suggest practical ways to realize what is happening, stop self-judgment, gain perspective, and heal past wounds. The result is an opportunity to change core beliefs about one's identity and potential. New to the third edition is an exploration of the importance of goal setting in maintaining self-esteem.

Chris Musselwhite, *Self-Awareness and the Effective Leader* (2007). In this article the author argues that when you are self-aware enough to openly admit missteps and concede that there is still plenty to learn, you turn mistakes into learning opportunities and give people permission to collaborate without fear, which ultimately leads to trust in the organization. Available at www.inc.com/resources/leadership/articles/20071001/musselwhite.html.

Chris Musselwhite and Randell Jones, *Dangerous Opportunity: Making Change Work* (2010). Based on fifteen years of research involving more than 10,000 managers, this book offers leaders insights into the different ways in which people react to change by way of their personal *Change Styles*. This book presents an invaluable model against which leaders can improve their self-knowledge by checking to see whether they themselves are following Gandhi's dictum to "be the change" they want to see.

Brian Roet, *The Confidence to Be Yourself* (2001), takes you step by step through a confidence-building process. Roet introduces the idea of a "spectrum" of confidence, one end being total confidence, and the other, insecurity and fear. His confidence-building technique encourages the reader to identify a realistic position on the spectrum and work toward full confidence. Roet includes case histories, exercises, and confidence boosters.

Martin Seligman, *Learned Optimism: How to Change Your Mind and Your Life* (1998). Seligman uses research he conducted on optimism as a basis for providing suggestions for individuals to move from pessimism to a more positive way of seeing the world. Positive psychology is in the field of cognitive science. Seligman's thesis is that the attitude of optimism has significant benefits for the individual and it can be practiced and learned.

Media Seminars

Jack Canfield, *Self-Esteem and Peak Performance* (1989), is an audio cassette seminar from CareerTrack Publications.

Hattie Hill-Stoks et al., *Women, Power and Self-Esteem: Take Charge of Your Own Well-Being* (1990), comes from Career Track Publications.

Web Resources

These websites have useful information for the following aspects of self-awareness:

Coaching

http://managementhelp.org/guiding/coaching/coaching.htm#anchor 200622. The author provides a library containing solid information about coaching that addresses: what is coaching, getting coached, coaching others, and other resources.

Journaling

http://42explore.com/journl.htm. This site provides an explanation about what journaling is under the subheading "The Basics" and provides a variety of website links containing useful journal writing information and resources. Another journaling site: www.journalingsaves.com. The author/creator of this website provides useful information on the benefits of journaling and the specifics of how to write a journal. She gives insights into how to get started journaling, how to stimulate your creativity, and how to dig deeper into your underlying values and motivations.

Mentoring

www.opm.gov/hrd/lead/mentoring.asp. The U.S. Office of Personnel Management provides this pdf document entitled "Best Practices: Mentoring."

It contains a definition of mentoring including types of mentors. This document suggests things to consider in developing and implementing mentoring programs as well as resources for mentoring.

Values exploration

www.whatsnextformylife.com/files/ValuesExercise.pdf. This pdf document is a values exploration exercise that helps individuals to rank their top values, determine how well they are honoring those values, and explore how to close the gaps between these espoused values and their actual values in use.

Notes

1. This story and others in the chapter are based on real people and events, but the names have been changed.

2. Chris Musselwhite, (2007), Discovery Learning, Inc., at www.discoverylearning. com.

3. Musselwhite (2007).

4. Weisinger (1998), 4, discusses how self-awareness is the basic building block of emotional intelligence. Sosik and Megerian (1999), 367, examine the impact on performance; Delmhorst (2006), 1, and Halverson et al. (2002), 3, look at 360 degree leadership evaluation; Lash (2002), 1, looks at top leaders and self-awareness; Goleman, Boyatzis, and McKee (2002), 30, discuss self-awareness as foundational for effective leadership.

5. Bennis (1989), 55–56.

6. Tannenbaum (1999), 221.

7. Cooke (1995), 1.

8. Ibid.

9. Ibid.

10. Gardner (1999), 180.

11. Gardner (1999).

12. Neill (1999), 209.

13. Porter (1999), 217.

14. Chris Argyris developed the "ladder of inference" in the 1960s. He is perhaps best known for his seminal work on learning organizations. A discussion of the ladder of inference can be found in Senge (1994).

15. Newell (2004).

16. Luft and Ingham (1955); Luft (1969).

17. Bunker (2001).

18. For Office of Personnel Management's (OPM) Executive Core Qualifications (ECQs), see 28 Senior Executive Service (SES) competencies on OPM's website at www.opm .gov/ses/recruitment/ecq.asp.

19. Hautman's website is www.selfcreation.com/awareness/index.htm.

20. Porter (2000).

21. Federal Executive Institute and Federal Consulting Group (2002), 1.

3 Effective conversations: The genetic code of relationships

Len Kill Kelley, Adjunct Faculty, Federal Executive Institute
Debra Robinson, CEO, Robinson Associates

"Poor communication" is one of the most frequently cited problems leading to dysfunctional relationships and lack of trust in organizations. Poor communication occurs whenever people don't know how to talk with each other. The effective one-on-one conversation is thus a key part of the "genetic code" for building solid interpersonal relationships. This chapter first presents the rationale for and dimensions of effective conversations in organizations. Such conversations require sharing facts and feelings in true dialogue, not the debate that too often ends up being a substitute for good communication in daily work life. Three skills sets are required for effective conversations: listening, inquiry, and feedback, and the chapter presents both a model for using these skills and practical tips for each skill set. When leaders use these skill sets effectively in conversation, both parties feel valued, understood, and can move toward a closure that meets both organizational and individual needs. The result is not only more trust but improved decision making and more commitment to common action.

The single biggest problem with communication is the illusion it has taken place.

—*George Bernard Shaw*

How often and in how many ways have we said, heard, or realized that our conversations are not working as we intend? It is almost a human mantra, "Communication could be improved." And in spite of our best efforts the mantra continues, follows us wherever we go, in endless repetition, with infinite variations on a theme.

Why do you suppose this is? What is so intractable about this issue? *Webster's* dictionary defines conversation as "an oral exchange of sentiments, observations, opinions, or ideas." The obsolete or archaic definition is "conduct" or "behavior." For our purposes the idea of conversation as much more than an "exchange" deserves exploration. Through our words and actions, we create our world. We use language and behavior to create relationships, emotional environments, moods—the very world we live in—and as leaders, the world that others inhabit as well.

No wonder that we so frequently hear that "communication" could be improved. It is so much more than the "exchange of sentiments, observations, opinions, or ideas." Arguably, the single most important skill for a leader is the ability to interact one-on-one successfully with others.

Why is talking together so hard?

In her book, *Turn Your Face*, Barbara Linney begins with a compelling story. One evening when her daughter was small, Ms. Linney was busy preparing dinner while her daughter was talking to her. Sensing that her mother was distracted, the small girl tugged on her mother's skirt and said, "Mama, turn your face." Ms. Linney's daughter knew, in the profound way that only children sometimes do, that her mother needed to stop what she was doing—to look at her—in order to associate and engage truly in a real conversation with her.[1]

What gets in the way of creating productive, engaging conversations? In most of our conversations, there is a lot going on that is not spoken. We get distracted by what we are not saying—what to share, what not to share, the anxiety that feels like a cannon ball just below the solar plexus, the rush to get to the point and move on to the next item on our to-do-list. When conversations are important, when large issues are in question, when we're having difficult conversations, we often fear the results. Fear invokes our fight or flight responses. This response distracts us—physiologically and intellectually. Consequently, we are often at our worst, just when we need to be at our best.

Kate is the manager of ten attorneys who are responsible for a heavy work load of cases that involve complex and difficult labor relations issues for a large agency. Kate has a case load herself, although a smaller one than her staff. Kate knows that she has two attorneys who negatively affect the rest of the staff. Both are highly competent attorneys. Jason, however, is slow and meticulous, always works alone and does not engage with the rest of the staff. He has problems maintaining the same workload as the rest of the staff primarily because he tends to be so slow. Sarah, who is an expert in an important area and a very good attorney, is the team cynic. Her cynicism has become more pronounced as the organization goes through significant changes and downsizing. It is beginning to affect the morale of the entire team negatively. Not only that, but Kate has just received feedback from her staff on a 360-degree review that indicates that they respect her technical expertise but do not believe she is handling the situation with Jason and Sarah very well. Clearly, Kate needs to have a difficult conversation with both Jason and Sarah. But how should she think about this conversation and what skills does she need to bring to bear on it?

The fundamentals

In their book, *Difficult Conversations,* Stone, Patton, and Heen suggest that in every difficult conversation there is an underlying structure. There are three elements to this structure: What happened, feelings, and identity. If we understand this structure, we can improve our approach to difficult conversations.[2]

This structure exists in all conversations. In most of our everyday conversations, these underlying structural concerns are not a problem. They become a problem when conversations become more intense because they are either really important or difficult. We all approach these underlying structures in very different ways. This is not evident until our conversations become fraught with meaning, evoke strong emotions, and/or create uncertainty.[3]

What happened?

First, there is the "What happened?" conversation. This conversation is about "truth." It's about my story and the other person's story. In this conversation, we tend to argue for our point of view based on our assumption that we are right; they are wrong. We do not stop to question the assumption. When we recognize that this conversation can be about different perspectives, interpretations, and values rather than about right and wrong, we have an opportunity to shift the conversation into an open, questioning space where we are trying to understand the other person, rather than judge. We can begin to have a learning conversation that is about what is important instead of what is true.[4]

Still in the "What happened?" undercurrent, we have yet another major player—intentions. Our intentions, as well as those of the other person, are invisible. We assume we know the intentions of others and when we do not, we assume bad intent.[5] We invent a story that supports our assumptions and our story becomes our truth. The other person is doing the same thing. The truth is that intentions are complex. The truth is also that if these are our stories, we can change them.

Finally, in the "What happened?" conversation, we play the blame game. We spend a lot of time and energy on who is at fault for the mess we are in. We know that it is not our fault, so it must be someone else's. This conversation is not productive. It produces fear, disagreement, denial, and little or no learning.[6]

Feelings

The second underlying structure of every conversation is the "feelings" conversation. Difficult and important conversations do not just *involve* feelings, they are *about* feelings.[7] If we did not care deeply, the conversation would be neither difficult nor important. By definition, we have to care to be in this conversation to begin with. We tend to discount emotion for the sake of rational conversation. We talk information, fact, and data. If we avoid the emotion (recall "sentiment" as part of *Webster's* very definition of the word "conversation") then we have not dealt with the issue. It will return over and over again.

We are victims of millions of years of biology. Whether we like it or not, we are emotional beings. We were emotional beings before we were rational beings. Emotions drive our behavior. What would happen if we simply accepted emotional responses as part of who we are? What if we embraced them in order to become curious about them?

Identity

The third and final underlying structure is the "identity" conversation. In the identity conversation, we look inward. It is about how we see ourselves. It is the internal story we tell ourselves about how what happened affects our self-esteem, our sense of self. When our sense of self is threatened, we can become distracted, lose confidence, feel paralyzed, and become defensive or offensive.[8]

Understanding these fundamentals that underlie effective conversations, Kate will have to seek to understand Jason and Sarah's stories, how they see the work situation and what impact it has on their productivity. She will have to suspend her assumptions about what is causing the problem with each of them as she seeks to truly listen to their views. As she listens, she will need to attend to their feelings, not just the surface aspects of the current situation. Finally, she will need to see how their identities affect the way they approach their work as well as whether her view of herself may be contributing to the problem she is having with them.

Searching for dialogue

The key to effective conversation is to be clear about our purpose—about our intent—the result we want to produce. We can choose our purpose, create our intent from one that aims solely to persuade and convince to one that is infused with curiosity and acceptance. This does not mean that we agree with everything being said. It does mean that we listen to the point of view being expressed so that we can hear without judgment. This is the way we open the door to real dialogue. William Isaacs defines dialogue as a "shared inquiry, a way of thinking and reflecting together,"[9] rather than an opportunity to make points or trade information.[10] The intention of dialogue is to "reach new understanding. . . . to create a new base of sharing meaning that can align our actions with our values and result in coordinated action."[11]

The roots of the word dialogue come from the Greek words "dia," which means "through" as in diaphanous, and "logos," which translates to "word" or "meaning." Hence dialogue is the flow of meaning from one person through another. It is building relationships by talking and thinking together—by developing associations with each other based on mutual respect and caring. It is our job as leaders to create networks of relationships.[12] Dialogue is not something we do *to* someone else; it is something we do *with* someone else.

Isaacs goes on to describe dialogue as a way to "kindle and sustain a new conversational spirit that has the power to penetrate and dissolve some of our most intractable and difficult problems."[13] It is a way to "manage the fire of our thoughts"; to build an environment where we can contain our intense emotions, reach our intellectual and spiritual selves, and find ways to turn that energy into creative and productive uses. It is an experience of shared inquiry; of thinking and reflecting together.[14]

Dialogue and debate

Dialogue is the opposite of debate. In debates the objective is to win the argument; in dialogue everyone wins or loses together. Dialogue is a conversation between equals who have a common purpose. Dialogue requires listening with compassion and an eagerness to grasp another's ideas. Debate does not. Dialogue requires divulging our deepest assumptions and accepting those of others with respect. Debate does not.

Why invest the time and energy to create dialogue when we have already said it is a discipline that takes practice? Isaacs suggests that all great failures in organizations stem from parallel failures in conversation.[15] Our most intractable problems, the barriers to high performance and great results, are directly related to our ability to think and talk with each other.

If we cannot recognize and shift our strongly held assumptions, we cannot create the more powerful commitment of acting together. We settle for compliance that does not require us to confront our assumptions. We begin and eventually we are defending not only the idea but ourselves. We argue for our positions (fight) or become silent and withdrawn (flight). We lose the ability to listen, to consider what others say, to be curious. Consequently, we cannot think together because we have lost the art of talking with each other. Dialogue is a vehicle to create mutual respect, trust, connection, understanding, and coordinated action. As leaders, we are no longer, if we ever were, in a position to accomplish anything alone. We need, not just compliance, but commitment and enthusiasm from bright, capable, smart people who work with us. It is our job to create an environment where we can all be our best selves and do our best work. One way to do that is through the practice of dialogue. When we practice dialogue in one-on-one conversation, it begins to create an environmental shift throughout the organization. This happens because as we shift our approach to conversations with one person at a time, we influence individual behaviors and those of the group. New skills and new ways of being together are created in the process of practicing dialogue.

Understanding the elements of dialogue

What are the crucial elements of dialogue? Daniel Yankelovich in the *Magic of Dialogue* says there are three essential elements and that without any one of the three, dialogue does not exist. First, in dialogue we must treat the other person as an equal. Dialogue is possible only after mutual trust and respect is established. As leaders in dialogue with those who report to us, we must leave our badges of authority at the door for that occasion. Power in dialogue does not work unless we're willing to share it with the other person. We have to be equal partners. We can deceive ourselves that we are treating others as equals when in fact we are not.[16] Pay attention to where you sit or stand, how you sit, what is your body position, what is your tone of voice, what is the expression on your face, how much air time are you taking up, how open are you to the other's point of view?

Second, we must listen with empathy—meaning that our purpose is to grasp the other person's views and that we can think their thoughts and feel what they feel.[17] When we truly listen, it is an invitation for the other person to enter into the conversation with candor and in trust that they will be heard without judgment and with acceptance. Listening with empathy means to hear not with just our ears, but with our hearts, with our body, with our eyes. How often do any of us have the opportunity to simply be with a person while they are speaking with us—to turn our face like the daughter in the story above requested?[18] We cannot listen with empathy if we are reading e-mail, taking phone calls, speaking to the person standing outside the door who just needs a minute, or thinking about the next meeting that starts in fifteen minutes (see Box 3.1).

Finally, Yankelovich says that in dialogue, we must bring our assumptions into the open. This requires both participants to examine the assumptions they bring to the conversation and reveal them to the other person. It requires both people to respect the assumptions they hear and treat them

---

Box 3.1 Interpersonal communication: The critical factor

"Interpersonal competence is fundamental to successful and effective leadership. What may be involved are the ability to communicate, the willingness and ability to promote individual relationships with others, authenticity, caring, the ability to handle conflict, and insight and empathy."

—*Bernard M. Bass,* Bass & Stogdill's
Handbook of Leadership, *1990*

with respect. [19] It does not require agreement; it does require acceptance, curiosity, and a willingness to explore the assumptions of each person and their effect on the situation. It requires a willingness to let go of assumptions and rethink our stories.

As Kate comes to understand what it takes to have an effective, if difficult, conversation with Jason and Sarah, she gains some confidence about addressing the issue. But that confidence must be matched with competence. She needs skills not just insight.

The requisite skills

Our mindset must be to use every conversation with another person as an opportunity to make our relationship with that person a little better than it was before the conversation. As leaders, we develop willing followers one follower at a time, day in and day out. It is only with these followers that we can achieve the results that meet the marker of "high performance."

These skills are bedrock as one considers the leader as an effective one-on-one communicator:

- Listening
- Inquiry
- Feedback

Listening is foremost. It certainly involves hearing. More specifically, however, the skill seeks to uncover the complete message that the speaker is communicating. Effective listening is an active process that employs all of one's senses to generate a common understanding of meaning between the two parties in a conversation. Success as an effective listener demands that the listener engage in self-control. Focusing completely on the other person and on what that person is communicating is the imperative.

Effective inquiry is the skill of making conscious choices to explore at greater depth matters that have arisen in a conversation. The communicator is reaching for understanding, for learning, about what stands behind the particular statements, views, opinions, or assumptions of the other party.

Feedback seeks to change or influence future behavior. It is a message delivered in the present, based on past observations or information, and should be guided by shared or clear interests. The demand upon the communicator presenting the feedback is to make distinctions in its delivery that draw on the totality of what has transpired between the two parties during the entire conversation.

FEI and executive communications skills development

The Federal Executive Institute (FEI) pioneered executive communications skills development for federal executives about twenty years ago. Inspired by Fred Nunes, an executive with the World Bank, FEI installed a case-based course in many of its programs that enables participants to practice specific techniques with videotaped feedback. The course is interactive, is oriented to the interpersonal challenges these leaders face, and provides a model for gaining willing followers.

THE OVERALL EXECUTIVE COMMUNICATIONS SKILLS MODEL AND ITS OPERATION Ellen Catalano, an adjunct faculty member at FEI, uses a house as a poignant metaphor for the successful conversation. We want a solid structure. We want the house to be inviting, with many points of access to its interior. We want clarity when looking through its windows. We want the free flow of ideas through its interior circulation. We want room enough to acknowledge concerns and reflect feelings. And, as we look at the people who call that house a home, we want commitment as an outcome of spending time together.

The Executive Communications Skills Model, or ECS Model, (see Figure 3.1) is a graphic depiction of how the leader can work to develop

Figure 3.1 The Model

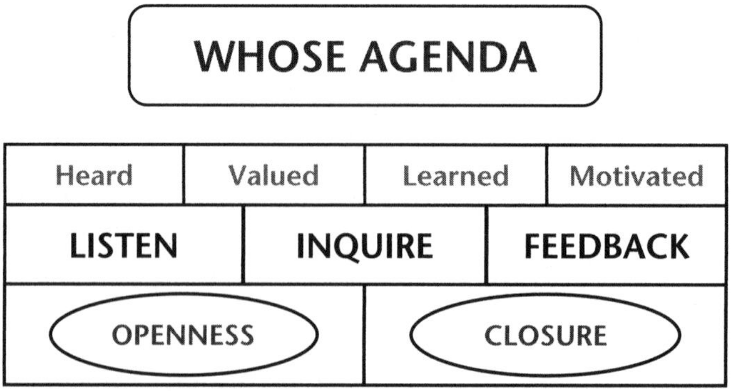

Heard	Valued	Learned	Motivated
LISTEN	**INQUIRE**		**FEEDBACK**
OPENNESS		CLOSURE	

WHOSE AGENDA

Source: Federal Executive Institute.

that commitment. Self-awareness and attentiveness are twin supports. An extremely important consideration is that it only takes one person to set a productive environment for that conversation. The ECS Model represents a conscious strategy to build relationships continuously with each interaction. Its key element is the joint pursuit of shared understanding in those relationships. That shared understanding also becomes an important guidepost for effective decision making. Over time, trust becomes a derivative.

"*Whose agenda*" in the model underlines the reality that both parties to a conversation, the leader as "A" and the other person as "B," bring their own agendas. Regardless of the fact that one person may have triggered the session, each party has his or her own interests, values, issues, viewpoints, and feelings as they relate to the subject of the interaction. These elements coalesce into separate agendas.

The ECS Model is a linear representation of a dynamic process. That is, although we will concentrate on understanding the model by segmenting its components, actual operation is iterative. Rather than always moving from Listen to Inquiry to Feedback, a real-world conversation is fluid. We can listen, do some inquiry, listen again, offer a little feedback, back off to listening and inquiry again, offer a little more feedback, listen again, etc. Nevertheless, the basic premise of starting with openness to reach closure, instead of starting with closure, remains solid. We want to strategically set aside our own agenda and be open to the other person's agenda.

When using the Listen skill in the model, A should be at maximum openness. A's goal in practicing the skill should be to have B coming away from the interaction feeling *heard* and *valued*. Person A is setting the mood and should be spending all of the available Listen time on B's agenda, trying to discover and clarify that agenda. A's agenda for all intents and purposes is off the table.

As we move linearly to the application of the Inquiry skill, A should still be at maximum openness. Somewhere in the deep recesses of his or her mind, A might be thinking about beginning to close but continues to build the dialogue. A's goal with effective inquiry is to generate *learning* on both sides of the table—that is, A should be learning about B's agenda as a consequence of successful listening and inquiry, while B should be learning from the kinds of queries A is posing.

At some point A will determine that he or she has a reasonable fix on B's agenda. Then it is appropriate to move to closure through a complete Feedback message. Rather than simply moving into A's agenda, however,

A should be seeking to merge *both agendas*. The goal of effective Feedback is to earn the *commitment* of B to go willingly where A needs to go as the leader.[20] The mutual willing agreement of A and B to action and to next steps is successful closure.

The ECS Model offers more than graphic depiction and technical understanding. Users can actually understand through practiced application where they are in a conversation. Moreover, the model enables individuals to manage their way successfully through an interaction, regardless of its difficulty. Most of us have developed our conversational skills through unreflective experience, patterning ourselves after people with widely varying abilities. The model offers a way for us to check our current functioning against a more thoughtful and powerful approach.

The listen skill: The foundational skill

Arguably, the Listen skill is the communications skill we most take for granted. Yet, it is at the epicenter of successful leadership. Klaus and Bass found strong positive relationships between the trustworthiness and informativeness of supervisors and their careful communications to subordinates; their two-way, rather than one-way, communications; and their attentive listening.[21] This trustworthiness, informativeness, and care contributed to their subordinates' role clarity, satisfaction with their supervision, and the effectiveness of their workgroups.[22]

What counts is not just what the speaker says, but what the listener hears, understands, or thinks he or she hears and understands. Acquiring that understanding, that full appreciation of meaning, is hardly passive. Instead, active listening is demanding, calling on the listener to concentrate intensively on the speaker. The true challenge, though, is for the speaker to suspend his or her agenda as it relates to the subject of the conversation. That means putting it aside. Concentrating on the other individual absolutely requires putting that person's agenda in the center, putting one's self in a learning mode, and doing everything possible to establish an atmosphere of trust (see Figure 3.2).

Active listening cannot happen unless you have a genuine interest in the other person. Not infrequently, that must come with a conscious effort to slow ourselves down. Being a successful active listener also means being a patient listener. Patience truly is a virtue!

As psychologists Carl Rogers and Richard Farson said, the skill "requires that we get inside the speaker, that we grasp, from his point of view, just

Figure 3.2 Focus on Openness

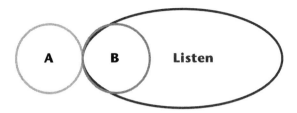

Listening challenge:

To put B's agenda in the center by using active listening skills

Source: Federal Executive Institute.

what he is communicating to us. More than that, we must convey to the speaker that we are seeing things from his point of view."[23]

In terms of the ECS Model, applying the Listen skill adeptly should cause the other person to come away feeling *heard* and *valued*. To do that, the listener must listen for total meaning. As Rogers and Farson describe so well, that message typically has two components: content and the feelings that underlie that content.

Content relates to the facts under discussion. As active listeners, we want to assure ourselves that we have a correct understanding of those facts. As a listener, presenting a complete summary of those facts to the speaker accomplishes two things: (1) it tells the speaker that we have been paying attention, that we understand; and (2) it affords the speaker an opportunity to clarify our understanding if our summary is not directly on point. Delivering that summary well also moves the conversation forward.

Every bit as important as the facts, though, and sometimes even more powerful, are the feelings emanating from the speaker during the conversation. It is these feelings that demonstrate the depth of emotional involvement that the speaker has in the subject. Reflecting these feelings back to the speaker can be a significant asset in convincing the speaker that the listener truly values what the speaker is communicating. That reflection can be as simple as an acknowledgment of concerns: "Fred, I can see that potential loss of young talent around here because of the coming cutbacks really alarms you."

Box 3.2   Naming a feeling

As one listens completely, the emotional element in a conversation acquires increasing definition. Reflecting feelings (such as those below) can enable the speaker to sense that he or she is *heard* and *valued* by the listener. For example: "You seem confused about the reasons for our new policy" shows the listener has paid attention to the speaker's concerns.

Excited	Concerned
Enthusiastic	Upset
Passionate	Confused
Driven	Irritated
Positive	Indifferent
Happy	Frustrated

Reflection of feeling is a step in building stronger relationships with people (see Box 3.2). Sensitivity to the feelings of others is a visible addition of substance. It can be a statement of our respect for the other individual. Hence, that reflection of feelings might be viewed as a deposit to the listener's account, which the listener, the leader, may well have to draw down in the future.

For many, reflecting feelings is not easy. Personal cultural roots, organizational cultures, personality profile preferences and a host of other considerations can get in the way. The "prize" that the listener is after is having the other person come away feeling heard and valued as a consequence of spending dedicated time in the other person's agenda. Another way to say that is both parties are working hard to be open to each other. They are paying complete attention to each other. They are truly listening to each other.

Many leaders pass through the FEI as session participants. Not surprisingly, doubters exist as the ECS Model course unfolds. Sometimes the doubt continues until they have tried the skills in the "real world" of their daily work. A notable success story is a retired major who came to FEI after accepting a position as a civilian in a Department of Defense facility. The major harbored significant skepticism about whether these techniques had any relevance in his new job. As a military officer he said, "We didn't do feelings in my branch of the service." Six months after graduation, he called and spoke with a faculty member about his experience. Despite his initial reluctance, he reported that he had employed these techniques deliberately and broadly. He said that he was "amazed" at how people now related to him. Feelings had become strategic.

VERBAL AND NONVERBAL COMMUNICATION. As we talk with another person, it is important to convey understanding and to recognize the ideas of that person at various times during the conversation. The importance springs from the listener's desire to have that person feel heard and valued. At the same time, the listener must be cautious. Understanding does not mean agreement with the speaker's ideas. The listener must be wary of miscommunicating.

We can convey understanding and recognition both verbally and nonverbally. As an example, verbally we can express that understanding directly: "Paul, the ideas that you're detailing come directly from the extended presentation you made at our program management meeting."

A second approach is to check your understanding: "Mary Ann, I think that I heard you say that the Nine-Mile Bridge is actually designed for articulated buses. Do I have that right?"

Summaries represent a third technique: "Mike, I heard you say that personal preference, the variety of network providers, and cost are the three principal reasons that the iPhone will never replace the Blackberry with federal managers."

Reflecting the message that the speaker has presented and the feelings that the speaker emitted in that presentation are another approach: "Ruth, I heard some genuine excitement in your voice as you highlighted that home porting the new aircraft carrier in New Orleans will be a major boost to the local economy."

Finally, the clarifying question can be helpful at this stage of the conversation. It demonstrates a spiked interest in more information about something raised by the speaker. The clarifying question simply tries to put a better box around something already on the table. As an example, if the conversation were about giraffes, a clarifying question might ascertain whether this was the standard giraffe: lanky, four legs, long neck, short tail, etc. If the listener got into the giraffe's pedigree or the number of bales of acacia leaves the giraffe ate each day, the listener would be much deeper into the ECS Model and would be applying the Inquiry skill.

Shifting to the nonverbal conveyance of understanding and recognition, we encounter a host of considerations that can come into play. Janet Bennet, who studies the effects that cultural diversity can have on interpersonal communications, defines nonverbal communication as including "all behavior that modifies, adds to or substitutes for spoken or written language."[24] She includes in that definition:

- Voice: tone, pitch, stress, and speed.
- Gestures: movements and postures.
- Eyes: threats and propositions.
- Space: formal, informal, and intimate distances.
- Touch: appropriate amounts of conversational contact.
- Time: importance of punctuality.

Most people characterize these elements as "body language." When nonverbal messages contradict verbal ones, the listener tends to trust the nonverbal message more than the verbal one.[25] Thus when the leader is communicating an oral message endorsing a follower's recommended course of action in an important issue area, while the leader avoids eye contact, speaks very quickly, drums his fingers, and checks his e-mail, the follower is certainly entitled to have reservations about the leader's understanding of the issue and his or her reliability as a backstop.

Accurate knowledge of body language is essential for interpersonal relations success in the business world or in personal life. Instinct, though, drives much of our understanding. Sometimes, we're just wrong. For example, while good eye contact is an asset in building relationships, research shows that specific instances of eye contact lasting longer than a few seconds can make us nervous. Further, Paul Ekman in *Telling Lies: Clues to Deceit in the Marketplace, Politics and Marriage,* has found that pathological liars excel at making eye contact.[26] Thus, while eye contact can be a useful skill and indicator in some cases, we should be wary of eye contact as a consistent measure of sincerity or truthfulness.

Being open and being perceived as open are twin considerations as one employs the Listen skill to set the mood for successful dialogue. As Nick Morgan stated in his article, "The Truth Behind the Smile and Other Myths—When Body Language Lies," most of us are not as good at decoding the emotions inherent in body language as we would like to think. He views body language as conveying important but unreliable clues about the intent of the communication. In his view, the more information you can acquire about the clues you are trying to decode, the more likely you are to be correct.[27]

Yet, despite some difficulties in using body language to communicate and interpret cues, it is important to let the other person know that you are listening. Nonverbal attending behavior does that. Such behavior encourages the other person to continue to provide information by establishing a very comfortable, conducive environment. By engaging in physical activity to demonstrate to the speaker that you are paying attention, you are conveying the message of being truly interested in the subject and in the speaker's views. While variations in culture always have to be considered, attentive American body language might encompass these basics:

- Be relaxed and remember that a smile at the right time can be of inestimable value.
- Lean slightly toward the other person.
- Maintain reasonable eye contact, unless it makes the other person uncomfortable.
- Nod to encourage the other person to continue.
- Employ silence creatively—give the other person an opportunity to consider and speak rather than filling pauses yourself.
- Be aware of your tone of voice, facial expression, and gestures.

When moving into a discussion with someone from a different culture, a little research into the communication basics of that culture can pay substantial dividends. Understanding at even the most basic level whether the individual is from a low-context culture (for example, Germany) where the explicit verbal message dominates, or from a high-context culture (for example, China) where such things as history, roles, and social norms pervade, can make a significant contribution to the goals of understanding and being understood. As an example, eighteen to twenty inches is the normal distance for face-to-face communication between two men in the United States. If talking to a woman, a man will back off another four inches. In Latin America, men feel comfortable at thirteen inches. Therefore, a U.S. woman in Peru might feel imposed on at thirteen inches. An individual from France might feel devastated were she to retreat to twenty-four inches.[28]

MAJOR IMPEDIMENTS TO ACTIVE LISTENING. Listening is hard work that demands the full attention and involvement of the listener. Multitasking may have a place, but it truly inhibits effective listening. The *distractions* in today's workplace represent the first major impediment. More often than not, those distractions or interruptions may be electronic (for example, reading e-mail, taking a phone call, or participating in an online conference). They make it difficult to concentrate on understanding. Clarification proceeds haltingly. Irritation flows into the speaker's sense of not being heard or valued.

The distractions might also be environmental, such as lack of privacy or uncomfortable surroundings. Such distractions create an atmosphere that works against developing mutual understanding and relationship-building. A prime example is being expected to listen about a significant matter while rushing to catch an elevator. Another example might be employing adjoining airline seats on a crowded plane as the time to unload unhappiness about the negotiation strategy underlying a pending contract.

An *evaluative mindset* and a *judgmental attitude* are additional inhibitors. When in the listen mode, one should be concentrating on acquiring good information. What is the speaker really saying? That means clarification becomes key to understanding what is important to the speaker. Evaluation and judging may have a role, but that role is farther down the line as one prepares to deliver a complete feedback message.

Inappropriate body language is another impediment. It may be defined as any nonverbal signal that inhibits the free flow of information. For example, many read the closed posture with crossed arms as a reluctance to engage the issue under discussion. Another may be a facial expression that appears to challenge what the speaker is saying. Still another might be sitting behind your desk when trying to have a difficult conversation, since the physical barrier of the desk might signal that you are the one with the power when you want to downplay that in the relationship.

Argumentative responses also impede productive dialogue, which should be a joint search for meaning. Debate can harden positions. When listening, the listener should be mounting a true search for clarification of the speaker's agenda. The listener's agenda is in suspense. Consequently, argument simply gets in the way of understanding by elevating the emotional element in the discussion. Not surprisingly, that emotional element probably arises from exposing the listener's agenda much too early.

Faked attention also takes a toll. There are very few people who cannot discern it and relegate it to the bin of disinterest. It does nothing to move the relationship forward. We said earlier that a genuine interest in the other person is essential to successful listening. The listener must want to learn to be successful in making the speaker feel heard and valued.

Mental wandering and drifting is similar. In both cases, the listener is not "in the moment" with the speaker. The listener is not actively involved in searching for understanding. The interaction can become mechanical, a lost opportunity for both parties.

Finally, *note taking too intensely* rounds out the impediments. While there is nothing inherently obstructive in taking notes, the listener should be wary of creating the impression of "keeping book" on the speaker. Something at the beginning of the conversation as simple as: "Talking with you is important to me. Do you mind if I take a few notes as we speak?" can maintain the open atmosphere so essential to successful interpersonal communication.

SUMMARY. Effective listening is the foundational skill in the ECS Model. Listening takes practice. It is the single most important element in building enduring relationships. When one listens well, problems are properly understood. There is less likelihood of arriving at second-best solutions. As importantly, listening well provides the opportunity to acquire some "social capital" or trust useful in future transactions with the speaker.

Artful inquiry

The inquiry skill is a natural expansion of the effective listening skill. Rather than focusing on clarification of matters already specified, the inquiry skill takes the listener to greater depth. It is a move beyond known or shared information to a greater shared understanding of the issues.

When using the Inquiry skill, the leader ("A") should still be at maximum openness. Person A certainly should be aware of his or her own agenda. Nevertheless, all of A's time and attention should remain concentrated on B's agenda.

The outcome that A is after in good Inquiry is *learning* for both parties. Person A makes a conscious choice to pursue understanding at more than a surface level. B, aware of the nature of A's inquiries, should appreciate much better the scope of A's interests. Therefore, there should be increased understanding by both parties, hopefully at a level that goes beyond facts. What A has is an excellent opportunity to understand and acknowledge B's feelings about the issues (see Box 3.3). It is here that the act of shaping questions can

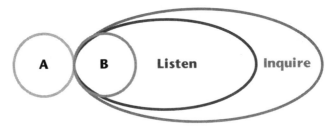

Figure 3.3 Focus on Openness

A   B   Listen   Inquire

Inquire challenge:

To understand and acknowledge B's
feelings **and get** information **about**
B's agenda.

Source: Federal Executive Institute.

pay major dividends. As we mentioned earlier, understanding at the emotional level magnifies awareness of B's intensity of involvement with the issue.

Effective inquiry is another step in the direction of building a long-term relationship with the other party. The person employing inquiry is demonstrating something beyond superficial interest. That person is bringing the other person into mutual problem solving. In doing that, problem solving can become a developmental experience for the other party and enable that person to become more independent in the future. The specificity of well-shaped inquiries and the thoroughness of the overall inquiry process can help the other party to deal with similar issues on their own. Enhanced problem-solving proficiency is a reasonable expectation.

By bringing the other party into a genuine problem-solving partnership, the person employing good inquiry skills is also working to establish mutual respect. As the problem solving proceeds, that respect can mature into commitment to a mutual solution, instead of simple compliance. That mutuality also leads to the person who applies well-developed inquiry skills having a willing follower in the future. Knowing that he or she is heard and valued as a consequence of skillful listening and that joint searches for solutions are de rigueur foster a willingness to go where the leader needs to go. The person who is taking full advantage of what solid inquiry offers is also compensating for the power imbalance. Position, relative rank, pay,

Figure 3.4 Inquire

An exploration process using questions and statements to:

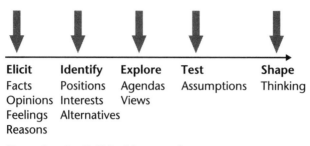

Elicit	Identify	Explore	Test	Shape
Facts	Positions	Agendas	Assumptions	Thinking
Opinions	Interests	Views		
Feelings	Alternatives			
Reasons				

Listen for the "gift" of key words and phrases that open the door to "B's" agenda

Source: Federal Executive Institute.

organizational stature, and other elements can impair interpersonal communication. That impairment has its roots in the perceived power of one person over another. Effective listening and inquiry can imply partnership, thereby somewhat offsetting that imbalance. Further, by withholding his or her own agenda, the leader can shape its eventual presentation to consider the learning occurring during the conversation.

Well-designed probing questions and statements are at the heart of effective inquiry. As depicted in Figure 3.4, inquiry is a series of techniques geared to thoroughly understanding the other person's agenda.

Betsy Poist, also an adjunct faculty member at the FEI, cites real-world archeological work at Jamestown, VA, as an example of the benefits of sound inquiry. A research team she encountered had identified the most likely area for study at a new dig. The archeologists carefully set a grid at the excavation site and methodically proceeded to try to unearth artifacts, small square by small square. Their assumptions factored into setting the dig's boundaries, and they met only limited success. One individual noted the existence of an old dry well beyond the boundaries of the dig. The archeologists stepped back from their assumptions to inquire into it. Lo and behold, they found it to be a magnificent resource, a veritable treasure trove. Members of the Jamestown community had used the hole for waste materials, and those materials survived the ravages of time protected in the well. In essence, the archeologists had tested their assumption that the well was insignificant and found that assumption wanting. One of the fundamentals of sound dialogue is that the assumptions that underlie a conversation should always be open to careful review.

Successful inquiry is dependent upon practicing some key behaviors:

- Asking open-ended questions.
- Asking one question at a time.
- Using active listening skills to identify key words or ideas.
- Using silence effectively.

ASKING OPEN-ENDED QUESTIONS. Open-ended questions cannot be answered with a simple "yes" or "no." They usually begin with who, what, when, where, why, or how. Since "why" can have significant parent/child history associated with it, or since "why" can put people on the defensive, staying away from that question is probably good advice. Any question posed with a "why" certainly can be shaped with a "what" or a "how."

Gerard Nierenberg in his *Fundamentals of Negotiating* offers some advice on formulating questions.[29] He points out that if the questioner is not careful, a question can invoke substantial anxiety in the person being questioned. A proper foundation for the question is important; for example, "You have a lot of experience here. How should we move ahead?" Further, he observes that questions should not offend or put a person in an uncomfortable position. With the well-designed open-ended question, the questioner should focus on the outcome of gaining information (for example, "What really excited the team over the last year?"), or causing the other party to think and provide a thoughtful response (for example, "What is the best way to capitalize on the success of your project?").

Statements can also serve the same purposes as open-ended questions; for example, "Help me to understand your concerns with the Finance Department." Properly used, such statements invite elaboration. That is a key to truly understanding the other person's agenda. Such statements also demonstrate that you have a sincere interest in the other person, reinforcing the valuing element of the listening skill.

In contrast, rhetorical questions demonstrate a lack of interest in the other person. By posing an answer as a question (for example, "Don't you think we ought to reorganize the Finance Department to solve that problem?"), rhetorical questions close off meaningful dialogue.

ASKING ONE QUESTION AT A TIME. Many people, particularly those with extroversion preferences, have a tendency to ask multiple questions in rapid-fire sequence. The questioner doesn't provide the other party with an opportunity to answer until all questions have finally stopped. Such questioners are actually thinking out loud, trying to identify the question they really want to ask. For example: "What is the problem? I mean, what are the origins of the problem and who was involved in identifying it? What are its implications and where is it most evident?" It is very difficult to keep track of the five questions just asked. The overwhelmed respondent simply picks the question he or she wants to answer or makes up a question to answer.

Taking a moment to think through the question you intend to ask can make the conversation much more productive. Clarity in the question drives clarity in the response. This approach also enables the questioner to guide the direction and pace of the conversation. It helps the questioner to manage his or her way successfully through the entire interaction.

USING ACTIVE LISTENING SKILLS TO IDENTIFY KEY WORDS OR IDEAS. While in inquiry, the person applying the ECS Model should be listening carefully, not structuring the next question. When engaged in active listening, one sometimes picks up a word or concept that jumps out of the conversation as a little different or curious. For instance, when someone is discussing the progress of a project and says, "This contractor brings a lot of baggage to the enterprise," inquiring into the baggage with a good, open-ended query has the potential to develop some relevant material. These key words or concepts, hooks if you will, can help to drill down into the other person's agenda. A simple "Help me to understand that a little better" can drive substantial learning.

USING SILENCE EFFECTIVELY. To some, any silence in a conversation represents space that they must fill. That action may arise from finding silence uncomfortable. Instead, silence can be a major aid to generative conversation. It is up to at least one person involved in the conversation to make that happen. When the silence occurs, letting it remain for a short while is offering the other party the opportunity to fill it with additional relevant material. More often than not, that happens. The person has the time to shape and articulate a thought. The other individual is simply being present, open to possibilities and prepared to press further into the other person's agenda. This creative use of silence is another manifestation of the self-control so essential to the listening skill discussed earlier.

SUMMARY. The skill of effective inquiry concentrates on acquiring a shared understanding of the issues using thoughtful open-ended questions and statements. The person practicing inquiry is trying to understand before trying to be understood. Effective inquiry is not a process of suggesting answers, giving advice or voicing opinions. It is not about interrupting the other party. Rather it is an extension and builds upon the centrality of active listening. Effective inquiry seeks to generate learning as an outcome for both parties to the conversation.

Effective feedback

When one has listened actively and inquired into the other person's agenda to truly understand it, the time has come to deliver a complete feedback message. The desired outcome is for that other person to leave the session motivated and committed to doing what the leader needs to get done.

Feedback is a message delivered in the *present* based on *past* observations and other information. It is guided by shared or clear *interests* and is intended to influence *future* behavior. As depicted in Figure 3.5, the ideal is to successfully merge your agenda with the agenda of the other person. Feedback is not an excuse to discount everything you have heard so that you can say what you wanted to say before the conversation even began.

There are essentially two types of feedback: (1) Affirmative, and (2) Constructive. The challenge in both cases is to deliver feedback in a way that enables the message to be heard, understood and accepted, while the person receiving the feedback feels valued, appreciated, and eager to succeed.

Affirmative feedback is intended to acknowledge accomplishments and other positive contributions. Two things typically inhibit gaining the most from affirmative feedback.

First, *it doesn't occur frequently enough.* There is a tendency in many of us to forget how much others like to receive positive reinforcement. Also, the press of business is such that we can take good performance for granted or fail to follow up on the exemplary.

Second, *it isn't specific enough.* General comments about good performance can have some value. At the same time, those general comments (for example, "That was a helpful analysis") can be viewed as a throw-away line, lacking any sincerity. At worst, it might be viewed as

Figure 3.5 Work Toward Closure

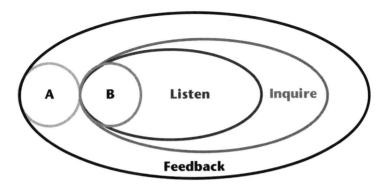

Feedback challenge:

To stay in both agendas for shared understanding and mutual commitment

Source: Federal Executive Institute.

manipulative. If the favorable comment has depth (for example, "That was a helpful analysis; I particularly liked the way the executive summary conveyed the seriousness of the contract problems that you covered so well in the body of the report"), then the other party has a greater appreciation for the value that you place on the work. That's the key to the feedback being a relation-builder and truly having some motivational staying power. Specific feedback also allows the person to know what they did that you valued, increasing the chances that they will perform similarly next time.

One of the objectives in constructive feedback is to help the other person gain some insight. In part, that may be information about how his or her behavior affects others or the mission of the organization. In essence, two conscious choices are involved. The provider of the feedback is making a conscious choice to deliver the feedback and the recipient is confronted with the conscious choice of changing his or her behavior.

Setting the stage for constructive feedback is essential. Effective listening and inquiry should have brought the person delivering the feedback to the point of having a reasonably thorough understanding of the other person's interests or agenda relative to the matter being discussed. A critical determinant becomes the receiver's readiness to receive constructive feedback. It is quite useful for the leader to begin with a summary of the content and feelings developed in listening and inquiry. The receiver's reaction to this summary can serve as a readiness guidepost. Is the receiver open or resentful? Open or rigidly defensive? Open or excessively emotional? This is a test of the leader's awareness of the receiver's reactions. If the receiver is not ready, then additional listening and inquiry are important in this or a follow-up session. Delivering the feedback anyway most likely will result in a very limited likelihood of any willing change in behavior as well as potentially negative effects on the continuing relationship with the receiver.

Assuming that the readiness guidepost demonstrates that the receiver is ready for constructive feedback, the content and feelings summary can serve as a fulcrum for launching into a complete feedback message. This is a message delivered from the leader's agenda that merges both agendas. The intent behind the message must be to help rather than threaten. It is here that the adage "soft on people, hard on the problem" is on point. Targeting the behavior, not the person, charts the route to improvement in both behavior and the relationship between the receiver and provider of feedback.

The first component of the complete feedback message is a sincere positive comment; for example, "Mark, you're a major contributor here. The creativity that you bring to your job helps to lead the team in product design."

Do not follow that positive comment with a "but," "however," or anything similar. Such language can destroy the positive comment by focusing the individual on the "post-but" commentary. After making the positive comment, just think "period" as punctuation or "and."

Next, present a clear description of the problem (not the person) and do that in a way that explains the constraints, is specific and uses "I" messages demonstrating that this is important to you; for example, "I've noticed that you've been 10 to 15 minutes late coming to our product development sessions two or three times a week" [Constraints].

After delivery of the clear basic message, it is important to highlight the consequences of the behavior on mission and to stress actionable behavior; for example, "What's happening is that we're losing some of that creativity that is a big part of your contribution. When you're late, we aren't really ready to work as a group. We lose time and don't get that quick, energized start. As a result, we're having to schedule extra sessions leading to delays in getting the new designs set. [Consequences] I need your help to turn this around. I need you to consider these sessions to be important and to set an example of timeliness. What can you do?" The mission consequences element is probably the single most important key to clear reception of the feedback message—it grabs attention.

In delivering effective feedback, it is important to avoid "beating around the bush," assuming clarity of your message, or ascribing motives. You probably don't have a clue about why somebody is engaging in particular behavior. What the person delivering the feedback is after is a commitment to change. Hence, closed-ended questions make sense as the feedback session concludes; for example, "We seem to have an understanding. Can I rely on you?" In fact, in some cases, it may make sense to install a continuing tie to keep behavioral change moving forward; for example, "I think we have an agreement. What do you think about getting together for a few minutes in a month or so to see how things are going?" This is a demonstration that the matter is so important to you that you are willing to invest more of your time to make sure that something happens.

Feedback is not about accusation. It is not about demanding improvement, and it is not about rushing to closure. As we stated earlier, the reality is that in applying the ECS Model, one bounces back and forth between its elements—some listening, some inquiry, some more listening, a little feedback, some more inquiry, some more listening, etc. What you're after, at the conclusion, is a motivated, committed follower, wanting to go with you where you need to go as a leader.

Feedback must be timely, specific, direct and relevant. If it is, the person receiving the feedback becomes empowered to make sustainable performance improvements. The person's value and worth are reaffirmed. The leader's stature is enhanced. These are all important outcomes. As important, however, is that the leader gets beyond uncertainty to closure.

Summary. The completeness of both affirmative and constructive feedback is the key to its success. That feedback should help its recipient to gain insights. The person should be ready to receive feedback. If the recipient gains both a direct appreciation of the behavior and its mission consequences, constructive feedback should lead to a commitment to change. Closure is the leader's goal, coupled with advancing the relationship between the parties.

Tips for leadership success

- True dialogue breeds success, a genuine exploration of assumptions, and trust. Leave your power and authority at the door. Engage as equals. Bring good will to your conversations. Be compassionate—our identities are tied up in our conversation. Maintain respect and dignity. Own your own contributions to and responsibility for the situation, and view others as partners who are as committed to the success of the endeavor as you are.

- To achieve true dialogue, listen, inquire, and engage in effective feedback. Be present in your conversations. This means putting everything else aside and focusing on the person speaking. Listen to your "voice in the head" so that you can tell it be quiet while you listen. Listen with your ears, eyes, heart, belly.

- When listening, focus on the person, the person, the person. Remember that feelings are important. Acknowledge the feelings that show up—yours and the other person's. Feelings drive behavior. When we acknowledge them, we gain powerful tools to create a productive exchange.

- Spend enough time in the other person's agenda to really understand it before you try to be understood. Listen for "what happened" as the other person tells it. Listen with a posture of acceptance. Accept does not mean agree. Accept what the speaker is saying as their point of view, their truth.

- Be curious. Put aside your judgments, your assessments, and your stories while you listen. Let go of "right" and "wrong." Let go of defensive reactions so as to create openness and interest. Have a learning-oriented, open communication in order to discover "what matters." Don't take the conversation personally. When we don't take it personally, we can let go of judgment.

- When in inquiry, use open-ended questions, one at a time, listening carefully for those key words or hooks that help you dive down into the person's agenda. Also, clearly state your assumptions and invite the speaker to do the same.

- The keys to effective feedback are the completeness of the message; its links to mission consequences; and a concentration on real closure, hopefully tied down with follow-through that demonstrates commitment.

- In feedback, acknowledge the reality of individual choice—as adults we always make our own choices.
- Always do your best and accept that your best shifts from moment to moment, day to day. Assume that others always do their best. Even if it's not true, the way you interact with them will shift the conversation.
- In conversation, it's okay to choose your purpose and keep your focus on it. And, throughout, be impeccable with your word. Language and words are powerful—they create. Use them with intention and in service to your purpose.

Resources for further learning

Books and Articles

Robert Bolton, *How to Assert Yourself, Listen to Others and Resolve Conflicts* (1986). Bolton offers a collection of interactive communication techniques that continue to stand the test of time.

Daniel Goleman and Richard Boyatzis, "Social Intelligence and the Biology of Leadership," *Harvard Business Review* (September 2008). The authors provide an examination of the biology of empathy and its implications for relationships.

Phil Harkins, *Powerful Conversations: How High Impact Leaders Communicate* (1999). This book integrates interactive communication and successful organizational leadership.

William Isaacs, *Dialogue and the Art of Thinking Together* (1999). A complete, thoroughly readable, discussion of conversations "with a center, not sides."

Michael P. Nichols, *The Lost Art of Listening* (1995). A comprehensive guide to reflective listening.

Kerry Patterson et al., *Crucial Conversations: Tools for Talking When Stakes Are High.* (2002). This book offers a best-practice inventory for day-to-day conversations that affect your life.

Douglas Stone, Bruce Patton, and Sheila Heen, *Difficult Conversations: How to Discuss What Matters Most* (2000). The authors, who worked on the Harvard Negotiation Project, offer a compilation of the mistakes people make in difficult conversations, coupled with strategies for converting those interactions into learning conversations.

Web Resources

Vital Smarts, www.vitalsmarts.com/crucialconversations_book.aspx. This site is for the authors of *Crucial Conversations* and also the book *Crucial Confrontations.* After registering on the site, you can gain free access to both print and audiovisual materials.

Consortium for Research on Emotional Intelligence in Organizations, www.eiconsortium.org/. Offering a range of research and practice papers on emotional and social intelligence, this site was established by the pioneers in this field. Daniel Goleman and Cary Cherniss currently serve as co-chairs of the consortium.

Dialogos, http://thinkingtogether.com. Dialogos was founded in 1995 by William Isaacs to promote the practice and development of strategic change through improved dialogue. Dialogos consultants and teams work with clients to transform their capabilities and move past the limits that have been taken for granted in the past.

National Coalition for Dialogue and Deliberation, www.thataway.org. This website brings people together to discuss, decide, and collaborate on tough issues.

Notes

1. Linney (2010), Introduction.
2. Stone, Patton, and Heen (1999), 7–8.
3. Patterson et al. (2002), 24.
4. Stone, Patton, and Heen (1999), 10.
5. Ibid., 11.
6. Ibid., 11–12.
7. Ibid., 13.
8. Ibid., 15–16.
9. Isaacs (1999), 9.
10. Ibid., 14.
11. Ibid., 19.
12. Yankelovich (1999).
13. Isaacs (1999), 6.
14. Ibid, 9.
15. Ibid, 3.
16. Yankelovich (1999), 42.
17. Ibid., 43.
18. Linney (2010).
19. Ibid., 44.
20. COMMITMENT means the same as ensuring the speaker feels MOTIVATED, as shown in the ECS Model.

21. Klaus and Bass (1982).
22. Bass (1990), 341.
23. Rogers and Farson (1987).
24. Bennett (2005), 15.
25. Remland (1981), 17–29.
26. Ekman (2001).
27. Morgan (2002).
28. Nierenberg (1973), 144.
29. Ibid., 116–118.

Coaching: A leadership imperative for the twenty-first century

RON REDMON, PRESIDENT, THE REDMON GROUP

Government leaders cannot do it all alone. They must develop the capacity of their employees. Coaching others is a tool that frees the leader to do the more strategic work of leadership. Becoming an effective coach requires skill in collaboratively establishing performance and developmental goals, praising and encouraging, using developmental questions, and providing feedback. The effective coach adopts a mindset that believes in the innate goodness of employees and their desire to learn and serve. The coach also demonstrates humility, empathy, optimism, curiosity, a respect for diversity, and a comfort with paradox and ambiguity.

IMAGINE HAVING ENOUGH TIME IN YOUR WORKDAY to try the leadership concepts, strategies, and tools offered in this book. For that to happen, one thing would have to change for many of us. We would need to find a way to stop, or at least slow down, the revolving door of people constantly coming to us with questions, particularly questions they can answer for themselves, given the right support.

The answer for leaders is not to lock their employees out, but to learn how to coach them. Coaching will cut down on many of the interruptions and allow the leader to put more thought and energy into leading. More important, employees who are coached attain higher levels of performance, take more ownership of their work, and become more self-directed. In short, they experience greater fulfillment—and so do their leaders.

When taken seriously, coaching requires practice and rigor, constant examination of one's attitudes and beliefs, and the willingness to learn as much as the people one coaches. Coaching opens doors to a new and deeper understanding of oneself, other people, and the world in general. At its most artful, coaching transcends skills and techniques. It is a way to lead people by engaging their minds, their hearts, their aspirations, and their highest selves. Indeed, the central proposition of this chapter is that the skills, behaviors, and mindset of coaching are no longer options for leaders; instead, they have become prerequisites for leadership success because of the nature and pace of change in the world and the necessity for genuinely new thinking.

This chapter will give you a sense of what is involved in coaching, context for its use in the workplace, and perspective on its role in twenty-first century leadership. It is not possible to explain in detail how to coach in these few pages. Instead think of this chapter as curiously dipping your toe in a pond. If it feels good, wade in a little—get a book from the resource list at the end and read more. If that further tantalizes, go for a dip in the pond—get formal training from one of the several excellent programs listed in the resources section.

What is coaching?

In 1980 the Department of Defense launched an advertising campaign to attract young men and women into the new all-volunteer army. The campaign slogan, "Be All You Can Be," quickly made its way into the popular lexicon. That slogan succinctly expresses what coaching is about. If you have had a relationship with someone who challenged you to be all you can be, who helped you find your own answers to whatever you were dealing with or working on (versus telling you what to do or what you should do), who left you feeling more able and sure of yourself, and who wanted to see you succeed even when you might have lost confidence in yourself, you were being coached.

For most people, the word *coaching* is customarily associated with sports. Of the many things an athletic coach does, assessing performance and developing talent are most similar to coaching in an organization. Both involve establishing performance and developmental targets; praising and encouraging; providing feedback on attitudes, skills, strategies, and results; and serving as a partner to their charges so they can hold themselves accountable for achieving agreed upon goals.

These two realms of coaching have had even more in common since the mid-1970s when Tim Gallwey's best-selling book, *The Inner Game of Tennis*, came out. Gallwey contended that the opponent within one's head is at least as formidable as the one on the other side of the net, and perhaps even more. The book spawned a revolution in the coaching of tennis and was followed by *Inner Skiing* and *The Inner Game of Golf*, sparking similar changes in those sports. All were predicated on the premise that if a coach can help a person remove or reduce the internal obstacles to better performance, the person's natural abilities, experience, and intuition will take over and unlock his or her untapped potential. At its core, Gallwey's approach was not to teach people, but to help them learn.

In the workplace, the grist for this learning consists of the issues and problems that occur in the course of employees' day-to-day activities. A vital role for an effective, trusted leader is to spot the learning opportunities embedded in these events, dilemmas, successes, and failures and help employees extract insights and lessons that can improve their performance in the future. Coaching is the vehicle for this learning. It is an exercise in critical thinking without being critical of the thinker.

The story of Bob and Lisa: A different kind of "two-minute drill"

> According to most studies, people's number one fear is public speaking. Number two is death. Death is number two. Does that sound right? This means to the average person, if you go to a funeral, you're better off in the casket than doing the eulogy.
>
> —*Jerry Seinfeld*

Lisa was honored to be selected as the new deputy division director. It meant being part of an entirely different operation and working for Bob, widely regarded as a masterful leader. Her only concern was that the job included periodic presentations to the bureau's senior management. Bob understood Lisa's concern. Earlier in his career he needed to participate in Toastmasters, a club where members learn public speaking skills, for several months before he was able to speak confidently in public and inspire his audience to action. He wanted Lisa to succeed, and quickly. Her speaking responsibilities were important to the job, and she had to get up to speed. She was a superstar among the technical ranks of their agency and clearly had potential for a bright future in management.

When they were identifying Lisa's performance objectives for the coming year, Bob said, "I recall from your interview for this position that the public speaking duties were of concern to you. What's your thinking about that now?" He listened carefully as she described how in her technical work she had done considerable writing, but had never been expected to speak in front of audiences larger than a division staff meeting.

"Frankly," she said, "I'm scared to death."

"I can identify," Bob remarked. "A little apprehension keeps us on our toes, but we certainly don't want your nerves to get in the way, so that's definitely something to work on. Let me ask you, what is it about public speaking that scares you?" Bob inquired in an empathetic tone.

"I'm scared I'll lose my place, embarrass myself, and the organization," Lisa replied. "I pride myself on being fully prepared, knowing my material inside and out. I've been told I'm actually quite articulate and that people enjoy hearing what I have to say. And I can't recall a time when I was stumped to come up with an answer to a question. It's nerves, I guess. Once I get nervous, it's hard for me to collect my thoughts and stay on message."

"Have you ever been this nervous about anything before?" he continued.

"It's been a while for sure," Lisa said, with a furrowed brow that told Bob she was pondering his question. "I guess it was back in eighth grade, being in the school play. Stage fright really got me."

"What did you do about it?" Bob's patient and focused demeanor as he asked his question signaled to Lisa that this conversation was important to him, and that he was sincerely interested in her situation.

"The thing that helped most was getting comfortable with the surroundings—the stage, the lights, staring out into that huge auditorium. Looking back on it, I can remember staying after school to practice walking out on the stage and taking it all in, over and over. I had my lines down cold. It was something about the space, the environment that unnerved me."

"Is there anything about that experience that could help with what you're dealing with here? Any ideas about what you might do?"

"Now that you ask, I suppose it could be the same thing happening again," Lisa speculated, her worried look brightening slightly.

"Go on," Bob said.

After a moment's thought, Lisa asked, "Do you think it would be possible to go with you to some meetings in the bureau director's conference room? I think it would help if I can be in there and start to get to know the senior officials a bit. And maybe I could chair a couple of my committee meetings in there to get used to the surroundings."

"I'm sure all that can be arranged. We'll begin next week. Let me know what else you come up with and anything more I can do to support you. In addition, I propose that you and I present together at the upcoming senior staff retreat. That will give you a target to shoot for that's coming up soon. What do you think?"

"Sure. That would be great, Bob. Thank you."

"I'm confident you'll get past your nervousness in short order, Lisa. By the way, if you want another resource, a chapter of Toastmasters meets in our building. I found that helpful when I was learning and would be glad to tell you about it sometime, if you like."

This two-minute exchange between Bob and Lisa is an example of a simple coaching conversation. Brief and straightforward as it is (and much of coaching can be), it contains a number of important elements common to all effective coaching. Notice what Bob did.

First, he used the occasion of performance planning with Lisa to focus on her developmental needs, making clear that he values continuous learning as part of her job.

Second, he listened attentively, seeking to understand what was going on with Lisa without assuming that he knew. His part in the dialogue was essentially to invite her to explore what she might do to help herself. Note that Bob's challenge with public speaking was not the same as Lisa's—an important detail that can be easily overlooked by a leader who does not listen attentively, but instead is consumed by her or his own thoughts and eagerness to dispense advice. Getting ready to speak is not listening!

Third, he picked up on Lisa's emotional state when she said, "Frankly, I'm scared to death." Masterful leaders know to respect employees' feelings. Emotions are part of a person's reality and can influence the choices he or she makes every bit as much as reasoning (this skill is part of "emotional intelligence" addressed in this volume's Introduction and is covered in depth in Chapter 3.) Instead of minimizing or dismissing the fear, Bob signaled that he understood how Lisa was feeling when he said, "I can identify" and added, "A little apprehension keeps us on our toes." Notice that he used *we* language rather than *you* language, which helped build rapport with Lisa before moving the conversation forward ("We certainly don't want your nerves to get in the way, so that's definitely something to work on"). Another important dynamic at work here is that an expression of feelings indicates there is trust in a relationship. Lisa felt comfortable enough with Bob to say how she really felt, which told him she would be open to his inquiries.

Fourth, Bob resisted the looming temptation to immediately offer Lisa advice, which kept the ball in her court. Her nervousness about speaking is her developmental challenge, not his. Just telling Lisa to participate in Toastmasters would have been quick and easy for Bob. But giving advice to people when one's intent is to foster development comes with an Achilles' heel. Advice relieves people of having to figure out a solution to their problem themselves (and, how often do employees *not* follow advice from their boss?). As a result, advice giving unnecessarily creates or reinforces dependency in a relationship. Advice (versus coaching) teaches the recipient to rely on the thinking of others, rather than thinking for himself. Part of coaching's power comes from a truism of human behavior: people are more motivated to pursue a strategy of their own making.

Certainly, situations arise when advice or direction is called for, such as when there is only one correct or proven best way to do something or time is critical. Those occasions, however, are more rare than leaders who operate in "tell" mode are willing to admit. Contemporary leaders too easily mistake convenience for urgency. Leaders of Bob's caliber know the difference and make time to develop employees.

Bob used an approach that is very effective when the goal is to help someone change behavior. He tapped into Lisa's past experiences by asking, "Have you ever been this nervous about anything before?" Answering the question helped her see that she could help herself rather than look to someone else for a solution. What she will carry away from their conversation is a lesson that goes well beyond an immediate step to resolve her nervousness. It is easy to forget just how much one has experienced in life, but not always easy to see how applicable these experiences can be to a current situation. A skillful question can help. Bob's question was an example of Gallwey's premise in action.

> The key to framing good questions, according to Kouzes and Posner (*The Leadership Challenge*, 2002), is to think about the "quest" in your questions. What do you want this person to think about? What do you want to learn? A questing mindset shows that you care about the other person. As the old saying goes, people don't care how much you know until they know how much you care.

A more complex issue or situation naturally would call for coaching of a more complex nature, taking an entirely different path and including a number of other coaching techniques and devices. It might involve exploring Lisa's assumptions about the matter at hand, what it would look like if things turned out the way she wanted (in other words, a preferred future), what the obstacles are for getting there, and what she would do if there were no constraints on her choices. The point of coaching, however, is always the same: thinking differently generates new possibilities for action, and new possibilities for action open the door to better results. Coaching's fundamental value-added lies in the increased self-confidence, self-direction, self-accountability, and self-correction that arise when one is in a process of discovery navigated by oneself.

Bob helped Lisa to suggest something specific she could do to get into action, offered his support, and proposed a commitment that she agreed to, which was to present together. The commitment, even though informal, was critical to Bob's effective coaching because it established a near-term benchmark by which both of them could observe Lisa's progress.

Most important, Bob entered this conversation with the intention of helping Lisa build her capacity for effective action. Although the issue at hand might not seem all that significant on the surface, it provided Bob with an occasion to establish an important boundary and a useful baseline in their new relationship. He shared Lisa's concerns and demonstrated support, while clearly expecting her to think for herself and be self-directed. This type of boundary setting is central to coaching. It makes clear where the responsibility lies for resolving the situation or issue without making the employee feel abandoned. Bob established listening and inquiry as a baseline norm for their interactions. Lisa will have far more complex issues to grapple with as she moves into her role as Bob's deputy. She now knows she can count on his interested ear, his probing questions, his support, and even his suggestions. She also knows he will not step in to rescue her when he believes she is capable of helping herself. That's coaching.

Of the many things that can be seen in this simple example, two stand out. First, Bob is highly purposeful in what he says. He clearly is aware of what he is trying to achieve and chooses his words and his tone with intent. This degree of rigor is true of all good coaching. Although coaching might appear to be a casual conversation, it is anything but. Second, we get several glimpses into the mindset that Bob brought to this conversation with Lisa. From those glimpses we can surmise pretty well what Bob believes and values and how he views the world generally. A leader's mindset is critical to effective coaching and is a major factor in its success, as much or more than the skills themselves. It is akin to an untrained eye watching a professional tennis match and concluding that the game is all about shot-making and stamina. An experienced observer, by contrast, knows that beneath what is apparent on the court lies a whole other world of deep concentration, self-control, and strategy worthy of a world-class chess match. So it is in coaching.

A mindset for coaching in the twenty-first century

> A rock pile ceases to be a rock pile the moment a single person contemplates it, bearing within the image of a cathedral.
>
> *—Antoine de Saint-Exupéry*

Saint-Exupéry's observation is a philosopher's way of describing a unique and powerful quality of the human mind—its ability to begin manifesting the potential that is all around us simply by noticing that it is there. It is a poetic expression of where coaching begins.

A mindset is a mental attitude, a way of looking at something. It reflects our beliefs and values and is informed by the norms of the culture and era in which we live. Our mindset reflects the theories we have adopted about how the world works and is shaped by the lessons we have learned. It is a window through which we see the world. In coaching, the primary pane in this window has to do with how we regard people. At the core of every successful and trusted coach's mind are three beliefs:

1. Most people are good at heart and try to do the best they can with what they have.
2. Most people have an inherent desire to learn and steadily improve themselves.
3. Most people are motivated by contributing what they do well to something larger than themselves and that makes a difference in the world.

Certainly, it cannot be said that these beliefs hold for every person, but they are reasonable assumptions upon which to build relationships with people, rather than starting from a place of doubt or skepticism. It is choosing Douglas McGregor's Theory Y over his Theory X.[1] According to the late McGregor, management professor, psychologist and business theorist at the Massachusetts Institute of Technology (MIT), organizations often work from assumptions that most people prefer to be directed, are not interested in taking on more responsibility, and want safety above all else. Such assumptions, he said, lead to the belief and corresponding actions, that employees are motivated primarily by money and the threat of punishment. He labeled these assumptions and beliefs Theory X. By contrast, McGregor postulated that people have the potential to be self-directed and highly creative if properly motivated; that they are not naturally lazy and unreliable. These beliefs he called Theory Y.

Perhaps McGregor's most enduring contribution to our understanding of organizational dynamics and human motivation were the lenses through which we can observe and understand the impact of a leader's assumptions about people on employee behavior. In addition to these beliefs about people, other panes in this figurative window include respect for diversity, humility, empathy, optimism, curiosity, and comfort with paradox and ambiguity.

Respect for diversity in this context extends far beyond appreciation for or tolerance of our differences in the familiar terms of race, creed, age, gender, religion, ethnicity, or national origin. It goes to the most fundamental aspects of who we are as human beings: how we think, how we learn, how we communicate, how we interrelate. It involves a wide array of variables, from personality type and the "multiple intelligences" in Box 4.1 identified by Harvard professor Howard Gardner to learning styles and the nature of one's emotional intelligence, to name just a few.[2]

Box 4.1 The theory of multiple intelligences

Howard Gardner is the Hobbs Professor of Cognition and Education at the Harvard University Graduate School of Education and adjunct professor of neurology at the Boston University School of Medicine. In his book *Frames of Mind: A Theory of Multiple Intelligences*, first published in 1983, he identified seven distinct intelligences that emerged from cognitive research and "documents the extent to which students possess different kinds of minds and therefore learn, remember, perform, and understand in different ways." According to this theory:

> We are all able to know the world through language, logical-mathematical analysis, spatial representation, musical thinking, the use of the body to solve problems or to make things, an understanding of other individuals, and an understanding of ourselves. Where individuals differ is in the strength of these intelligences—the so-called profile of intelligences—and in the ways in which such intelligences are invoked and combined to carry out different tasks, solve diverse problems, and progress in various domains.

This is not to suggest that a leader must become a psychologist. However, a leader of people will not succeed without a basic understanding of the core theories of human behavior and motivation, as well as an awareness of the many ways in which each of us is unique. It means noticing those differences and seeing them, not as things to be managed, but as wellsprings of new thinking that can improve a product or service or how we work together.

This story from a vice president of the World Bank makes the point. She had just announced at an all-hands meeting the forthcoming flattening of her sizable organization to put employees closer to their customers. An employee approached her after the meeting to express her deep consternation at this news. The employee, a native of India, had been raised in that country's system of castes, within which people are born, marry, and die, and which people accept as the way to keep society from disintegrating into chaos. As a result, she could not contemplate, much less appreciate, how the organization could function without hierarchy. She was truly shaken at the thought. It was an eye-opener for the leader—a highly capable, well-educated, thoughtful woman—and a lesson that she says she recalls regularly to remind herself how different we can be in very fundamental ways, especially in terms of what resides in our heads.

Humility is not always associated with leadership but is certainly a main ingredient of wisdom. Consider John Wooden, UCLA's Hall of Fame college basketball coach. He was frequently quoted as saying, "It's what you learn after you know it all that really counts."[3] Leaders who leave space in their thinking for new ideas, new perspectives, and perhaps entirely different assumptions to arise, regardless of their years of experience, demonstrate true humility. That space in one's thinking is what people notice when they say someone is "open." It attracts us because we experience it as an invitation; we are drawn into it. It is comfortable to be with people like that; it is easy to trust them. Humility is an elixir for relationships that truly great leaders and coaches demonstrate. When Max DePree, the iconic former chairman of the board of Herman Miller, left Switzerland after working there for some time, his Swiss coworkers presented him with a fireman's hat inscribed, "I don't know for sure." As he recounts the story, "They apparently thought it unusual to have an American manager who admitted that he didn't know everything. I still try to remember how much there is that I don't know."[4] A leader at the pinnacle of corporate America who can admit to not always having the answer should be an example for leaders at every level everywhere.

> Make your ego porous. Will is of little importance, complaining is nothing, fame is nothing. Openness, patience, receptivity are everything.
>
> — *Rainer Maria Rilke*

Out of humility arises empathy, the capacity to imagine oneself in another's place and understand the other's feelings, motives, needs, and actions. This is not necessarily to agree with or condone them, but to better understand the individual behind them. In *Sacred Hoops*, championship basketball coach Phil Jackson shares what empathy looks like at the highest level in his world.

> Pro basketball is a macho sport. Many coaches, worried about showing any sign of weakness, tend to shut down emotionally and ostracize players who aren't meeting their expectations. This can have a disturbing ripple effect on the players that undermines team unity. In my work as a coach, I've discovered that approaching problems of this kind from a compassionate perspective, trying to empathize with the player and look at the situation from his point of view, can have a transformative effect on the team. Not only does it reduce the player's anxiety and make him feel as if someone understands what he's going through, it also inspires the other players to respond in kind and be more conscious of each other's needs.[5]

There, in the words of a coach/leader whose name is synonymous with success (eleven NBA titles as a coach and two as a player) in the take-no-prisoners world of professional sports, is an important lesson: empathy reduces apprehension, builds trust, and inspires others to greater awareness of their teammates as human beings. Without humility, empathy, and genuine respect for people, coaching will be perceived as manipulation—a crass attempt to use legitimate principles, methods, techniques, and skills to deceive or convert another to one's point of view. In the end, such attempts are only destructive.

In the mindset of every great leader and great coach the proverbial glass is half full. They are optimistic about the future, hopeful in the face of adversity, and confident in their abilities and those of their team members. They see and appreciate what is, rather than lament what is not. From this simple tenet an entire philosophy about organizations, called Appreciative

Inquiry (AI), was born. Its father, David Cooperrider, professor at the Weatherhead School of Management at Case Western Reserve University, describes AI as "involving the systematic discovery of what gives 'life' to a living system when it is most alive, most effective, and most constructively capable."[6] AI is about what inspires, what energizes, what encourages and sustains. It is about possibilities for the future, not blame for the past. Planting the seeds of one's coaching, indeed one's leadership, in the soil of AI is to adopt a new paradigm that breaks with a long, and at times painful, tradition of thinking of organizations and the people in them as a set of problems to be fixed.

At the core of AI sits curiosity, and curiosity is the "juice" behind coaching. This curiosity is not nosiness, but a genuine, respectful desire to understand how others think. Understanding how others think permits us to view the world through their eyes, to appreciate what they see as possible or impossible, and to comprehend how they arrived at their conclusions. By understanding others' thinking, one is positioned to posit an alternative perspective, to observe something that is missing, to offer a distinction that might lead to different thinking. Curiosity (without judging) opens this door by gently piercing the veil of the conditioned mind, which is the province of knowledge and therefore, by definition, is limited to what is already known.

What is not known is the domain of imagination. Imagination is stimulated by curiosity, one's own or another's. No less an intellect than Albert Einstein said that imagination is more important than knowledge. As he elaborated in a now-famous observation, "The significant problems we face today cannot be solved by the same level of thinking that created them." In other words, we must think anew, we must think differently, if mankind is to progress. Thinking differently, or "outside the box," as we are regularly implored, is easier to say than to do. The classic nine-dot exercise is simple proof. The goal is to connect all the dots in a three-by-three matrix with a single line without lifting the pencil from the paper. Trying it for the first time, most people are stumped. It demonstrates the grip that conventional thinking has on most of us. (See the solution to the nine-dot exercise and an explanation on page 127.)

Curiosity, then, is crucial for leaders to understand their colleagues' thinking, as well as their own, so that issues and problems can be addressed in new ways. As Einstein suggested, this is not problem solving by using what we know; rather, it is about challenging our assumptions, examining our biases, removing our filters, and imagining a future not extrapolated from the present or the past.

> A shoe manufacturing company sends two marketing reps to a region in Africa to assess the potential for new business. One sends back an e-mail, "Situation hopeless. No one wears shoes." The other writes back enthusiastically, "Fantastic business opportunity. No one has shoes."

Finally, today's leader must be comfortable with paradox and ambiguity, two constants in our complex and continuously changing world. Paradoxes—seeming contradictions—are all around us, for example, the ever-present call to do more with less. Paradoxes compel us to step out of our familiar mental models to consider "both/and," not just "either/or" thinking. Paradoxes beget possibilities. At Toyota, this principle has been put to use at the corporate level. In a December 2006 interview with the *Detroit Free Press*, Matthew May, author of *The Elegant Solution: Toyota's Formula for Mastering Innovation*, made this comment: "In order to drive innovative thinking, Toyota purposefully sets strategic goals in direct conflict with one another and demands simultaneous achievement. Why? Because these competing goals cannot be met without everyone thinking differently. The artful setting of opposing stretch goals mandates innovation."

Ambiguity is a lack of clarity, a state of uncertainty, the shades of gray that color relationships and much of what leaders deal with in organizations. To be uncomfortable with ambiguity is to need more structure, control, or assurance than the world usually provides. Structure, control, and assurances certainly have their place in organizations, but in the extreme they can extinguish the energy in a human endeavor, reducing it to rote process, and constrain an organization's ability to respond with adaptability and flexibility.

These hallmarks of the mindset of a coach, in whatever context or vocation, afford us a way to see the people, events, and circumstances around us in the light of flux, potential, and possibility. Just as important, they generate and continuously recycle trust in our relationships. Who does not trust someone who accepts and respects us just the way we are? Or is humble, has empathy for our wants and needs, curiosity about our views, and demonstrates hope and strength in the face of the world's challenges?

This kind of mindset is critical to one's authenticity, one's credibility in coaching, and to the quality of trusted leadership called for today.

A culture that supports coaching

To optimize the power of coaching throughout an organization a leader must create a climate in which it is valued, welcomed, and expected. A coaching-rich culture can lead to transformational change for individuals and the whole enterprise. The preconditions for such a culture are trust, alignment, a priority of learning, and the institutionalization of commitments.

Trust

My colleagues make it abundantly clear in other chapters that effective leadership in democratic institutions is grounded in and relies on trusting relationships between the leader and his or her followers. The components of that relationship are one's trustworthiness and behaviors that signal a willingness to trust others. Trustworthiness was addressed eloquently by Terry Newell in Chapter 1, citing a quote from Abigail Adams, the wife of one president and the mother of another. It bears repeating here: "Great Learning and superior abilities, should you ever possess them, will be of little value and small Estimation unless Virtue, Honor, Truth and Integrity are added to them." In short, character trumps knowledge or talent. We must earn the right to be trusted by others by demonstrating our worthiness of their highest regard.

In a leader's relationship with an employee, behaviors that signal willingness to trust include:

- Creating "space" in which the employee can do his or her job free of unnecessary interference;
- Steadily assigning more responsible duties and providing the means to accomplish them; and
- Making it clear that one believes in the employee to achieve what is expected.

For some leaders these behaviors might require letting go of a comfortable way of interacting with others in order to take a risk on someone else.

Risk begets trust. These behaviors reflect a commitment to employees that goes beyond the mechanics of adequate supervision.

> How many of your direct reports would agree with the statement,
> "My leader wholeheartedly wants to see me succeed"?
> If not all of them would, what would be different if they did?
> Would you say that is true of your boss?
> How does that make you feel?

When leaders make the success of employees paramount, healthy, effective organizations are grown. This is not altruism, but strategic, bottom-line leadership. Larry Bossidy, former CEO of AlliedSignal, said it well when he observed, "In the end, we bet on people, not strategies."[7] Coaching is the most effective way for leaders to secure that bet.

Alignment

When Jack Welch was CEO of General Electric, he often visited its corporate university at Crotonville, NY, to tell program participants his expectations of them as members of the GE management team. One of their primary tasks, he said, was to continuously define and clarify for their employees what he called "the field of action." He would draw a rectangle on a whiteboard and label the four sides *mission, vision, values,* and *results.* The point was that unless employees are on the same "field"— they understand these four essentials of the organization in roughly the same way— they are not aligned and are therefore prone to misunderstandings, suboptimization of their efforts, and even failure.[8] Alignment is a simple and useful construct for leaders, and it is especially beneficial for creating a culture in which coaching can take root and thrive. It ensures a foundation of shared understanding and precludes the development of alternative assumptions about purpose, direction, and expectations.

Learning as a priority

Learning is the fertile soil in which coaching takes root. In his book, *Competing for the Future*, internationally renowned consultant and London

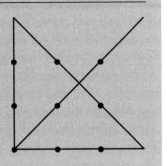
School of Business professor Gary Hamel asked, "Are we learning as fast as the world is changing?" This is one of the most profound questions a twenty-first century leader can contemplate. Consider the implications for an organization if the answer to that question is no.

In 1995 Dr. Janet Woodcock, director of the Center for Drug Evaluation and Research (CDER) at the Food and Drug Administration (FDA), understood those implications better than she might have liked. Her organization was under intense scrutiny by a Congress grown impatient with CDER's inability to adapt to changes in the pharmaceutical industry vis-à-vis FDA's regulatory responsibilities. Legislators were pushing to constrain the center's authority and slash its funding. Woodcock told her management team that the only thing worse than being shut down entirely would be for Congress to make them "irrelevant." She rallied her team to rethink their long-held assumptions about CDER's role and how it worked, create a culture of learning, and embrace innovation. In essence, she coached her organization to a new understanding of itself, to a different way to be (see Box 4.2). What she and they accomplished over the next two years literally became a case study in public sector leadership and the value of learning as a strategic priority to drive change.[9]

The coaching lesson here is that for any individual, team, or organization to adopt new behaviors (meaning to change), they must first make learning a priority. Otherwise, new behaviors will result from extrinsic motivators such as a willingness to please the boss, a desire to get along, or a "this too shall pass" mentality. Extrinsic motivators evaporate once the stimulus is gone and often leave behind a residue of ill will and cynicism. With learning as a shared priority, the groundwork is laid for coaching to make sense and be appreciated by employees.

Once learning has been established as a priority, organization members need to make a practice of exchanging constructive feedback with one another on a regular basis, preferably in real time. Feedback is central to what can be the most important learning in any organization—what we learn about ourselves, the human players in the narrative. Coaching is the catalyst that converts that feedback into action, which leads to improvement. Without the mechanism of purposeful language provided by coaching, feedback remains little more than information and data about one's behavior that can lie fallow for want of tilling and nurturing.

Creating such an organizational culture can be difficult for leaders who focus predominantly on the immediate or the near term. Such is the pressure where priorities are continually in flux, where players regularly change, or the prevailing value is "What have you done for me lately?" Difficult or counterintuitive as it might seem, creating a learning culture is precisely the work that leaders must undertake to ensure the future success of their organization. It requires taking a longer view, making the explicit commitment to developing people, respectfully challenging one another's thinking, being persistent about seeing new possibilities, and freely offering and receiving feedback. The best tool of all is the leader's own example. We know it is possible to create such a culture because the U.S. Coast Guard has done it (see Box 4.3).

Commitments

A commitment is a pledge or a promise to do what one says one will do. Without a commitment to action, coaching can easily dissipate into little more than an interesting conversation with no practical effect. Commitment to action generates momentum through steady gains and ultimately brings success. As in the case of Bob and Lisa, a commitment can take the form of an informal, almost tacit, agreement or something more formal or structured. What is crucial is employees understand and embrace the significance of commitments and honoring them becomes institutionalized in the organization's culture. Without meaningful commitments, energy and time are squandered, morale suffers for lack of direction and accomplishment, and mediocrity prevails.

Box 4.3 An organizational culture for the twenty-first century[*]

The U.S. Coast Guard has a mission that spans more than 120,000 miles of coastline and inland waterways. It operates with fewer people than the New York City Police Department and with an annual budget that is less than the cost of a new aircraft carrier.

How does it do so much so well with so little? The answer, according to Admiral James M. Loy, former Coast Guard commandant, is " . . . simple and cultural. The foundation is commitment to leadership development. All personnel, from the youngest recruit to the senior-most admiral, are immersed in the culture of leadership and expected to practice it on a daily basis."

This culture is based on a leadership model developed at the Coast Guard Academy and has as its foundation character and values, including integrity, respect, commitment, honor, and trust. Standing on this foundation are fourteen core competencies, some traditional, such as vision and goals, expertise, teamwork, decisiveness, and some of more recent vintage, such as connectivity, empowerment, and coaching/mentoring.

What is the upshot of this culture? In Admiral Loy's words, "All this preparation eventually meets the serendipitous filter of opportunity. People must be coached to keep their eyes and ears open to new possibilities, cracks in the competition's armor, and new niches in the marketplace. This approach is affirmed by the success and efficiency of the Coast Guard. It is the values-based leadership culture that explains how the organization can be agile enough to shift its focus during a major natural disaster. It clarifies how the Coast Guard was able to save 33,000 lives while other response organizations were waiting for someone to lead."[*]

[*]Donald T. Phillips and James M. Loy, *Character in Action: The U.S. Coast Guard on Leadership* (Annapolis, MD: Naval Institute Press, 2003). The lives saved refer to the Coast Guard's work during and after Hurricane Katrina.

What makes coaching a leadership imperative for the twenty-first century?

The Chinese have an aphorism: "May you live in interesting times." Indeed we do, most especially the leaders coming into their own early in this new century. Their leadership challenges include the exponential explosion of knowledge; rapid globalization along with increasing awareness of the impact of our actions on others far away; higher degrees of interdependence that necessitate collaboration across time, space, and organizational and national boundaries; the technology-enabled availability of data and information at every level and in every corner of the organization; the technology-facilitated fluidity of work schedules and sites; and the constant arrival of new technology itself; a workforce more educated than at any time in history; a workforce composed of a dizzying blend of salaried employees, contractors, grantees, and partners of all kinds in an unprecedented mix of cultures and generations; the talent wars and the exodus of expertise and wisdom of the Baby Boom generation—all in a vortex of swirling priorities and a mind-numbing demand for speed and more speed. If these factors were not challenging enough, in large bureaucracies like government, this new reality is occurring within antiquated structures, with antiquated processes, and often with antiquated notions about what leadership needs to be.

In 1989 Peter Vaill, among the most influential organizational change theorists of our time, coined the term "permanent whitewater" to characterize the conditions he saw emerging as we moved into the information age.[10] Little more than two decades later, we have already moved beyond the information age into what is being called "the intangible economy." This modern economy is driven not by access to raw materials, transportation, and physical markets, but by the flow of data, images, and symbols. In this economy, brick and mortar are no longer assets of choice; rather, they have been replaced by brand, intellectual property rights, human capital, and knowledge transfer.[11] The twenty-first century—in which every aspect of life is immersed in the technologies of Facebook, iPads, iPhones, iPods, LinkedIn, Twitter, XBOX, Wikis, and Wii—is a whole new world compared to the era of black and white television in which many of today's senior leaders came of age. This degree of change in a stunningly brief period of just half a century constitutes a fundamental transformation in history. As you read this, other turbulent changes are occurring in many fields and most institutions.[12] For example, no one fully knows what will be revealed through the Human Genome Project, only that a transformation in biology is under way. Our basic understanding of life is literally under a microscope. What we do know, however, is that transformations require and result in new thinking. That was Einstein's point. We also know that thinking does not transform itself. It requires a catalyst, a mechanism. Coaching is one such mechanism that is readily available to leaders all the time, everyday.

In these periods of seismic shifts in history, human behaviors lag well behind all other changes. To minimize this lag and maximize effectiveness, today's leaders must adopt new paradigms for their role in the enterprise. The command and control style of leadership that emerged in the industrial era (and remains even now in too many dark organizational corners) is at best futile and at worst damaging in light of the challenges facing twenty-first century leaders. To succeed in a world that does not stand still, organizations can no longer consider it a luxury to have self-directed and self-correcting employees at every level. It is an imperative for their very survival. To develop such employees, leaders must tap the passion, aspirations, knowledge, experience, talent, and potential of everyone around them. They must lead by example. They must lead by calling forth. They must lead as coaches.

Conclusion

Coaching is a set of skills for a leader's toolkit: deep listening, inquiry that broadens and deepens thinking, mindful presence, encouragement, goal setting, and the willingness to hold employees accountable for their own commitments (for starters). Coaching also can be a way for leader and employee to frame their relationship, to move beyond the boss-subordinate paradigm based in power to a truly adult-adult alliance grounded in trust, shared purpose, values, aspirations, and goals. At yet another level, coaching can be the means to more fulfillment, both for the person doing it and the person receiving it. In business terms, coaching provides a path to greater employee productivity, and by extension, organizational effectiveness.

At an even higher order of impact, coaching can be a catalyst for transformational thinking, a new way of approaching problems that goes to the underlying premises and assumptions by which individuals, organizations, and society operate. No matter how one thinks about it, coaching is an act of connecting—connecting leader and employee, connecting an issue or situation to a larger context where its significance is clearer, connecting cognition and emotion, head and heart, and connecting what exists to what could be.

Coaching is an uncommonly positive, powerful, and strategic tool for a leader in relationship to employees and the organization as a whole. It is positive because it affirms the employees, seeks the best in them, and calls upon them to clarify and operate from their values and aspirations to be their best selves. It is powerful because it relies on the employees' thinking, intuition, wisdom, and experience, enabling them to see new possibilities and make informed choices, where perhaps all they knew before was "this is the way it has always been done." It is strategic because it looks forward, calls for systems thinking, and is about learning and change. Coaching can stop the revolving door of people coming to us with questions, particularly those that they are capable of answering for themselves with the right support. It can provide us an entry into being a new kind of leader, enjoying the paradox of greater impact with less control.

Bill O'Brien, the highly respected CEO emeritus of Hanover Insurance, had this to say on the subject of twenty-first century organizations and leadership: "Our traditional organizations are designed to provide for the first three levels of Abraham Maslow's hierarchy of human needs—food, shelter, and belonging. Since these are now widely available to members of modern society, these organizations do not provide anything particularly unique to command the loyalty and commitment of people. The ferment in management today will continue until organizations begin to address the higher order needs: self-respect and self-actualization."[13] No doubt Einstein would have added "new thinking."

This is the imperative leaders must address in the twenty-first century if their organizations are to remain relevant. Ultimately, coaching is a tool, a process that brings the full potential of a leader's team to bear on the enormous challenges of organizations and of our time. What would be different if your employees were coached?

Tips for leadership success

> When their work is done, of the great leaders people will say, "We did it ourselves."
>
> —Lao Tzu

The following principles are offered as considerations for those interested in integrating coaching into their leadership practice.

- Coaching is grounded in the leader's beliefs and expectations about other people and a trusting relationship with employees.

- The primary purpose of coaching is to develop the capacities of the other person. The focus of the conversation is the task or situation at hand, and therefore coaching can occur at any time.
- The larger context of the coaching is a common understanding of the organization's mission, vision, values, and desired results that is shared by both the leader and the employee.
- The leader who coaches sees herself more as a resource for people than as a manager of processes or things.
- Coaching is about possibilities, as opposed to established ways of doing things; it is therefore a vehicle for learning and organizational change.
- As with leadership, the most powerful coaching is by example. Leaders who coach must be models of whatever they expect from those they coach as well as open to coaching themselves.[14]

Resources for further learning

For a broader foundation on coaching as a leadership competency, consider reading:

Chalmers Brothers, *Language and the Pursuit of Happiness* (2004). Written by a certified personal coach, this book explores how our internal and external conversations influence moods, motivations, and relationships, and define human potential.

Marshall Goldsmith, Beverly Kaye, and Ken Shelton, eds., *Learning Journeys* (2000). This compendium of life stories and lessons from a veritable who's who of leadership practitioners and thinkers demonstrates the importance of learning how to learn as a foundation for success.

William Isaacs, *Dialogue and the Art of Thinking Together* (1999). Isaacs is the master of an essential element of twenty-first century leadership: being able to talk together in honest and generative ways. A must read.

Michael Marquardt, *Leading with Questions* (2005). Marquardt asserts that leaders model the way by asking questions that elicit thinking in others and by demonstrating their willingness to learn and change. He examines every side of this approach to leadership and the implications it has for organizations and the people in them.

Susan Scott, *Fierce Conversations* (2004). Two of Scott's lessons pertain to all of us: (1) the conversation is not about the relationship; the conversation is the relationship, and (2) never mistake talking for the conversation. Real stories, easy to read, and immediately applicable.

Richard Strozzi-Heckler, *The Leadership Dojo* (2007). Combining experience in the Marines, as martial arts expert, and executive coach for AT&T and Microsoft, Strozzi-Heckler places powerful emphasis on commitments and self-cultivation, two key elements of a successful coaching mindset and leadership style.

Laura Whitworth, Henry Kimsey-House, and Phil Standahl, *Co-Active Coaching* (2007). A veritable coaching handbook that helped define the field, this book has strong appeal for those interested in a professional pursuit of coaching expertise. For even the more avocational coach, the Toolkit section alone provides some seventy-five pages of exercises, worksheets, action plans, and resources.

Rosamund Zander and Benjamin Zander, *The Art of Possibility* (2000). Many talk about transformed thinking; the Zanders deliver. With lessons from their experiences in art, business, music, and psychology, they help us understand how to turn our thinking on its head and see the world from radically new perspectives.

For more specifics about how to coach, coaching styles, and coaching language, consider the following:

Thomas G. Crane, *The Heart of Coaching: Using Transformational Coaching to Create a High-Performance Culture* (2001). Best choice for busy executives interested in learning enough to get started. Includes helpful graphics to make coaching as straightforward as possible and immediately applicable in small doses.

Robert Hargrove, *Masterful Coaching* (1995). A timeless and seminal work in the field that is at once practical, philosophical, educational, informative, and entertaining. Simple to read, very advanced in concepts and techniques.

James M. Hunt and Joseph R. Weintraub, *The Coaching Manager: Developing Top Talent in Business* (2002). A clearly written, practical compendium of basic and advanced coaching skills and techniques along with useful scenarios and case studies from the authors' research and experiences in a coaching program for MBA students at Babson College.

Doug Silsbee, *Presence-Based Coaching* (2008). The title says it all—Silsbee offers a solid foundation for authentic human connection grounded in profound mindfulness and appreciation of the other. The book's engaging style combined with practical exercises and sample conversations takes the reader beyond technique into an understanding of what really makes coaching powerful, even transcendent.

Web Resources

Below is a selection of coach training programs the author knows personally and is comfortable recommending. All are certified by the International Coach Federation (ICF), the discipline's governing body, as meeting its rigorous standards. You can explore coaching at their website, www.coach-federation.org. Note: some programs include forms of coaching, such as life coaching, or aspects of coaching, such as starting a practice, not needed by leaders in organizations.

Coaches Training Institute, San Rafael, CA, www.thecoaches.com.

Georgetown University, Washington, D.C., www.lifecoachcourses.info/leadership-coaching-certificate-program-georgetown-university.

The Hudson Institute, Santa Barbara, CA, www.hudsoninstitute.com.

Newfield Network, USA, LLC, Boulder, CO, www.newfieldnetwork.com.

New Ventures West, San Francisco, CA, www.newventureswest.com.

Notes

1. McGregor (1960).
2. Gardner (1983).
3. Wooden and Jamison (1997).
4. DePree (1992).
5. Jackson (1995).
6. Cooperrider (2005).
7. Bossidy and Charan (2002).
8. GE videotape of one of Welch's appearances at Crotonville, loaned to the consulting team of the Federal Quality Institute, Washington, DC, in 1993.
9. The author served as the principal organizational development consultant to Dr. Woodcock and her senior leadership team during this period. Woodcock's efforts are chronicled in "Growing Leaders for Public Service," by Ray Blunt, from *The Business of Government,* November 2003, published by the IBM Center for the Business of Government.
10. Vaill (1989).
11. Goldfinger (1994) is credited with having first coined the phrase, by which he meant, "The source of economic value and wealth is no longer the production of material goods, but the creation and manipulation of dematerialized content." In 2000 the European Commission published "The Intangible Economy—Report of the European High Level Expert Group on the Intangible Economy," which added this observation (p. 5), "The 21st century business landscape is often characterised as 'old economy' plus internet. As a metaphor this has the appeal of simplicity, but is misleading. Today, the pursuit of competitive

advantage requires a radical shift of mindset away from our old-world business models and practices. The clarity of 20th century markets was based on a system of fixed boundaries, with one-to-one trading relationships, linear value-chains and balance sheet accounting concepts. The economy today operates without fixed boundaries, and this has far-reaching implications for companies, financial markets, public institutions and regulators."

12. See "The 2007 SHIFT Report—Evidence of a World Transforming," by the highly regarded Institute for Noetic Sciences, Petaluma, CA, at www.noetic.org.

13. Senge et al. (1994), 24.

14. From the training course, "Coaching Skills for Executives," created and taught by the author at the Federal Executive Institute, Charlottesville, VA.

5 Leading for team success

GAIL FUNKE, LCC ASSOCIATES

Effective leaders are leaders of people, and in organizations, people must often work in teams. Knowing the principles of working with teams is thus invaluable for today's (and tomorrow's) leader and helps to attain results: employees who trust their leaders are more likely to remain with the organization, to engage in the (extra) discretionary effort that can make such a difference in today's constrained world, and to work more effectively with others to accomplish organizational goals. This chapter provides a primer for creating and working with teams. It looks at why the use of teams is so vital, the macro-level factors that leaders who create teams must consider, and the micro-level features that those in the team must address. Among other topics covered are how to create a team, who should be on the team, when to use teams, and how to ensure that your team will flourish in the most effective manner possible. A section on virtual teams offers guidance for this increasingly common strategy.

Teams strengthen the performance capability of individuals, hierarchies, and management processes.

—*Jon R. Katzenbach and Douglas K. Smith,*
The Wisdom of Teams

"IS EVERYONE HERE?" Miriam queried. A series of responses confirmed that, indeed, everyone was here. "Here" in this case, and increasingly in both public and private sectors, was a *teleconference*. Miriam's team not only was meeting virtually, but in fact had never had a face-to-face meeting! "We just can't afford the down time that travel would create for our team," Miriam commented. "Besides, we'd never get to the distant regions anyway, so they'd continue to either feel left out or constantly saddled with a travel burden."

137

Miriam's experience—and success—with virtual teams didn't just happen. She carefully studied the principles and practices of teams in general and virtual teams in particular, including the formation process. The subsequent teleconferences followed a specified protocol, much as a face-to-face team would.

How can leaders understand the value of teams and teamwork and skillfully implement and use this approach? How can leaders effectively initiate team-based approaches in both their immediate environments and in the virtual world of geographically dispersed teams? And what are the organizational *sine qua nons* for becoming an effective user and implementer of teams? This chapter explores the meaning of teamwork, the factors necessary for its effective implementation, and how one major learning institution, the Federal Executive Institute (FEI), fosters the understanding and use of teams and the tools necessary for creating a team-compatible organization environment.

The chapter discusses the several levels of learning and understanding that are necessary for the effective use of teams in the public sector. Success with teams rests on the central tenet of this book: the building of trust and the establishment of relationships. Without these foundational steps, the leader cannot hope to use teams effectively. We then turn to institutionalizing teams in the greater organizational structure, to specific activities for building and maintaining teams, and to special applications, particularly for virtual teams.

The case for teams

The opening vignette reminds us that even in an era of profound technological change, teams remain an essential part of corporate and government life. As team specialist Jon Katzenbach emphasizes, teams represent the simplest, most straightforward process change an organization can make to improve its productivity, reduce duplication, and raise performance.[1] In government, where stagnant budgets and declining discretionary funds are the order of the day (and the future), teams can improve output without requiring more resources, and the benefits can be quite substantial. Further, government and private-sector annals are replete with examples both of near disasters when teamwork and cooperation were missing and glowing successes when collaborative teams were present.

If groups and teams can accomplish far more than the same number of individuals working independently, if their use can mitigate the effects of flattened public-sector budgets, and if teamwork and "groupwork" indeed constitute the template of the twenty-first century workforce, what are the individual and organizational implications for future leaders? Often tempered by independence and autonomy, today's leaders must undergo a sea change to prepare proactively for the challenges awaiting them. The hallmarks of today's executive environment are complexity and interdependence. Leaders simply cannot accomplish their agendas without engaging people in true collaborative association: leadership requires that others be substantively engaged in the "production process." Furthermore, public-sector leaders confronted with static or shrinking budgets can actually create leverage with a team-based environment and accomplish far more than in an atomized, "stovepiped" arrangement, in which organizations themselves rarely if ever interact and see more advantage in maintaining their turf than in collaboration and cooperation.

Countless situations and structures throughout government would benefit from greater or more efficient use of teams and teamwork: the response to Hurricane Katrina, the BP oil disaster, the strategies for managing BRAC (base realignment and closure) mandates, the recent federal health care legislation, agency reorganizations—the list is seemingly without end. Yet we encounter a patchwork of application. Some agencies—the National Aeronautics and Space Administration (NASA), for example—make extensive use of teams, but others do not, are coming late to this opportunity, or see teams as of limited use. Why?

The answer lies in our leaders and in our organizational history.

> For most of my career in government, I believed that I needed to do it all—in other words, to set out the plan and direct the work; but as I moved up to leadership positions, I couldn't do that—there simply weren't enough hours in the day. Then I came to FEI and discovered that real leaders are not necessarily responsible for doing the work; but they are responsible for seeing that the work gets done.
>
> *—Participant in the Leadership for a Democratic Society program, Federal Executive Institute*

> I need to allow my team to do the work it's good at—to lead where I can and to get out of the way the rest of the time (most of the time). I'll admit this is a stretch for me but the results already seem to be worth it.
>
> *—Naval Air Systems Command Team Leader*

Figure 5.1 Leadership at the "T"

Strategic leadership
- Strategic thinking
- Political savvy
- Vision
- External awareness
- Influencing/negotiating

Team leadership
- Team building
- Interpersonal skills

Technical leadership
- Professional and technical skills

The FEI uses a model represented as "Leadership at the 'T' "—a construct that depicts and contrasts the skills necessary early in one's career with the skills necessary for leadership positions assumed later in one's career (see Figure 5.1).

As one rises up the leadership ladder (represented by the T's vertical bar), the balance shifts from reliance on personal skills, such as technical expertise, to interpersonal skills, working with others, and building teams and coalitions. At the top (the T's horizontal bar)—the strategic leadership level—one's success depends most heavily on the ability to work in a team framework within and across organizational boundaries. Paradoxically, the early contributors to executive success must be modified as one works in an increasingly group-oriented environment.[2]

Leader, first know thyself and build trust

> The journey of 10,000 miles begins with a single step.
>
> —*Aphorism*

> Trust is the foundation of real teamwork. [T]here is nothing soft about it. It is [the most] critical part of building a team.
>
> —*Patrick Lencioni,* The Five Dysfunctions of a Team

If trust is central to effective teams, leaders need to understand its meaning and importance and practice it in their daily work life. Yet many leaders "go it alone," trusting no one and relying solely on themselves. Or, they fail to understand the process for building trust, both for themselves and for the people with whom they work. Trust in this context is not merely assuming someone will not steal from the office or will show up on time even when you are not there (although that is certainly part of it). Rather, the trust we emphasize here is the willingness to be vulnerable, to abandon a position of "always right," to be willing to admit when you are wrong or need help. For the executive used to solo performance this adjustment can be major and life-changing. In the public sector, "going it alone" has been a long-standing characteristic, handed down through generations of public servants.[3] Leaders must know themselves well enough to understand if they are engaging in this tendency as well as know how to generate the trust essential to breaking from this limited and limiting paradigm.

The work of building teams must begin with this knowledge in mind. On most teams, some personal disclosure can be a powerful tool in creating the trust necessary for progress and high performance. This disclosure must fit with the team and organizational culture. The willingness to self-disclose, be open, and be vulnerable is critical to team cohesion and performance. And it all starts with the leader. The usual result of a disclosure experience is that team members see firsthand the results and achievements of groups that create and maintain a high level of trust. For example, a leader who discloses his or her hopes and fears, or organizational and professional challenges and setbacks, may see a result in increased group acceptance and openness.

When carefully calibrated disclosure is practiced at FEI in executive development programs, participants very quickly forge teams that are strong, enduring, productive, and grounded in trust. Strong trusting teams are not about agreeing all the time, but about having firm foundations that allow members to air their concerns and disagreements openly and then resolve them together. Both the teams and the individuals involved are strengthened by the process.

Another important outcome of this process is that government executives understand that trust and relationships *precede* rather than follow task and content. Clarity on work tasks does not in any way cause trust and sound relationships to occur. In fact, often groups who put the cart before the horse in this fashion find that later they cannot resolve even the simplest disagreements because they neither learned nor practiced trust and never developed effective relationships that transcend the work at hand.[4] This is often the most difficult phase of team leadership. It is important for team members to know that this is "real work," perhaps not the work they are used to but perhaps the most essential work they will do.

This process often causes considerable discomfort for public executives, who, although they accept and understand the necessity for teamwork and groupwork and the foundation of trust and relationships, are concerned about their personal abilities in championing such an approach at their own agencies. Among their concerns typically are personality preferences and their approach to influence. For example, individuals with a preference for closure may be uncomfortable with the open-ended process of team formation or the use of a consensus model.

Self-awareness is a key to team and leadership success. One success measure is the ability to participate in and lead team development. Leaders who understand their own styles will be more effective and build stronger teams. Personality or style preferences can be addressed through the use of the Myers-Briggs Type Indicator (MBTI), the DISC,[5] or other valid and reliable instruments.[6] The MBTI identifies innate preferences that are manifested through behavior along four main dimensions: (1) one's source of energy (internal/Introvert or external/Extravert); (2) information gathering (detail/Sensor or big picture/Intuitive); (3) decision making (impersonal/Thinker or personal/Feeler); and (4) approach to work and life (decisive and systematic/Judger or open and spontaneous/Perceiver). The capital letters combine to form sixteen types, and each type brings gifts and skepticism to the team process. Knowing one's MBTI and that of the group allows teams to self-diagnose opportunities as well as pitfalls, which are discussed later in the chapter. For the leader, this kind of information can be invaluable in implementing and supporting teamwork in the agency. Type is a tool for insight, not for avoidance.

The DISC is another instrument helpful to the team leader that specifically addresses how people interact, deriving four distinct styles along two dimensions. The dimensions of the DISC shown in Figure 5.2 that help us to identify our personal styles are whether we are *people or task oriented* and whether we are *reserved or active*. Depending on the combinations of these dimensions, the four possibilities are:

Figure 5.2 Spectrum of DISC possibilities

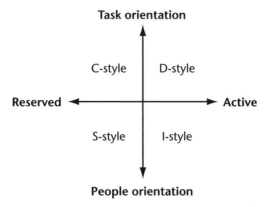

- D-style (Dominance)
- I-style (Influence)
- S-style (Steadiness)
- C-style (Correctness)

The Dominant style will be active and task-oriented, focused on goals, results, and oneself. Terms such as "assertive," "bold," and "fast-paced" come to mind. The Influencing style also will be active, but with an orientation toward people and focused on others, team spirit, and the future. Here, terms such as "accepting" and "agreeable" are more descriptive. The style of Correctness (earlier-Conscientiousness) is reserved and task-oriented and focused on task specifics such as facts, analyses, and details (questioning and skeptical), while the style of Steadiness is people-oriented and reserved, focusing on agreements and principles and the team itself, with descriptors such as "thoughtful" and "calm." It is easy to see that a mix of styles could lead at best to a lively team and at worst to a conflictual one. Too many similar types on a team will rob it of its diversity and contribute to the dreaded groupthink phenomenon.

Leaders need to be aware of several things when utilizing such instruments as the MBTI or the DISC with teams:

- A team with a preponderance of the same preferences or styles may suffer from easy unanimity and lack challenges to its decision-making process and actual decisions; paradoxically, this could also lead to clashes amongst strong personalities. In this situation, the leader needs to see that provocative questions are asked, alternatives considered and all members heard.

- Using style preferences to plan teamwork can be extremely useful to the success of the team. The instrument gives team members a neutral language when addressing conflicts and concerns.[7]
- Each member of the team has a great deal to contribute. The leader can help this happen.[8]

In essence, the effective leader is aware of the value and pitfalls of preferences and uses them to the team's advantage.

The complex environment and effective utilization of teams

> Our leadership views our unit as a "bunch of cowboys" — talented but independent, and less effective than they could be in a more concerted effort.
>
> — *Department of Defense civilian commenting on the need for his team to work together*

> The task was likely to be long and strenuous, and an ordered mind and a clear programme were essential if we were to come through without loss of life.
>
> — *Ernest Shackleton,* South[9]

One need only look to evolving work patterns and dependencies to appreciate the growing need for teamwork and groupwork. A quarter century ago, more work was accomplished by individuals working alone than is the case today. We are simply more dependent on other groups and people to accomplish our agendas. This dependency creates the need for people to understand how to (truly) work together. Working together is not "we are in the same location, and I do my work, you do yours"; rather, it is more of "my work is your work" and vice versa.

A successful team or group approach appears tantalizingly easy, yet nothing could be less true. Teams are more than collections of individuals who formerly worked independently and now work together. Their effective utilization requires a broad systems approach not only to the work itself but also to the organization within which the work is conceived and executed. The capable leader will analyze the work environment to best employ team/group approaches. Since so much work is group or team-based, one should err on the side of using teams. Because of the synergy of teams, all can provide creative, strategic input. Teams can take many forms: large, small, long-term, short-term, and each has its own purpose. So, once having committed to the team approach, the leader then forms the team(s) to best suit the needs of the project or organization.

This section provides the background and principles around team formation that the leader must know to be her most effective in utilizing this powerful production process. Some considerations are in order as we proceed. First, team-based environments require special attention to human relations and morale. People are being asked to assume new and different responsibilities that can feel like additional work, perhaps without a financial incentive. Long-standing research tells us that money is overrated as a productivity motivator, while recognition and appreciation are underappreciated for their effectiveness.[10] The skillful leader will pay diligent notice to recognition and be attentive to teams without micromanaging them. Second, as with many new initiatives, teams are often "expensive now" but "cheap later." When learning the team protocol, including the sometimes difficult task of working collaboratively, progress may seem slow. The attentive leader recognizes this phenomenon and knows that once the team reaches a trusting "steady state," this duality will dissipate. Third, the question often arises of how long it takes for a team to gel. The not surprising answer is: it depends. If the work is long-term, complex, or the relationships strained, months may elapse, depending on the methodology used to form the team. But as we will see later in this chapter, specific, tested methodologies can get any team off to a more rapid and effective start.

Five questions to ask when using a team approach

Leaders considering the use of teams in public-sector settings need to consider several questions to best design and launch a team-based effort.

1. *WHY SHOULD A LEADER FORM A TEAM?* This question is essential. In government, the overriding issues are flat budgets and the need for agency effectiveness. But an argument can be that teams can actually do

more! Eight branch chiefs that teamed up at a large federal agency found that not only was their workload more bearable, but also their influence with higher management increased and some outputs actually went up—deadlines met sooner, better reports, and so forth. At a more individual level, the leader had better be ready to answer the "why" question before proceeding too far. Bear in mind also, that additional benefits often emerge as the team does its work, and the synergy takes over.

2. *ARE THE WORK TASKS INTERDEPENDENT; CAN THEY BE, OR SHOULD THEY BE?* Trying to answer this question can be confusing at first because the work initially is being performed separately. In addition, potential team members who are skeptical of teams or unwilling to work with others may create all kinds of reasons why the work at hand does not depend on others for their success.[11] The Department of Defense (DOD) team referenced earlier believed they had no reason to interact, much less have mutual dependencies. They believed their individual jobs were totally different, even though all were in the same branch. A long-standing culture of independence reinforced this belief. Thus, it is important to ask the question and answer it truthfully—which may require some thought and discussion. If it was apparent that the work tasks were interdependent, perhaps the team approach would have been tried a long time ago.

3. *IS THE WORK SHORT TERM OR LONG TERM?* Katzenbach points out that many high-functioning teams engage productively and at high energy levels for a limited time because of the nature of the work and the excitement of the potential outcome.[12] In these short-term cases, the project itself may generate sufficient energy to motivate a group to form a team and conduct the work. The leader's task is to keep the group focused on the goal. In these tactical situations, relationships and trust are not inessential, but they take a secondary role to the goals of the team. When the project is finished, the group disbands. If the project is likely to take a long time, however, the leader must give care to building relationships and trust, or the team will be unable to sustain itself as conflict and controversy arise—and they will. The lack of this foundation will endanger the team's work.

4. *WILL THE PARTIES EVER WORK TOGETHER AGAIN?* Trust and sound relationships are essential if the individuals on the team are likely to encounter one another in other groupwork situations. Interagency task forces may have two or more members from a cooperating

organization, or a division may implement a matrix approach. As a result people could encounter each other in a variety of team situations, and if the initial experience was negative or unproductive—in other words, no trust and poor relationships—the second round will be worse.

5. *WHAT IS THE NATURE OF THE RELATIONSHIP BETWEEN THE VARIOUS INDIVIDUALS?* Warm, personal, and trusting relationships tend to endure. People in such relationships may disagree, but they know what to do to resolve their differences. Poor prior relationships will only endanger the work of the team(s) if not addressed at the beginning. If the situation is openly hostile, individual coaching and other activities may be warranted in addition to team development activities for the group. Individuals who perceive their relationships with others as "either/or" may need to be treated more directly,[13] transferred, or given other duties if not resolved.[14]

The macro environment

> I never realized that I'd need to make so many other organizational adjustments to use the team approach. But once I did, things went even better. For example, the "Teamwork" award has been really popular and motivating.
>
> —*FEMA branch chief*

Teams do not operate in an organizational vacuum. Ignoring this fact can doom teams to fail. Only when the organization is in complete alignment with the work process will the work products be of the quality desirable and necessary for the future. Once the decision to employ teams is made, the diligent leader will give careful attention to the total organization and the processes within the organization that either support the team approach or are not harmonious with it and must be changed. For example, many federal agencies perpetuate processes and systems that reinforce and reward individual effort. This culture encourages teamwork opponents to "ride out" the leader who dares to change the status quo. Leaders can, however, ensure that the team approach becomes firmly ensconced in their organization. Following Weisbord's Six-Box Model, [15] they will find several leadership principles to which they can turn (see Table 5.1). This model is immensely useful as a framework for team management as it includes all functions of the organization and gives the leader explicit guidance on how to manage these functions.[16]

Table 5.1   Six-Box model

Organizational element	Definition
Purpose	Goals and vision of the team; how its work relates to the overall organization
Relationships	How we manage and coordinate the work of the team with the rest of the teams and the overall organization
Helpful mechanisms	Resources and organizational support systems
Rewards	How appropriate behavior is recognized and rewarded
Structure	How the work of the organization functions: time, tasks, physical space, work schedules
Leadership	Keeping the "boxes" in balance
Environment (a "seventh" box)	Everything else, including the way the organization relates to its external customers—in essence, this is not a "box" but a surrounding element

Source: Weisbord (1978). "Environment" may be considered as the box that contains all the other boxes and wider external forces. Weisbord does not list it as a "box," reserving that term for what takes place *inside* the organization.

1. Purpose. The leader (the word *leader* in this section refers to the overall leader of the organization or work unit; the team leader is discussed under micro issues) always clearly articulates the purpose of the team, its overall goals, the relationship of its work to the overall organization, and the congruence of goals if multiple teams are being used. Even the team name is important: eschew names such as "Red Team" and "Team A" whenever possible, as they have a way of trivializing the team when the name could be a source of pride or dignity. Reminders from the leader about team goals are in order as well. The leader is aware of the team's progress and when it may require redirection. In addition, the leader keeps the overall agency work unit informed of the rationale for teams, how they will be deployed, and the goals they support. This information is written and posted in ways consistent with the agency's culture, for example, on a communal bulletin board.

2. Relationships. The leader orchestrates the management and coordination of the team(s). The leader ensures that teams do not work at

cross-purposes, that they communicate with each other, that organizational processes support the teams, and that the teams appropriately interface with people and technology as necessary to carry out their work. The leader also gives attention to relationships within the team, whether the members are a group of peers or come from several organizational levels. With respect to the work at hand, teams are essentially groups of equals, which may require orientation for members accustomed to a hierarchical environment. Supervisors and team leaders may require additional training from an expert in collaboration and conflict management. One easy strategy is to create cross-team groups that meet with the leader regularly to report about how the teams are working and on what. As the teams become more sophisticated, the leader may not need to attend every meeting.

3. Helpful mechanisms/support systems. Overall organizational alignment dictates that the leader pays attention to the many subsystems within the unit that could either support or derail the team. The team may need a budget to promote its work, to rent rooms, hire facilitators and specialists, and create and copy reports. Performance evaluations (see rewards section) will need to be aligned with the responsibilities of group as well as individual accomplishment. Policies and procedures, such as permission for off-site activities, may need to be changed. The serious leader realizes that teams may not initially know what resources they need or that they will be provided. Sometimes the existing office space configuration will need adjustment to better accommodate the team.

4. Rewards. This element is critical because incentive systems tell us what is truly valued and expected. Many organizations utilize teams extensively, but maintain individual performance as the standard for end-of-year evaluations. This practice effectively removes any incentive for the individual to cooperate in a team environment.[17] Are interim rewards or recognition provided for the work of the team? Is the team treated with respect and its work valued? People laboring in the relative anonymity of a cooperative environment still benefit from the reinforcement that may more regularly accompany individual effort. Is the team accorded "safety" in the work environment? In other words, is the leader building trust, making sure that people can feel free to speak up and do their best work. Is status associated with the work of the team, and do individuals on teams have the same chances for advancement, increased responsibility, and other rewards? This element is not easy to address, although the adage "what gets measured gets done" would apply here. The individual performance evaluations "exceeds

fully successful" or "outstanding" need special attention in a team environment so that recognition of individual accomplishments does not overshadow appreciation of group (team) work. This is the opportunity for the leader to identify special behaviors, for example, "The work of the team is implemented and functions as a model for other teams."

5. Structure. How do the various structures of the organization support the work of the team? The leader decides what type of team is needed and allocates the workload of the team and its charge/goals (task structure), assures that the team has dedicated time and space to do its work, and manages potential areas of conflict that the team's work may engender. Most importantly, the leader assures that the work and needs of the team(s) are integrated into the overall organization, that the work of the team "fits" with the other work of the unit. It is in this domain that the leader ensures that the originating work unit of the team member understands the responsibility of this individual and facilitates arrangements for the unit's work to be done in the absence of the individual. The surest way to a dysfunctional team is to neglect the necessary work restructuring that must occur if the day-to-day work *and* the team work are to get done. Not addressing this problem is a common error, but one easily avoided with some thought and collaboration with employees. A city administration almost doomed the team approach by making two major mistakes: expecting team members to stay late to finish work that went undone while they attended team meetings and expecting other workers in the team member's department to attend to that person's work as well as their own. Strategic thinking and planning beforehand prevents these common errors.

6. Leadership. This box references the leader, who keeps all the boxes in balance. Any initiative benefits from the holistic view of this model, and savvy leaders constantly remind themselves to pay attention to everything that is going on. In the end, the leader manages all these boxes and enables the team to do its best work, unfettered by inappropriate disruptions or internal snafus.

7. Environment. The environment box is the "everything else" category. In some ways it is not really a box because it surrounds the total organization. It captures the external environment for the team, including customers, suppliers, competitors, and regulators. For example, under a team approach, the formerly one-on-one meetings with customers may be replaced with the whole or part of the team participating in such interactions. External actors must then be made aware that decision making is now diffused and that the people they deal with may change depending on

which team member is acting as representative. Outsiders must be told that the team has full support, and the leader minimizes internal team management disruptions through boundary management, either intra- or interorganizationally.

Some considerations

Culture and gender

> I decided to use a team approach at my new office in Texas. We had used teams very successfully in Florida, and I was excited about the prospect. Imagine my surprise when I encountered resistance, even hostility! My predecessor did not believe in teams. It was a tough road, and I learned a lot. We're doing OK now.
>
> —*NASA senior manager*

Leaders, federal or otherwise, need to assess their organization's culture before championing or adopting a vast team approach if one is not in place. The senior manager from NASA had experienced success with her teams, and it was her preferred method of operating. This enthusiasm was not initially shared at her new location. Simply barging in with the assumption that others will see teams the way you do will not always gain goodwill. The careful executive evaluates the organization's culture before taking the leap. For senior federal executives who change jobs on an average of every two years, this is sage advice. Adopting a team approach in your new organization should be addressed using principles of organizational change.[18]

Culture and gender can overlap, since each leader has the opportunity to shape his or her organization's atmosphere and processes and may use personal preferences and background to inform that shaping. Writers Carol Gilligan, and more recently Alice Eagly and Linda Carli, have all noted that women's style may be more circular, connected, and communal (relationship-oriented), and less agentic (task-oriented).[19] Women *tend* to favor the relationships of the organization while coming later to the tasks at hand. This tendency may not always work to their advantage, particularly in task-centric cultures. Pat Heim, author and consultant in the area of management and gender differences, characterizes this tension as women's desire to keep the organization "flat" rather than hierarchical.[20] Good leaders, regardless of gender, recognize the joint importance of relationship and task, and assure that attention is given to both.

To facilitate or not facilitate?

> Gail, can you please come and help up straighten out our team?
> We tried to run the offsite ourselves and after two days of fight-
> ing realized that we could not do it ourselves—we had too much
> invested. We need your help!
>
> —*Excerpt from a telephone conversation of the branch chief of*
> *a scientific agency, following a highly contentious meeting*

Often, and especially when well-planned, teams and their leaders believe they can manage their groups themselves. While this can be the case, there are parameters for when and when not to engage professional team facilitation services (see Table 5.2).

Table 5.2 **Team facilitation guidelines**

Parameter	*Self-facilitate*	*Professionally facilitate*
The group functions well and the meeting is primarily about non-contentious issues.	The leader can safely run this type of meeting.	
The group has never met before, and there is reason to believe that there could be conten-tious issues or at least uncharted territory.		This allows the leader to be a full participant in her/his new group,[1] and permits the necessary development (and practice) of group norms.
The agenda for the team's work is critical and highly time-sensitive		All should participate and there is no room for redoing the meeting if things do not go well.
Some external or in-ternal critical event has impacted the team		All should participate, espe-cially the leader.
The meeting will focus on scheduling and simi-lar issues	The team needs to manage itself when possible, taking ownership of its work.	

[1.] The leader simply cannot play two roles, that of participant and facilitator at the same time. To attempt this is to court trouble and resentment as the two agendas become inseparable.

Who do you want on your team?

> When I interviewed for the job, my (future) boss talked a lot about my MBTI type, my decision-making style, and my general approach to life and work. I soon noticed that there were real differences between us. I observed this out loud and his response was one I'll never forget: "Good!" he said, "we don't need two of me."
>
> —*Head of a public health department in Miami, FL*

There's an old adage that we tend to form romantic relationships with our opposites, but hire those who are like us. Whether true or not in affairs of the heart, this practice could be deadly in the workplace—many processes, including our ability to form effective teams would be adversely affected. Too frequently, teams can devolve into a monoculture, as individuals seek a comfort level with others with their worldview. Whether the MBTI or DISC styles, gender, race, ethnicity, or other consideration, teams must guard against subtle processes that weed out needed diversity. Lack of diversity has the potential to affect many team processes, not the least of which will be people-task dichotomies, communication styles, decision-making protocols, and attitudes toward conflict. Some teams will not actually be "voting" but the effect can be the same if there is a virtual isolation of the "different" members of the team. It is important for teams to be sure that all viewpoints are heard, and to "invent" them if the team itself lacks the proper diversity. Teams often use designated roles such as "devil's advocate"[21] to tease out differences.

The micro environment

> My role in the project was only to manage the relationships of the work team. Someone else managed the technical work. I made it clear from the outset that I would require as much autonomy for my role as the other manager did for his. I got it, and we came in early and under budget.
>
> —*A winner of the 2006 Federal Executive of the Year Award (and FEI graduate)*

In addition to macro or organization-wide issues, the leader must attend to the internal dynamics of team functioning. The more attention the leader pays to the fine details of the team, the less he will need to worry about its work. In the work setting, this begins with the posture the leader takes with respect to teams. For example, initiating the use of teams involves familiarizing individuals in the organization with the unique responsibilities and opportunities of working in a collective environment. Counterproductive attitudes such as the notion that collaborative work is inappropriate and results in loss of professional identity will need to be addressed. The leader may need to reassure individuals about this with visible evidence such as revised performance evaluations and changes in policy directives. Training and team monitoring may be needed until the team has reached a trusting "steady-state," particularly around roles and decision making. It is impossible to overestimate the value of this up-front work. A team with the firm foundation of trust coupled with strong relationships will outperform its less-prepared counterparts. This extra effort is worth it later. For example, FEI participants spend one-quarter of their month-long program building trust and forming relationships. Many of these teams are still active years after graduating.

The following features shown in Table 5.3 provide a useful construct for managing teams, particularly within the complex external environment of the government executive

1. Membership. Team membership should be representative of the skills necessary but also provide a venue for contribution from across the organization. Top-heavy teams may contribute less to the overall product than teams that are representative of all organizational levels, depending on the team's charge. On the Manhattan Project, Robert Oppenheimer

Table 5.3   Basic team definitions

Team element	Components
Membership	The kinds of people, groups, and viewpoints that should be represented on a team
Roles	The sets of constructive or destructive behaviors that help or hinder the team in its work
Teamwork	The team stages of sharing; levels of cooperative behavior
Team process	Activities necessary to start and then support the team over time

would not have wanted a team representative of all organizational levels, and his approach might work well in agencies with a strong scientific focus, such as the National Science Foundation, the National Institute for Standards and Technology, or the National Institutes of Health.[22] In many units where the work is not strictly scientific or the need is for policy implementation, cross-representational teams function well and provide substantial side benefits. First, the team representatives are goodwill ambassadors to their work units, relieving management of the difficult task of "translation" when seeking to inform the broader organization about the team's work. Second, the very act of representation serves to quell the voices of the office "disagreers": seek to people your team with a cross-section of naysayers as well as supporters. Third, the team leader thus receives regular communication about what is going on back in the units. Representation takes many forms; better to have your potential adversaries or opponents inside the tent rather than outside engaging in target practice.[23] In some cases, it may be useful to include contractors on certain teams and in certain activities. One agency took this approach because contractors were intimately involved in the agency's work and sat at desks in the same work space. To exclude these individuals would have meant losing valuable input and sacrificing hard-earned cooperative camaraderie. Preestablished ground rules can handle concerns about contractors being privy to certain internal functions (that is, budgets). In this case, the contractors were aware of the sensitive issues and did not attend sessions that addressed them.[24]

2. Roles. Teams function differently from traditional, hierarchical organizations. As such, many members will be unfamiliar with what is essentially a "flat" structure. The team leader is not "the boss."[25] Higher leadership must clarify this role with the team leader and the team itself. The role of team leader is unique and does not/should not involve actual authority over members of the team. The team leader coordinates, facilitates, convenes, serves as liaison with management, conveys information, and otherwise helps the team do its work. Because all teams have many functions, the team roles may change over time and according to the situation. Again, as we move from a hierarchical, manager-centered formulation, the leader needs to be familiar with and familiarize his teams with the various roles that each can/might play. There are several team taxonomies, and two are discussed here as representative of key team roles.

Creative, supportive, and administrative roles. All of these roles are essential to effective team functioning. During a given team meeting, individuals might play all of these roles, and all are essential for beneficial results. Creative behaviors include idea generation, suggestions that lead to addressing problems from different perspectives ("What would we do if we knew we couldn't fail?" "What if we had an unlimited budget?") and reframing ("Perhaps our problem isn't lack of resources, but poor deployment of resources."). Supportive behaviors are just that: cheering on an idea, being the first follower, thinking of ways to apply the idea, or generally boosting the team. Administrative behaviors help keep the team on track and include the people who serve as timekeepers, interface with other affected groups, keep records, and handle communication. The team leader is responsible for making sure these behaviors occur, either naturally or through a process.

Task, relationship, and self-oriented behaviors. In this construct, the first two behaviors are positive; the third refers to self-centered behaviors that undermine the team. Task behaviors include keeping the team on track, paying attention to the task, keeping time, and monitoring progress. Relationship behaviors are trust-centric and directed at keeping the team functioning on an emotional level, making sure everyone is included, that all ideas are heard, and that the well-being of the team members, not just their task accomplishment is addressed. The aforementioned Executive of the Year award winner essentially had this task as her full-time job for several months. The public-sector leader should pay the most attention to this angle because government employees are usually task-oriented, not relationship-oriented.

Self-oriented behaviors are destructive, directed at enhancing the person rather than furthering the work of the team, and lethal if not addressed early. Self-oriented behavior is a key team dysfunction.[26] Sometimes such individuals can be brought into the fold and sometimes they cannot. After a period of reasonable effort, perhaps involving individual work with the team member, the leader must make the hard decision: removal from the team or even the organization.[27]

3. Teamwork. The team is working toward higher and higher levels of collaboration, shown here in order from the first stage of sharing information to the most advanced stage of sharing power and decision making.

- Share information.
- Share ideas, jointly problem solve.
- Share resources.
- Share power, decision-making authority.

Initially, team members share information, an important first step. Many blissfully stovepiped organizations have little internal knowledge about what others are doing and as a result perform at less than optimum levels. The extent of the knowledge in a room with ten team members is tenfold the individual, which, albeit a tautology, still bears repeating. This stage of the team (see "Orientation" below) contributes to establishing trust and expanding the knowledge domain. Much has been written on team interpersonal processes, and it all begins with a "Who am I/Who are You?" dialogue. At this stage, teams begin to engage in conversations and activities that give them a chance to "try their wings" in more complex situations.

Once trust and information sharing have been established, the next stage begins the real work of the team as it engages in creative activities and addresses the charge for which it was formed. At this stage the team synergy is formed, and approaches and solutions transcend individual input. The trust-building stage is the necessary precursor, however, as the environment must be safe for the creative energy to emerge. It is important to note that the stages of team development are often iterative. A more challenging activity may lead some members to revisit trust as the opportunities for conflict increase. The team is then reminded of its purpose, its ground rules, or norms, and, ideally, addresses the conflict or difficulty in an open fashion.[28]

Sharing resources is a considerably higher level of team attainment as it indicates that the team has started to view itself as an entity, rather than a collective. The final stage, the apex, comes when power and decision making are shared. All team members sees themselves as part of a whole, a whole that is larger than its parts and means that each member of the team trusts the other members to act in his or her behalf and vice versa.[29] It also means that the team can function at full effectiveness when not every member is present. Given the complex and demanding nature of government work, this point is crucial, since a leader can be called away at a moment's notice to deal with external stakeholders. The team's work cannot cease when this happens.

4. Team process. There are several major team processes that, if followed, will increase trust, create positive relationships, and improve the success rate of the team.

Orientation. All teams need a formal orientation. It may be brief or extensive, but it needs to happen. Without it, the work of the team may be slowed and the full value of the group never realized. Orientation is usually the first meeting, at which the leader (of the organization or work unit) gives the charge, reaffirms the organizational goals that the team's work supports, outlines time and resource parameters, establishes meeting times, articulates arrangements for work coverage, and so forth.

Norms. These are the critical ground rules by which the team agrees to "live." Norms are generated by the team and can/should include confidentiality, shared speaking time, respect, and active listening. The generated norms provide a scorecard that the team can use to evaluate its behavior; when a norm is violated, the team usually will engage in some corrective behavior and a reaffirmation of the norm. Teams often add to the list of norms over time.

A targeted trust-building activity also helps speed the team toward its work. This should match the expected duration of the team. In other words, a long-term team needs to spend more time on such matters than a team with a one-month deadline. These activities can involve disclosure, which can take many forms, from highly personal to moderate revelations. As discussed previously, disclosure builds trust in the group and forges a separate *team identity*, which greatly improves team functioning and results.

Conflict management. If the subject matter is likely to be contentious, and/or the commitment of all team members is critical for implementation, outside professionals or serious attention to conflict is essential.[30] During its active years in the 1980s, the National Coalition for Jail Reform engaged a professional from the American Arbitration Association to begin each semiannual meeting with a session on the consensus rule that the group agreed to as part of its norms. The work of the coalition was at once delicate, conflict-prone, and critical. This one protocol step allowed it to accomplish major reforms.[31]

Shared responsibility. The agreement that the team's work goes forward regardless of how many are in attendance is an essential part of the team process. This not only encourages attendance but also eliminates a common problem that many teams face—essentially redoing their work every time they convene. This problem is a major cause of team disaffection and dysfunction and has the effect of allowing one person or a small number of people to "hamstring" the team. When the work moves forward, people stay engaged and the team stays productive.[32] But this cannot substitute for organizational commitment to teams. Sometimes leadership must adapt agency processes to accommodate team schedules.

Ongoing assessment. Regular team assessments of team health, progress and protocol on task and creative and administrative behaviors are necessary. Leaders can use the frame of task, relationship, and self-oriented behaviors to assess how they contribute to or degrade the life and work of the team. The norms developed in the first stage also provide a useful barometer of the team's functioning. Occasionally, some type of conflict management or resolution will be necessary (see midcourse corrections below), or the team may simply need to validate its direction and work thus far.

Midcourse corrections. Any number of problems may beset a team as it progresses: it may need new members and/or a member may leave, necessitating a skill check and recruitment. The mandate may be altered. The working environment may change. The boss may be transferred. The time may quicken (or lengthen). The decision-making process may break down. In the case of new or subtracted members, the operative concept is "new team." A change in the team's composition essentially creates a new team because the relationships and skill mix are different. A new, albeit brief, orientation for the team is in order. The norms may be affirmed rather than reconstructed, but the essential concept is that the team once again views itself as the unique entity that it is.

Certain midcourse strategies, such as the classic "force field analysis" or conflict management training, may be useful tools for the team (see Figure 5.3). In force field analysis, the team analyzes its present state of operations and then identifies driving and restraining forces that are keeping it in the present state, rather than in a more desirable future state—the completion of the team project.[33] Next, the group identifies the actions it can take to mitigate the restraining forces (a more productive strategy than increasing drivers that may already be at their maximum). For example, absenteeism may be slowing the work. The team may be meeting too infrequently and spending excessive time on catching up. Some team members may lack the authority to speak for their work unit. There may be petty disagreements. The team may need additional training in how to use a consensus model. While after-action reviews have their place, midcourse corrections can prevent the train from proceeding to the wrong station in the first place.

Decision making. In general, if long-term commitment to the decision is required for effective implementation and acceptance throughout the organization, the consensus rule works best. Majority votes are best used

Figure 5.3 Force field analysis

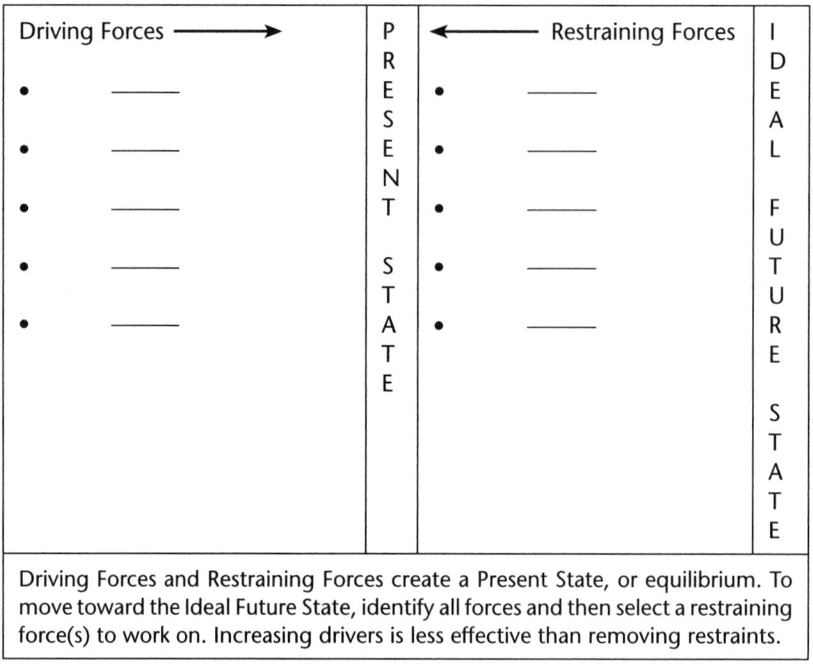

Driving Forces ⟶	PRESENT STATE	⟵ Restraining Forces	IDEAL FUTURE STATE
• ⎯⎯		• ⎯⎯	
• ⎯⎯		• ⎯⎯	
• ⎯⎯		• ⎯⎯	
• ⎯⎯		• ⎯⎯	
• ⎯⎯		• ⎯⎯	

Driving Forces and Restraining Forces create a Present State, or equilibrium. To move toward the Ideal Future State, identify all forces and then select a restraining force(s) to work on. Increasing drivers is less effective than removing restraints.

for short-term situations with no stakeholder impact. Unanimity is difficult to achieve under the best circumstances, though always worth a straw vote to check positions. The team can develop its own decision rules but needs to recognize that the enticing efficiency of a majority vote in a contentious situation only creates winners and losers, the latter often feeling no compunction to support a decision they oppose.[34] So, consensus is time-consuming in the beginning and very speedy at the end. Consensus differs from unanimity in that the final decision may vary from the original proposition but is one that the entire team can live with—an important consideration The group polls its members, who identify the offending portions. Then, concessions, language adjustments, and additions are made until each person agrees not to dispute the decision. One of the most helpful parts of the consensus process is that the team is reminded of (and affirms) what its goals and outcomes are. This "eye on the prize" helps keep the group on track and softens the way to consensus.[35]

Team member contributions. Sometimes, team members do not all pull their weight. A lack of effort may create resentment on the team and raise the possibility of inferior products because the team composition usually reflects the skill mix necessary for optimum results. This problem needs to be addressed in the norm-setting stage even before the team starts its work. Assumptions need to be clarified, including queries such as "Will everyone here be able to fully participate? What will we do as a team if this is not the case?" The norms help create the space for the team to have a productive discussion if someone is not contributing. The ways to address this situation are too numerous for these pages but include direct statements ("Mary, it appears that you're not going to be able to put in the time on this team. Would you like to recommend a replacement?") or a slightly more indirect approach ("As we write our final report, it appears that we are each going to need about fifteen hours to do this. Is there anyone for whom this is a problem? Would you like to still be listed as a 'contributing' member?"). A professional facilitator can help in this situation. Again, the possibility of nonparticipation reinforces the need for regular meetings and a reorientation time for each, however short. Without these strategies, problems fester under the surface and can undermine a team's productivity.

Team communication. Each team needs its own communication strategy. However structured, the team needs to speak with one voice, which may require writing scripts for team members who report back to their groups or units, or the appointment of a single team spokesperson. It may require that all team members are present at certain larger meetings to reinforce solidarity. Any question put to an individual member that the team has not addressed should not be answered but instead brought to the larger group. Regular and frequent communications are necessary, because when a group of people meets privately there is always great curiosity about what has transpired.[36]

Virtual teams

> Our team has consistently met in person, and many members were on what seemed like perpetual travel. Then we got the word that (1) our travel funds would decline substantially; and (2) the top brass was questioning the wisdom of so much travel. This unhappy confluence led to some very creative sessions in which we were able to reconceptualize our work

and develop and adopt very effective processes for meeting virtually.

—Team leader of a major technology development operation for the U.S. Army

Home is where the site is.

—Jessica Lipnack and Jeffrey Stamps, Virtual Teams

Once an anomaly in team thinking, virtual teams are as much a part of organizational life as in-person teams. They are not a "lesser" substitute for face-to-face meetings. Often virtual settings are the only way in which many individuals in organizations can ever meet. They permit full-partner participation by remote offices and employees. Since alternative worksites, long-distance work, telecommuting, and regional or branch offices are now mainstream arrangements, and because new technology allows us to simulate a meeting environment that approaches an in-person model, the typical processes of an in-person meeting can and should be emulated in a virtual setting. Many forces drive the move to virtual teams or geographically dispersed teams including the value of collaborative work, the importance of knowledge management, the necessity to include geographically dispersed members, and time constraints. In addition, the nature of government work and difficult budgets dictate cost-effective and time-sensitive ways to work together. One agency was able to maintain its services in the face of budget cuts by adopting a (more) virtual approach to what had been extensive travel schedules and costs. The time and money saved by this rethinking (and it was a major rethinking for an organization that relied, even thrived, on travel) more than compensated for the budget cuts. Many opposed this "new" approach, but open-mindedness prevailed, and now the virtual approach is central to its operations. Another organization was able to makes its teams more broadly representative because the virtual setting alleviated additional travel costs. Bear in mind that the steps, process, and organizational requirements for trusted team formation are still necessary, albeit modified for the virtual environment.

Virtual work includes geographically dispersed management, individual projects (requiring group input), group projects, and community of practice teams. The latter is a group tied by common and critical interests, for example, the defense intelligence community, where acting individually could produce dangerously suboptimal results. Virtual work allows agencies and organizations to reap the considerable benefits of more teamwork with individuals and groups who do not work near each other. In other words, through attention to the special considerations of virtual teams below, the public-sector leader can implement teams throughout his agency and even across organizational and geographic boundaries.

1. Virtual team components. The components include virtual leadership (the leader is physically distant from the group); virtual operations/operating agreements (the team determines how it will function, for example, by teleconferences, videoconferences, or periodic in-person meetings, and how attendance/participation is structured); the team charter (the team norms, goals, outcomes—what the virtual group actually commits to—which is a fairly time-consuming activity); and the virtual team process (similar to the activities discussed above except that the members are dispersed).

2. Initiating the virtual team. Although the work of the team will be geographically dispersed, an initial face-to-face meeting is much desired. Trust and relationship-building activities are best conducted in person. If the work of the team is highly sensitive, there really is no other way. At the initial meeting, team members get to know each other, affirm or reaffirm their individual, then collective visions and mission, and engage in the various activities that start to build trust. Confidentiality is particularly critical, as the team has only this opportunity to address it directly.

Because the team's face-to-face time is so limited or possibly nonexistent, this initial session becomes more crucial and the topics more diverse, as the team must also address potential derailers, meeting schedules and protocol, and other issues that would be handled by traditional teams in ongoing, in-person meetings.

At this initial session the team develops its charter or working agreement. It is a statement of the group, its members, its internal name, and the things to which it has agreed, beginning with its purpose and its goals. Deciding the team norms and other operating principles and procedures are the next steps. Since technology often results in the use of groupware, training and basic protocols should be provided for those new to the format and electronic communication. It is also during this period that participants can voice their hopes and fears about the team and its virtual nature. If members can first meet face-to-face, time is well-used to set in place methods for the team's virtual work.

3. Operational practices of the virtual team. In addition to the practices outlined above, the team also needs protocols for defining success, trouble-shooting, conflict management, integrating new or additional members (including definitions of membership), recognition and rewards, and com-munications. Sustaining the work of the virtual team is more problematic than for on-site teams because the initiation and actual convening of a meeting can be cumbersome. In addition, the integration of the products of the team must be discussed so that all have ownership, make contributions, and receive appropriate credit. A virtual team can have spokespersons, as long as the team agrees on the products put forward. If the virtual team spends sufficient up-front time on these issues, its work is much more likely to go forward than if these steps receive scant attention.

4. Technology. The technology available for maintaining virtual teams is excellent and continues to improve. At a minimum, teleconferences work to keep all in touch, but chat rooms, private websites, virtual team buildings (with different "rooms" for different activities), and video tele-conferences (VTCs) significantly enhance the work of the team. All of these strategies work to promote team cohesion and success.

The easiest way to approach virtual teams is to remember that the team should follow all the steps of a face-to-face team. For example, good man-ners should prevail in any setting. No one should need to be reminded to use the mute button on the phone, to refrain from eating or using the com-puter, and to devote one's full attention to the group. The team may need some initial reminders about participation, including a go-round or other mechanism to ensure 100 percent input. This is more critical virtually because without a "script" or other verbal or written commitment, a team member is not seen by the group and could conceivably deny support after the meeting. Another extra decision-making mechanism may be to verbally refer to one's position on an issue, for example, I am giving this thumbs up, or I have only one finger up, so I have reservations, etc.

Summary

The results are in: teamwork and group work are the way that work will be accomplished in the twenty-first century. By following the principles described here, wise leaders can ensure that their operation will be success-ful. Most employees, public or private, want to do their best work all the time. Since many early career experiences rewarded individual work over collaborative efforts, early team leadership can require much vigilance. It is important for managers to pay close attention to the environment and approach team implementations strategically. For the trusted team leader, proper orientation activities, modifying organizational processes to more support teams, midcourse corrections, and emphasizing relationship alongside task are pivotal responsibilities. When properly attended to, teams will help the public-sector leader strengthen his or her organization to better serve the American people. Diminishing budgets, increased public scrutiny, and ever more complex missions demand that today's public servants do nothing less.

Tips for leadership success

- Trust and relationship building precede task and content activities.
- Virtual teams adhere to the same principles as face-to-face teams.
- Trust building and adhered-to team norms are essential to team success.
- Adjust processes to accommodate the team's long-term or short-term focus.
- Be flexible as the team, its relationships, and its tasks evolve.
- Revise and adjust organizational processes, such as time and budget, to support and reinforce teamwork.
- Whenever a team member arrives or departs, a whole new team results.
- Routinize team processes, both face-to-face and virtual, in the overall organization.

Resources for further learning

Nancy J. Barger and Linda K. Kirby, *The Challenge of Change in Organizations* (1995). An explanation of reactions to change from the perspective of the MBTI. Yields insight into how different types might respond to new initiatives, such as teams.

Leslie Bendaly, *Games Teams Play* (1996). Contains more than fifty games and exercises to help teams develop productive ways of working together.

William Bridges, *Managing Transitions: Making the Most of Change*, 2nd ed. (2004). Quite simply the best book on transition available. Essential in understanding human reaction to new initiatives.

Alice H. Eagly and Linda L. Carli, *Through the Labyrinth: The Truth About How Women Become Leaders* (2007). Excellent study of gender-based styles, as well as implications for organizations that lack diversity.

Carol Gilligan, *In a Different Voice* (1982). The original volume on gender differences in group approaches and conduct.

Sally Hegelsen, *The Female Advantage: Women's Ways of Leadership* (1995). Studies of evidence and application of Gilligan's findings in the workplace.

Elizabeth Hirsh, Katherine W. Hirsh, and Sandra Krebs Hirsh, *Introduction to Type and Teams*, 2nd ed. (2003). Team building using the Myers-Briggs Type Indicator.

Jon R. Katzenbach and Douglas K. Smith, *The Wisdom of Teams* (2003). All around good advice and insight.

Jon R. Katzenbach, David C. Garvin, and Etiene C. Wenger, *Harvard Business Review on Teams That Succeed* (2004). Excellent "for future reading" compendium of articles on team issues. See also *Harvard Business Review on Building Better Teams* (2011).

Patrick Lencioni, *The Five Dysfunctions of a Team: A Leadership Fable* (2002). Easy to follow with an excellent framework and actionable advice.

———, *Overcoming the Five Dysfunctions of a Team* (2005). Builds on the original work.

Jessica Lipnack and Jeffrey Stamps, *Virtual Teams: Reaching Across Space, Time, and Organizations with Technology* (1997). This is one of the fine books on virtual teams, with good overall explanations and assistance.

Deborah Mackin and Deborah Harrington-Mackin, *The Team-Building Tool Kit: Tips and Tactics for Effective Workplace Teams* (2007). Ideas for team motivation and accountability.

Abraham Maslow, "A Theory of Human Motivation," *Psychological Review* 50 (1943): 370–396. The original work on creating safe workplaces and the hierarchy of human needs.

Larry Osbourne, *Sticky Teams: Keeping Your Leadership Team and Staff on the Same Page* (2010). Team principles and lively vignettes from different team challenges.

Ernest Shackleton, *South* (1998). Reprint of Shackleton's 1914–1916 diary of his 600-day struggle to keep his men alive in the Antarctic and the teamwork required to do so.

Marvin R. Weisbord, *Organizational Diagnosis: A Workbook of Theory and Practice* (1978). Excellent (and still the best) reference on organizational functions. Essential to know when instituting organizational change.

John H. Zenger, Ed Musselwhite, Kathleen Hurson, and Craig Perrin, *Leading Teams: Mastering the New Role* (1993). Another helpful reference.

Web Resources

Both of the following sites contain considerable information, from a variety of sources, on teams, team building, and how to manage teams:

http://managementhelp.org/grp_skll/teams/teams.htm.

http://humanresources.about.com/od/involvementteams/a/twelve_tip_team.htm.

Notes

1. Katzenbach and Smith (2003).

2. Executive coaching can be an invaluable asset for emerging team leaders. Its confidential, one-on-one, organizationally focused approach helps keep leaders "on track" as they navigate through their organizations. For more on coaching, see Chapter 4.

3. One of the advantages (and sometimes a disadvantage) of the public sector and its bureaucracy is its ability to sustain itself independently of the individual, so that the nation's work is not subject to the vagaries of new hires and subsequent frequent or dramatic organizational and policy changes. The downside is that many practices become institutionalized and are hard to alter without considerable individual and group work.

4. Team development is not a journey for the timid. It is very tempting to start with the so-called "real work" rather than the relationships because the latter are often difficult to facilitate and the person may be met with resistance. This road is fraught with danger. Once on task, it is hard to get back to trust and relationships. Many retreats and off-sites stop at this point, with no foundation or tools for future unpredictable obstacles.

5. *Dominance, Influence, Steadiness, and Correctness.*

6. The MBTI, one of the most widely used preference instruments in the world, has myriad applications, including insights for leadership. Based on the theoretical work of Swiss psychologist Carl Jung and his U.S. followers, Kathryn Briggs and her daughter Isabel Briggs-Myers, it uses a detailed self-report instrument to identify innate preferences about perception, energy, and lifestyle. It is extremely useful not only for self-awareness but also for understanding others. Its value in team formation, communication, and maintenance is unparalleled. The DISC, now known as the "Extended DISC" is a behavioral instrument that has been in use for a considerable period of time, and is extremely useful in assisting individuals to be aware of style differences and their impact on others.

7. The MBTI and the DISC are excellent for teams. They are nonintrusive, yet address the strengths and blind spots of the group, provide an excellent structure for problem-solving and in general afford the team a common language for talking about itself and to each other. This cognitive orientation avoids the suggestion of intimacy about teams that is off-putting for some.

8. See Hirsh et al. (2003), for a thorough and insightful approach to understanding and applying type to teams.

9. Possibly the greatest work on leadership and the team approach ever written. *South* was Shackleton's diary for the fateful attempted Antarctic crossing of 1914–1916. The attention to teamwork resulted in a 100 percent survival rate.

10. Pink (2009).

11. An organizational culture that has emphasized competition as a way of enhancing productivity will be especially taxed to embrace a cooperative approach.

12. Katzenbach and Smith (2003).

13. This was the case for two individuals at the aforementioned DOD unit. Only when one of the two engaged in a disclosure did the other begin to appreciate the constraints and demands of the position. They subsequently arrived at a more cooperative and productive working arrangement.

14. Lencioni (2002) observes that sometimes it is necessary to invite people to leave the team, or—in some cases—the organization. It is always a difficult decision because in the short term the group is affected adversely. Most leaders who employ this last-resort strategy are pleasantly surprised by the team's acceptance. They saw it coming too.

15. Weisbord (1978).

16. The leader keeps all the boxes in balance and is aware of the environment.

17. One government agency, seeking to use teams more effectively in a contentious and competitive office environment, was advised to incorporate team cooperation and behavior into the annual employee performance reviews. The manager demurred, claiming that the evaluations would then "not be useful in other jobs." The group is still contentious and uncooperative.

18. The work of Bridges (2004) on managing transitions is always relevant here. Moving from an individual to a team approach can invoke the same sense of loss and identity and require the same kind of adjustment process that accompanies other organizational changes. Move forward but tread carefully.

19. Writing in *Through the Labyrinth: The Truth About How Women Become Leaders,* Alice Eagly and Linda Carli Ably (2007) contrast these styles and offer ways to negotiate through complex organizational structures.

20. Heim (1995).

21. The "devil's advocate" is a fabricated role in which a team member adopts a posture of questioning and asking "what if" questions. For foundational research on its impact see Schwenk and Cosier (1986).

22. Oppenheimer's leadership of the Los Alamos team is legendary for his genius in managing the egos and motives of a disparate group of gifted scientists. His story is probably most instructive for managing elite teams.

23. A federal agency planned a division team retreat involving the DC office and two regional offices as well. At the regional offices were many naysayers who did not support the coming together. At the insistence of the (outside) facilitator, these individuals were encouraged to attend (the branch chief was all for leaving them home) and many of them became outspoken champions of the retreat and the team approach.

24. This is where an early affirmation of public service values can help career employee and contractor alike in understanding the purpose of the team and its work.

25. A federal agency using a team approach mistakenly appointed an individual as team leader who refused to accept that in this role he was not the boss. The team required many hours of intervention because this particular person was unable and/or unwilling to relinquish control. The better choice for this intractable individual would have been

removal. As it turned out, the team never achieved its potential, and its resentment of the leader never abated. His retirement brought many sighs of relief. In a contrasting situation, a team leader in a different agency carefully orchestrated his role and interaction with the team, making it very clear when he was "on the team" and when he was guiding it.

26. See Lencioni (2002), *The Five Dysfunctions of a Team* for more insights and scenarios.

27. A Federal Highway Administration team member consistently degraded the team and its members. The team functioned well when he was absent. At two off-sites (the second being necessary only because of his lack of cooperation and an unfortunate way to spend taxpayer dollars), the rest of the team finally gave up on converting him into a committed team member and developed strategies to isolate him. It was a suboptimal approach, perhaps, but one that let the other, high-performing team members maintain their energy and organizational commitment. He finally left and was never missed.

28. FEI spends considerable time on experiences that allow teams to move through the phases of "Forming, Storming, Norming, Performing."

29. Some elected (and other) groups with low trust never move out of the "committee of the whole" into subcommittees because no one trusts a subunit to act on their behalf. It is a cumbersome yet common phenomenon.

30. Each team member brings a set of knowledge, skills, and abilities (KSAs) to the effort. In addition, they bring presuppositions, attitudes, and concerns about the work of the team. Ignoring these in the process stage creates deeper problems in the decision-making and implementation phase.

31. For example, the membership ranged from the American Civil Liberties Union to the Sheriff's Association and the National Association of Police Chiefs—not groups that normally interact, much less see eye-to-eye. Yet they agreed on many positions in their work with the coalition and achieved necessary reforms in the nation's jails.

32. A federal training facility that was using cross-functional teams for the first time encountered this problem repeatedly. At each meeting the (essentially) new membership would revisit decisions and change them, resulting in virtually no progress. A subsequent team, seeking to not make the mistakes of the past, adopted the "go forward" position as one of their ground rules, and the team performed at a very high level.

33. From the work of Kurt Lewin (1943), force field analysis is a powerful tool in many settings.

34. This model in effect allows team members to go back to their units and undermine the group decision unless the team agreed to support every decision. Usually, with voting, the true attitude of the minority comes out in unproductive ways, such as "this is what they decided."

35. It is helpful at every meeting to reaffirm the team goals, verbally, using a timeline or whatever device helps keep members centered. Team members have other responsibilities, and this reminder helps people focus on the work at hand.

36. Ben Bissell, a noted change management authority, used to comment that in the absence of information, people simply make up their own—with the concomitant clean-up problems for the team because denying a negative is practically impossible.

6 Building high-performance organizations

John W. Pickering, Principal, Commonwealth Centers for High-Performance Organizations
Gerald S. Brokaw, Principal, Commonwealth Centers for High-Performance Organizations

Sustained high performance is always the goal, but many managers lack the tools to accomplish it. The High-Performance Organization (HPO) Diagnostic/Change Model presented in this chapter asks managers to consider three conceptual Change Levers (leadership, vision, and values) and three applied Change Levers (strategy, structure, and systems). Collectively, these levers offer a systemic approach to sustained high performance. Yet making these levers work requires addressing seven related diagnostic questions: (1) What is high performance for us? (2) How would we know if we were high performing? (3) According to whom are we high performing? (4) Why do we need to be high performing? (5) Is what we are doing the right "what"? (6) How good are we at delivering our products and services? and (7) How are we going to treat each other, our partners, customers, and other stakeholders? The last question opens up the critical area of leadership philosophy, values, and work culture. In the end, managers who do not have a philosophy that builds shared leadership, based on treating others as valued partners (rather than compliant followers), cannot hope to succeed.

Knowing is not enough, we must apply. Willing is not enough, we must do.

—Goethe

THIS BOOK IS ANCHORED IN THE FACT that trust is the product of relationships—relationships between individuals, between top management and the entry-level workforce, and between citizens and government. Consider, however, the following two situations. You are the top manager of a large Navy industrial facility that must improve performance dramatically or be closed. To accomplish this, you have to downsize the civilian workforce by half or more and set aside years of tradition to change production processes. And you must do so while dealing with multiple unions. Or you have just become city manager in a medium-sized eastern city. The city council is supportive but is pushing for the city to be more responsive to rapidly evolving public needs for services and the public's demand for more participation in decisions. At the same time, however, you have inherited a set of senior managers focused exclusively downward into their own units; the mindset of the organization is largely "stovepiped"; it's "our unit first and the heck with everyone else." These are real scenarios faced by managers in organizations we have worked with over the past thirty years. How do you build and maintain trust in situations like these? Managers will often say, "I have a technical background! No one prepared me to deal with this kind of challenge!"

Such reactions supply the departure point for this chapter, which distills lessons found in the literature and applied practice base from the fields of organizational development, change management, and process improvement to produce a handy roadmap leading to higher performance. Our approach—which we call the High-Performance Organizations (HPO) Diagnostic/Change Model—assumes that (1) after years of observation, federal, state, and local government and nonprofit organization managers and employees are experts on their own organizations; but (2) they may not have been exposed to an extensive organizational theory background and so need a framework to effect change; and (3) they want to be part of a positive change process, continually driving their organizations toward becoming higher performing organizations.

The HPO Diagnostic/Change Model

The High-Performance Organizations Diagnostic/Change Model was developed in the early 1990s and has been evolving ever since, as we work with organizations. The academic theory and applied lessons from well-run organizations that underpin the model are not new. They are loosely based on the causal model of Rensis Likert, a pioneer in organizational behavior;

Figure 6.1 The high-performance organizations diagnostic/change model

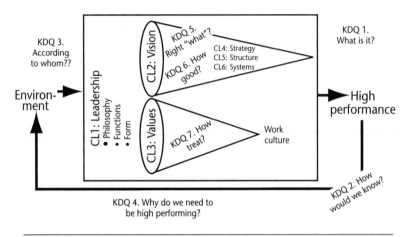

Key: CL = change lever   KDQ = diagnostic question

author and researcher Marvin Weisbord's six-box model; the McKinsey Company's Seven S model; and others in the management literature.[1] The model has been refined and expanded over the years, based on our work with scores of federal, state, and local government organizations, nonprofit agencies, and a few private-sector entities. The HPO model (see Figure 6.1) is a classic systems model—input, throughput, output, feedback. Inside the model, it moves from the three *conceptual* Change Levers of leadership, vision, and values, through the three *applied* levers of strategy, structure, and systems, to affect organizational performance. There is also a feedback loop to our organization's environment, which is critical to secure the support of those outside the organization for our continued efforts to improve performance.

To make the model more "diagnostic" in nature, we later added seven Key Diagnostic Questions (KDQs) to integrate with the model's six Change Levers:

KDQ 1.   What is high performance for us?

KDQ 2.   How would we know if we were high performing?

KDQ 3.   According to whom are we high performing?

KDQ 4.   Why do we need to be high performing?

KDQ 5. Is what we are doing the right "what"?

KDQ 6. How good are we at delivering our products and services?

KDQ 7. How are we going to treat each other, our partners, our customers, and our stakeholders?

The interaction between the KDQs and the change levers produces a thought process and roadmap for improvement. One final point: the black box surrounding the model represents the organization, but when we ask managers or employees to name their organization, they are confused. Do we mean their immediate unit, their branch, division, or their larger organization? The answer, naturally, is yes. They need to apply the model and the KDQs to themselves personally, to their immediate unit, to the intermediate units above them, and to the organization as a whole. Then they need to ensure alignment or "nesting" of the answers to the KDQs at each level of the organization, one into the other.

The seven key diagnostic questions

One way to understand the model is through the seven Key Diagnostic Questions (KDQs) that can help an organization evaluate its foundational assumptions and causal reasoning. These KDQs can lead an organization to define more completely the work required in each of the change levers. This chapter examines each of the KDQs in considerable detail as well as several Change Levers.

KDQ 1: What is high performance for us?

Members at all levels of an organization must agree on the answer to KDQ 1—for the organization as a whole, for their individual units, and for themselves. Without agreement, individual members of the organization, acting alone and in isolation, have little chance to accidentally arrive at a common understanding of what high performance is or how to achieve it. If individuals, units, and the organization as a whole are not aligned on what high performance is, then no matter how talented or committed the individual members are, the organization will be unlikely to achieve the outcomes and impacts it seeks. Yet, from the way many organizations operate, this appears to be exactly what they believe will happen. They seem to be saying: "Hire good people, let them figure out on their own what high performance is for them, and then start off in that direction." Instead, organizations that want to begin moving toward higher performance must establish a collaborative process for articulating and sharing a common organizational vision of what high performance is, for creating nested visions indicating how each unit fits into the whole, and for aligning individual members in the organization with these nested visions.

It is, moreover, not enough for an organization to define high performance as just "wanting to be the best"—especially if it is the organization, acting alone without customer participation, that gets to define what best means. Consider the all too common mistake made in the apocryphal story about the dog food factory that wanted to make the best dog food in the world and hired the world's foremost experts to produce excellent (in their view) dog food. There was only one problem: dogs would not eat the food. In this respect, our use of the term *high performance* appears to be similar to what leadership researcher and writer Jim Collins means by the term great in his book *Good to Great.*[2] It is possible to be merely good, maybe even the best among a mediocre lot of competitors, but it takes substantially more to be great or, in our language, high performance.

KDQ 2: How would we know if we were high performing?

Organizations seeking high performance must, as a part of understanding what high performance is, address a second question: And how would we know if we were high performing? This question implies a system of measurements that will let us know if we are moving in our intended direction. I want to emphasize, however, that this is the *second* question, not the first. We have seen some organizations trying to implement a performance measurement process without first agreeing on what high performance is.

We often run an in-class exercise to illustrate that most people have a good intuitive notion of what high performance looks like, in other words, a generic definition of high performance. We point out that they have experienced organizations all their lives and that each of these encounters—whether a good experience or a bad one—adds to their notion of what high performance in organizations means. To help them uncover these sometimes unconscious attitudes and beliefs, we select a type of organization, for example, a laundry/dry cleaners, and ask participants what they think high performance means in this example.

Immediately, participants begin yelling out things like: "I want my clothes back; I want them clean; on hangers with light starch; no broken buttons or crushed lapels. . . ." Others say: "I want them to treat me in a friendly and respectful way; I want the laundry close to where I work or live; I don't want to take vacation time to go to the laundry—they need to be open when I'm not at work; they need to handle problems well; I don't want to have to go to the manager to get satisfaction; the first person I deal with should be able to handle the issue." Eventually, someone says: "And I want it at a competitive price; I don't want to have to pay the price of the shirt to get it back!"

At this point, we ask: "So who were you in this exercise?" They answer: "The customer." So then we ask: "What if you are a residential neighbor of the laundry? Would your ideas of what high performance means change?" The answer: "Absolutely: I want it quiet, and 'green,' and good at handling traffic, and clean, and well-designed. . . ." Finally, we ask: "What if you were a long-term investor in the laundry; would your definition of high performance change again?" Again, the answer is: "Sure. Now I want profit!" When we explore what produces profit, we find that the laundry needs to be good at generating revenue and minimizing costs. Few of our participants would agree that generating profit is the primary objective of the public/nonprofit sectors; rather, most would say that accomplishing the mission is the primary objective. On the other hand, if we look at the causal sequence involved in achieving these objectives, we see that things are not so different as they seem in these two different worlds: the business world would say they need to focus on serving customers to generate revenues and on minimizing costs to generate a profit, and the public/nonprofit sectors would say they need to generate revenues and minimize costs to accomplish the mission. As a result, we can use many private-sector approaches, thought processes, and tools in the public sector; we just have to recognize that the ultimate objectives are different in the two worlds.

Out of the laundry exercise, the class generates a generic definition of high performance, which includes the following factors:

Factor 1: Quality of products and services (meeting the wants, needs, and expectations of customers with excellent execution quality)

Factor 2: Outstanding customer value (satisfaction, responsiveness, service, timeliness, convenience, courtesy, competence of staff, problem resolution)

Factor 3: Sound financial performance (generating revenue, minimizing costs, good business model, efficient systems)

These generic factors are common in almost every organization we work with and can produce a lively discussion of whether a unit/department/

organization can define and measure these factors as they relate to the specifics of their situation. The three factors are not mutually exclusive—that is, when we are talking about one of them, it almost always overlaps one or both of the other two factors. Let's explore each of these in more detail.

Factor 1: Quality of Products and Services with Excellent Execution Quality. Quality of products and services requires a focus on the customer's wants/needs/expectations and on the organization's support systems/work processes—two very different perspectives that result in two different dimensions of quality. The first dimension is a focus on the customer and requires that we produce products and provide services that meet the customer's wants, needs, and expectations. Moreover, it demands that enough interaction take place between the supplier and the customer to ensure that a clearly defined agreement exists about what will be delivered. We call this dimension design and features quality. Visualize it as a vertical scale with the bottom labeled "modest design and features quality" and the top labeled "complex design and features quality." Using a car analogy, think Corolla-level features—outstanding fit-and-finish, repairability, and reliability, but modest design and features, compared to Lexus-level features—all the same features as Corolla, but offering more complex design and features. This does not mean the Corolla is a poor choice. It simply has fewer features and therefore costs less. What is appropriate—Lexus, Camry (the midpoint on the scale), or Corolla—is a decision for purchasers based on their needs, preferences, and budget (see the vertical scale in Figure 6.2).

If we deliver too low on the design and features quality dimension, we will have dissatisfied customers, who are likely to complain that we are delivering poor quality. On the other hand, if we deliver too high and try to charge the customer for the additional features, we will again have dissatisfied customers, who could say we are forcing them to accept excess features they do not want to pay for and accuse us of trying to bait and switch, running up the bill, or gold-plating. If we exceed their wants/needs/expectations and do it for free (that is, at no additional cost to the customer), we may have delighted customers, but we also run the risk of inflating our customers' expectations beyond our ability to deliver in the future. And we may be providing more complexity than our customer wants, needs, and/or expects, leading them to describe our products or services as cumbersome, not intuitive, or too hard to use.

Figure 6.2 The definition of quality

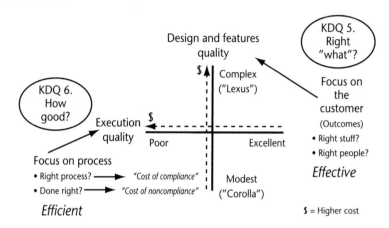

We may want to make the business decision to add features we know a customer wants and not charge them as a way of cementing a relationship or seizing market share, but we need to clearly understand the implications of doing so. It is critical to reach agreement on the level of design and features quality the business is going to deliver (or, if multiple levels are required for varying customer needs, then the agreement is around when to deliver each level). To leave it up to each individual is to invite the delivery of a full spectrum of products and services varying from poor design and features quality through gold-plating, most not pleasing the customer and potentially wasting resources. One way to do more with less is to stop gold-plating and apply the saved resources to increased production. We will revisit this dimension of quality when we discuss KDQ 5: Are we delivering the right "what"?

The second dimension of quality is execution quality. It reminds us of the work of W. Edwards Deming, Joseph M. Juran, and others in the world of "quality" programs (for example, Quality Circles, Total Quality Management, and today's LEAN/Six Sigma in manufacturing).[3] This dimension requires us to have excellent execution quality, defined as the ability of the organization to perform flawlessly a best-practice process. We must also be as near flawless as possible in our planning, design, engineering, and production processes and in our people training and development, procurement, contracting, facilities, and other support systems.

We can visualize execution quality as a horizontal scale, running from left to right, with the left end of the scale labeled "poor execution quality" and the right end as "excellent execution quality" (Figure 6.2). The two questions to ask ourselves about our organization on this scale are: Do we have the right process (best-practice processes for delivering the design and features required) and are the processes being done right? (is there excessive rework, scrap, warranty?). If our processes are not best-practice, we would have a high cost of compliance; in other words, doing an inefficient process perfectly is still inefficient. If, however, we have a best-practice process but execute it poorly, we would incur the high cost of *non*compliance because doing a best-practice process poorly is also inefficient. If we were delivering excellent execution quality, we would be running the appropriate best-practice processes in a near flawless way. Another way to do more with less is to move to the excellent (right) side of this dimension. We will revisit this discussion of "How good are we?" briefly under KDQ 6.

FACTOR 2: OUTSTANDING CUSTOMER VALUE. Customer value in the HPO model has to do with the relationship side of our interaction with customers, citizens, and others. Recall in the laundry example that seminar participants said, "I want them to treat me well; I want the laundry located close to where I live or work; I don't want to take vacation time to go there." What if the laundry owner was to give us back perfect clothes and then insult us as we walked out the door? The quality was perfect, but the relationship was not, and it is the relationship part that constitutes customer value. Customers will use terms such as *dependable, reliable, convenient, responsive, satisfying, fast,* and *pleasant* to describe their desires on this factor. The problem here is that one size does not fit all; instead, each customer selects from this market basket of items those she desires, and the supplier needs to figure out what items they are and deliver them.

Before we can do this analysis, we need to identify our current and future customers, understanding that they come in lots of different flavors (especially in the government world) and that they often have conflicting wants, needs, and expectations. We address how to do this analysis when we get to KDQ 3: According to whom?

FACTOR 3: SOUND FINANCIAL PERFORMANCE. Financial performance relates to our ability to generate revenue, minimize our costs, evaluate profitability, generate accurate contract estimates and winning bids, and justify our investments. Doing this analysis in the public sector can be difficult. Historically, government organizations have focused primarily on design and features quality and not on execution quality, customer value, or financial performance. Indeed, in many cases, the government's financial management systems (budgeting, procurement, contracting, and so forth) have not been designed to provide units with the information they need to make sound financial decisions. Think of the messages these systems send to us: "Here's your allowance to run your program—we really don't care what you need; this is all you get. It's based on what you got last year plus or minus a little, depending on economic conditions and administration priorities. Don't overspend your allowance (but the numbers are always late to you, so you won't really know how you're doing). Don't underspend your allowance, or you'll lose it and get less next time. And don't steal a nickel of it." But, by implication, you could waste a billion of it! Rarely do we see a demand that a unit demonstrate that it is best-practice, that it has a sound business model, that its causal model has been tested, and that it can show that it produces the mission's desired outcomes. To be fair, at the federal level the Government Performance and Results Act (GPRA) and the Office of Management and Budget (OMB) Program Assessment Rating Tool (PART), and the President's Management Agenda (in the George W. Bush administration) are efforts to improve the system, but much more needs to be done—especially at the unit level of organizations.

In the HPO model, high performance is defined as the simultaneous delivery of all three of these elements—quality products and services, outstanding customer value, and sound financial performance. We call the simultaneous delivery and continuous improvement of these factors "Pick 3," and because we want these three factors to be delivered over time, the expectation is really Pick 3+, where the plus is consistent and sustainable performance over time. It is a rare organization that performs at the Pick 3+ level.

Over the years, we have worked with many organizations that have performance metrics, but often they are not capable of answering the most fundamental questions: What are we trying to achieve (our desired outcomes and impacts) and how would we know if we were? Organizations tend to measure what is measurable, which can translate, especially in the public sector, into a focus on activities and tasks, intended to demonstrate compliance with legislation or regulations—to show to Congress, the city council, or the public that work is being performed (a focus on activity). We would argue that high performance in the public/nonprofit sectors translates into mission accomplishment at a level defined by the organization's vision (a focus on outcome).

KDQ 3: According to whom are we high performing?

The third KDQ requires us to do a thorough analysis of the environment outside the black box from Figure 6.1. The box represents us: our unit/ department/organization. The environment includes customers and other stakeholders who can affect us as an organization. In the public and nonprofit sectors, the concept of customer appears to be more complex than in the private sector. Customers certainly include those who use the products and services we produce (our beneficiary chain customers), but they also include our food chain customers (those who provide us with funding and/or policy direction), our partners (people and entities inside and outside our unit/organization with whom we must work to produce value for our beneficiaries), and our competitors (those with whom we can or do compete). In addition, customers include stakeholders who do not belong in the preceding categories, but who can influence us in sometimes positive, but more often, potentially negative ways. They include the press, regulatory agencies, investigative entities such as inspectors general, and the Government Accountability Office. The power of this analysis, referred to as strategic customer value analysis (SCVA), is that we are now able to see where overlaps and conflicts exist between what one beneficiary customer or funding source wants/needs/ expects and the desires of others. Figure 6.3 places these actors into a graphic display, showing the interactions between *us* and the various flavors of *them*.

In addition to understanding where we are today relative to customer expectations, KDQ 3 often leads us to develop a more collaborative relationship with our customers, for it is not only important that we understand their wants, needs, and expectations today, but that we understand what their requirements are likely to be in the future. If we are to remain high performing, we will need to build strategies that increase our value to our customers over time and that will deliver the outcomes required by our vision and mission.

Figure 6.3 Strategic customer value analysis (SCVA)

KDQ 3. According to whom are we high performing?

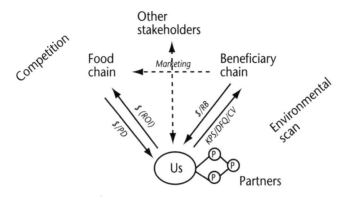

Key: $ = Money; PD = Policy direction; ROI = Return on investment; RB = Repeat business; KPS = Key products and services; DFQ = Design and features quality; CV = Customer value; P = Partners

KDQ 4: Why do we need to be high performing?

The fourth KDQ gets at a critical factor in successful change efforts: the issue of organizational energy to sustain our improvement efforts over time. What if we cannot answer this question to the satisfaction of our workforce? Employees will not support the change effort for the time required for our performance to improve. If the literature on large-scale organization change is correct in saying that sustained effort is required for five to seven to ten or more years to achieve lasting organizational change, then we will need to tap a variety of energy sources. University of Michigan professor Noel Tichy, former GE organization development adviser, argues that all of us need to develop a "teachable point of view"—a succinct, personal, and compelling set of arguments capable of being delivered with passion to ourselves, our coworkers, our subordinates, and others reminding us of the importance of improving our performance.[4]

When we ask participants why their organizations need to be high performing, nine times out of ten the first answer will be some version of "threat to our survival"; in other words, we'll lose to our competitors; our citizens will be dissatisfied and elect a micromanaging council; we'll be outsourced. So when we ask, "A threat to your survival is an energy source?"

the response is a resounding "of course!" But what kind of energy source is it? It is negative energy. And if an organization is under threat to survival for a long period of time, those employees who can leave do so to escape the stress, while others hunker down and seem to say "kill me, already." This drop in morale leads to lower, rather than higher, performance over time. We have described threat to survival as a "short-term, nonrenewable energy source." So what else is available as an energy source?

The second reason for needing to be high performance is self-pride: "I need to be part of something high performing just because I need it for me." When asked if this one is a renewable energy source, the answer is yes. But when asked if self-pride can be injured by the organization, the answer is again yes. The good news, based on our experience, is that even when self-pride has been injured, most people will come back to us when allowed to experience self-pride again.

These two sources can be used in almost any kind of organization, but pressing our participants, we often ask: "So you're telling me there's no difference between the mission of your organization and that of a tobacco company?" Now, many private sector firms have moral purposes equivalent to public/nonprofit sector organizations: Johnson & Johnson is a good example. But the one energy source that the public/nonprofit sectors generally have in abundance is higher moral purpose. It matters whether we are high performing or not because the missions we have are critical to society. When we ask why we had to work so hard to discover this energy source, many participants will respond that they don't talk about it out loud, but it's what keeps them doing what they're doing. When we ask participants if their organizations use this energy source effectively, some say yes and can explain how, but most generally say no, we could do better.

KDQ 5: Is what we are doing the right "what"?

The fifth KDQ begins to integrate the thinking and analysis done to this point into a more concrete set of specifications. We saw this question earlier when we were discussing design and features quality (see the vertical scale in Figure 6.2). To be able to answer this question effectively we must engage the following more specific questions:

- What are/should be our key products and services (KPS) to meet the wants/needs/expectations of our customers—now and in the future?

- Are we providing our products and services to the right customers? If we have the right products and services, but the wrong customers, maybe we should fire some customers and get some new ones? On the other hand, if we have the right customers and wrong KPS, then we need to change the products and services. Are we *effective* in serving our customers?
- Do we produce excellent customer value, according to the beneficiary chain, food chain, partners, and other stakeholders?
- What is or should be our organization's unique niche? (To answer this one it is helpful to ask: Who would miss us if we were gone?)
- What should we take responsibility for accomplishing in the near term (next three to five years) and the longer term (ten to thirty years)? What is/should be our major impact or outcome goal?
- How do these efforts contribute to achieving our larger vision—our definition of high performance?

The product of this particular effort is clarification and revision of our core purpose and reason for being—essentially we must confirm, revise, or construct our mission and unique niche. An example comes from the U.S. Environmental Protection Agency's Office of the Inspector General (IG). Historically, the purpose of the IG had been to ensure that the agency complied with law and regulation and that efforts were undertaken to prevent fraud, waste, and abuse. While important, the inspector general and her staff realized that these activities were insufficient. Greater emphasis was needed on the intention of Congress in establishing these laws. Results (outcomes/impacts) mattered. Effectiveness mattered, and to that extent the IG's office refocused its efforts on making a contribution to the improvement of the environment and human health. Compliance to law and regulation was necessary, but mindless compliance that produced no outcome/impact benefits was also wasteful. To address this new emphasis area, the IG established the Office of Program Evaluation to determine whether EPA's programs would result in the impacts and outcomes intended, even if all the statutory and regulatory directives were executed perfectly.

KDQ 6: How good are we at delivering our products and services?

We looked at the sixth KDQ when we were discussing execution quality (see the horizontal scale in Figure 6.2). Are we as *efficient* as we can be in delivering our main products and services? Do we have the right business strategy (business model) and organizational structure? Are our systems and processes best-practice and executed flawlessly? Note that the last three items mentioned here (strategy, structure, and systems) are the three applied Change Levers in the HPO model (see Figure 6.1).

Let's begin by looking at our overall business strategy/business model. If we were a small business making a pitch to the bank to secure a loan, we would need to lay out a convincing argument that we really know our business, that our business model is robust—that it will work no matter what economic or other conditions we encounter—and that we have considered whether we should do all the work ourselves versus outsourcing or partnering. Do you recall People Express Airlines, the first of the low-cost airlines? It had great values, was a fun place to work, and *Harvard Business Review* couldn't write enough case studies about it. But here was their business strategy, their niche: low-cost vacation travel. Not a robust enough strategy, as it turns out. Let me add one main word and a connector word to that strategy statement: low-cost business and vacation travel. So, now what airline are we talking about? Southwest. How are they doing? They modified the strategy of People Express into a robust business strategy and then delivered flawlessly. In the business strategy/business model area, we might want to ask ourselves the following more specific diagnostic questions:

- If our strategy/business model is the very same one that got us here, is it capable of getting us to the next level as well? Will it allow us to effectively and efficiently accomplish our vision, mission, and strategic goals?
- What is our competitive advantage based on?
- Do we know our key business functions? Do we need to close out some business lines to better align with our future direction and to generate resources to fund new initiatives?
- Do we have a sound approach to strategic outsourcing decisions? How do we handle "surge" demand and/or surplus production capacity?
- Can we explain our key business assumptions and our causal model for getting results?

The next factor for examination is organizational structure. We need to evaluate our current structure and change it if we believe a different organizing principle would allow us to fulfill our vision and strategy. Most organizations we work with have inherited a stovepiped structure from their industrial model past, so examining structure might be threatening to the established order. Specific diagnostic questions we may want to ask in the structure area are:

- Is our structure sophisticated enough to perform our work? Or should we explore more complex structure models, including matrix, business centers, process/product focused structures, and so forth?
- Have we broken our work down correctly so as to most efficiently deliver our products and services? Are cross-cutting projects and processes under control; in other words, do we have a clearly accountable project/process owner? This is particularly critical when multiple organizational stovepipes are involved.
- Have we provided for the integration of the parts of the organization to produce a seamless higher-level whole?

Finally, we must review each of our support systems and work processes. What we are looking for here is an assessment of the extent to which the systems and processes aid us in improving our performance. Too often, we assume that these systems and processes are givens and that we can do little to improve them. This assumption may sometimes be true, but before accepting that, we would want to seriously test our ability to affect them. In some organizations we have contracted with, it takes two hours to secure the contract, while in others it takes two *years*! Why the difference? The answer is that some organizations have found ways of complying with the Federal Acquisition Regulations while making the acquisition system serve their end values—they have improved performance dramatically by aligning the support systems and work processes with their vision. The systems and processes we would want to assess are our:

Support systems. These include human resources, financial management, procurement, contracting, information technology, facilities and equipment, communication, legal services, vehicle maintenance, and research and development laboratories. If these groups are not at their peak form, people in the organization will not believe that improvement is being taken seriously. We find that improvements in support systems speak louder than any other action an organization can take in making employees believe that management means what it says.

Work processes. Do we have best-practice work processes tailored to the appropriate design and features quality level delivered flawlessly? Are we continuously improving? If necessary, can we reengineer a process from the ground up?

Work management and control processes. Does every member at every level of the organization have the systems and skills to monitor and take appropriate corrective actions on our key success factors?

In the Navy's industrial facility mentioned at the beginning of this chapter, they had to work all seven KDQs, but the two that drove most of the improvement were KDQ 6: How good are we? and KDQ 7: How do we treat each other and our customers? We will address the second of these below, but in the "how good are we" area, they had to reinvent how naval shipyards performed ship modernization projects. They introduced the discipline of project management and established a project-management college to prepare the workforce; installed matrix management and built an integrated top leadership team (see more in the Tips section below); and renegotiated an international labor contract to allow the use of cross-trained work teams to complete most of the work on the ships. The shipyard turned a $20 million "profit" on the first ship modernization completed under the improvement process, and, over a three-year period, this yard became the Navy's number one performer.

KDQs 1–6: Addressing the first six Key Diagnostic Questions using the HPO model's visioning change lever ·

An organization's vision work is, perhaps, the most time consuming of all the Change Levers. During it, the organization has to deal with six of the seven KDQs. It is important to understand that vision work is *not* just about developing another vision statement. Let's face it: most units and organizations have enough vision statements. What they often do not have is a shared vision—that is, when members of the organization are asked where the organization is headed, they all point in the same direction and know their part in getting there.

In the HPO model, visioning moves from a more abstract, broad, and long-term focus, through a more focused set of activities, including strategic thinking, strategic planning, tactical/operational planning and execution, and monitoring and recovery. We refer to this process as the vision to performance spiral (see Figure 6.4). As Figure 6.4 indicates, the process

Figure 6.4 The vision to performance spiral

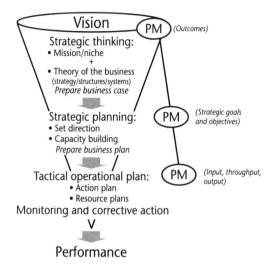

Key: PM = Performance measures

resembles moving down a funnel or spiral from broad and general to near-term and specific. Near the point of the spiral, individuals should know what they are doing each day, with whom, and what resources they will use to move them and the organization toward the accomplishment of their vision. Each level of the organization—from unit through the whole—needs a vision that is nested into the next higher level. Creating the vision does not come only from the top; it needs to come up from the units as well. A docking process then meshes these ideas into an integrated, aligned vision for the organization.

At the top of the vision spiral, units/organizations need to address KDQ 1: What is high performance for us? and KDQ 4: Why do we need to be high performing? This discussion focuses on what our *end values* are and what they should be. What is the higher moral purpose we are seeking; what is our desired future state; what outcomes/impacts are we seeking; who would miss us if we were gone? As an organization begins to settle on its desired future, we will begin the process of asking KDQ 2: How would we know? We ask this question at every level of this spiral. At the top of the vision spiral, we are future-focused, so the measures will also be future-focused. Because we cannot measure *now* whether we are *there*, the indicators are trailing or lagging indicators. Because they are trying to measure the end values we are seeking, they may also be called outcome or impact measures.

The following is an example from an Army laboratory of a vision statement being turned into a set of measurable statements. In other words, we would seek specific outcome/impact measures for each of the ten numbered parts:

[This laboratory] is (1) <u>recognized</u> as a (2) <u>premier Research and Development organization</u> that is (3) <u>sought out by customers and partners</u>. We (4) develop and maintain a <u>relevant and vibrant research program</u> that includes a (5) <u>robust reimbursable portfolio</u>. We are a (6) <u>highly skilled, adaptable team</u> with (7) <u>unique facilities</u> that enable us to (8) <u>perform cutting-edge research</u>. We operate in an (9) <u>efficient and effective manner</u>. We (10) <u>provide comprehensive solutions</u> to the nation's and the warfighter's toughest challenges.

As we drop down a level in the spiral, we call the next level strategic thinking, which has two parts: mission/niche thinking and theory of the business thinking. Strategic thinking is an "opening up" activity. We prefer that organizations think before they plan. We also warn organizations not to let "perfect" get in the way of "good enough." Because visioning is a cyclical process and will come around again in a year or so, we do not have to be perfect in our execution of these steps—we just need to be better this year than before. Strategic thinking includes:

Mission/niche thinking, which looks at KDQ 5. Are we doing the right "what"?—where we look at our key products and services, design and features quality, and customer value—and KDQ 3: According to whom are we high performing?

Theory of the business thinking, which looks at KDQ 6. How good are our processes at delivering our mission/niche?

We are now ready for the next level down in the spiral: strategic planning, which is a "closing" activity. The two parts of strategic planning are set direction and capacity building:

Set direction. It sounds simple. We decide where we're going and let everyone know. Yet it often becomes more complex. What if stovepiping is widespread in the organization, with many of the units going in whatever directions they want? If we want the organization to be going true north, and three-quarters of the organization is not, what must we do to redirect those units? We have found that many organizations are good at *adding* new strategic initiatives during the strategic planning process, but we have rarely found an organization very good at *shutting down* programs, units, and/or business areas when they are not going true north. In addition, the field of "change management" (sometimes defined as managing the "people-side" of change) is often overlooked when major changes are planned in an organization's direction, systems, or processes. People in organizations must be prepared for such change if it is to succeed.

Capacity building. As we exited the strategic thinking level in the spiral, we asked ourselves a series of fill-in-the-blank questions: Do we have the right _____ to achieve our vision? The missing part of the question could be key products and services, business strategy/model, partners, structure, systems and process, facilities, equipment, information technology, data, and people with the right competencies. What if the answer to any of these questions is no, and it is a serious, vision-blocking no? Now what? We have to address the issue. This is where capacity building comes in. For us, hope is not a strategy; rather, these issues must be dealt with seriously in the strategic plan, or it will not be taken seriously by employees and first-level managers.

Time for more measurement work: at the strategic planning level, we are still looking for trailing or lagging indicators, because we are dealing with strategic goals and objectives that will be measuring events three to five years or more in the future. These measures are closer-in than the outcome and impact measures at the top of the spiral, but they are still in the future.

As we reach the lower levels of the spiral and engage the tactical/operational/project planning level, the work shifts from leadership work to no-fooling, near-term, task/management implementation, grind-it-out work. At this point many organizations fail. Too often, when the strategic plan (the one with the glossy cover) shows up at the unit level, it is viewed with suspicion. Lack of participation in the strategic planning process by units at all levels often results in either direct opposition or passive-aggressive behavior at the unit level. This is precisely why we argue that units need to "run the spiral" at their level and to participate in a top down/bottom up, docking process to align the plans at each level. The two parts of tactical/operational/project planning are action planning and resource planning.

Action planning. If we are dealing with an actual project at this level, then this step creates the project plan. Usually, the plan includes a work breakdown structure and uses other techniques from the project management body of knowledge such as schedule and resource estimation, earned value, and variance analysis.[5]

Resource planning. In addition to detailing the actions/events/activities that need to occur, the unit/organization must create a matching resource plan. What if we have a brilliant causal sequence, but it will cost $1 million to execute it, and we have only a quarter of that available to pay for it? The resource plan must cover personnel, facilities, training, and other costs. Once the resource plan matches the action plan, we will be able to track the accomplishment of the scheduled activities against the estimated expenditures.

In the measurement area, we are now ready to establish some leading indicators: measures that will predict whether we will achieve our outputs and, thereby, our goals, objectives, and outcomes/impacts. The two most common are *input* measures (did we get the personnel we estimated as required for each activity in the causal sequence; did we get the required facilities, equipment, training, data, information technology?) and *throughput* measures (were the milestones accomplished when we said they would be with the resources we estimated?).

The concluding step in the vision to performance spiral is called monitoring/recovery. After the near-term, detailed, applied planning process, we turn to the actual implementation and execution. Ask the following questions: Are we on-budget and on-schedule (with the required design and features quality, execution quality, and customer value also being delivered)? If an emergency occurs or we are not on budget and on schedule, what are we going to do to recover as much of the plan as possible? What corrective actions are necessary? Did we learn anything from missing our estimates that should be factored into the planning/estimating process next time?

KDQ 7: How are we going to treat each other, our partners, our customers, and our stakeholders?

KDQ 7 is far too often overlooked in organizations. Described by some as soft or touchy-feely, it does not get the serious consideration it deserves to sustain a culture of customer satisfaction, continuous improvement, and accountability. If an organization is expected to sustain the kind of effort needed to become and remain high performing, it must, as part of that effort, consider and sustain the appropriate *means values*. These are the values that guide how we get to our desired ends values (higher moral purpose). The three types of means values we work with are:

1. Leadership philosophy is a statement of beliefs explaining the assumptions upon which management actions are based and judged. It answers the questions: What do we believe about the nature of people and their attitudes toward work? What motivates most people, once their basic needs have been met? What is the distribution of knowledge and creativity and, as a result, how will decisions be made? What is the nature of the work? Leadership philosophy imposes boundaries on the behavior of managers and team leaders with hierarchical authority over others and, as a result, will be a major determinant of work culture.

2. Individual behavioral values are a larger, overarching set of values describing how members of the community treat each other, their partners, customers, and stakeholders. They provide a standard for judging interpersonal behavior and answer the questions: "How are we going to treat each other and, by extension, our customers?" These values help define the human side of the organization's work culture.

3. Operating systems values state how we want the organization's systems and processes, such as the support systems—human resources (HR), purchasing, information technology (IT), and technical work processes—to treat the people in the organization. These values define the technical side of the organization's work culture. How organizational systems/processes *treat* employees often speaks louder than anything managers say. What if a manager says to the employee, "You're empowered, but don't forget the thirty-seven signatures to buy the pencil." Does the employee hear "We think you're responsible" or "We don't trust you"?

These means values must be translated into well-understood criteria for them to guide and even limit our decisions, actions, and behaviors. The work culture they create is a leading indicator of future results. What if we have a wonderful strategic plan and a perfect performance measurement system, but a really rotten work culture? Can we get to sustained high performance?

Addressing KDQ 7 using the change lever of the high performing organization model's values

In the HPO model, we take organizations through a thought process, the values to work culture spiral, designed to produce a statement of values and a plan to implement and enforce them. Although the values spiral looks only at KDQ 7—How do we treat each other, our partners, our customers, and our stakeholders?—we find that many technically oriented organizations are challenged by this work. The work contained in the values spiral is critical to a central thesis of this book: The need to build relationships and trust among the players within an organization and between the organization and the external world is critical. The values spiral is all about building trust. Like the vision spiral, the values spiral proceeds from high-level, conceptual work down the spiral, with each lower level becoming more near-term and more specific. We begin the values work by addressing the three means values that are the building blocks of our organization's work culture: leadership philosophy, individual behavioral values, and operating systems values (see Figure 6.5).

Leadership philosophy is perhaps the major determinant of the trust level that will exist between the workforce and management. In the roughly left-to-right flowing causal sequence defined by the HPO Diagnostic/Change Model in Figure 6.1, leadership philosophy is in the number one position. If an organization does not get leadership philosophy right, almost nothing downstream in the model works. We use the work of three organizational behavior research pioneers—Douglas McGregor, Rensis Likert, and Peter Block—as the theoretical base from which to

Figure 6.5 The values to work culture spiral

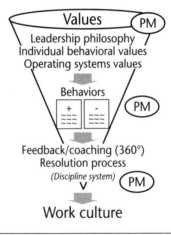

Key: PM = Performance measures

view, discuss, diagnose, and finally initiate change in an organization's leadership philosophy.[6]

How organizations behave toward employees, customers, suppliers, and other stakeholders determines their leadership philosophy. At one extreme, for example, are organizations that see people as not liking to work; as not being ambitious or wanting responsibility; as not doing a good job unless directly and closely supervised or motivated by coercion, threats, and punishment; and as lacking in knowledge, talent, and creativity. Such organizations are likely to design control-oriented, multilayered hierarchies that tell workers exactly what to do at all times. Workers are not to be consulted or involved in designing work processes because they will be seen as having nothing to say. Work is reduced to discrete tasks, and workers are directed to perform the tasks exactly as directed by the supervisor or by a work rule set in a rigid, highly regulated, management-defined process. Workers are asked to check their brains at the door and are discouraged from making suggestions for improvement. "It's my way," says the boss, "or the highway." This belief set loosely corresponds to what McGregor called Theory X, Likert called Systems 1 and 2, and Block called the bureaucratic cycle.

At the other extreme are organizations that see people, generally, as wanting to do a good job because it is a core human need; as wanting to be part of something meaningful; as being motivated (once basic needs are satisfied) by challenge, responsibility, achievement, recognition, personal growth, and advancement to more challenging work; and as being knowledgeable and creative or capable of being made so by development. Such organizations view good problem solving, continuous study and improvement of work processes, and innovation as requiring consultation with and involvement of a wide range of knowledgeable employees. Under these beliefs, work is seen as integrated processes needing knowledgeable, broadly skilled, and talented workers who collaborate to ensure that jointly held objectives are accomplished. This belief set represents the essence of Theory Y in McGregor's approach, Systems 3 and 4 in Likert's work, and Block's entrepreneurial cycle.

The following is an example of a leadership philosophy statement developed by the senior management team of a municipal government and modified by the workforce through a consultative process:

> *We, the employees of [a medium-sized] City Government, want to do*
> *a good job. We will excel if we are part of something important, are*

consulted and involved in all aspects of our work, are provided the tools to do our jobs, and are recognized for our efforts. Knowledge, experience, creativity, and cultural diversity abound in this organization. We will use these resources to achieve [our] vision.

Each of us has an important role in the "work of leadership" and the "work of management." Our work will be characterized by shared information, continuous learning, and personal responsibility. We will provide an atmosphere of competence, teamwork, trust, confidence, and respect. Our organization will succeed with clear goals and purposes. We will be mission-centered. We will make our policies and actions clear, purposeful, and consistent with our values at every level of the organization.

Addressing the individual behavioral values and operating systems values is less theory-driven and more experiential. In these areas, we normally use a brainstorming process to generate the values that the organization wants to embrace. After defining them, organizations generally synthesize these three means values—leadership philosophy, individual behavioral values, and operating systems values—into an integrated statement of their values.

Once we have described the values of our unit or organization in conceptual terms, we are ready to move to the next level of the values spiral: behaviors. To illustrate the need for becoming more specific, we often pose this question: What if we have successfully developed the best set of values known to humankind, we've posted them on the wall all over our organization, and then we watch them get violated every day? Most participants will agree that this result is worse than not having developed them in the first place, because now people can see clearly that their values are being violated instead of simply suspecting it. To stop the values work after developing the values statement, then, is to increase cynicism in the organization.

The behaviors level of the values spiral asks participants to become more specific about what behaviors they want to see from each other that support the values and what behaviors they do not want to see anymore that violate the values. A federal regulatory agency that went through this process produced the following example. It looks at one of the eight values they articulated, open communication and credibility or being believable and honest, and lists some of the behaviors that were desired and not desired:

1. Productive behaviors

- Share information up, down, and across (information should be shared with necessary individuals/teams, especially with people whose performance will be affected; inform people of the reliability of the information).
- Tell the truth. Use qualifiers, for example, "As far as I know . . ." when information is uncertain since things may change; say when you can't say; inform people if the situation changes and why.
- Actively listen (eye contact, no interrupting, undivided attention) even when you don't want to.
- Acknowledge/admit lack of information/knowledge (say when you don't know or don't understand).
- Avoid use of offensive language; important that one knows the audience/individual (no racial slurs, off-color jokes, religious/ethnic jokes, or religious profanity).
- Give and solicit frequent, polite, and constructive feedback (be specific; suggest how to improve; give positive feedback).

2. Counterproductive behaviors

- Vindictive or malicious comments.
- Being overly critical.
- Condescending tone or attitude/belittlement of employees.
- Aggressive/threatening voice tone and/or body language.
- Hidden agendas.
- Manipulation for personal or professional gain.

The final steps in the values spiral are feedback and coaching and resolution. In these steps, units need to find mechanisms for holding team members accountable for living the values. A number of organizations we've worked with have turned their behaviors-level work into 360 degree feedback instruments, which are generally used initially in a developmental way to help the person being assessed improve her performance and behavior. Eventually, these instruments feed into the appraisal process. Coaching is frequently offered as a way for individuals to see how others see them and to explore how they might improve. Resolution requires us to deal with those who choose to violate our shared values. Without this step, we don't really have values, no matter how many places they hang on the wall. We may have to ask managers to relinquish their hierarchical authority and become a nonmanager or ask that violators—whether managers or employees—"make a contribution to some other organization." This step is the ultimate test of whether we want to have a high-performance work culture or not.

Finally, just as we ask KDQ 2—How would we know?—at every level of the vision spiral, we must also ask the same question at every level of the values spiral. At the top of the spiral, for example, we might use Likert's *Profile of Organizational Characteristics* or a similar survey to assess our unit's or organization's leadership philosophy.[7] At the behaviors level, we can design customized instruments to deliver 360 degree feedback or we can develop less formal methods of feedback where individuals deliver the feedback face-to-face. Methods also are available to assess organizational/unit work culture, such as the KEYS instrument from the Center for Creative Leadership and the Organizational Assessment Survey (OAS) from the U.S. Office of Personnel Management.[8]

In our example of the Navy industrial facility, KDQ 7—How do we treat each other?—was a foundational part of the change process. The new commander of the shipyard when we began the improvement process there (he was also responsible for bringing us in to help) had been at the shipyard earlier in his career. Unfortunately, in that incarnation, he was seen as a "take-no-prisoners" kind of manager (System 1 in Likert's typology). Before we could make progress in the change effort, we needed to help him alter his leadership philosophy. Between the time he left the shipyard after his first tour of duty and his return as shipyard commander, he had participated in a number of executive development programs, including Harvard's Kennedy School, the University of Virginia's Darden School, and a program conducted by the Naval Sea Systems Command. These programs had convinced him that his leadership philosophy was not going to serve him well in the future, and, based on this insight, he engaged us to help with his personal transition. After the commander began to change his style, one of his more difficult tasks was to get the others in the yard to see him as different, rather than the person he had been.

Tips for leadership success

Although this chapter has not been a full treatment of the HPO Diagnostic/Change Model, it has tried to lay out a good deal of the diagnostic thinking required to drive organizational improvement. As we work with organizations, several additional lessons we have learned and tips for success may be useful to keep in mind:

- **Get organized for change:** We have yet to encounter a successful organizational improvement effort that happened "accidentally." It seems that many organizations believe that sending their employees to training will, by itself, somehow result in performance improvement. Our experience is that *training does not equal change.* Instead, improvement requires a concerted effort by management to make it happen. It is necessary to build "change mechanisms" at every appropriate level of the organization in which individuals agree that a portion of their "real jobs" involves working on improving unit/microbusiness/organizational performance. The "roadmap" presented in the HPO Diagnostic/Change Model will not, by itself, cause anything to happen. We need "leadership teams" at every level of the organization who will seize the roadmap and "make it happen." It is critical that top management be involved in driving this process—a "demand function" is needed (the demand is *not* "do what I tell you," but rather is "you can't tell me you won't get organized and skilled to help improve the organization").

    Further, members of such leadership teams (especially top teams) must adopt a "stewardship" mindset, in which their focus is on the success of the whole, rather than just their units. We believe stewardship can be treated as a leadership competency and can be assessed (have the individuals worked to support cross-unit projects or organization-wide process improvements; do the individuals contribute to the success and improvement of other members of the leadership team; do the individuals identify this leadership team as their "primary team," as opposed to the units that they head?). In the example that started this chapter in which a city manager inherited a group of department heads who were definitely not stewardship-minded, our first order of business in their improvement process was to begin building an integrated top leadership team. Indeed, we have rarely seen an organization achieve sustained improved performance without a successfully integrated top leadership team (remember, however, that "top" in our material is relative; top can mean a project, division, department, or organization leadership team).

- **You may need some help:** We frequently find that senior managers (especially those with technical backgrounds) need some help with the change process. Our experience is that at about the 300-person level, an organization begins needing one or more part- or full-time change professionals on staff—people with organizational development, change management, business analytic thinking, project management, and team-development skills. Experienced change agents can "staff" the senior leadership team's efforts and can deliver "just-in-time" training, change-team facilitation, and encouragement/reinforcement/coordination. These change agents also can build a network of part-time change agents dispersed throughout the organization. In addition, they can play a "sensing function," pulling information together from all the different parts of the organization that touch a microbusiness (for example, support staff from HR, IT, finance/budget/procurement, facilities, legal, equal employment opportunity (EEO), etc.). Based on this information, a picture of the microbusiness begins to emerge that can suggest (in consultation with the managers and members of the microbusiness) what specific interventions may be useful to significantly improve the unit's performance. Finally, they can integrate with any outside contract support secured to help with the change process; this will continue to increase the in-house staff's skills and may raise an alert to problems with the contractors.
- **Consider "recontracting" everyone's job to also include leadership, management, and team/networking skills and responsibilities:** Many organizations we deal with are using human resources systems from the early 1900s in which work is seen as a discrete set of tasks that an individual employee is to complete (implicitly without regard to the whole). This "task-only" focus often is called the "industrial model" of work. It does not require the workforce to focus on the whole, on "owning" unit or organizational outcomes or impacts, or on the networks that must work smoothly to yield performance. The future will require a workforce that sees work differently and possesses a wider range of skills: leadership skills, management skills, technical skills, and team skills. These individuals will need to integrate themselves into, and care about the results of, the networks of which they are a part. For organizations to de-layer, broaden spans of control, be more flexible and responsive, and

reduce the cost of overhead, they will need "high-performing" employees at every level of their organizations. We've called this concept the "networked talent model."

Resources for further learning

Books

Mark Graham Brown, *Keeping Score: Using the Right Metrics to Drive World-Class Performance* (1996). This is a useful book for public/nonprofit managers who have not been exposed to measurement theory.

William Cohen, *Drucker on Leadership* (2010). This book offers a thoughtful look at Peter Drucker's writings on high performance.

James Collins, *Good to Great: Why Some Companies Make the Leap—and Others Don't* (2001). This is one of the best books on moving organizations toward high performance.

————, *Good to Great and the Social Sectors* (2005). Collins's excellent monograph, which accompanies his book above, adapts his concepts to the public and nonprofit sectors.

Jeffery M. Hiatt, *ADKAR: A Model for Change in Business, Government, and Our Community* (2006). This book proposes a personal and organizational change management approach called ADKAR, an acronym for awareness, desire, knowledge, ability, and reinforcement.

Robert S. Kaplan and David P. Norton, *The Balanced Scorecard: Translating Strategy into Action* (1996). Another good resource on measurement and performance management.

Daniel Pink, *Drive* (2009). This recent book on motivation, is a major contribution to the thinking on how to create work cultures and engage employees.

Web Resources

Project Management Institute, www.pmi.org. Many public-sector managers, especially those with a technical background, seem to lack exposure to the concepts of project management and to the people side of project management, often called change management. The body of knowledge surrounding project management is well established and relatively ubiquitous, and this institute is the widely acknowledged keeper of this body of knowledge.

Prosci, www.change-mangement.com. This website has an impressive amount of material in the change management area.

Balanced Scorecard Institute, www.balancedscorecard.org.

Notes

1. Likert (1961); Weisbord (1976); Peters and Waterman (1983). Note: We prefer to use the "older" seminal works in the organizational development, change management, and other literature in our HPO Diagnostic/Change Model, and then, if the client is interested, show how more modern material builds on the base laid by the giants in the fields we cover.

2. Collins (2001).

3. See Deming (1986); and Juran (1988). LEAN Manufacturing is Toyota's approach to quality and process improvement, and Six Sigma is Motorola's. The Capability Maturity Model (CMM) and CMM Integrated (CMMI) were developed by the Software Engineering Institute at Carnegie Mellon University.

4. Tichy (1999).

5. For an overview of the project management body of knowledge, see the Project Management Institute website at www.pmi.org.

6. See McGregor (1960); Likert (1961); Likert (1967); Block (1991).

7. Adapted from Appendix 11 in Likert (1967).

8. The KEYS instrument is available from the Center for Creative Leadership in Greensboro, NC, at www.ccl.org; the Organizational Assessment Survey is available from the U.S. Office of Personnel Management at www.opm.gov/employ/html/org_asse.asp.

7 The diversity opportunity

TOM GORDON, FOUNDER AND PRINCIPAL, TAGA CONSULTING
ALLISON LINNEY, PRESIDENT, ALLISON PARTNERS
KRISTINA ENERGIA NARANJO-RIVERA, MAXWELL SCHOOL OF CITIZENSHIP AND
PUBLIC AFFAIRS, SYRACUSE UNIVERSITY
MICHAEL RAWLINGS, SENIOR FACULTY, FEDERAL EXECUTIVE INSTITUTE

With each passing day, diversity increasingly defines public-sector organizations—both in the people making up the organizations and the citizens they serve. A complex and at times daunting demographic mix of race, religion, ethnicity, sexual orientation, lifestyle, disability, generation, and gender means that diversity is more salient than ever in America's democratic, pluralistic society. A real, resilient, and deeply rooted culture of trust can exist in organizations when leaders understand and harness the diversity around them. Similarly, government leaders who respond to diversity in inclusive and creative ways in their programs and policies can foster trust from the public. Indeed, the Constitution's call for justice for "We, the People," demands nothing less. Leaders who seize the diversity opportunity will not only continue to honor the spirit and letter of laws regarding equal opportunity, but they will ensure their organizations reflect the diversity that is America and that they value the perspectives and talents that diversity brings. For them, diversity and inclusion are not just a nice thing to do; they are a business necessity aimed at achieving even more positive organizational outcomes. Responding to the challenges of diversity is difficult work, of course, but leaders can master how to achieve it in both their relationships with others and in the strategic and tactical approaches they take to lead their organizations.

The leadership imperative is to define what is right and to do it.

—*Barbara Jordan*

Bᴏʙ ɪs ᴀᴛᴛᴇɴᴅɪɴɢ ᴀ ᴅɪᴠᴇʀsɪᴛʏ ᴄᴏɴꜰᴇʀᴇɴᴄᴇ at his boss's request. His boss was "too busy," but Bob felt that "political correctness" required him to show up even though his plate was full too. The conference dived eloquently into the nation's changing demographics and the need for paradigm shifts in how to staff, groom, advance, and leverage talent. Bob has come to accept the "business case" for diversity, but he's struggling with something he can't quite pin down.

At lunch with two other attendees, Jackson and Rachel, his concern gets clearer. "These diversity conferences are phony and hypocritical," Jackson says. "The big boys don't really care about all this. By sundown tomorrow, this diversity stuff will have all been forgotten."

Rachel agrees wholeheartedly: "Did you notice—five men spoke and took charge of the morning; but only one woman shared the main podium? It's like back at work. I'm conspicuously invisible in my branch. I'm routinely ignored for strategy and policy input. White men still run the show—and that's a fact."

These conferences are ducking a core diversity issue, Bob realizes. Diversity needs a strategy, trusted leadership, and a home. Pontificating won't get it done. The real problem is that no one trusts our top leaders, our chain of command, to define the right diversity direction, to lead by example, and to rally us to get there. Trust is the real issue. And trust doesn't just fall from the sky—or emerge from attending a conference.

"I wonder what would change the game," Bob blurts out. "What?" Jackson and Rachel say. "Oh. nothing," Bob replies. But of course he knows it's not "nothing." He sees the diversity opportunity. He's more willing than when he showed up for the conference to give it a serious try. But how do you get there from here, he wonders?

Being a trusted leader means facing diversity challenges just like this—and innumerable others fraught with various levels of hope, intensity, complexity, worry, and emotion. For the public-sector leader, a critical realization is that diversity led well builds unparalleled trust, and diversity led poorly or ignored destroys trust and cripples collective effort. Public-sector leaders—especially given the constitution of their organizations and the citizenry they serve—must proactively approach diversity. They must know how to build diverse teams, manage diverse organizations, and respond to increasingly diverse constituents. They must approach diversity as people, process, and performance opportunities.

Saying this is easy, of course. Yet many public-sector leaders feel like Bob: anxious as well as excited about the diversity challenge. These leaders face fears of being politically incorrect, of saying the wrong thing, of unintentionally offending, and even of litigation, which can transform a mindset of opportunity into an attitude of timidity and even hostility. Their minds may be cloudy and sometimes even clueless about what matters to their fellow citizens. Well-intentioned but poorly implemented diversity initiatives and dialogues have left many leaders frustrated and fatigued. Their own identities and sensitivities may distract and absorb them. Thus they remain ill-prepared, with little discretionary energy for in-depth reflection and conversations about the right and smart things to do.

Today's trusted leaders must rouse themselves from such worries and transform difficult diversity scenarios into practical productivity and advantage. This chapter pairs essential conceptual frameworks with key tools for seeing and seizing the diversity opportunity. The aim is to equip public-sector leaders with an actionable and practical "diversity GPS" to help them navigate the amazing contours of our diversity landscape.

Diversity: What is it?

The word "diversity" conjures up an astonishing array of thoughts and reactions. It can spark considerable consternation and confusion. Defining diversity is a knotty leadership challenge itself: definitional variance about a topic that literally means "variance" can hamper dialogue and delay trust-building. We define diversity in its broadest and most powerful sense as the inclusion and tapping of all of the human potential in a group, be it a team, organization, or society.

The Department of Defense (DOD), which has been working on the diversity opportunity since President Harry S. Truman ordered integration of the U.S. Armed Forces in 1948, recently crafted a similar definition, the result of the work of its Military Leadership Diversity Commission, a cross-service initiative mandated by Congress in 2009. For the DOD, "Diversity is all the different characteristics and attributes of individuals that are consistent with Department of Defense core values, integral to overall readiness and mission accomplishment, and reflective of the nation we serve." As the commission notes, "[T]he definition acknowledges that individuals come to the military not only with different cultural backgrounds but also with different skills, experiences, and talents. It also acknowledges that these differences are operationally relevant. With proper leadership, diversity can increase military agility and responsiveness."[1]

In this same vein, for this chapter *diversity* includes, but is not limited to, variations in age, race, ethnicity, economic class, gender, sexual orientation, religion, disability status, marital status, parental status, language, and geographic origin. Diversity is human complexity, visible and subtle. It is our significant descriptors or identities—human attributes that attract attention and stimulate how we assign respect, regard, and enact rules of engagement for ourselves and others. For our demographically vibrant public-sector organizations, diversity describes the people mix, talent pool, our varied constituents, and our wide-ranging stakeholder demographics.

Diversity as a leadership opportunity thus directs us to respect, explore, and leverage what we notice about human "form" to enhance engagement—and through that organizational performance. Diversity leadership focuses and fuels employees to deliver their best talents and perspectives for themselves and those they serve. When leaders emphasize inclusion, people feel safe, connected, respected, and successful—and trust blossoms.

The public-sector leader's obligation: Being faithful to America's promise to its people

The diversity opportunity is not new; it draws on the guidance, obligations, and wisdom of our nation's cherished political principles and traditions. Indeed, the Declaration of Independence and the U.S. Constitution are foundational documents for public-sector leaders seeking to achieve the diversity opportunity. They highlight how and why public servants have moral, political, intellectual, and strategic obligations to pursue diversity's full promise.

Diversity and inclusion have always been at the center of America's national aspirations and values. The Framers made a promise of equality to the nation's citizens and provided a mechanism to achieve it. Much of our history—and the practice of government—has been involved with both. Martin Luther King Jr. said on the steps of the Lincoln Memorial in 1963 that "[W]hen the architects of our republic wrote the magnificent words of the Constitution and the Declaration of Independence, they were signing a promissory note to which every American was to fall heir." King also was said to have quipped once that: "The Constitution is an amazing document. It worked exactly for those it was meant to exclude—blacks and women." His words capture the fact that the Constitution provides a vision and a method for government leaders to pay off on that promissory note. Slavery, along with the treatment of the Native American population and the subjugation of women and other groups, have been among our nation's greatest failures, but the Constitution offered a way to correct them. In this broad sense, every leader in government is charged through the Oath of Office with delivering on the promise of America.

The Declaration of Independence was an exception in world history; it proclaimed as self-evident that "All men are created equal. . . ." It would take the Constitution in 1787 to give this vision a concrete blueprint. The Preamble sets the stage with its ringing call to "establish Justice" and "secure the Blessings of Liberty" to *all Americans*. The Constitution's rules and tools then enable leaders in government, often pressured by leaders in the broader society—such as King himself—to realize the vision.

No one at the Constitutional Convention had completed a "diversity awareness" course. Yet all understood that different interests—what James Madison in *Federalist* No. 10 called "factions"—were inevitable and that liberty depended not on extinguishing them, which was impossible, but on allowing (and managing) their free expression. The convention believed that the best decisions would emerge from the greatest diversity of views. It is for that reason that the Constitution could not get ratified until it was clear that a Bill of Rights protecting freedom of expression, religion, the press, association, and the right to petition the government would be added.[2]

The Framers, however, were not doe-eyed believers in the power of reason. They knew that power could still allow majorities to tyrannize minorities, just by getting enough votes to have their way. So they set up tools—separation of powers, checks and balances—to protect the politically weak.[3] In their wisdom, they also recognized the need for adaptation and change, and enshrined this in an amendment process. It was this process that, in time, abolished slavery and extended the franchise to African Americans, women, and eighteen-year-olds. Yet even these amendments do not diminish the ongoing need for protections of equality under law. Most of our antidiscrimination legislation, administrative regulations, and policy statements reflect this need to protect individuals and classes, to right wrongs and to prevent further wrongs—in short to honor our diversity.

Thus, the Constitution offers a useful case study in leading diversity. It provides lessons for government leaders in their work today. Briefly, these include the following:

- *Vision and values matter.* Were it not for the vision of "all men created equal" and "a more perfect Union," it is unlikely that generations of Americans would have persisted in building a society that respects differences. Visions of diversity and inclusion that are bold, clear, and reflect deeply felt values drive people to commit to their fulfillment.
- *Actions must be consistent with values.* Leaders who say one thing and do another forfeit trust. The Framers ignored this point when they took abolishing slavery off the table in order to reach consensus. It took a Civil War and the Thirteenth through Fifteenth Amendments to correct their lack of moral courage.
- *Encourage dissent.* It is not hard to manage a bunch of people who think the same way. But for leaders in a democratic society, diversity is essential. It is also messy. The ability to manage rather than suppress diverse views becomes a critical diversity leadership skill.
- *Establish ground rules to manage diversity.* The Framers did not know how to solve all the problems the nation would face. So they crafted a process that dispersed power so that dialogue with others is essential and checks and balances so that the leader's ability to act depends on communication, argument, and the consideration of differing points of view. Leaders in government can establish ground rules in their organizations to do the same.
- *Communicate the view that diverse organizations perform better.* Despite the difficulty of leading diversity, few people would trade our government in for the other choices. How many well-performing dictatorships exist in the world? Heterogeneous groups perform better than homogeneous ones. Within organizations, this has an important corollary for leaders: hire people who are different than you and who don't think like you do—and then communicate in word and deed that you are glad you did.

Whom do we serve?—The constitution of America's diversity

If government leaders are to deliver the American promise through leading in a diverse society, who comprises that society they have taken a constitutional oath to serve? The historical imagination conjures up a homogenous America of colonial patriots who shared a common culture, religion, and value system. That's a picture that never was—America was diverse before the Pilgrims landed and its diversity has only grown. To talk meaningfully about how to capture the diversity opportunity, some attention to the current kaleidoscope of America is necessary. While we focus here on demographic differences, it is important to keep in mind our broad definition. Diversity is present not only in what we can see but in our personalities, talents, professions, and values. If it takes leadership skill to craft a coherent agency policy among the differing demands of racial and ethnic groups, for example, it takes leadership skill as well to get the lawyers to talk to the social scientists, to get both to talk to political appointees, and then to converse with information technology (IT) specialists to build the technology to implement that policy. Diversity is everywhere we look—and that is a good thing.

We focus first on "the changing face of America," and then on the changing workforce of government itself, the latter as an example of how diversity in government is integrally connected to diversity in society.

The changing face of America: Who is "American"?

In the United States, we do not define citizenship by ethnicity or race. Being born here confers citizenship, and naturalization is open to those born elsewhere. Our Constitution guarantees basic rights to "persons," even those not citizens. What follows, given the limitations of space, is a brief snapshot of several aspects of the diversity that is our nation. The aim is to sample the contours of the landscape, not draw a comprehensive map.

- In 2009, 12.5 percent of the U.S. population (38.5 million people) was foreign born.[4] California tops the nation with 9.9 million foreign-born residents. Six states (California, New York, Texas, Florida, New Jersey, and Illinois—in rank order) account for nearly two-thirds of them.[5]
- The increase in foreign-born residents is not confined to traditional "border" states. Increases of greater than 50 percent in the foreign-born population between 2000 and 2007 were recorded in South Carolina, Nevada, Arkansas, Tennessee, Alabama, and Georgia.[6]
- In 2009, 20.0 percent (57.1 million) of Americans spoke a language other than English at home, up from 17.9 percent in 2000.[7] Indeed, Americans reported more than 103 ancestry groups to describe their origins.[8]

- Between 2010–2050, the number of Hispanics in the U.S. population will increase by 167 percent, compared with 18 percent for non-Hispanics and a total growth of the U.S. population of 42 percent.[9]
- Americans from other nations are also increasingly part of the labor force that the government fosters and protects. From 1970 to 1980, 10 percent of the new entrants to our labor force were immigrants.[10] From 2000 to 2005, immigrants accounted for 78.5 percent of labor force growth.[11]

Melting pot or salad bowl?

We have traditionally viewed America as a melting pot. A salad bowl may be a better metaphor, reflecting the need to gain from the unique contributions of the people and cultural traditions that form America rather than asking them to give up their identity in an undifferentiated stew:

- As of 2010, the U.S. population consisted of 50.5 million Hispanics/Latinos (16.3 percent of the population). By race, the population in 2010 consisted of 38.9 million African Americans (12.6 percent), 14.6 million Asian Americans (4.8 percent), 2.9 million Native Americans/Alaskan Natives (0.9 percent), 540,013 Native Hawaiians/Pacific Islanders (0.2 percent), 19.1 million (6.2 percent) who were "some other race," and 9.0 million (2.9 percent) who classified themselves as of two or more races. More than a third of Americans are what we traditionally have considered minorities.[12] Indeed, the term "minorities" is increasingly being replaced by "people of color," to recognize the literal fact that these groups are often no longer in the numerical minority in places where they live and work and also because "minority" contrasted with "majority" too often implies in some minds a subordinate status that ignores the richness of opportunities that diversity brings.
- The Arab population in the United States is growing. In 2009, there were nearly 1.7 million Arabs in the nation, a figure that more than doubled since 1980.[13]
- Nearly one in ten of the nation's 3,143 counties has a population that is more than 50 percent racial/ethnic minorities.[14] Racial/ethnic minorities are thus in some places becoming the new majority.

- In thirteen of America's twenty-five largest cities, more than 20 percent of residents are foreign born.[15]
- The labor force is seeing similar shifts. According to the Bureau of Labor Statistics, by the year 2030, non-Hispanic whites are expected to constitute 60.6 percent of the labor force, Latinos 18.8 percent, African Americans 13.8 percent, and Asian Americans 8.6 percent.

How old are we?

We are an aging society. This has profound implications for how those in government must lead.

- The "sixty-five years old plus" age group will be the fastest growing segment of American society, projected to increase to about 76 million people by the year 2030 (about 21.2 percent of the population in 2030 compared to about 12.9 percent in 2010).[16]
- There were 2.2 million Americans eighty-five years old and older in 1980. That figure will rise to 8.7 million by 2030 and 19.0 million by 2050.[17]

We are also a society with many generationally based cultural differences. As these generations express their needs and come into contact with each other, leaders in government will have to respond with different kinds of services—and sensitivity, in the workplace and beyond. To capture the diversity opportunity means navigating among the values, needs, and demands of at least four generations: Traditionalists (born between 1922–1943), Baby Boomers (born between 1943–1960), Generation X (born between 1960–1980), and Millennials (sometimes called "Generation Y" and born since 1980).[18]

What about gender and gender roles?

Since the 1970s we have seen dramatic changes in the role of women in American society.

- In 2009, 1.64 million women were enrolled in graduate and professional education, more than double the number in 1976. By comparison, 1.54 million men were enrolled.[19]

- Women's progress toward earning an equal share of first-professional degrees has been notable. In 1970, 5 percent of law degrees, 8 percent of medical degrees, and 1 percent of dentistry degrees were awarded to females; in 2008 the corresponding percentages were 50 percent, 47 percent, and 45 percent.[20]
- In 2007, of the people on active duty in the U.S. armed forces, 14 percent or 198,400 were women. In 1950 the figure was 2 percent.[21]
- Women still lag in such fields as engineering and the sciences and are still underrepresented in many other fields.[22] They comprise less than 20 percent of the "traditionally male" jobs of mining and construction and account for only 20 to 30 percent of the jobs in agriculture, transportation, and manufacturing.[23] Women make up only 20 percent of the membership of private-sector executive teams.[24] The pay gap between women and men persists; as a recent White House report revealed, women at all levels of comparable education still earn only 75 percent of the pay that men get.[25]

There have also been profound changes in gender "expectations" about child-rearing practices. These changes also demand corresponding changes in how government serves society.

- 55.3 percent of women with children less than one year old worked outside the home in 2008, compared to 31 percent in 1976.[26]
- Between 1990 and 2007, the number of households with children under age eighteen grew by 12 percent for married couples, but by 67 percent for father households with no spouse present and by 29 percent for mother households with no spouse present.[27]

What about people with disabilities?

As we age, more of us will have disabilities.

- In 2006, 15.1 percent of Americans over five years of age had a disability. Disability prevalence varied dramatically by age: 6.3 percent of Americans between ages five and fifteen; 12.3 percent for those between sixteen and sixty-four, and 40.9 percent for those sixty-five and older.[28]
- As society ages, the total number of people with disabilities grows: 54.4 million people in 2005 compared to 43 million in 1990.[29]

What religions do we follow?

Our currency says "In God We Trust," and Americans are generally a religious people. Indeed, visitors from Europe to the United States are often surprised by Americans' widespread participation in and fervor for active religious observation. But our motto hides a wide diversity of religious practice:

- In 2007 Americans identified their religious preference as follows: Protestant—51.3 percent (Evangelical churches, 26.3 percent; mainline churches, 18.1 percent; historically black churches, 6.9 percent); Catholic, 23.9 percent; Jewish, 1.7 percent; Mormon, 1.7 percent; Buddhist, 0.7 percent; Muslim, 0.6 percent; Hindu, 0.6 percent; and Unaffiliated, 16.1 percent.[30]
- The number of adults who identify themselves as nonreligious/ secular has increased 138 percent from 1990 to 2008. Corresponding increases for those who identify with some other religions are: Islam (156 percent), Buddhism (194 percent), and Hinduism (156 percent).[31]
- Religious diversity, if not managed well, can lead to workplace problems. The federal Equal Employment Opportunity Commission reported in 2008 that religion-based charges of discrimination have increased 83 percent in the past decade.[32]

What about sexual orientation and lifestyle choices?

Increasing diversity also manifests itself in (more openly expressed) sexual orientation and preferences for living arrangements. The "two parents with children" household that many associate with the post–World War II era is now just one of a wide range of patterns in which Americans choose to live.

- Married-couple households are on the decline percentage-wise: 80 percent of households were married couples in the 1950, but that dropped to 49.7 percent of households by 2009.[33]
- Between 2000 and 2008, the number of opposite sex unmarried partner households increased 16 percent to nearly 5.7 million. From 2000 to 2006, the number of same sex unmarried partner households increased 31 percent to more than three quarters of a million.[34]

- Although good data are hard to obtain, especially because sexual orientation is kept private by choice and fear of reprisal, according to DiversityInc.com, 3 to 10 percent of the U.S. population was gay or lesbian in 2001.[35]
- Support for same-sex marriage or civil unions is growing in U.S. society, from only 22 percent in 2004 to 42 percent in 2009.[36] Domestic-partner benefits in 2008 could be found in 286 (57 percent) of Fortune 500 companies, compared to 200 (40 percent) in 2003 (though not for U.S. government employees and those in most states).[37]

Leading a diverse society

A life dedicated to public service means we have to understand the "public," how it is changing, and the needs that its diversity brings. To build trust, leaders in government who grasp the kinds of changes suggested above should ask themselves such questions as:

- What are the implications of all of these changes for the services government needs to provide?
- How can we attract the most highly qualified Americans to government service—so that diversity in government mirrors the diversity of society?
- How can we best draw on language diversity in America to help us accomplish the agency mission?
- What conflicts might we anticipate among generations competing for limited services and tax dollars?
- How can we benefit from an increasingly healthy older workforce, many of whom wish to continue to contribute even after official retirement?
- How do our web and social networking services need to change to reflect and respond to an increasingly multicultural, multigenerational citizenry?
- How will the services we now offer need to be changed or adapted to meet the needs of a growing number of people with disabilities?
- How will pressures from, and the needs of, those with varied religious beliefs show up in such governmental services as education, health care, housing, transportation, and homeland security?

- How can we make all in the workplace who are different feel safer for the expression of their difference so that they are included and thus can become even more productive?
- What needs will a wider range of living patterns generate that government must meet in housing, child care, worker benefits/protections, and retirement/survivor benefits and rights?

The changing face of the federal workforce

If America is changing, so is the government workforce. We focus briefly on changes at the federal level. What is happening in some states is most likely even more dramatic.

As Table 7.1 demonstrates, the federal government civilian workforce is becoming more diverse. The percentage of the workforce classified as minority jumped in the past two decades from a little more than a quarter to more than a third. Every group except Native Americans and Alaskan Natives comprised a larger percentage of the federal civilian workforce in 2009 than they did in 1990. While data are not available on the proportion of the civilian workforce that is gay, lesbian, bisexual or transgender, scholarly research suggests that 65,000 gays and lesbians now serve in the armed forces, and that there are about 1 million gay and lesbian veterans.[38]

Table 7.1 **Diversity in the federal workforce**

	Federal work-force 1990	Federal work-force 2009	Civilian labor force 2009	Census 2010 and 2009 American Community Survey
Women	43.1%	44.2%	45.9%	50.7%
Men	56.9	55.8	54.1	49.3
Black/African American	16.6	17.8	9.8	12.4
Hispanic/Latino	5.4	8.0	13.4	15.8
Asian American/ Pacific Islander	3.5	5.5	4.3	4.7
Native American/ Alaskan Natives	1.8	1.8	0.6	0.8
Two or more races	N/A	0.5	1.3	2.4

Sources: U.S. Office of Personnel Management/U.S. Census Bureau.

If we ask how representative the federal workforce is of the nation it serves, we can see that the most glaring disjunction is that the federal workforce significantly underrepresents the nation's Hispanic/Latino population, causing potential problems in the ability of government to understand and serve this growing segment of American society, and to be trusted by it. This underrepresentation is true as well when we note that, as of 2006 (the last year for which data are available), 6.8 percent of the federal workforce has a disability, compared to 15.1 percent of Americans overall.[39]

While government seems to mirror society fairly well in other demographic groups, a different problem emerges when we examine how well people of color and women are represented at the highest levels of the civil service, where officials presumably exert the greatest influence on the design and direction of government policies and programs, including those on diversity within government itself. According to the most recent government data, African Americans comprise only 6.4 percent of the most senior civil service positions even though they account for 17.8 percent of all federal workers. Women represent only 30.4 percent of senior workers while making up 44.2 percent of the federal workforce. Hispanics make up only 4 percent of senior civil servants yet comprise 8 percent of the federal workforce and 15.8 percent of the U.S. population.[40] These figures explain, in part, why President Barack Obama is planning to issue an Executive Order to enhance the hiring and development of those underrepresented in the federal workforce and to make the senior civil service far more diverse.

Finally, following social trends overall, the federal government also has recently committed to ending the "Don't Ask, Don't Tell" policy regarding the service of openly gay, lesbian, and bisexual Americans in the armed forces. This signals an important step toward diversity and inclusion as well, and it will have implications for leaders.

These data—and other data we saw for the nation as a whole—suggest a number of questions that leaders in government might profitably ask to ensure that they realize the diversity opportunity within their organizations. For example:

- How can government enhance its recruitment of Hispanics and draw on their culture and language skills to enhance government services?
- How can leaders in government develop, recognize, and promote more women and people of color into senior positions to take advantage of their skills and perspectives for serving an increasingly diverse society?

- What accommodations will we need to make to attract those with disabilities to the workforce—and help them be most effective? How can we advance more of them into senior positions?
- What workforce policies are needed to support men and women who don't want to trade off raising children for meaningful work?
- What difference will it make to recruiting and retaining Lesbian, Gay, Bisexual, and Transgender (LGBT) individuals if organizations guarantee their partners the same benefits afforded other couples for health insurance, retirement, relocation expenses, etc.?
- What will we be asked to do and how will we respond in regard to religious accommodations and practices that our employees expect in the workplace?

Realizing the diversity opportunity

We have thus far explored what we mean by diversity and America's shifting demographics. We've also framed the constitutional imperative for diversity and seen in that charter some lessons for how those in government can realize the diversity opportunity in their organizations and for the citizens they serve. We move next to some of the practical tools available for realizing the diversity opportunity.

Perhaps the most powerful tool is a different mental model or paradigm. Our tacit mental models govern how we think and so orchestrate and constrain us—what we do and what we can achieve. For example, traditional institutional paradigms sponsor and assign highest priority in government to budgets, tasks, and performance results not to the diverse demographics of people and their partnership potential. Budget-centered, task-dominant, and performance-focused paradigms have their place, but they tend to place greatest value on so-called "hard deliverables" or tangible outcomes. Leading diversity then appears as a "soft" deliverable, making investments in it less likely or positioned as marginal, suspect, invisible, and unworthy of leadership's top priority. When this happens, leaders do not routinely recruit, develop, promote, leverage, reward, and retain diverse talent. They do not routinely challenge collusion and exclusion. They do not provide in-depth feedback to diverse audiences or practice listening to them—either inside the organization or among the public.

We offer a new paradigm—which acknowledges the importance of both "hard" and "soft" considerations and which argues that they are complementary ways of leading. In our view, fostering diversity is the way to

Table 7.2   Leading diversity

	Protecting Differences	Affirmative Action: Advancing Differences	Multicultural Diversity: Celebrating Differences	Deep Diversity: Engaging Differences
Origins/ theory base	• Federal law	• Executive orders • Politics • Leader values	• Cultural studies	• Socio-technical theory
Unit of analysis	• Group	• Group	• Group	• Individual • Organization
Typical inter- ventions	• Complaint process • Awareness and process training	• Set-asides, quotas, and targets • Developmental programs • Awareness training	• Ethnic celebrations • Diversity councils • Awareness training	• Establishing the business case • Production analysis and problem solving
Focus of activity	• HR and management processes • Organizational learning	• HR and management processes • Organizational learning	• Human community	• Primary work of the organization
Payoffs	• Diminished social and organizational bigotry	• More people have a voice • Different people have a voice	• Greater appreciation of differences	• Heightened productivity, creativity, and commitment
Possible down- sides	• Resentment • Exclusion	• Resentment • Exclusion • "Entitlement" • Backlash	• Overtaxing of group identification • Overlooking of individual uniqueness	• High cost in money • High cost in time

Source: John G. Corlett Ph.D., Federal Executive Institute, 2000.

achieve ever-higher levels of organizational results, not a detriment to doing so. We think that the model shown in Table 7.2 offers a helpful presentation of such a new paradigm. Crafted by Dr. John Corlett, formerly with the CIA and now an organizational consultant who has taught at the Federal Executive Institute and the University of Virginia, this model suggests four different approaches to leading diversity. All have merit, but as we move from the left to the right, we move toward ever-more powerful ways of achieving organizational results.

Diversity traditionally has meant righting wrongs and protecting differences—the aim of most of the architecture for diversity in government organizations. Equal employment opportunity (EEO) laws and regulations are necessary and important—and will continue to be—but they are not sufficient for fully realizing the diversity opportunity. The same can be said for affirmative action (AA), without which the workforce in government organizations—not to mention the composition of colleges, universities, and many other American institutions—would not come close to looking like America.

The first step beyond EEO and AA is to appreciate differences. Differences become not just something to protect but a resource to learn from and learn about. Finally, when we *engage* differences, we see diversity as a resource not just for celebration but for accomplishing the work of the organization and the society. We anchor the business case for diversity not in the need to comply with law and regulations or the need to appreciate our employees or fellow citizens—as important as these are—but in the hard realization that results that are quantitatively and qualitatively better emerge from it.

Collectively, these four approaches offer a powerful way for leaders to think and act. There is general agreement that the more diverse an organization or a team, the more creativity and ideas flow forward and the more robust the problem solving and decision making become. Furthermore, it is reasonable to assume that as employees see that fair recruitment and effective integration into the workplace are encouraged, they will more energetically commit to the mission. This is true for both domestic and international agency goals. While Chapter 13 focuses on the need for diversity leadership in U.S. international efforts, it's worth noting here that if we bring those with international perspectives and cross-cultural skills into our agencies, we will enhance our ability to build better relationships globally.[41]

Admittedly, this all sounds nice, and many public-sector leaders intellectually accept these premises. But they can get exhausted by the challenge of actually realizing diversity's promise. Diversity management efforts often fail. The promise of creativity and innovation dissolves into conflicts that cannot be resolved. Diversity training sessions energize people for new behaviors, but then colleagues retreat to their silos and silences. Leaders agree that all people should have a chance to work in the organization as long as they are qualified, and that everyone should have access to the American dream, but then quietly wonder why white male candidates are overlooked while "diverse" candidates are promoted too early or positions remain open when not enough "diverse" external candidates can be found. "Diverse" candidates tire of having colleagues wonder if they are qualified. Leaders or their colleagues may have dealt with an EEO allegation of discriminatory practices when they felt deep in their hearts that they were being fair and unbiased. Leaders see employees from an underrepresented group whose ideas are shot down and then later embraced when someone from the majority culture suggests them; sometimes the leaders *are* those employees who feel shot down. Or leaders find that they or some of their employees are constantly struggling to be included in the "sidebar" meetings where the real work takes place and somehow never get invited. Leaders want to serve diverse elements of the public better, with greater sensitivity and more helpful products, but almost every time they try they get criticized. As leaders, we agree with the promise of diversity, but can it really work?

We need a few clear examples of best practices to help turn the diversity opportunity into reality.

Best practices in government

Many government agencies have developed approaches to realizing the diversity opportunity, even if none may have mastered what is always a work in progress. The 2010 annual *Best Places to Work in the Federal Government* rankings, compiled by the Partnership for Public Service using employee survey data from all federal agencies, has a subcategory titled Support for Diversity. The two large agencies that top the "best" list are the Nuclear Regulatory Commission (75.5 out of a possible score of 100) and National Aeronautics and Space Administration (NASA) (71.2). Looking at agency subcomponents and their scores, NASA centers take five of the top seven spots.[42] Of these, Goddard Space Flight Center in Greenbelt, MD, ranks highest.

Goddard has been at work on the diversity opportunity for more than a decade. It has a "Business Case for Diversity" which makes clear that the focus is on center performance, and its definition of diversity is inclusive, not focused on demographics alone (see Box 7.1). Its efforts are led by a Diversity Council chaired by the deputy center director and composed of a special assistant for diversity, representatives from management of all Goddard units, unions, and nearly a dozen advisory committees that focus on everything from veterans' to women to minority to gay and lesbian concerns. The council has crafted a Diversity and Inclusion Strategic Plan that focuses on diversity leadership, recruitment and retention, education, communication, performance management, measurement, and accountability.

Box 7.1 Goddard Space Flight Center's business case for diversity

Policy statement

It is the policy of NASA's GSFC to develop and maintain a vital and effective workforce by involving employees in the creation of a work environment conducive to their best performance according to the Center's values and goals. Our objective is to foster an organizational climate where employee diversity and mutual respect are catalysts for creativity and team effectiveness.

Definition of diversity

Diversity includes a number of important human characteristics that affect an individual's values and opportunities and perceptions of self and others at work. These characteristics include, but are not limited to age, ethnicity, gender, ability, race, sexual orientation, religion, and family status. They also include secondary characteristics such as: geographic location, military experience, work experience, income, religion, first language, organizational role and level, communication style, family status, work style, and education.

Source: http://diversity.gsfc.nasa.gov/diversity.cfm.

Among Goddard's innovative practices are a Diversity Dialogue Project (DDP) and the Goddard Opportunities Bulletin Board System (GOBBS). The DDP is "a facilitated dialog process in which small groups of employees come together in an open, non-judgmental and comfortable environment to discuss differences based on many dimensions of diversity that are brought into the workplace on a daily basis." The GOBBS is a program that enables managers and supervisors to advertise special opportunities to employees. These opportunities are details or one-time-only efforts that have an objective, a start date, and an end date. Employees can even identify a specific skill or experience to receive targeted announcements (for example, engineers or professional/administrative) through the system. The GOBBS does not replace the merit selection process but offers short assignments to enable employees to acquire and demonstrate skills to make them more visible and valuable across the center.

The range of activities that can be undertaken to realize the diversity opportunity in any government organization is limited only by the business case for diversity and the imagination (see Key Results Areas in Box 7.2). A few additional examples of agency efforts demonstrate the possibilities.

Box 7.2 Leading diversity in your organization

Key Results Areas

Organizational leadership and culture

1. The diversity of the top management team reflects America.
2. The organization's explicit values emphasize diversity and inclusion.
3. Leaders model through word and deed that they value differences as an asset for success.
4. Top leadership is evaluated on measurable success in diversity efforts.

External relationships

5. Products and services are tailored to respond to needs of differing external/internal customers.
6. Websites and social networking applications reflect a commitment to diversity and inclusion.
7. Messages about policies, programs, and services are tailored to needs and abilities of diverse audiences.
8. Training is given to those who work with international clients to be effective in other cultures.

Diversity mission and goals

9. The "business case" for diversity is articulated for employees verbally and in writing.
10. Diversity goals address external customers and employees.
11. Diversity efforts are linked to the organization's strategic and performance plans.
12. A diversity plan exists for the organization, with measurable objectives.

Structure and resources

13. A specific person has overall operational responsibility and the charge is more than EEO/AA.
14. The lead person for diversity has ready access to top management.
15. A budget exists for the organization's diversity initiatives, and resources are adequate.

Human Resource Systems

Recruitment and hiring

16. An active program recruits a workforce that reflects the clients the organization serves and will serve in the future.
17. The organization provides incentives to recruit new hires from under-represented groups.

Training and development

18. Competencies needed for the success of diversity goals have been identified.
19. Training is provided to help people learn these competencies.
20. Mentoring is provided to help retain and develop all employees.

Team development

21. The organization assembles teams reflecting the diversity of the customers served.
22. Teams are given training and support to achieve high quality results.

Employee satisfaction and retention

23. Employee satisfaction data are analyzed by demographic groups and the results are used to improve.
24. Fully accessible workplaces and reasonable accommodations exist for those with special needs.
25. Why employees resign, by demographic group, is tracked, and data are used to make needed changes.

Rewards

26. Success on diversity goals is measured in the performance plans of supervisors, managers, and senior leaders.
27. The organization rewards people/organizations to recognize their contributions on diversity goals.

Vendor/supplier services

28. The vendor/supplier base reflects the diversity of the population the organization serves.

Source: Terry Newell, Federal Executive Institute, 2000.

National Park Service — Creative collaboration for diversity recruitment[43]

In 2007 Jill Hawk, chief ranger of the National Park Service's (NPS) northeast region, faced the dual challenge of an impending wave of retirements and the need to diversify the workforce. Within five years, 55 percent of rangers in the region would be eligible to retire. Furthermore, she recognized the need to change the 80 percent white demographic composition of staff to better represent the communities NPS serves.

Seizing the retirement-recruitment transition as a strategic opportunity, Hawk partnered with Temple University's criminal justice program to codevelop ProRanger, an internship program designed to train and retain diverse, dynamic young law enforcement professionals. The program was designed to attract students that reflect a diversity of race, gender, aptitudes, and interests. Students attend a preprofessional training academy, gain practical work experience, and are put on a fast track to employment with NPS. In turn, national parks are infused with a diverse, well-trained talent pool. The ProRanger model now also operates in NPS's Inter-Mountain Region, through a partnership with San Antonio College. Of the first twenty-one cadets selected there in 2010, 80 percent are ethnically diverse. Their program includes two years of training, mentoring, a summer internship in the parks, and attendance at a Law Enforcement Academy to prepare participants for their NPS jobs.

U.S. Census Bureau — Diversity and the 2010 census[44]

In conducting the 2010 census, the U.S. Census Bureau defined three diversity goals: (1) achieve employee diversity from leadership to field workers; (2) utilize a diverse partner pool to build public awareness; and (3) ensure contract opportunities for disadvantaged and underrepresented groups.

The Census Bureau began by assessing the diversity of its leadership, benchmarking against leadership diversity in the federal government as a whole. It found the bureau's representation of people of color exceeded benchmarks, while female representation fell short. This information was used to inform recruitment strategy. Leadership succession planning was crafted to reflect greater racial, ethnic, and gender diversity.

The Census Bureau also partnered with 140,000 state, local, and tribal governments and community organizations to "recruit, hire, and deploy a diverse workforce that looks like and can relate to the people being counted."

Local field staff hiring efforts targeted diverse racial and ethnic groups, multilingual individuals, women, senior citizens, and retirees best able to relate to local populations. Furthermore, to improve data collection on hard-to-enumerate communities, the bureau collaborated with trusted partner organizations and community leaders. Examples include the Mexican American Legal Defense and Education Fund, the National Association for the Advancement of Colored People, the American Association of Retired Persons, and several religious organizations. Additionally, the communications strategy included contracting advertisers expert in marketing to historically undercounted groups.

The Census Bureau also crafted provisions to honor socioeconomic diversity, such as ensuring public assistance benefits would not be reduced as a result of census income earnings. The Department of Commerce set prime contracting goals to incentivize the awarding of contracts to small businesses owned by women, veterans, people with disabilities and socially and economically disadvantaged companies.

Similar examples can no doubt be found in state and local governments, and other chapters in this book also offer powerful approaches. Chapter 8's attention to collaboration across organizational boundaries offers concepts and tools for fostering excellence across the diversity represented in different organizational functions and organizations themselves. Chapter 12's focus on e-governance demonstrates the power of web 2.0 technologies to engage diverse public audiences in crafting government policies and programs. And Chapter 3's attention to effective conversations demonstrates the potential to talk productively across all of our human differences. Indeed, we have focused thus far on realizing the diversity opportunity at the macro-level of organizations. Chapter 3 reminds us that we also need to focus on the diversity opportunity at the micro-level of one-on-one relationships. If it doesn't happen there, it's not likely to happen on a wider scale. We now turn to diversity at the individual/relationship level.

Diversity conversations

> Be the change you wish to see in the world.
>
> —*Mohandas Gandhi*

We lead through words. Until leaders talk, they can accomplish little. Yet talking about diversity, for many leaders in government, seems fraught with worry and a paucity of skills. As professors Martin Davidson, Robin Ely, and Debra Meyerson suggest, the promise of diversity in the workplace is often unrealized because a politically correct culture has led to an inability to have real conversations about difference. "Sensitivity to race, religion, or gender is a good thing," they write, "but too often it is driven by fear. Rather than walk on eggshells, managers can learn to develop more productive, meaningful relationships at work."[45] These relationships, as we have seen so often in this book, depend on productive dialogue. Davidson, Ely, and Meyerson argue that such dialogue around diversity means having the ability to deal with identity "abrasions."

For example, Maria, a supervisor, holds a briefing for her new team, using PowerPoint slides, without stopping to realize that Art, a near-blind team member, gets lost in the briefing because he cannot read key information on several of the slides. Shortly after the meeting, she hears a rumor that Art was hurt at her insensitivity, although Art never says a word. Art may, in fact, be reluctant about speaking up, and whether or not he does, how Maria responds to the situation will determine whether she can lead and build trust or fail and produce cynicism within the team. She knows she meant no disrespect to Art, and she feels a little defensive about this with her new team. Her feelings about the situation are thus also a key factor in what happens next. As Davidson, Ely and Meyerson put it:

> Assaults to people's identities occur daily in most organizations: A white person confuses the names of two Asian-American coworkers; a black executive is addressed less formally than her white male counterparts; a woman's idea is misattributed to a male colleague. Repeated experiences of this kind diminish people's sense of how much others value and respect them. Offense at a perceived slight may or may not be well-founded, but an attempt to discuss the possible insult risks, for example, the charge that one is overly sensitive. Such assaults occur on the flip side as well, as when members of majority groups are accused of being prejudiced or of treating others unfairly. Because they often have meant no harm, they tend to respond defensively, upset by any suggestion that their moral goodness is being questioned.[46]

These authors offer five principles for seeing such possible abrasions as opportunities and handling them well:

1. *Pause:* Slow down. Don't respond right away, since such a response may show anger, hurt, or another unhelpful emotion. Take a time-out to consider how best to proceed.
2. *Connect:* See the situation in a broader context. Focus outside yourself, connecting with broader diversity, organizational, and even societal goals and needs. Doing so can help you put your personal feelings aside in favor of the greater mission.
3. *Question yourself:* Look inside before going outside yourself. What does the situation say about you, what you might have missed, how you might be seeing (perhaps wrongly) the other person, what you might have to learn? This is the self-awareness work discussed in detail in Chapter 2.
4. *Get genuine support:* Find people who can help you approach this in a positive way, whose perspectives you trust to be honest not self-serving to your possible desire to be in the right. Draw on their ideas and talents to help craft a productive way to proceed. Finding a coach, as discussed in Chapters 2 and 4, may be very useful for this.
5. *Shift your mindset:* View the abrasion as an opportunity, not an attack. Find a way to reformulate the issue that allows you to approach it with the core question: "What can I do and say that will move us to a better place?"

In applying these five principles Maria might proceed something like this. Instead of immediately approaching Art to defend herself or confront the issue (which may also be awkward for him), she decides to take time to think about it. As she does so, she realizes that her "insensitivity" proceeded from a lack of understanding about Art as well as about people with disabilities in general. Since her team serves a broad section of the American public, through its programs and publications, she realizes that she may not be alone and that the unit, not to mention the broader organization, could benefit from a more proactive approach to people with disabilities. She thinks about reframing the situation with Art into a broader, team goal aimed at her employees and the public. She'd like Art to play a key role in this effort, but she's worried about whether that would be typecasting him in a way he does not want. So she contacts Ed, an executive coach she used in her last job, and asks his help in deciding how to approach Art respectfully and productively. All this takes just a few hours, and then she asks Art if she might talk with him in the morning.

A second way to foster conversation around differences is through storytelling. Storytelling is how kids bond at school or summer camp and traditionally how elders bond with and instruct the young in their families and communities around the dinner table or at play. It can also be a powerful, if indirect, approach to honoring and building on an organizational team's diversity.

At the Federal Executive Institute, each executive entering the Leadership for a Democratic Society (LDS) program joins a facilitated small team of leaders from various agencies. Within the first several days of the program, after spending time on a series of self-reflective questions, each executive relates his or her personal leadership journey to the other members of the team. One of the most powerful components of this process is sharing a time when the individual felt different. This exercise creates mutual understanding, enhanced respect, and team bonding. It also indirectly reprograms us to stand back, listen, observe, and test assumptions about how we perceive other individuals in our teams and community against the reality of their story. Each individual has a story, and making the time and space to hear those stories creates an appreciation for the diversity that frequently leads these teams to bond and support each other long after they leave the program. For example, hearing of the abject poverty in which a colleague was raised, and the obstacles overcome, breaks down barriers and builds understanding. In a similar way, learning that a naturalized U.S. citizen born in China, a brilliant and strong female leader, experienced neighbors drowning girl babies in order to have a chance to have a male child forever changes the team's perception and appreciation of that person's life journey and leadership style. Storytelling in this fashion forges strong bonds of trust.

Another approach is to encourage individuals to use public records from federal, state, and local sources to explore their own place in the American story and then to share their journey with others. The National Archives and Records Administration[47] is a useful source for individual, family, and community records, and those from outside the United States can often access comparable sources for records research. This allows people to gently move beyond the surface of stereotype and into the richness of each individual's background. Individuals can research themselves, their families—by birth or adoption, their communities, towns, etc. This exploration typically leads to increased self-awareness and to an appreciation of how we, as Americans, are uniquely connected.

Discussion groups can be created using formal or informal meetings, and with the creation of simple norms, powerful and productive interactions can occur. Mysteries are solved, questions answered, a sense of belonging occurs, and a connection to the American Dream and the national journey is strengthened. Storytelling based on different experiences of shared history is being used in organizations and groups throughout the world for conciliation and to strengthen relationships in diverse groups.

A diversity "GPS"

At the beginning of this chapter, we focused on Bob's effort to lead a diversity and inclusion effort that could live up to the values and promise of the diversity opportunity. We suggested that he could use a Diversity GPS system to help guide him. Such a system helps the leader maintain constructive intention, stay the course and calibrate decisive, mission-relevant directions. Trusted leaders don't try to drive out or control diversity dilemmas and disturbances. They proactively and correctly respond to diversity and inclusion challenges. They may stumble and get punched or surprised, but they don't rest immobilized and lost. They navigate toward success.

Beginning with self-awareness, the heart of all leadership, a Diversity GPS should center on four key, interdependent concepts, as shown in Figure 7.1. A few case scenarios suggest the power of these four "I" concepts: identity, intelligence, impact, and innovation.

As you read the cases, think about how to apply each of the four "I" concepts:

- *Identity* amplifies self-direction, self-regard, and your continual answer to the leadership question: "Who am I now—really?"
- *Intelligence* is not about yesterday's knowledge, but tomorrow's applications of compelling perspectives and learning.
- *Impact* reminds us to look for real leverage and, relative to goals, to produce desired change. Impact literally means to hit with force or to move something.
- *Innovation* means to renew something through changing one's vantage points and perspectives as well as revamping critical techniques, resource supply lines, or tools.

Figure 7.1 The Diversity GPS

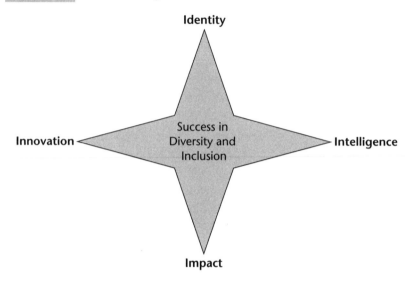

As you read this first case, think about what you might do if you were the leader:

You lead a team and join some team members for a routine lunch that suddenly becomes quite heated and polarizing. On the TV in the corner, a passionate commentator begins to describe and dismiss diversity/inclusion strategies as "liberal nonsense, left over from another era, that's going to take us down the road to socialism and outright reverse discrimination; diversity is nothing but code talk for affirmative action quotas; don't look at the 'numbers,' just let things change on their own; as "cream tends to rise to the top."

You notice that the mostly young, junior-level, race-, and gender-mixed team members are signaling visible approval for the commentator's position; particularly around the idea of diversity's "lowering standards," "being divisive," and fueling "reverse discrimination." One team member of similar age and cultural background as you is vigorously arguing against the commentator's view. This person almost calls one of his women colleagues a nasty slur, but he stops suddenly out of deference to you. Instead he grimaces, sighs "What's the use?" and skips out on lunch in frustration.

The trusted leader would not dismiss this debate as trivial, idle chatter. Nor would a leader instantly join one side of the argument versus the other. Piling on or heroic rescue won't address the fundamental challenge. Similarly, rushing to turn off the TV, scheduling "diversity awareness" training, lobbying for more ethnically diverse food options at lunch, or demanding that the team attend a Black History Month program won't address the core issue either.

The Diversity GPS suggests that you start with *identity* to work your way through the four interlocking concepts. This team doesn't clearly grasp where you stand on diversity as integral to mission success. Are you clear about diversity as essential, not optional? Some team members are certainly confused about diversity: diversity isn't divisive; stereotypic judgments and exclusions are. Diversity doesn't lower standards. Looking for the best global talent and treating people respectfully raises the performance bar for all individuals and the organization. The team, however, may not yet appreciate your diversity priorities. You must do more to strategically embed diversity and inclusion into the team's identity.

How might you proceed? Your diversity GPS starts with you, your life, and your self-portrait. As the Oracle at Delphi urged the ancient Greeks, "Know thyself." People will follow you, your clear sense of self, and your diversity-relevant behavioral example long before they develop a mature grasp of your philosophical tenets, command of details, and strategic plans. Take a 3x5 index card and write down your top three strategic priorities for your team and agency success. Identify how diversity, led well, advances each strategic priority. Think of two personal stories, core values, experiences, or defining moments that have most influenced your commitment and support for diversity. Write them down. You have to develop your own business case; you have to be authentic. Deliver the business case via your stories and personal "ah-ha's" and share it across several, different audiences and settings.

Here is a second short case. Once again, think about what you would do if you were the leader:

After a meaningful diversity awareness event, you've decided, as team leader, to spotlight "leadership, diversity challenges, and culture change" as a standing agenda item for selected performance accountability meetings. This represents a systems change. You've asked the group to practice some intelligent scanning prior to the next meeting in the interest of discovering some concrete, diversity, and inclusion strengths and gaps.

One staff person, an informal, junior level leader in the group, pulls you aside for a "permission to speak freely" session. Sue tells you that some staff are nervous about the pending diversity discussions because they don't want to "step on anyone's toes" or "offend any minorities." At the same time, they'd love to talk about how turf, cronyism, and double standards are crippling team effectiveness.

Also, they don't want to offend you by spotlighting your leadership approach. In fact, Sue reports, two team members are still stuck on the fact that less than six months ago, you branded diversity as headquarters' "ceremonial fluff" and the "flavor of the moment." Not to mention, they notice you "still tweet and multitask in staff meetings" and don't pay much respectful attention.

"With your senior leadership circle being all white men," Sue continues, "I thought I'd gently ask you to slow down a bit, because, frankly, we don't know what's got you so pumped up about it, and you aren't looking so credible and squeaky clean." Sue gulps and stares anxiously past your left shoulder, praying that she hasn't offended you or ruined her generally "favored status" with you.

Fearful reactions and resistance sometimes show when leaders announce and attempt diversity changes. Support is even harder to come by when leaders don't provide a credible rationale. Sue is simply the canary in the coal mine.

The team doesn't believe that you're really serious about establishing diversity and inclusion respect and practices. One "I" concept, *innovation* (adding the topic to each meeting agenda), won't carry the change. Busted for discrediting diversity, you also first need to own your past indiscretions. You don't have to be perfect, but you do have to be transparent, *intelligently* adaptive, and full of an honest rationale for why you and the team must change. Trusted leader alert: don't wait to be called on it. Develop in advance the business case and personal *identity* elevator talk. And obviously, marching into the future with a racially homogeneous senior leadership team is not the best positioning for credibility, constituent service, and dealing with impending Baby Boomer attrition.

So, digest Sue's feedback. Take out that 3x5 index card. Recall your best case for the diversity opportunity. Be prepared to show the team the *impact* that realizing that opportunity can have. Then, find an appropriate time to ask the disgruntled team members (many from groups formerly known as minorities) to share their concerns. Never shame the feedback "messenger" with defensive dismissal or labeling. Ask them to frame their concerns in a story about their deepest values, pressing obstacles, and the specific support they need.

As these minicases highlight, thoughtful application of these four key elements—identity, intelligence, impact, and innovation—can offer an important part of the "Diversity GPS" today's leaders need to navigate thorny diversity and inclusion issues. No resolution will be without discomfort; no solution will be perfect or permanent. But practiced regularly (along with the framework provided (page 233) for productive conversations) the diversity and inclusion compass in Figure 7.1 will promote positive change.

Toward e pluribus unum

Leaders in government have a constitutional responsibility to be faithful to the soaring phrase on the Great Seal of the United States, *e pluribus unum*—"out of many, one." A "more Perfect union" demands that we come together as a nation and that we honor and build on our differences. We can be diverse and united at the same time. In fact, we dare not be less.

Trusted leadership, then, will require comprehensive and continual self, institutional, and paradigm inspection. Like the rest of us, however, leaders are partially "blind." We are all cultural fish *and* agents of choice—thriving, surviving, thrashing about, swimming to priority targets here or there—seldom appreciating the influences of past and current paradigms, our personal power, our change opportunities, or just how culturally wet we are. To lead diversity, we must vigilantly know, grow, think and act deeply, plunging beneath the surface of things—the better to define what is right and to do it. We must move America's democratic and constitutional society adaptively and sustainably to places the nation otherwise would not go.

The DOD knows what is right to do and is doing it. The department wants to be "the gold standard" of the federal community for disability hiring and programs. Steven King, the Director of Disability Programs, has taken the lead. Leveraging DOD's commitment, he has implemented a series of activities to harness the diversity of those with disabilities.[48]

During National Disability Employment Awareness Month in October 2010, the DOD hosted the 30th annual Disability Awards Ceremony, celebrating the Department of Labor's chosen theme: "Talent Has No

Boundaries: Workforce Diversity INCLUDES Workers with Disabilities." The ceremony honored "outstanding work and service" by people with disabilities, with awards presented to "wounded warriors."

The DOD has also established programs, such as "Hiring Heroes," an initiative designed to expand employment opportunities to disabled veterans and conducted in tandem with other government agencies. Though the DOD already leads federal agencies in veteran hiring, regardless of disability status, it has a five-year plan to employ 36,000 people with disabilities, a goal aligned with the presidential directive to hire 100,000 disabled employees across federal agencies during that same time period. This is particularly important given the sharp rise in veterans returning with mental disabilities. Ongoing DOD efforts also include promoting voluntary disclosure of disability by current employees to more effectively gauge the efficacy of disability diversity initiatives.

Through these efforts (and the earlier commitment we saw from the DOD in its Military Diversity Leadership Commission), the seeds of a comprehensive approach to diversity and inclusion have been planted. Much work is ahead. Through such action to create innovation and mission victories, trusted leaders embody and demand active, identity-empowered, impact-seeking, intelligent, and innovative thinking. The United States is a democratic ideal that an amazing diversity of people have fought, struggled, and died to preserve. Thus, perhaps it's fitting that the DOD has taken such a leadership role.

Ideals, never guaranteed, must be sustained. Trusted leaders throughout government are needed now to see the diversity opportunity, capture it, and establish it more solidly within the American experience. Public-sector leaders especially must show that they dare to shape the new America. They must champion and leverage diversity for competitive advantage. They must sponsor equitable institutions and work ecologies (rules, roles, role models, rewards, symbols, etc.) that model opportunity and inclusion. The demands of government and governance in the twenty-first century and the needs and expectations of the American citizenry demand nothing less.

Tips for leadership success

- As with leadership in general, realizing the diversity opportunity first involves self-awareness and a dedication to learning. Understand your own identity, roots, insights, and blind spots about diversity. Also, dedicate time on your learning journey to understanding and building relationships with people who are different.

- Approach the diversity opportunity holistically. It's not just a matter of hiring some new people. As a leader you need a systemic approach that focuses inside the organization (recruitment, orientation, training, mentoring, rewards, team development, etc.) as well as outside (suppliers, outreach to the public, web presence, etc.).
- Listen. This means opening dialogue about differences and their impact on your work and the work of those you lead. This has an inside dimension. Foster diversity conversations among employees, groups of employees who share similar concerns, and about how to serve diverse segments of the public. It also has an outside dimension. Talk with the public about how you can be more responsive and effective in meeting the needs of diverse audiences.
- Benchmark best practices. A lot of excellent work is being done in government, in the private sector and elsewhere. Learn from it through reading, visits, conversations, conferences. You don't need to invent everything yourself.
- Establish concrete and measurable goals. Like everything else, what gets tracked gets attention and resources.
- Consider a diversity coach—someone with wide background in this area and special skills in diversity conversations. Such a resource can build your comfort level and your skills in approaching and dealing with tough issues that are almost certain to arise.

Resources for further learning

Books and Reports

Martin Davidson, *The End of Diversity as We Know It: Why Diversity Efforts Fail and How Leveraging Difference Can Succeed* (forthcoming 2011).

Susan Hannam and Bonni Yordi, "Engaging a Multi-Generational Workforce: Practical Advice for Government Managers" (2010). This research report covers six trends in our multigenerational workforce and offers practical advice to lead across this diversity.

Allan Johnson, *Privilege, Power, and Difference* (2005). This well-written book with practical examples shows how power and privilege exert themselves in our social systems and what we can do about the negative effects.

Robert Kegan and Lisa Lahey, *How the Way We Talk Can Change the Way We Work: 7 Languages for Transformation* (2002). The authors describe and present self-assessment exercises on four personal (internal) and three social languages that shape how we talk to ourselves and others and how we act to bring about change in the world.

Peter Senge, *The Fifth Discipline: The Art and Practice of the Learning Organization* (2006). This is the updated version of Senge's classic focus on the power of personal mastery, mental models, shared vision, and team learning in improving our understanding and ability to change organizations—and ourselves.

Harriett Washington, *Medical Apartheid: The Dark History of Medical Experimentation on Black Americans from Colonial Times to the Present* (2008). This book traces medical experimentation on blacks over the course of U.S. history. It is a powerful exposé (and lesson) in how our mental models and prejudices can allow us to violate core moral values.

Cornel West, *Race Matters* (2001). In eight powerful essays, West confronts key aspects of the black experience in America and American race relations.

"Best Practices in Achieving Workforce Diversity" (2000). U.S. Department of Commerce and National Partnership for Reinventing Government Benchmarking Study. While this report is from the Clinton administration and thus dated, it contains useful ideas of what is both possible and has been done, drawn from looking at more than 600 public- and private-sector organizations. Available at http://govinfo.library.unt.edu/npr/library/workforce-diversity.pdf.

"From Representation to Inclusion: Diversity Leadership for the 21st-Century Military" (2011). Final Report of the Military Leadership Diversity Commission. This detailed report of how to foster diversity and inclusion in the armed forces was a "predecisional" document as of the writing of this chapter. The final may well be available now. For this draft, go to http://mldc.whs.mil/download/documents/Draft%20Report/MLDC%20Final%20Report%20Predecisional%20Draft%2022DEC2010.pdf.

"Global Diversity and Inclusion" (2009). Society for Human Resource Management. This survey of forty-seven countries provides information on diversity and inclusion readiness and practices. The United States is ranked fourteenth on the Global Diversity Readiness Index, with a score of 61.5 (out of 100). Available at www.shrm.org/Research/SurveyFindings/Articles/Documents/Diversity_and_Inclusion_Report.pdf.

Web Resources

Leveraging Difference, http://leveragingdifference.com/. This is the website of Dr. Martin Davidson and includes books, news, and articles about his work and his weekly blog, "In My Opinion."

StoryCorps, www.storycorps.org. StoryCorps is an independent nonprofit whose mission is to provide Americans of all backgrounds and beliefs with the opportunity to record, share, and preserve their stories. The site shares the stories of others and offers guidance on how to record your own story.

There are many websites devoted to specific issues and programs for enhancing the inclusion of different groups. Rather than list them all, we offer a few examples.

Human Rights Campaign, www.hrc.org. The Human Rights Campaign (HRC) "represents a grassroots force of more than 750,000 members and supporters nationwide. As the largest national lesbian, gay, bisexual, and transgender civil rights organization, HRC envisions an America where LGBT people are ensured of their basic equal rights, and can be open, honest, and safe at home, at work and in the community." For the federal government organization dedicated to this topic, go to www.facebook.com/group.php?gid=300522658414.

Federally Employed Women, www.few.org. This is a private group whose aim is to represent the interests of women who work for the federal government and the District of Columbia.

National Association of Hispanic Federal Executives, www.nahfe.org/vacancies.php. The aim of this group is to move more Hispanics into the Senior Executive Service of the federal government.

NTL Institute, www.ntl.org. For more than sixty years, the NTL Institute has pioneered in the development of individuals and groups to respond effectively to issues of diversity and inclusion. It has individual training courses as well as a Diversity Leadership Certificate Program.

Notes

1. "From Representation to Inclusion: Diversity Leadership in the 21st Century Military," Final Report of the Military Leadership Diversity Commission (2011, predecisional draft), iv, at http://mldc.whs.mil.

2. It is important to note that the First Amendment prevented the national government from infringing on these rights. The states were not proscribed from doing so. It took the Fourteenth Amendment and court cases emerging from it to ensure these rights against state infringement.

3. James Madison makes this point forcefully in *Federalist* No. 51, when he says that: "It is of great importance in a republic not only to guard the society against the oppression of its rulers, but to guard one part of the society against the injustice of the other part.... If a majority is united by a common interest, the rights of the minority will be insecure."

4. U.S. Census Bureau, *American Community Survey Briefs: Place of Birth of the Foreign-Born Population,* at www.census.gov/prod/2010pubs/acsbr09–15.pdf.

5. Ibid.

6. U.S. Census Bureau, *American Community Survey, 2007.*

7. U.S. Census Bureau, *American Community Survey, 2009,* at http://factfinder.census .gov/servlet/ADPTable?_bm=y&-qr_name=ACS_2009_1YR_G00_DP2&-ds_ name=ACS_2009_1YR_G00_&-redoLog=true&-_caller=geoselect&-geo_id=01000US&- parsed=true&-format=&-_lang=en.

8. U.S. Census Bureau, *American Community Survey, 2009,* at http://factfinder.census. gov/servlet/DTTable?_bm=y&-geo_id=01000US&-ds_name=ACS_2009_5YR_G00_&-_ lang=en&-redoLog=false&-format=&-mt_name=ACS_2009_5YR_G2000_B04003&- CONTEXT=dt.

9. U.S. Census Bureau, at www.census.gov/population/www/projections/summary tables.html.

10. Sum et al. (2002). Immigrant workers and the great American job machine: the contributions of new foreign immigration to national and regional labor force growth in the 1990s.

11. Khatiwada, Sum, and Barnacle (2006).

12. U.S. Census Bureau, U.S. Census 2010, at www.census.gov/prod/cen2010/briefs/ c2010br-02.pdf.

13. U.S. Census Bureau, *American Community Survey: We the People of Arab Ancestry in the United States Special Report, 2005,* at www.census.gov/prod/2005pubs/censr-21.pdf; U.S. Census Bureau, *American Community Survey, 2009.*

14. U.S. Census Bureau, U.S. Census 2010, at www.census.gov/prod/cen2010/briefs/ c2010br-02.pdf.

15. U.S. Census Bureau, *American Community Survey, 2006.*

16. U.S. Census Bureau, *U.S. Census Bureau Current Population Reports, 2009;* P25– 1130, at www.census.gov/prod/1/pop/p25–1130.pdf.

17. U.S. Census Bureau, *Current Population Reports,* P25–1138, at www.census.gov/ prod/2010pubs/p25–1138.pdf.

18. "From Vets to the Net: Leading Across Generations" FEI presentation by Pete Ronayne and Dana Brower.

19. National Center for Education Statistics, Table A-8-1. Number and percentage distribution of actual and projected post baccalaureate enrollment in degree-granting

institutions, by sex, attendance status, and control of institution: Fall 1976–2019, 2008, at http://nces.ed.gov/programs/coe/2010/section1/table-gre-1.asp.

20. National Center for Education Statistics, Table A-42.1. Number of master's, doctoral, and first-professional degrees awarded by degree-granting institutions, percentage of total, number, and percentage awarded to females, and percent change, by selected fields of study: Academic years 1997–1998 and 2007–2008, at http://nces.ed.gov/programs/coe/2010/section5/table-gfs-1.asp.

21. U.S. Census Bureau.

22. Figure below generated using data from the National Science Foundation S&E Degrees: 1996–2006 Detailed Statistical Tables, NSF 08–321, October 2008, at www.nsf.gov/statistics/nsf08321/pdf/nsf08321.pdf.

23. U.S. Bureau of Labor Statistics, 2009.

24. "Results of Menendez's Major Fortune 500 Diversity Survey: Representation of Women and Minorities on Corporate Boards Still Lags Far Behind National Population," August 4, 2010, at http://menendex.senate.gov.

25. *Women in America: Indicators of Social and Economic Well-Being*, March 2011, 32. Full report available at http://kezi.com/files/Women_in_America.pdf.

26. U.S. Census Bureau, *Population Profile, 2005*; U.S. Census Bureau, *Fertility of American Women Report, 2008*, at www.census.gov/prod/2010pubs/p20–563.pdf. U.S. Census Bureau, Population Profile, 2005.

27. U.S. Census Bureau, *Living Arrangements*, at www.census.gov/population/www/socdemo/hh-fam.html.

28. U.S. Census Bureau, *American Community Survey, 2006*.

29. U.S. Census Bureau, *Americans with Disabilities Report, 2005*, at www.census.gov/prod/2008pubs/p70–117.pdf.

30. Pew Research Center, *Pew Forum on Religion and Public Life, 2007*.

31. U.S. Census Bureau, *Statistical Abstract of the United States: 2011*, at http://search.census.gov/search?q=religion+projection&filter=0&entqr=0&output=xml_no_dtd&ud=1&client=subsite&proxystylesheet=subsite&hq=inurl%3Awww.census.gov%2Fhhes%2Fwww%2Fdisability&subtitle=hhes-disability&sort=date%3AD%3AL%3Ad1&oe=UTF-8&ie=UTF-8.

32. Equal Employment Opportunity Commission, 2009, at www.eeoc.gov/eeoc/statistics/enforcement/religion.cfm.

33. U.S. Census Bureau, *American Community Survey, 2009*.

34. U.S. Census Bureau, *Married and Unmarried-Partner Households by Metropolitan Residence Status: 2000*, at www.census.gov/prod/2003pubs/censr-5.pdf; U.S. Census Bureau, *American Community Survey, 2006*.

35. DiversityInc.com, 2001.

36. CBSNews.com, May 26, 2009.

37. Human Rights Campaign, 2009 www.hrc.org/issues/workplace/benefits/11612.htm.

38. "104 Retired Military Brass Against 'Don't Ask, Don't Tell,'" at www.cnn.com/2008/POLITICS/11/17/dont.ask.dont.tell.

39. See www.opm.gov/feddata/factbook/2007/2007FACTBOOK.pdf 44.

40. 2009 Federal Equal Employment Opportunity Report, U.S. Office of Personnel Management, Washington, D.C.

41. While the focus in the discussion of the Leading Diversity Model is on the government organization and how to realize the diversity opportunity within it, the model applies conceptually to how government leads in the broader society as well.

42. See http://bestplacestowork.org/BPTW/rankings/demographics/sub/diversity.

43. Davidson (2010).

44. U.S. Government Accountability Office (2007).

45. Ely, Meyerson, and Davidson (2006), 78–87.

46. Ibid., 79.

47. See www.nara.gov.

48. This description is drawn from two sources: (1) OEDP news release. "U.S. Labor Department Office of Disability Employment Policy Announces National Disability Employment Awareness Month Theme." May 13, 2010; www.dol.gov/opa/media/press/odep/ODEP20100630.htm, and Federal News Radio (1500 AM). "DoD celebrates 'Talent Has No Boundaries'." Interview with Stephen M. King, at www.federalnewsradio.com/?sid=2191279&nid=15.

8 Collaborating across organizational boundaries

RUSS LINDEN, PRINCIPAL, RUSS LINDEN & ASSOCIATES

Government organizations rarely succeed on their own, but building effective collaborative relationships with other organizations is not easy. For collaboration to thrive, there must be a shared purpose; a desire to collaborate; the involvement of the appropriate people; an open, credible process; champions for the effort; and open and trusting relationships among the principals involved. These provide the foundation for success. Other essential components are demonstrating the stakes involved, developing a constituency, and using collaborative leadership skills. Government leaders who have mastered these strategies may still find barriers to success, such as a lack of enthusiasm by some of the principals; a good start that stalls; a history of distrust of others and/or a tendency to focus on one's organization and needs instead of seeing things from a broader perspective; and those participants who just won't "play well with others" or even refuse to join the effort. All of these potential problems can be anticipated and addressed.

COLLABORATION—working across internal and external organizational boundaries—is one of the most critical challenges facing government in the twenty-first century. The reason is that most of the nation's major problems—immigration, global warming, pandemics, health care, terrorism—are complex by nature and cannot be solved by one unit, one function, or one technical area of expertise. Indeed, as public administration scholar Donald Kettl writes, "It is virtually impossible to find any public program that matters in which a single government organization's jurisdiction can capture the features that determine success."[1]

Complex problems can be addressed effectively only when people from different disciplines and different functions work together to deal with them. And when such collaboration occurs, the results can be truly impressive. Consider the following two examples.

The Integrated Air Defense System (IADS) is a virtual team from intelligence, defense, and related agencies that have found ways to collaborate at both the analyst and manager levels. It includes analysts from different agencies who use technology to share information and conduct analysis on the air defense systems of countries that pose threats to the United States. The IADS team has three types of customers: warfighters, policymakers (Congress, the Office of the Secretary of Defense, the Air Force chief of staff), and the acquisition community.

IADS was created in 1995. In the aftermath of the Gulf War, the need for more integrated analysis had become apparent. Prior to IADS, the different intelligence agencies produced their own independent reports on particular aspects of other countries' air defense systems. One agency would report on a country's early warning radar, another would analyze its surface-to-air missiles, but no agency could describe how the country's air defense worked as a system. As one analyst put it, "the customer got parts of a jigsaw puzzle and had to put the pieces together."

Intelligence analysts and managers discussed the problem and agreed on the need for an integrated approach to studying air defense systems. Two well-respected intel managers, Phil Davis and Phil Lathrop, spent months working on the formation of a virtual team of analysts from across the community. Some intelligence agency leaders felt threatened; this new program wouldn't belong to any one agency, and it would require new resources. Davis briefed Joan Dempsey, then the deputy director of the Defense Intelligence Agency. She agreed that an integrated approach was needed, and she suggested a two-part structure to address the agency leaders' concerns. In addition to an Analyst Group (which would perform the studies on other countries' air defenses), there would be a Coordinating Group made up of managers from the agencies providing analysts. The Coordinating Group would identify the priority countries for the analysts to study and identify analysts to work on each task. The agency directors approved the structure. The IADS planners spent many more months detailing the concept, briefing agency leaders and showing great sensitivity to the politics and personalities involved, and the new IADS program was launched.

The two-part structure has worked well. Twice a year the Coordinating Group identifies the highest-priority countries for analysis, based on the perceived threat a country poses and on customer requirements. The managers on the Coordinating Group then commit their agencies and their appropriate analysts to those priorities. The actual studies are done by those in the Analyst Group. They create a schedule for producing reports, and the analysts needed for each report begin their work with a face-to-face meeting. After that, 90 percent of their communications is achieved via technology.

By all accounts, IADS has been a clear success, providing its customers with the kind of timely, integrated reports on threats to the nation that they require. One of its successes occurred in the fall of 2001. Immediately following the 9/11 attacks, IADS analysts went to work on an analysis of Afghanistan's air defenses. Within just three days the group produced a product that was ready for the warfighters and that was used in the U.S. invasion of Afghanistan several weeks later. It was an incredible challenge; the analysts had to produce a huge amount of work, in very little time. They started with virtually no information on the Afghan air defense capabilities. And they had to get it right.

Several customers remarked on the group's performance after 9/11. As one of the IADS analysts noted, "There's no way we could have produced a quality product so quickly before IADS. It was only possible because of the years of experience working together on the Analyst Group and the existing structure to pull in whatever resources we needed. Sure, Afghanistan didn't possess an integrated air defense system. But it had a lot of ways to shoot aircraft down. And its assets were not organized in any obvious way, which actually made it harder to analyze.... Our intelligence agencies needed a huge amount of data and analysis, immediately." And IADS delivered it.

Another example of collaboration is the justice information system begun by Gov. Tom Ridge of Pennsylvania. In 1996, Ridge was in his second year as governor, and he wanted to make good on a key campaign promise to make a major reduction in crime. He believed that information sharing in the law enforcement community could make a significant difference in reducing crime, but that information was not being shared quickly or easily among the sixteen state agencies involved in law enforcement. Ridge decided it was time to act.

His administration made available $11 million to design the justice information network (soon dubbed JNET). Ridge formed a steering committee made up of leaders of the sixteen agencies. It met with a contractor and began designing the new system. The JNET Lab was soon in place, and by 1998 it had created a pilot system that was used by selected units. By 1999 the first phase of JNET was completed, and all sixteen agencies were using it.

JNET quickly proved to be a big success. Using open Internet and web technologies to link agencies using a common web browser, JNET helps federal, state, and local officials access each other's files. Through JNET, these agencies can:

- Access offender information.
- Access digital mug shots.
- Use secure e-mail.
- Access driver's license information.
- Access searchable online reference libraries.
- Use various criminal justice websites not available to the public.
- Exchange photo images.

None of these functions was possible prior to JNET. Before, it took several days to obtain hard copies of photos, suspects' criminal histories, and outstanding warrants. And sometimes the information simply was not shared at all. This information is now available to JNET members in real time. By helping law enforcement agencies share information and collaborate, JNET has helped law enforcement agencies get a number of criminals off the streets. It is making a difference in providing public safety services for Pennsylvanians.[2]

IADS and JNET are stories about successful collaboration. These short summaries make collaboration sound fairly straightforward. In fact, both projects had to overcome huge obstacles: middle managers who were threatened by a perceived loss of power, huge egos and turf concerns, and tensions between headquarters and the field, to name just a few. But the stories also reflect three common approaches to collaboration.

Three general paths to collaboration

> A crisis is a terrible thing to waste.
>
> —*Paul Romer*

Informal, bottom-up. Collaboration often starts informally, at the working level where employees are faced with important demands but don't have the knowledge and resources necessary to meet those demands by themselves (as happened with IADS). As the collaboration proves mutually beneficial, it sometimes expands into more formalized agreements.

Formal, top-down. A more formal, top-down path also can be used. When an important need arises that one unit cannot meet on its own, the leaders sometimes form a coalition, create a governance structure and charter the effort, find a senior champion, develop a game plan, and start producing results (the JNET story).

Crisis. And sometimes a crisis spurs collaboration. The need is immediate and urgent (and often public and visible). No one party can fully meet the need; only a collaborative approach will work. That was the story at the Pentagon immediately after the 9/11 attacks. The collaboration that occurred during the weeks that followed was extraordinary. A triggering event in the JNET story was the death of a police officer. While Ridge was campaigning for governor in 1994, the officer was killed by a man who had been arrested several times using at least six aliases. Just five days before the shooting, the man was picked up on a parole violation but was then let out of jail. The lack of a comprehensive information system allowed his release, and the resulting tragedy provided some of the urgency that led to JNET. IADS also resulted from the need for comprehensive and integrated information; that need was made crystal clear during the Gulf War.

Each of these three approaches can produce quality services and products for the customers, and each can fail to produce such benefits. Crises don't always produce collaboration; just ask the survivors of Hurricane Katrina. But what ultimately determines if such efforts succeed?

Major collaboration drivers

Certain factors are almost always present when collaboration succeeds. I think of these factors as the basics of collaboration: necessary (but not sufficient) for it to thrive. There are six basics, and each was present in the two stories introducing this chapter:

1. *A specific, shared purpose that the parties want to meet and cannot achieve on their own.* The law enforcement agencies in Pennsylvania had a great need to exchange accurate, real-time information, but had no mechanism to do so prior to JNET. And prior to IADS, the intelligence community

agencies were clearly unable to meet the need for analysis of other countries' air defense systems, if they continued working alone.

2. *A desire by the parties to meet now and a willingness to contribute something (people, resources) to the effort.* Collaboration rarely works unless the agencies or units at the table place a priority on the shared purpose. Governor Ridge's commitment to public safety (plus the officer's murder) made JNET a high priority in Pennsylvania.

3. *Appropriate people at the table.* This task is often one of the trickiest. It is not always obvious who the appropriate people are. Collaboration scholar David Chrislip offers a useful method for identifying the necessary people on a collaborative effort. He asks who has *influence* on the particular issue, and who has a *stake* in it? I have revised his formula a bit and offer it in graphic form (see Figure 8.1).

The horizontal dimension in Figure 8.1 identifies those who have something to contribute to the initiative—influence, expertise on the issue, or both. The vertical dimension addresses those who have a stake in the issue. Starting in the upper-right quadrant: those with something to contribute, and with a high stake in the issue, are clearly important players (and often champions for the effort) and must be at the table. Just as obvious, perhaps, are those in the lower-left quadrant; they have little if anything to

Figure 8.1 **A tool for identifying stakeholders**

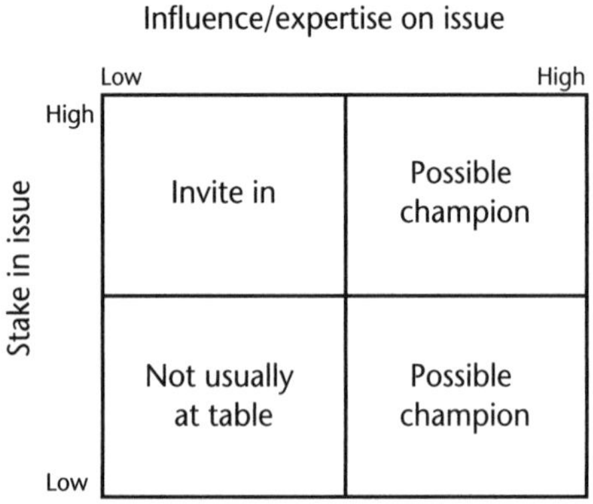

Influence/expertise on issue

	Low	High
High (Stake in issue)	Invite in	Possible champion
Low (Stake in issue)	Not usually at table	Possible champion

Source: Adapted from *The Collaborative Leadership Fieldbook* by David Chrislip (San Francisco: Jossey-Bass, an imprint of John Wiley & Sons, 2002), 75.

contribute, and are not affected by the initiative. They may not need to be present.

In the lower-right quadrant are those with much to offer, but with little at stake. They sometimes are champions for the effort, because they often have high credibility (because they have little at stake, they can be impartial in dealing with conflicts). Those in this lower-right quadrant could include people in administrative offices: finance, budget, policy shops, information technology (IT) units, office of general counsel.

Finally, those with little to offer but with a big stake in the issue are in the upper left. They must be invited in because they do not have much clout. These could include customers, partner agencies, and units with few resources.

JNET and IADS are both excellent examples of bringing the appropriate people to the table. Unlike many collaborative projects, JNET and IADS actually involve two tables, two key groups that manage the initiative. In addition to a steering group of civil servants from each of the sixteen law enforcement agencies that helped create the actual network, JNET had an executive council made up of political appointees from these agencies, which dealt with high-level policy issues and provided support for the effort. And the decision to create a Coordinating Group of intelligence agency managers was one of the keys to IADS's success. Without this group, it's unlikely that IADS would have seen the light of day given the highly competitive nature of the intelligence community.

4. *An open, credible process for working together.* Once the right people are meeting, how well or poorly will they work together? Collaboration, again, is about working across boundaries. People from different organizations and cultures may have very different styles of problem solving. They may not know each other at the outset and do not have a basis of trust. It is important that they feel a primary allegiance to their home office or agency, but how to get them working well together? An open, credible process is necessary to overcome these and other hurdles. Such a process includes agreed-upon ground rules, a skillful convener, transparency (agreement to make important decisions at the table), clear roles, a clear plan with timelines and measures, and joint ownership of the process.

It takes considerable patience at the outset and a smart convener or facilitator to develop a credible and open process.

5. *A champion or champions for the effort.* By champion, I mean someone who takes formal or informal leadership for the initiative, who has the

credibility and clout to help it succeed. In large, complex collaborations, there are often two levels of champion—a senior champion (Governor Ridge for JNET, Joan Dempsey for IADS) and a working-level champion (such as a manager working on the JNET steering committee or the IADS Coordinating Group). Champions are critical in helping the group overcome the myriad hurdles involved. I have seen few significant collaborative efforts succeed without the focus and energy of a committed champion.

The most effective champions are passionate about the issue being addressed, have good political and people skills, and know how to get others involved, so that the champion does not seem to be pushing her own perspective all the time. Dealing with power issues and finding senior level support are critical to most collaborative initiatives.

> When it comes to collaboration, it's all about trust.
>
> —*Tom Martin, Captain, Virginia State Police (Ret.)*

6. *Forming open, trusting relationships among the principals.* "We had to put our money on the table, and our hands behind our backs!" That is how one senior manager described the efforts of a coalition of agencies trying to collaborate on early childhood issues. It took a lot of trust, which was not easy to form given the parties' history of competing for resources.

Trust is almost always an important factor in successful public-sector collaboration (indeed, it is the theme of this entire book). Harvard Business School professor Rosabeth Moss Kanter found the same in her research on private-sector alliances around the world. After conducting more than five hundred interviews, she concluded that positive business alliances cannot be controlled by formal systems. Rather, they need a "dense web of interpersonal connections."

When trust exists, the other collaboration basics become easier to establish. People can be candid about their offices' interests in the initiative, about their level of commitment to it, and about what's on the table and what's not. When trusting relationships do not exist, chances for success are low. Many U.S. managers have been surprised by how critical it is to form trusting relationships when working overseas. Allen Hard, former faculty member at the Federal Executive Institute, consults frequently in Southeast Asia. As Hard notes, "in these countries, the unspoken rule is 'relationships before work.'" Successful collaborative leaders understand this, and they look for opportunities to build trust among current and potential partners.

Jay Gregorius, a Drug Enforcement Administration official, has had great success forming collaborative relationships in the law enforcement community. As Jay sees it, "we're all in the relationships business" (see Box 8.1). If we

---

Box 8.1   Trust and the search for the D.C. sniper

It was October 20, 2002, and the D.C. sniper was still at large, creating fear among millions of people in Maryland, the District of Columbia, and northern and central Virginia. Fourteen people had been killed, and law enforcement agencies in dozens of jurisdictions were working overtime to find the killer or killers. Jay Gregorius, assistant special agent in charge of the Drug Enforcement Administration's (DEA) training academy, and others at the academy were looking for a way to help. Tracking down snipers is not part of the DEA mission, but Jay is a big picture guy, and he is passionate about the importance of relationships and trust in law enforcement. So he called the sheriff of Stafford County, a rural county not far from the scenes of some of the attacks.

"I didn't know the sheriff at the time," Jay recalled, "but I wanted to help. I figured he must be stretched to the limit because of the fear and media exposure given to the sniper. Besides, I live in his county. So I called him, explained that I supervise several agents, that we're trained law enforcement officers, we carry guns, and that we'd do anything at all that would help him. He wasn't used to getting this kind of call, and wasn't sure what we could do. But he told me that his deputies were spending a lot of time sitting at freeway exits off I-95, and that when the next attack came (if it was along the I-95 corridor), he'd close off every exit ramp and his deputies would have to inspect every vehicle.

"I told him that our agents could help with that task. In fact, our agents would do whatever he needed, whenever he needed them (including evenings and weekends). Further, I explained that the DEA agents would be taking orders from him and his deputies; they would be in charge, we'd be there in a support role. Well, local government officials don't usually hear that from the feds, but he really appreciated the offer; he accepted it; and the next day our agents were at the freeway exits, working with the sheriff's deputies.

"The snipers were caught a few days later, so this didn't go on too long. But my agents (who weren't excited about this initially) really liked working with the sheriff's deputies. The sheriff, of course, was delighted. Since that time, he and I have a great relationship. He'd do anything for me, and vice versa. That's how we run our office, and that's one way we build relationships."*

---

*Author's conversation with Jay Gregorius, September 2005.

understand that, we'll continually scan the environment and be aware of opportunities to partner with and help others. One of the unusual aspects of Jay's story is that he found a way to form a relationship and start building trust in the middle of a crisis. People in the emergency management world believe that whenever possible, the time to establish relationships is *before* you have to work together.

> You don't want to meet someone for the first time while you're standing around in the rubble," says Jarrod Bernstein, a spokesperson for the NYC Office of Emergency Management. "You want to meet them during drills and exercises." New York, says Bernstein, has very tight relationships with state and federal officials in a variety of agencies. "They're involved in all our planning and all our drills. They have a seat at all the tabletop exercises we do.[3]

Bernstein's insight is important: meetings and training sessions provide better opportunities for establishing trusting relationships than when you are "in the rubble." But Gregorius's insight is also powerful. It is best captured by Stanford University economist Paul Romer's remark quoted above: a crisis is a terrible thing to waste.[4] Collaborative leaders would prefer to avoid crises, but they understand that crises create opportunities— resources become available, rigid rules and regulations are relaxed, and leaders are focused on the problem.

Veterans of successful collaborative efforts report a number of ways they have established trust with individuals trying to collaborate:

- Value others' input; use it whenever possible.
- Model openness; use self-disclosure and "I messages."
- Set aside time to work on relationship building (meals, trips together, off-sites, etc.).
- Use "careful listening" to learn underlying interests; seek common ground.
- Share accurate information, both requested and not.
- Engage in joint training (among some of the units trying to collaborate), which helps form bonds across agency boundaries.
- Take on small, work-related projects together (to build bridges and help people learn others' skills, knowledge, and interests).

- Make good on commitments.
- Earn trust by sharing credit, keeping confidences, and being trustworthy.

Going beyond the basics

The six factors discussed above form a strong foundation for successful collaboration, but more is usually required to ensure success. Other strategies that promote successful collaboration include demonstrating the high stakes involved, developing a constituency for the initiative, and effective use of collaborative leadership skills.

Demonstrating the high stakes involved in the initiative

As noted at the start of this chapter, crises provide one of the three common paths to collaboration. It is no surprise that such conditions usually bring out excellent performance. During a crisis the priorities are clear, the goal is vivid, the consequences of getting it wrong are high, and the situation is often very visible to others.

To get some of the collaboration basics in place—in particular, having the appropriate people at the table—collaborative leaders must be clear about the high stakes involved in the initiative: the payoff to customers, the impact on the safety of the community, the need to deal with major budget cuts, and so forth. The IADS leaders had no difficulty demonstrating the stakes involved in producing integrated analyses for the warfighters and policymakers who depended on them, and that helped them get the right people involved in doing their studies.

The point is not to create false emergencies; most of us have experienced them, and they only lead to cynicism. Rather, it is about clarifying for the people at the table what the real stakes are, why the stakes are high, and why this initiative will have such a huge impact if it is done right (or wrong).

The following are examples of how to demonstrate the high stakes of an initiative:

- Bring in customers to meet with those trying to collaborate. Hearing the voice of the customer can be a strong motivator for change and action.

- Look for ways to link the initiative to the agenda of a senior leader. When leaders see how a collaborative effort can further their work (or address a problem that has been consuming their time), they sometimes become strong champions for the effort.
- Seek resources for the initiative. Many people are more concerned about what they might lose in a proposed collaboration than its benefits. When collaborative leaders line up funding for the project, as Tom Ridge did for JNET, it sends at least two messages: (1) the leadership is doing its homework and has gotten others to invest in the project; and (2) there may be some tangible rewards for getting involved. And that brings us to the WIIFM question: What's in it for me?
- Give the principals at the table an answer to the WIIFM question. Whether it is asked out loud or not, those invited to collaborate certainly will be asking themselves the question. How do they justify spending this time; what is the payoff for doing so? Whether this is a selfish question or not, it is a supremely human one that has to be answered candidly (see Box 8.2).

Developing a constituency for the initiative

One of the many concerns that confronted the JNET leaders when they started working on their information system was that the next governor might torpedo the effort. Two previous efforts to create an information sharing network for Pennsylvania's law enforcement community had failed. Even if they got JNET up and running, what would guarantee that the next governor would support it?

The next governor (who happened to be of the other political party, which created even greater concerns) gave JNET full support. So did the state legislature. They did so for many reasons: it was fully operational, it was producing results, and all the agency heads supported it. They also backed it because JNET had developed a strong constituency at the local government level. As JNET grew, it was shared with the counties in the state. Many of the counties started sharing the system at no cost with the small towns and townships within their borders. JNET gave these county and local agencies valuable data via a system none of them could have built for themselves. The local elected officials became strong JNET supporters and told their state legislators how important it was to continue funding it.

Box 8.2 Making the WIIFM question clear

Here's how Brian Swann, an Alcohol, Tobacco, and Firearms agent, answered the WIIFM—what's in it for me?—question. He managed to demonstrate both the stakes involved and the payoff for working on the initiative. He leads a joint task force that is working to reduce violent crime in a large eastern city. Task force membership is a full-time commitment. The task force works effectively only if it includes federal, state, and local law enforcement officers, but Swann was having a hard time getting the local police chief to commit talented officers for the task force. He said:

> Law enforcement folks are often competitive and territorial—they'll fight for money, for more personnel, etc. Why should the police chief give me his best people? What's in it for him to do that? So I talked with the police chief about our task force's need to have one officer from each precinct in his city's high crime areas. I promised the chief, "you give me good, young, aggressive people for two years, and I'll give you back officers ready to be detectives. I'll train them, they'll get great experience and lots of support. And when you get them back, they'll be able to handle the toughest, most complex cases." That answered the "what's in it for me?" question, and we received very good people from that PD.*

*Author's personal communication with Brian Swann, ATF team leader, February 2006.

Any new governor trying to radically change JNET would have faced fierce resistance.

By constituency, I mean a group of people or organizations that are materially benefiting from the initiative and have a vested interest in its success. Constituents of a collaborative project can include customers, senior leaders, special interest groups, state and local agencies, and private-sector firms. The key is to identify them, involve them, listen and use their ideas when possible, and show them how your work can help them.

The politics of collaboration can be tricky. Some agencies have stakeholders that do not like collaboration. Think about it: If you lead a special interest group that has successfully lobbied Congress to create a certain program, once that program is up and running, you want the people managing it to succeed. You also want them to be accountable. And you want the funding to remain intact. If someone suggests that the program office work closely with other offices, your reactions might well be negative—where is the accountability if it is spread over several units? What happens to the program office's line item in the budget? Is collaboration just the first step toward a merger?

In addition, collaboration is not a positive word for everyone (few people become labor union leaders because they promise to collaborate with management!). Collaborative leaders therefore must develop the ability to do what the great public administration theorist Harlan Cleveland suggested years ago: *they must learn how to think politically, without becoming political.*[5] And that includes paying close attention to developing strong constituencies for the collaborative effort.

Using collaborative leadership skills

> Nothing starts without men; nothing lasts without institutions.
>
> —*Jean Monnet*

Jean Monnet, an early champion of the European Union, understood that most successful collaborations begin with individuals, men and women who are strongly committed to a shared goal and use their enthusiasm and persistence to gain support. Over time, these individuals seek to institutionalize their accomplishments, so that the project is not overly dependent on inspired people. But, at the start, it usually does take inspired people.

What do we know about those who effectively lead collaborative efforts? David Chrislip offers an important insight. Collaborative leaders, he writes, "lead as a peer, not as a superior."[6] That is, they typically do not have the formal authority to demand action; they are often at the same pay grade as the others at the table. Collaborative leaders rely on informal skills and tools—the arts of persuasion, negotiation, consensus building, personal appeal, and skillful listening—to help a group find common ground and move toward their goal. Collaborative leadership is not the same as traditional hierarchical leadership. We will always need good hierarchical leaders, but there was no way that Mike Geraci, a very collaborative leader at the Department of Transportation, would have successfully implemented his creative idea for reducing crime and traffic accidents by using top-down leadership (see Box 8.3).

Box 8.3 Collaborative leadership

Mike Geraci is an unusual civil servant. A former police chief with more than thirty years' experience in law enforcement, he long ago developed a strong interest in traffic safety and its impact on overall public welfare (which is not that typical in law enforcement). He notes that "from 9/11/2001 to 2010, we had approximately 100,000 fatalities due to crime in the United States. During the same period, we had over 300,000 deaths on the highways! Clearly both crime and traffic contribute to the social harm in our communities and both deserve the development and implementation of effective counter-measure strategies by law enforcement."

In addition to his strong interest in traffic issues, Mike is a natural collaborator. In 2007, when he came to the National Highway Traffic Safety Administration (NHTSA) to head up the Office of Safety Programs, he quickly sought partners who shared his dual interest in traffic and crime. He assigned NHTSA staff member Earl Hardy, a former North Carolina trooper, to take the concept and develop a formal strategy for the program.

They called it Data Driven Approaches to Crime and Traffic Safety (DDACTS). The concept was simple (if counterintuitive): highly visible traffic enforcement, at the right place and at the right times and most importantly for the right reasons, will have a deterrent effect and may lower traffic crashes and reduce crimes simultaneously. The goal of DDACTS is to reduce the incidence of crime, crashes, and traffic violations in communities across the country.

Geraci and Hardy then met with Department of Justice (DOJ) officials, who wholeheartedly supported the data-driven concept. Two DOJ agencies, the Bureau of Justice Assistance and National Institute of Justice, agreed to become equal DDACTS partners. Soon, seven DDACTS pilot project sites were underway.

This is how DDACTS works. A local law enforcement agency analyzes where and when certain crimes occur, and when and where traffic crashes occur. The department creates geo-maps with both sets of data and looks for the overlaps—the "hotspots" in the community where (and when) both criminal activity and traffic crashes occur. Then they devise their strategies and countermeasures to address the

Box 8.3 *(Continued)*

problems. Focusing on the traffic data results in the deployment of high-visibility traffic enforcement at the hot spot areas during the hours of greatest need. For example, Baltimore County (one of the pilots) can now deploy its officers on the corridors that impaired drivers use most often, during the days and times when they are using those roads.

The results in the DDACTS pilot communities are very impressive: in Nashville, violent crime dropped 12.5 percent and fatal crashes declined 15.6 percent in the target areas since using the data-driven approach. Baltimore County saw a 16.6 percent reduction in burglaries and a decline in robberies of 33.5 percent in the target areas. Most of the other pilot communities saw similar reductions.

When Geraci talks with local law enforcement leaders about DDACTS, it's a true partnership. Rather than the all-too-common federal approach of "here's the program, here are the requirements, we'll give you money if you follow our procedures, and we'll be monitoring," Geraci invites local officials to customize the approach to their circumstances. DDACTS is a partnership that meets all of the stakeholders' needs. And Geraci's approach—from concept and marketing the idea to implementation and giving others the credit—is all about collaborative leadership.

Challenges to collaboration

At this point, a reasonable response might be "Yes, but. . . ." Indeed, the hurdles to collaboration are numerous, and many issues and challenges arise. Here are some of the more difficult ones and different ways to address them.

Lack of enthusiasm or commitment by some of the principals

The lack of commitment is a common concern. It often occurs when the initiative is led by one agency or office that has a huge stake in it and others are asked (or told) to help out. It also occurs when members of the collaborative group worry that the initiative seems to be a threat to one of their agency's interests. Such people attend the meetings primarily to play defense and to protect their home agency.

Successful collaborative leaders are not surprised by such behavior; indeed, they should expect it. Collaboration, especially in the early phases, can pose real or perceived threats to certain members' units. And those who are not threatened by the initiative still may have many unanswered questions at the start, which dampens their enthusiasm.

To deal with this problem, the initiative's leaders can try these suggestions:

1. Talk candidly with other principals about the WIIFM from their point of view. What would make this project valuable to them and their agencies or offices? Recognition? Access to resources available in the initiative? More control over the way the initiative is being run?

2. Talk with principals individually, outside of the group meetings, to find out what concerns they have about the effort. Do they worry that it is a threat to their turf, mission, or autonomy? Do they see it as a potential loss of control (often a huge issue)? Obtaining such information can help collaborative leaders clarify what is "on the table" and what is off, to allay people's concerns.

3. Use some of the methods listed above, in the section on Demonstrating the High Stakes Involved in the Initiative: Find a senior leader who champions the project, bring a customer to the table who will be materially affected by the team's work, find new resources for the project.

4. Create some early wins. Busy, successful people want to be associated with success. Build that into your plan.

A good start that stalls out

Losing momentum is a concern with a variety of projects. After several positive meetings, statements of support from leaders, and clarification of goals and roles, things slow down. Members either send their deputies to the meetings, or no one comes at all. The priority project seems to be OBE—overtaken by events.

Some collaborative leaders have avoided this dilemma when they:

- Plan the project in "chunks" so that it produces a series of small, visible products over time. JNET was designed this way. Every few months the network's planners created some new functionality that was available on the desktops of the participating members and their colleagues. Creating a network in chunks provides many benefits; one of them is that it maintains momentum. In addition, the members gain a sense of group identity (they say "we" more often, and "you" and "I" less).

- Celebrate the delivery of these products. It helps when people mark successes.
- Shine a light on the problem. This is one way to use a strategy noted earlier: demonstrating the high stakes involved. Shining a light can be done by quantifying the cost and risk of the problem, by involving a variety of external stakeholders who want the problem addressed, by bringing in the media to discuss the problem and what is being done to address it, and by enlisting the involvement of senior leaders.

A history of distrust and conflict among the principal agencies

How do individuals work well on a collaborative team, when their offices or agencies have been feuding for decades (as has been the case with the CIA and FBI)? The reasons for interagency feuds and turf battles are plentiful and well established. What exacerbates these tensions in collaborative efforts is that employees have stronger allegiance to their home agency (or office) than to the collaborative group they have joined. No matter how compelling the project's vision, most people keep firmly in mind that they will be going back to their boss and worksite and that their career interests are primarily rooted there.

A strategy for dealing with preexisting distrust and conflict is to help people identify with the initiative's larger purpose. Talk about that larger purpose, why it matters to real people, and the cost of not achieving the purpose. These discussions help focus team members on their reason for being at the table.

Other examples of this strategy include:

- Periodic rotations. Moving people around helps them see the larger picture. In organizations such as the Department of Defense, military personnel do not rise through the officer ranks unless they have had several rotations through joint commands (where they work with members of all four armed services).
- Co-located facilities. The Service First initiative is a partnership of the U.S. Forest Service and Bureau of Land Management. The two agencies share information, staff, and resources in many parts of the

country. The partnership also includes more than twenty co-located units, where staff from both agencies work together and sometimes integrate key functions to improve customer service. One trend at the state level is to create fusion centers, where intelligence, law enforcement, and emergency management personnel from different agencies work together to anticipate and deal with threats to the country. These centers are proving useful in building trust across different agency cultures.

- Joint training. Such experience often helps break down agency and interpersonal barriers. Like rotations and co-location, joint training gives participants a chance to move beyond stereotypes. Relationships form that can be used when sudden challenges occur. Indeed, some of the law enforcement and emergency management managers who responded to the 9/11 attack on the Pentagon had been through many training sessions together; their relationships were critical to their extraordinary collaboration during and after the attack.[7]

- Joint task forces. In today's law enforcement and intelligence communities, joint task forces are common. When people from different agencies work together every day on high-stake issues, they tend to overcome stereotypes and forge strong bonds.

A unit-focused versus agency-focused organizational culture

One of the most common complaints in government (and in many large private firms, for that matter) is the reluctance of personnel to widen their focus. And it has some similarities to the previous issue.

Tribal loyalties can be incredibly strong. For many reasons, people at work usually find it more compelling to relate to their immediate unit than to the entire organization. The problem is that what is good for the individual units is not always what is needed for the enterprise.

I have observed a variety of efforts to address the problems created by strong tribal loyalties. Usually, when employees start letting go of their "silo mentalities" and adopt an agency-wide focus, a strong leader helped by making it a priority to move the culture in this direction. The following is an excellent example.

In December 1997 Treasury Secretary Robert Rubin asked Dick Gregg to take over the troubled Financial Management Service (FMS). The agency was in disarray, plagued by internal feuds, rigid stovepipes, divisions among senior leaders, and failure to implement an important law passed by Congress in 1996. Congressional leaders were upset, and the previous leaders were ousted. Gregg brought in Ken Papaj, his former deputy at the Bureau of Public Debt, and set about changing things at FMS.

Gregg articulated the necessary changes at the outset. At his first meeting with senior managers, Gregg recalled, "I said that we would speak with one voice, not several, that information would be shared widely, and issues would be dealt with early and directly. I emphasized that we would have a few common objectives and that we'd do business from an agency-wide perspective."[8] In his meetings with the senior managers, Gregg made clear his intention to make major changes and his expectation that the managers would support those changes. Within a month, two of the managers left; they were not forced out, but it was clear that they would not be able to function in the new environment. During the following months some other senior managers were moved to different roles, as Gregg brought in people whose leadership style fit the culture being created.

Gregg and Papaj made a number of other changes during the next year: they emphasized the values of teamwork and agency-wide perspective in performance appraisals, and they saw to it that managers took them seriously. They formed matrix teams to get people working with others from different functions. Gregg and Papaj also spent countless hours meeting with small teams of employees to discuss the new direction, explain how it would affect employees, listen to the questions and concerns, and respond candidly.

The results of these and many other changes were striking. FMS developed a true culture of collaboration. The changes were done in firm but humane ways. And when Gregg retired in spring 2006, it was clear to everyone at FMS that this culture was on solid ground.[9]

People on the collaborative team who "don't play well with others"

Many collaboration issues are organizational and structural, but some are personal. Some people simply prefer to work on their own. Some become rigid and protective in groups. And then there are those like the person that collaboration theorist Michael Shrage describes. Shrage tells of a man who was being interviewed for a senior position. After being told that the company was committed to a team concept, he was asked if he was a team player. "You bet," he answered. "Team captain!"[10]

Entire books have been written on this topic, so I will not try to give simple solutions to this challenge. One point to emphasize, however, is the importance of being clear at the outset about what is expected of the people in the collaborative group. One good approach is to ask the principals at one of the first meetings to think about similar groups they've served on in the past and describe the behaviors that were helpful and those that weren't. This technique can lead to a decision on group norms: What are the behaviors we need (and behaviors we cannot accept) to succeed? When the group members develop their own norms, these norms can be especially powerful. They still must be enforced, and it often helps to have a skillful facilitator to do that. But the first step is to discuss and agree on the acceptable behaviors and get them from the group.

The following norms can be especially helpful in dealing with difficult people:

- Candor, and no retribution for being candid.
- Mutual respect: we will be tough on the problem, not on each other.
- Park your ego and your agency (or unit) identity at the door.
- Everyone contributes; nobody dominates.
- The 70 percent rule: When making decisions, we will be satisfied if we each can get about 70 percent of what we want; holding out for 100 percent means we will never agree.

Another approach is to meet some of the ego needs of the principals early on as a way to reduce posturing at later meetings. Here is how one manager does it, especially if she knows she will be dealing with some huge egos. When she convenes a group for the first time, she goes around the room and introduces each person. She takes the time to talk about their current and past roles, some of their accomplishments, their wonderful skills, why she is so pleased that they are with "our group." She will talk about the varied contributions each can make to the team. If she does not do that, she has found that those with large egos will try to impress the group (and irritate other people in the process). By doing the introductions for them, she has found that posturing and egotistical behavior diminishes. She satisfies some of their ego needs for them, in a fair and efficient way, and the group then moves into the substance of their issue.

Finally, it's often important to bring in trained facilitators to convene and support collaborative teams, especially when there are major-league egos involved. Collaboration usually involves plenty of challenges; dealing with extremely difficult people may be one challenge too many for most team leaders. It's sometimes best to leave that to a professional.

Agencies or offices that refuse to join

As noted earlier, one factor for successful collaboration is to have the appropriate people at the table. But what are your options when one of the principal parties refuses to play?

A project manager at the National Aeronautics and Space Administration (NASA) had to contend with this problem a few years ago. He was the champion for a complex initiative that involved two NASA labs, the Air Force, and some aircraft companies. He started by talking informally with people at each organization to learn what they thought they might get out of the project and any concerns they had. Most seemed interested, but he was not certain about the people at one of the NASA labs. The project manager decided to take what I call an "outside-in" approach. He worked with personnel at the organizations that were most interested (even though they were not as vital to the project as the reluctant NASA lab). They developed goals, a project plan, and identified resources for the project. The project manager did not approach the NASA lab until the other partners were firmly on board. He then went back to that lab and explained what was in place. Managers there got interested in the project; they saw that it was a serious venture, were impressed by the stature of the interested organizations, and did not want to be left out.

A constitutional system that engenders distrust

The design of the U.S. government may be the biggest challenge to collaboration today. We are so used to our division of powers and legislative oversight that we take our fragmented system for granted, but this system is hardly a prescription for getting things done. The Framers were willing to put up with a government that was slow and clumsy because their overriding purpose was neither speed nor effectiveness (and it certainly wasn't efficiency!); rather, it was to prevent tyranny. As Donald Kettl writes, "At the very beginning, the founders decided there were two things they did not want: a single government that consolidated the states ... and a government that consolidated governmental power in a single executive."[11]

The result: fragmented authority. We divide power between the federal and state governments, and within each level we divide power among the legislative, executive, and judicial. Moreover, we give each branch powers over the others. Add to that multiple oversight agencies and it's amazing anything ever gets done! The Framers' goal of avoiding tyranny has been a brilliant success. But the system's way of doing so makes it very hard to move all the players in the same direction.

The U.S. constitutional system is a challenge to collaboration, but the complexity of today's problems requires the involvement and coordination of multiple skillsets, mindsets and organizations. The major issues on the public's mind—the global economy and its impact on jobs, immigration, health care costs, global warming, the growing tribalism around the world, and terrorism—all require extensive collaboration. Developing the most effective options can be accomplished only by a coalition of specialists from different backgrounds and organizations, often with active public involvement.

This last issue is, in my view, the most profound problem facing government today. We are using a system of government based on eighteenth-century structures to deal with twenty-first century challenges. These challenges do not honor traditional boundaries. And the ways we address them must reflect new ways of thinking and organizing.

The answers will not be found in the powerful new IT tools that dazzle us, even though technology will be important to our success. The answers will not be found in moving boxes around on organizational charts. Nor do I believe that merging multiple agencies will lead to serious breakthroughs. The answers are being found, however slowly, in the efforts of many informal leaders throughout government who invite others from different units to work together on complex problems. These noble collaborative leaders are experimenting, taking risks, using the methods noted here and by many others, and they are slowly creating the strategies and ways of thinking that are necessary to work across boundaries.

Some of their efforts are leading to new organizational forms such as fusion centers, which were briefly described in the section, *A history of distrust and conflict among the principal agencies.* They share sensitive information, analyze it, and function as one unit to prevent and deal with natural and man-made threats. And because they work next to each other and work on common challenges, they are forming the trust that is critical to collaboration. Other efforts are leading to more informal solutions, such as the development of human and IT networks within certain professional communities to share knowledge and develop answers to vexing problems. One of the most interesting is "Intellipedia," which is loosely modeled after

Wikipedia, the online encyclopedia. Intellipedia is a self-governing system using content submitted by its consumers. Intelligence community analysts send postings to Intellipedia on a variety of topics. The content is subject to peer evaluation; if flawed information is submitted, others point it out quickly. (Unlike Wikipedia, Intellipedia's contributors are not anonymous, which provides accountability.) So far, Intellipedia is providing a secure and quick method for analysts at all levels and agencies to engage on important topics and emerging issues.

The collaborative pioneers who are creating these and other new forms are helping us see the world differently, and that is absolutely necessary. America's fragmented government system, for all of its blessings (and there are many), makes it very difficult to see the world holistically, find patterns, think systemically, and deal with complexity. Although it is not yet clear where these new forms will take us, what is clear is that today's major challenges will be met only through the power of collaboration.

Tips for collaborative success

In summary, those attempting to lead collaborative efforts should always keep in mind the following six "basic" conditions that form the foundation for collaborative success:

1. A specific, shared purpose that the parties want to meet and cannot achieve on their own.

2. A desire by the parties to meet now and a willingness to contribute something to the effort.

3. Appropriate people at the table.

4. An open, credible process for meeting.

5. A champion or champions for the effort.

6. Trusting relationships among the stakeholders.

These conditions can be difficult to achieve, so successful leaders use certain approaches to create this foundation. They can:

1. Demonstrate the high stakes involved in the effort.

2. Develop a constituency for the effort.

3. Use collaborative leadership skills.

Resources for further learning

Books and Articles

To stretch your thinking about macro trends in the economy, technology, politics, and why collaboration is so central to the nation's future, two excellent books are: Thomas Friedman, *The World Is Flat* (2005), and Harlan Cleveland, *Nobody in Charge: Essays on the Future of Leadership* (2002). Two excellent books devoted entirely to the topic of networks are *Governing by Network: The New Shape of the Public Sector*, by Stephen Goldsmith and William D. Eggers (2004), and *Unlocking the Power of Networks: Keys to High-Performance Government*, edited by Stephen Goldsmith and Donald F. Kettl (2009). To learn how leading thinkers in public administration view collaboration and its increasing role in public management, see *Public Administration Review* 66 (Special Issue, 2006). The entire issue is devoted to the topic of collaboration. Here are more books on related subjects:

James E. Austin, *The Collaboration Challenge* (2000). The author offers guidance on forming alliances between nonprofits and businesses.

Stephen M. R. Covey, *The Speed of Trust: The One Thing That Changes Everything* (2006). This is one of the best books on the development of trust in interpersonal relationships and organizational cultures.

Joel DeLuca, *Political Savvy* (1999). Exploring the political aspects of collaboration, how to form coalitions, and how to use influence in ethical ways, this excellent book describes the art of lining up support, connecting projects to others' agendas, and using relationships in positive ways.

Stephen Dent, *Partnering Intelligence* (1999). A fine book that describes collaboration from a private-sector perspective.

E. Franklin Dukes et al., *Collaboration: A Guide for Environmental Advocates* (2001). The authors focus on the process of forming collaborative groups, and how to establish collaborative norms.

Donald Kettl, *The Next Government of the United States: Why Our Institutions Fail Us and How to Fix Them* (2009). This insightful book emphasizes the increasing role that networks will play in the future of government.

Russ Linden, *The Quest to Become 'One': An Approach to Internal Collaboration* (2005). This report, published by the IBM Center for the Business of

Government, focuses on large federal departments and agencies trying to become "one" (gain internal alignment around common purpose).

Russ Linden, *Leading Across Boundaries: Creating Collaborative Agencies in a Networked World* (2010). This book provides more about this chapter's particular approach to collaboration, with a special emphasis on leadership.

Web Resources

Mashable, http://mashable.com/. This site has up-to-date information on social networking products, information and services.

Leader to Leader Journal, http://www.leadertoleader.org/knowledgecenter/journal.aspx. This journal has fine articles on many aspects of leadership, including collaboration.

Notes

1. Kettl (2006), 13.

2. The development of the JNET system is an instructive example of what it takes for collaboration to work across multiple agencies. Several other states have studied JNET and built their own systems using a similar framework. For more on JNET and how the collaboration developed, see Linden (2002), chap. 4.

3. Walters (2005), 5. For more on the importance of forming relationships prior to crises, see Moynihan (2005) on leveraging networks during emergencies, and the after-action report by Titan Systems Corporation (2001), A-31, on responses to the 9/11 attack on the Pentagon.

4. Friedman (2005a), 306.

5. Author's personal communication with Harlan Cleveland, (2001).

6. Chrislip (2000), 23.

7. Titan Systems Corporation (2001), 12.

8. Linden (2002), 205.

9. For more on the transformation of the Financial Management Service under Dick Gregg, see ibid., chap. 12.

10. Shrage (1990).

11. Kettl (2006), 11.

9 Career-political relationships: Going beyond a government of strangers

Robert Maranto, 21st Century Chair in Leadership, Department of Education Reform, University of Arkansas*

Career public servants and political appointees are here to stay, and they must work well together if government is to succeed. An effective collaboration starts with recognizing that the negative stereotypes each has about the other are mostly wrong. Beyond that, political appointees must approach their career counterparts with respect, seek to understand their agencies, build partnerships, and focus on what appointees do best—craft overall strategy and manage externally. Career officials must seek to understand and appreciate the appointee's view of the world, extend a helping hand, keep their organizations in working order, and be tolerant of initial appointee missteps.

Their fanatic conservatism is fine with me! It is simply misplaced in what should be a bipartisan agency. . . . My problems are not ideological. They won an election. I'll help implement policies I don't necessarily agree with. Basically, however, most of the Reagan people couldn't operate a bingo game.

—*A career executive in 1987*[1]

If there truly is a move in the future to eliminate that agency or fold it back into ____, I would speak up in favor. Very little was accomplished on a day-to-day basis. When you come from a White House environment where things happen so quickly, you are always in a reaction mode and you never go to your superior and say this can't be done—you find a way to accomplish it, and in ____ I was unable to accomplish anything in nine months and had Mr. Bush been reelected I knew I could not stay in that job, because I couldn't accomplish anything.

—*A former George H. W. Bush political appointee in 2000*[2]

* I wish to thank Jason O'Brien, Grant Reeher, James P. Pfiffner, and the Federal Executive Institute for helping on this project, as well as the literally hundreds of government executives whose insights follow. I further thank Hugh Heclo, whose *A Government of Strangers* (Washington, D.C.: Brookings Institution, 1977) provided the title and many of the ideas presented here.

As THE OLD SAYING GOES, in Washington the search for the scapegoat is the easiest hunting expedition. In politics, "political hacks" and "lazy bureaucrats" make great scapegoats. A long line of political folk wisdom and some scholarly writing suggests that U.S. political appointees are less expert, more politically driven, and more corrupt than career public servants.[3] Similarly, career bureaucrats are often thought to be unrepresentative, devoted to increasing their budgets, and unwilling to take direction.[4] The reality is that political appointees and career public servants must work together. When they build relationships of mutual respect, public value is more likely. In this chapter, I first outline reasons why decreased trust in government has little to do with the quality of political or career officials and why negative stereotypes about both groups of professionals are (mainly) wrong. Second, I review ideas about how political appointees can better work with, rather than at cross-purposes with, their career bureaucrats to foster bureaucratic change and ultimately better serve the public. Finally, and most important, given the audience for this book, I suggest what career officials can do to foster good relationships with the political appointees in their agencies— what a public servant can do within his or her own sphere of influence. After all, as Leo Tolstoy put it, "Everyone thinks of changing the world, but no one thinks of changing himself."[5] Or as Linda Bunker, University of Virginia education professor and sports psychologist puts it: "To succeed, executives must focus on the behaviors they can control—rather than lamenting the failures of bad karma or bad others."[6] Chiefly, political and career leaders must put themselves in each others' shoes to better serve them and ultimately the public.

Why everyone hates the bureaucracy

For decades, American politicians, media, and interest groups have railed against "the bureaucracy," by which they usually mean career civil servants. As far back as President Andrew Jackson, citizens considered the Washington bureaucracy in particular corrupt, lazy, and unrepresentative (out of touch). After all, bureaucrats live on taxes coercively collected, while most people suffer the vicissitudes of the free market.[7] Further, bureaucrats are a technocratic, at times quasi-aristocratic elite certain to draw resentment in a populist nation. Antibureaucratic sentiment has waxed and waned in the American political life cycle.[8] Since the 1950s the mood has been mostly antibureaucratic, with, to varying degrees, Presidents Dwight Eisenhower,

John F. Kennedy, Richard Nixon, Jimmy Carter, Ronald Reagan, and Bill Clinton all trying to become chief executive by running against their future employees, the permanent executives. One result of these campaigns by out-parties is the inclination of the winner's political appointees to view career officials with skepticism.[9]

Few analysts have conducted systematic treatments of public trust of the government, and not all of those who have done so have asked good questions. Still, most agree that public distrust in government cannot be blamed on the U.S. bureaucracy. Family breakdown, the polarization of culture war politics, and more sensationalist media coverage clearly played roles in decreasing public trust in government (and in other institutions). The inevitable comedown after phenomenal U.S. success in World War II also explains declining trust.[10]

I suspect four additional factors. First, the largest declines in public trust in government generally and the bureaucracy in particular occurred in the late 1960s and early 1970s, when homicide rates tripled, total tax bite (federal, state, and local) went up by about 25 percent, the United States lost a major war in Vietnam, and a president resigned in disgrace. In short, to some degree the level of public trust in government reflects objective conditions related to government, if not necessarily bureaucratic, failures.[11] Similarly, President George W. Bush's popularity soared after initial successes in Afghanistan and Iraq and foundered after later failures in Iraq and New Orleans. As I write this, President Barack Obama's popularity is waning because of stubbornly high unemployment and near record deficits.

Second, as numerous scholars have pointed out, a plethora of new ethics laws in the wake of Watergate may have made government somewhat more honest, but also had the unintended consequence of producing more scandals. As ethics laws and regulations proliferated, politicians and bureaucrats who in the past would have been lionized today wind up in jail, disgraced, or at least under investigation by congressional committees, inspectors general, general counsels, or independent counsels. Moreover, the media and public have difficulty distinguishing minor from major transgressions. The problems of the new ethics regime are neatly captured by the titles of noted scholarly works such as *The Pursuit of Absolute Integrity* and *Innocent Until Nominated*.[12] Political appointees are among those most victimized by the new ethics regime, which has made for ever greater delays in appointments. Like most of his recent predecessors, President

Obama imposed what David Lewis[13] calls "the strictest ethics rules of any incoming president," slowing the pace of his appointments.

Third, public education has changed in ways unlikely to enhance trust in government. In the past, textbooks portrayed an overly positive view of American life, more heritage than history. In contrast, public education may now accentuate the negative, emphasizing sins rather than triumphs and lacking the context of realistic foreign comparisons. Further, public education has not imparted the basic facts of American government.[14] For example, few Americans know that very little public money goes to public employees, welfare, or foreign aid, but that the budget deficit is driven by spending on middle-class entitlements.[15]

Finally, during the Depression, World War II, and the early Cold War, most American families included public servants, usually soldiers. Direct experience demythologized government, so citizens understood both its strengths and its limitations. Such public service generally led Americans to hold more positive views of government and to see government as "theirs" in a way that merely writing (tax) checks or cashing (entitlement) checks does not.

The truth about bureaucrats: They're (mostly) good

As Charles Goodsell shows at length in his classic *The Case for Bureaucracy*, contrary to popular misconceptions, American bureaucrats are reasonably representative of the public, both demographically and ideologically.[16] Further, U.S. bureaucracies generally do a good job delivering public service, with remarkably little corruption. Customer satisfaction surveys show that frequent users of agency services give high marks to the U.S. Postal Service, the Social Security Administration, and to regulatory organizations such as the Food and Drug Administration, Federal Aviation Administration, and the Environmental Protection Agency (EPA). Even the Internal Revenue Service, an organization with the truly impossible job of interpreting and applying millions of words of tax code, gets reasonably high ratings from taxpayers and very high ratings from professional tax preparers.[17] An improved environment, safer workplaces, and longer life spans all represent government (as well as private sector) success stories.[18] As I report, there is substantial evidence that the Clinton-Gore reinvention efforts have made the U.S. government more efficient and innovative than ever. The George W. Bush administration continued reinvention, albeit with less fanfare. Early indications suggest that the Obama administration is acting likewise.[19]

The good news about the U.S. bureaucracy applies particularly to the executive levels. In my three years serving in the higher civil service, I rarely encountered public servants who in dedication and smarts were not more than a match for the professors I knew during two decades of university teaching. Public servants are not only talented, they also recognize their roles as *public* servants, accountable not merely to their own preferences but to the political leadership of their agencies, to Congress, and ultimately to the American people. I frequently heard government executives speculate about whether one or another action furthered the public interest, something I rarely hear state university professors talk about. Regarding bureaucratic flexibility, considerable scholarship shows that for the most part, career bureaucrats do accept legitimate political direction.[20]

Despite widespread views that a declining talent pool is sapping the strength of the public service in a "quiet crisis" of ever-increasing incompetence, the intelligence and capability of the career and noncareer executives I worked with rarely failed to impress. In the best review of the evidence, political scientists Joel D. Aberbach and Bert A. Rockman report that "evidence on behalf of a 'quiet crisis' is itself very quiet."[21] Measures of education, class background, and job satisfaction show little evidence that the higher civil service grew any less expert from 1970 to 1992.

Moreover, for decades surveys have found political appointees giving rather high marks to their career executives. Kathryn Newcomer surveyed sixty-nine former political appointees who also had private-sector experience. She found that political appointees from the Johnson, Nixon, Ford, Carter, and Reagan administrations rated career executives as comparable to, or better than private-sector managers on technical skills, managerial skills, and cooperativeness, though all saw government managers as less likely to take initiative than their counterparts in the private sector.[22] (Arguably, the last point is not negative, given constitutional constraints.) My own 1987–1988 mail survey of Reagan appointees found that they rated their career executives as highly competent, and generally willing to take direction.[23] This result mirrors the Aberbach and Rockman 1991 survey, in which overwhelming majorities of political appointees report that their career executives have good management skills, try to improve government, and work hard to carry out administration goals.[24] Similarly, Judith E. Michaels's survey of George H. W. Bush appointees found that nearly 75 percent saw career executives as competent, and nearly 66 percent saw them as responsive.[25] Though George W. Bush was a very different president than his father, Ed DeSeve's 2008 survey of sixty-six high level "W" appointees showed that nearly nine of ten thought it important to work with career officials.[26]

Naturally, we can find exceptions. As my own work and that of Robert Durant[27] suggests, when political leaders impose policies in opposition to the core values or practices of agencies, career subordinates sometimes respond by failing to share information or by leaking to Congress or the press. At times, therefore, political appointees are justified in using relatively hard-nosed tactics to "tell" rather than "sell" their policies. Currently, there are indications that the Obama administration may need such an approach to push the U.S. Marine Corps to implement full inclusion of gays and lesbians.[28]

Political hacks as the "folk devils" of government

If the permanent bureaucracy has a (mainly) undeserved bad reputation, political appointees are even more beleaguered. As Domonic Bearfield explains in his brilliant essay, "The Demonization of Patronage," the reaction against politically appointed public servants often takes the form of a "moral panic," an "exaggerated reaction of a society to events and phenomena that challenge or upset traditional norms and values."[29] Moral panics focus on "folk devils," which attract public outcry and government action. Bearfield discusses the scapegoating of two Massachusetts Port Authority executives, who had been appointed by the governor. The press blamed them for the 9/11 terrorists' use of Boston's Logan Airport. The two political appointees had substantial management and law enforcement experience, had improved Logan, and did not contribute to the failures of 9/11. The press and politicians nevertheless hounded them from office. Their political experience and connections to governors made them immediately suspect to reporters conditioned to consider career officials as competent and political officials as hacks.

As I detail elsewhere, many public administration academics subscribe to the dominant journalistic view of political appointees.[30] Although less biased than denizens of the ivory tower, some career public servants hold the same views. Indeed, Georgetown University's Joseph A. Ferrara and Lynn C. Ross see the hapless political hack as the same sort of political myth as the infamous "$400 hammer" or the "welfare queen."[31] In my own time in government, I saw many career executives stereotype political appointees based on limited data, just as people stereotype those of other races.[32] One Clinton appointee recalled, "At first my agency tried to bury me. They didn't know what to make of me since I came in as a special assistant, so they put me in the back with a little office and tried to ignore me."[33] Although most career executives get along just fine with the political appointees they work with, some still see politicos in general as incompetent, fanatical, and corrupt. The good ones, the folks they know, are simply exceptions to the rule. For example, EPA careerists seemed to experience productive working relationships with most of their political appointees from the second Reagan term and the George H. W. Bush and Clinton administrations. Yet when asked about EPA political appointees generally, career executives often focus on the very controversial appointees under Reagan's first EPA administrator, Anne Burford. Indeed, when career officials approve of the political appointees, and when those appointees support more resources for the agency, career officials often consider them "apolitical" rather than "political."[34] I once gave a presentation on political appointees before an audience of career executives and one brave and effective Clinton politico, Cynthia Brock-Smith, who had befriended many of the careerists. Several of the career executives disputed my arguments that most political appointees do a good job, often adding comments to the effect that "we don't mean you, Cynthia. . . . You're one of the good ones."[35]

Stereotypes do not explain everything. To my knowledge, only two published works, both reflecting on the Reagan presidency, have systematically examined how relations between political appointees and career executives change over the course of an administration.[36] Defense agencies had missions that President Reagan prized, and largely for this reason political appointees and career executives saw career-noncareer relations as starting well and staying that way. In contrast, domestic agencies fell into two patterns. In a handful of agencies with highly controversial first-term Reagan political appointees, such as the Federal Emergency Management Agency (FEMA), Office of Personnel Management (OPM), National Highway Traffic Safety Administration (NHTSA), and EPA, relations started badly, as the appointees with some talent but little political acumen tried nonincremental changes in agency scope and missions. Relations improved rapidly once these agency chiefs were replaced with less polarizing and often more expert figures. In most domestic agencies, career-noncareer relations remained both stable and mixed for careerists; for political appointees, a rough first two years were followed by gradual improvement.[37] Notably, friends in government suggest that career-noncareer relations in the George W. Bush administration generally improved in the second term as polarizing leaders in the Defense Department, CIA, and elsewhere were replaced.

In part, gradual improvements usually result from personnel changes because, as a longtime political appointee, a veteran of two administrations, put it, the most ideologically zealous and least politically skilled political and career officials eventually "kill each other off." More important, however, as George Mason University political scientist James P. Pfiffner and former career government executive Paul Lorentzin have taught me, over time political appointees and career executives get to know each other and overcome the stereotypes each side holds about the other to build productive working relationships.[38] This shift comes about because most of those on each side of the divide are competent, idealistic grown-ups. Consistently, career and noncareer officials ranked public interest motives, such as "the ability to work for desired policies" and "serving my country," above pay, benefits, and other more self-serving motives.[39] Career officials view the public interest through their agency prism, while political appointees typically view the public interest through party or ideological lenses. Yet over time, through persuasion, education, negotiation, and sometimes direction by the appointees, competing views can be reconciled.[40]

In truth, new political appointees typically know far less about their agencies than career public servants who have served for decades. Even so, in sharp contrast to the stereotypes about appointees, very few incompetents survive an incredibly elaborate vetting process involving the White House, cabinet secretaries, the FBI, many and varied interest groups, the Washington press corps, and for high-level positions, the U.S. Senate.[41] As a Clinton Office of Presidential Personnel official put it:

> I've heard some people say that we select people for jobs by throwing darts at a dart board. Sometimes I wish that were so, but in fact it is an incredibly complex process of matching up the people to the job and going from the White House to the agencies to the secretaries to the FBI and the ethics checks back to the people. I'm against the wall. I'm working 15 hours a day five days a week; 12 to 15 hours Saturday, and two or three hours Sunday.[42]

The limited data available suggest that the vast majority of political appointees have considerable talent. As Judith Michaels found, 53 percent of George H. W. Bush's PAS (presidential appointees, Senate confirmed) officials had an MD, LLD, or PhD, and 78 percent had some sort of advanced degree. Sixty-five percent were over age fifty, and 49 percent had prior budgetary responsibility of greater than $1 million. Fifty-one percent reported losing income to join government. Moreover, the variety of experience political appointees bring to their new jobs helps their agencies break down traditional bureaucratic "stovepipes" and build new partnerships across sectors: 41 percent of Bush appointees (and far more in most administrations) had their immediately prior positions outside Washington. Most came from the private sector or from academia.[43]

Obviously, lower-level noncareer Senior Executive Service (SES) and Schedule C officials have fewer credentials. Still, tens of thousands want to join a new presidential administration, but only a few earn jobs. Those few typically have the competence and desire to help government. Or as a Clinton appointee told me, "Remember that every political appointee has something you don't," most typically experience in state government, business, or a congressional staff. A young Reagan-Bush appointee I interviewed started in a low level White House job, developed a good track record, and then gained advancement to higher levels in the White House and finally to an SES position in an agency, based on performance:

> [My political boss] knew I could handle people older than I was and I had experience in management. Even though I was young, they knew I would do whatever it took to learn that job and so for the first six months I lived at the White House, from eight in the morning until ten at night, until I reached a comfort level and really changed that office. . . . They knew they could use me confidentially as a sounding board [and] took a chance on me because she knew that I had what it took, which was loyalty and being willing to do whatever it took to learn the job, which I did, but that is certainly not the way a career person gets their job, and I can see how that would be frustrating to career people. I would never have survived the personnel office in an agency because I didn't have the "credentials" for the position, but in the White House it is a make or break position—you either do well or you don't.[44]

A mail survey I conducted in 1994 found that large pluralities of career executives considered appointees in their own agencies competent.[45] Similarly, Aberbach and Rockman interviewed career executives in

Washington, finding that 60 percent agreed that political appointees "bring valuable experience to the job"; 52 percent agreed that appointees "have good leadership qualities"; 59 percent agreed that appointees view their jobs as vehicles to make "positive, long term improvements to government service"; and 91 percent agreed that appointees "work hard to carry out administration initiatives and priorities," though fewer than a third thought that political appointees did a good job at internal agency management.[46]

To be fair, most political appointees are not responsible for internal management, which is left to career public servants and military officers. Instead, political appointees do *political* work: strategic planning, budgeting, regulation developing (or delaying), as well as dealing with interest groups, members of Congress and congressional staffs, the media, and state and local officials. The number of political appointees has roughly doubled since the Kennedy administration, but congressional staffers have more than tripled, and interest groups and Washington-based reporters have increased faster still. Since the 1970s Washington's *political-industrial complex* has been a growing sector of the economy, as anyone familiar with Washington housing costs knows. Political appointees have actually lagged behind the rest of the sector.[47] To reduce the number of political appointees, we would need to reeducate career public servants to play more political roles, with the attendant political risks. To my knowledge, none of those who propose reducing the numbers of political appointees have considered how to do it.

At the same time, David Lewis's very sophisticated, Neustadt award-winning *The Politics of Presidential Appointments* makes a powerful case using the Office of Management and Budget (OMB) designed Program Assessment Rating Tool (PART) data that programs led by political appointees are on the whole not as well managed as those run by career executives, in part because appointees have less internal agency experience and in part because they serve for shorter periods and their posts are frequently vacant.[48] While as Lewis admits large numbers of appointees are valuable, it seems likely that some reduction in their numbers would improve government. Further, it seems that appointees are most effective when they focus on goal setting and the management of external stakeholders rather than internal management. Quite possibly, government works best when both career and political officials understand their proper roles.

What political appointees can do

If neither political appointees nor career bureaucrats are demons, and if in fact they can come to respect each other, we must ask what each side might do to build trust and hasten relationship building. For their part, presidential political appointees must approach their agency bureaucrats with respect rather than seeing them as stereotypes.[49] Agencies with similar organizational charts can have very distinct cultures. A wise political appointee (or indeed any newcomer) should immerse himself or herself in the agency's culture as an amateur anthropologist. As Anne M. Khademian writes, components of culture include organization members' views of their mission, customers, commitments, and partners.[50] To this, defense analyst Andrew Krepinevich, a former Army major, adds an organization's goals and the standard operating procedures through which to achieve those goals.[51] In addition, components of culture include the agency history and how officials interpret that history. As UCLA management professor William Ouchi points out, culture includes the degree of loyalty to the organization.[52] To understand an organization's culture, one must spend time reading its history and listening to its employees, overseers, and customers. A wise political appointee will consult everyone who previously held the position not only to understand how they succeeded or failed but also to get a scouting report on the best (and worst) career employees.

Studying the agency takes time, and for better or worse most PAS officials serve for months in an unofficial capacity as consultants before formal confirmation. These months can be useful for on-site reconnaissance.[53] Without careful study of agency culture, new appointees are apt to botch communications. One hilarious example occurred when Jim Miller, President Reagan's choice to head the Federal Trade Commission (FTC), tried to explain his goals to FTC career executives. Miller, a flamboyant and highly capable former academic, introduced his agenda to a trumpet fanfare while dressed in a devil's outfit; he then assured the staff that he was not the devil. Unfortunately, this did not impress serious FTC attorneys.[54]

Capable appointees see part of their job as campaigning inside the agency to partner with career bureaucrats and persuade them to join the administration rather than wait it out. Appointees must listen, and, as Ferrara and Ross put it, appointees must also "communicate, communicate,

communicate."[55] For example, I interviewed a Reagan appointee who found that career executives knew little about Republican ideology, so he held a sort of seminar for them:

> I recommended readings that would give a full picture of Reagan policy and where it was coming from. I had a series of brownbag lunches just to kind of sit around and informally talk about policy ideas, and I found these lunches invaluable for idea exchange and clearing the air. I think every [PAS] can do this.

Skillful politicking avoids gaffes. Like veterans, farmers, ethnic groups, and other constituencies, bureaucrats can be extremely sensitive. Career EPA staff disliked Carol Browner, Clinton's appointee as administrator, because she had made the mistake of criticizing career EPA officials during her confirmation hearings. As a Clinton EPA appointee lamented years later, "I don't know that she's ever recovered from the point of view of careerists."[56] Donald Rumsfeld, George W. Bush's first defense secretary, offered an even more extreme example in freezing out military officers. As Dale R. Herspring writes, "Bureaucracies have a strange way of seeming to obey the person in charge even when they are being insulted, as with [Rumsfeld], but they generally have the last laugh by jettisoning most of the changes he made as soon as he is gone."[57]

In sharp contrast, numerous FEMA career and appointed officials I interviewed admired Clinton era Director James Lee Witt's ability to persuade career executives. A Clinton FEMA appointee marveled that:

> Written mission statements, I used to think that was all bull, but the employees here needed that. There was this tension about whether we are a Cold War agency and can't talk about what we do even with each other, or we are a disaster relief agency that talks constantly with stakeholders, and is wired and interconnected, and [Director] Witt resolved that. . . . He's been real accessible, communicating his vision to the employees with lots of feedback. Of course, we're doing something most of the American public believes that government should be doing.

In addition to understanding the broader culture, capable appointees should get a feel for the change agents and laggards within their organization and how to unleash the former and encourage or work around the latter. A good example is Steven Kelman, the Clinton appointee who led the OMB's Office of Federal Procurement Policy. Kelman conducted surveys and focus groups to identify those within the system who backed procurement reform, and spent considerable time plotting with the pro-reform Procurement Executives Association. Once reformers within government showed that procurement reform could work, Kelman reinforced their efforts by publicizing successful innovators, rewarding them, and training others. Kelman also increased pressures for change by building alliances with powerful actors outside the organization, particularly in the media, Congress, and in the defense industry. Similar strategies were used successfully by FEMA's Witt, the National Aeronautics and Space Administration's Daniel Goldin, the Veterans Health Administration's Kenneth W. Kizer, and U.S. Mint director John Martino.[58]

As explained above, in general appointees achieve the most by focusing on strategic initiatives and managing an agency's external politics. Although appointees must attempt to persuade career officials, they typically lack the time and knowledge to manage the day-to-day affairs of the agency. The exception occurs when appointees seek to reform agency core practices, which may necessitate more coercive signals. In such cases, research suggests that a single unexpected bonus, promotion, or exile to a turkey farm can send a message through an entire organization.[59]

Yet coercive means, if used too often, can prove counterproductive. Political appointees must understand that a small minority of careerists will do more to hinder than help. A few careerists may not fully share information, and squabble with each other. One Clinton appointee in an agency not known for good management complained that two important career deputies had not been on speaking terms with each other for some time, a situation the appointee was not informed of before joining the office. The matter resolved itself when one retired. The same appointee reported that the first day on the job, one deputy greeted his new boss by saying, "You're the tenth _____ I've worked under," implying that an eleventh would be along soon enough![60] Fortunately, this leader did not allow these individuals to turn the appointee against the civil servants generally.

Finally, appointees must understand their own strengths and weaknesses, building on the former and overcoming the latter to serve the public, a theme of many of the other chapters in this volume.[61]

What career public servants can do: Managing one's own government of strangers

For better or worse, large numbers of political appointees are here to stay, and career civil servants cannot control how well those far above their pay grades manage a presidential transition. They can influence the micro-level political transition within their organizations and how to use those transitions to build social capital within the agency. Certainly, those micro-level transitions will often be difficult. As noted above, Americans are populists: they suspect experts and hierarchies.[62] Donald Devine, a political scientist who became Reagan's OPM director, explains that such suspicion is a deep part of our collective political culture and safeguards democracy: those in positions of expert authority are not always right.[63] Politics is a cutthroat business, making politicians doubly suspicious people. Combined, these tendencies ensure that incoming administrations distrust the bureaucrats who served predecessors of the opposing party, especially if the incoming party has long been out or represents a fundamentally different governing philosophy, as in 1933, 1953, 1961, 1969, 1981, and 1993.[64]

Only the very centrist George H. W. Bush administration—in some respects the first third term since Franklin Roosevelt—had the sort of kind and gentle transition in the bureaucracy that bureaucrats would want. As one career executive recalled of the 1989 transition: "It wasn't so much Bush One as Reagan Three."[65] Arguably, the Obama transition has also been relatively peaceful, in part since the President seeks to expand the missions of traditional domestic agencies and respects the expertise of the military in wartime.[66]

But such nontransitions are rare. As populists, Americans like political change. Thus, career executives must master change readiness, both psychologically and administratively. What can career executives do to hasten the eventual cycle of accommodation between the civil service and political appointees? How can career leaders help make political appointees more effective in managing the broader Washington political environment (reporters, interest groups, the White House, and congressional staffs)? After all, if the political appointee thrives, so does the agency.[67] Borrowing from others, I offer the following advice to career executives who want to do their part to smooth political transitions.

First, avoid stereotypes

Too often, career executives believe the harsh stereotype that political appointees are political hacks. Certainly, presidents always have a few "must-place" appointees whose clout exceeds their talent: the odd New Hampshire party official who helped win the primary or the child of a major contributor who wants to go slumming in government. As David Lewis reminds us, patronage is not dead. Such appointees, most typically schedule C's, concentrate in low priority areas in which technical credentials are not needed.[68] But as longtime Navy career SES Harvey Wilcox points out, such officials typically wind up supervised by career officials who can keep them out of trouble. And a few such scions develop into effective leaders, rising in government or the private sector.[69] Career leaders can help in their ascent.

As noted above, in sharp contrast to the stereotypes, the data show that PAS officials are well-educated and have substantial experience. Lower level Schedule C political appointees are less qualified, but even so, politics is a competitive business, and successful campaigns are not run by fools. Those few who have proven themselves in a political campaign usually have dedication, intelligence, and commitment to public service. Even if they start out with limited knowledge of the executive branch generally or the agency in particular, most are smart enough and industrious enough to learn the ropes and make a real contribution. Even political ambassadors, which journalists and members of Congress love to attack, may in practice prove necessary. As an Office of Presidential Personnel official told me, Congress simply does not appropriate sufficient funds to support major embassies, which makes the recruitment of wealthy (and one hopes charming) campaign contributors a practical necessity. Political ambassadors such as Nixon contributor Walter Annenberg (London), George H. W. Bush contributor Peter Seccia (Rome), and Clinton contributor Pamela Harriman (Paris) were all successes in other fields and capably represented their presidents and their nation.

Sometimes stereotypes do come true. Presidential personnel decisions may prove perilous if the agency is not an administration priority. Just as career bureaucrats develop turkey farms to bury their own low performers, so too do presidents.[70] If one's agency serves as such a dumping ground, career leaders may have little choice but to grin and bear it and find a way to make callow political appointees as effective as possible. For solace, one can remember that unlike career turkeys, political turkeys lack tenure. If they screw up publicly, Thanksgiving dinner could come at any time.

Second, do reconnaissance

Every political appointee brings something to his or her post. It may be knowledge of the budget process or public relations skill. It may be business experience. It may be connections with the White House, OMB, Congress, or an interest group. It may simply be a fresh pair of eyes with new insights about the agency. Whatever it is, find out what talents new appointees bring, if possible even before they come on board, and think about how they can help the agency. But understand that they may have their own ideas and ultimately must define their own roles.

During the reconnaissance period, seek contacts in the appointee's previous workplaces to get inside information. If the appointee has published anything, read it, which is easy to do in our online age. To find ideas about how to make a personal relationship work, see if you have anything in common. Finally, remember that like Army generals, nearly all political appointees have had patrons (mentors). Study the particular patron as best you can. For a Hill staffer, this is almost invariably his or her boss, the member of Congress. I have found that appointees from the Hill whose mentors were humane and professional behave likewise; unfortunately, not all members of Congress are humane and professional.

Third, put yourself in their shoes

As one careerist put it, it is difficult to understand how lonely and unsure a new political appointee can be. If appointees are new to Washington, this may be true of their private lives as well. One Clinton appointee who moved to Washington from the West recalled that "it is very hard to make friends here. The legislative branch is very social, lots of receptions, a lot of people in their 20s, but in the executive branch people work a lot of hours and have families. You can't really socialize too much with your subordinates. It's not appropriate, so that part, leaving behind my parents and my brother and his family and my support network since high school; that was hard."

And a Clinton EPA appointee complained:

It's completely different from a job and hiring situation anywhere else, because you don't really know what the job is, and your boss, the administrator, doesn't really know what the job is, and your boss is negotiating back and forth with the White House. In any other sector, before you are hired you would actually have discussions with the person you are working with about what their vision for this job is, to clarify the expectations of what you can achieve. I was not the only one who did not have that discussion. From my colleagues, I don't think any of us did.[71]

By exercising empathy, career public servants can better understand, respect, and serve political leaders.

Fourth, make the first move

Political appointees' biggest complaint about career executives is the same one careerists have about them: a failure to communicate. Or, as one career senior executive told me in 1993, "The trouble with the civil service during a transition is that we're just too civil. We don't say anything." As noted above, each organization has a unique culture, so new appointees may not know how to talk to career executives. Nearly 70 percent of the Clinton appointees surveyed agreed that careerists should "initiate contacts with appointees, who may not know how to work with the bureaucracy."

During the pre-appointment process, try to see that your agency's general counsel or personnel people are keeping your appointee-designate advised as to his or her status. Offer to help with the ethics regulations. If the appointee is moving to Washington, try to arrange help. As soon as the appointee comes on board, or even before if possible, career executives should request get-acquainted meetings to explain what career officials do, to see what the appointee needs, and to find out the appointee's preferred style of interaction—in person or by memo. Provide a booklet with everyone's picture and basic information. Particularly for appointees who have never supervised large numbers of people, the last step can be invaluable.

Making the first move gives executives the chance to show political appointees that they know who's boss—appointees are in charge, and career public servants are there to help. In addition, career officials should ask new appointees to orient careerists as soon as they are comfortable doing so, to make sure that everyone understands the new agenda. If careerists don't know what appointees want, they can't help them get it; nor can they advise political appointees to protect them from running afoul of law or Congress. Again, see what you may have in common. One longtime career SES greeted a new cabinet secretary by pointing out that they were both from Chicago. Mentioning that made a personal connection and signaled a common way of viewing administration and a willingness to acknowledge that the new secretary might want his own person in this transferable SES position. In the end, the new secretary stuck with his incumbent career SES, a practice more typical than not.

Part of that first move should be developing an orientation plan for the new appointee, if at all possible after consulting with the appointee regarding what sort of information he wants and in what form. Some political leaders are more comfortable with paper orientations, while others prefer personal time. Orientation is the first part of what may be a three- or four-year relationship, so get it right by copying from those who have done a good job orienting past appointees. Indeed, doing a good job orienting incoming officials, who often express confusion regarding the budget process in particular, may help one's own advancement. Appointees (and others!) find government budget and personnel procedures particularly obtuse, so help is usually appreciated.

As part of any orientation, career leaders should attempt to put new appointees in touch with their predecessors. New political appointees are literally "home alone," particularly if they come from outside the Beltway. Forty-five percent of Reagan political appointees reported not knowing any of their agencies' political appointees before joining government; 35 percent of Clinton appointees said the same. Fewer still knew career officials. At the same time, 81 percent of Clinton appointees reported a desire to consult their predecessors. Accordingly, the regular briefing materials for new appointees should include the names and whereabouts of all those who previously held the position, regardless of political party or administration. PAS officials, in particular, may face a stressful wait of several months from the time they are designated to the time they actually take office, so they have ample time, as well as the desire, to consult predecessors. Because most political appointees give their career bureaucrats high marks, you probably have more to gain than to lose from having the new boss consult the old one. In general, political appointees of different parties will agree about which career officials are speedy and which are speed bumps.[72]

Naturally, you may not wish to share everything with new appointees, at least not during the first days of the relationship. Just as it is bad form to badmouth an ex-girlfriend to a new one, criticizing the last administration to members of the current one will have them suspect that come the next administration, you'll be saying the same things about them. Then, too, you might not want to show that picture of you getting an award from an ex-president of the other party—at least not right away.

Fifth, keep your house in order

New political appointees bring fresh eyes to the agency. Part of their job is to question agency practices to bring improvement or at least ensure accountability. The process may not be fun, but if your house is basically in order, the scrutiny should cause little long-term discomfort. Wilcox writes:

> There's a natural tendency for appointees confronted with issues they don't yet understand and a staff they don't yet trust to call for outside help. One of the first projects most new appointees wanted to discuss with me was how to contract for a consulting firm or a renowned expert, and in their shoes I might have done the same. It's hard to argue against taking a fresh look at an old issue. Just try not to take it as a personal affront.[73]

In Wilcox's case, new Navy secretary John Lehman dispatched Yale law professor Robert Bork to grill career attorneys on contract procedures. This resulted in no changes, but did assure Lehman that the Navy's house was in order, at least regarding submarine contracts. All this recalls the old Air Force saying: The two biggest lies are when the inspector general says "we're here to help you," and you reply "we're glad you're here." Yet without such outside pressures, none of us would serve the public half so well.

As part of keeping your house in order, *practice maximum feasible transparency*. From years of interviewing hundreds of officials in dozens of organizations, I know my subjects are lying to me when they tell me that everything in the agency is "great" because they have a "great bunch of people" wonderfully effective at "interfacing with others to provide terrific public service." Often, they are also lying to themselves. In the real world, organizations do some things well, some things tolerably well, and some badly or not at all—sometimes for reasons beyond anyone's immediate control. When a bureaucrat says his or her agency is heaven on earth, that person loses credibility. And I have to think that most political appointees are at least as smart as I am.

Sixth, forgive them their trespasses

Just as career executives often stereotype political appointees, political appointees often join government with their own negative ideas about bureaucrats, particularly if the president's party has been out of power for some time. Usually, negative views of bureaucrats soon become positive, but this may happen more quickly if you remember the biblical admonition that "a soft answer turneth away wrath." Like the rest of us, political appointees simply make mistakes. When they do, do not correct them in public.

Related to this, as Wilcox advises, *forgive every appointee at least one reorganization* as a way of marking his or her territory:

> Every appointee will have an impulse to reorganize. Whether that springs from a campaign promise to cut fat or whether it's to accommodate new agency duties, reorganizations are every bit as certain as death and taxes. But they're rarely as momentous.[74]

Indeed, wise career leaders should offer to lead the reorganization to make sure it goes well. Sometimes reorganizations really can bring improvement. Indeed, savvy change agents within an organization will often develop ideas in hopes of finding a new appointee with the interest and clout to make them happen.[75]

Political appointees often offend career executives by doing things demanded by their role as appointees representing the president to the agency rather than (or in addition to) the agency to the president. Appointees have an obligation to point out when the agency could better serve the public, and highly effective appointees such as James Lee Witt, Jim Miller, John Lehman, Steve Kelman, and Jim King actually began with policies that many agency insiders objected to.[76] As a Clinton EPA appointee put it, "Sometimes I have to say that OMB has a point there: maybe we are getting too much money." While perhaps true, I doubt that saying this won any friends inside EPA.

Seventh, as Colin Powell says, never step on enthusiasm

In general, political appointees join government more for patriotism (and ego) than for money.[77] Although they probably know less about the agency than career officials and may hold a different view of the public interest, they want to do a good job. As survey research shows, they are frustrated by the many constraints that frustrate all government executives.[78] Help them figure out how to overcome those constraints and buck them up when they get discouraged. At the same time, not all their ideas will be practical. When you disagree with an appointee, explain why in terms of external forces or standards. Rather than simply criticizing, say: "You have a good idea, but right now the congressional committee won't accept it. How might we develop a strategy to change that?" Sometimes, with sufficient effort and planning, political and legal obstacles really can be overcome.

Eighth, don' t get in the line of fire

As scholar and occasional political appointee Richard Haass explains in *The Bureaucratic Entrepreneur*, political appointees exist in part to take risks for the agency and for the president's agenda. Their short tenure frees them to battle Congress and take on the press. The killing hours that politics requires are acceptable because appointees are running three-year sprints rather than thirty-year marathons. Finally, as politicians, political appointees are more likely to do politics better than career officials can hope to. Career executives are in a different position. They should support their appointees but also understand and explain the limits of what battles they can fight, given that careerists may someday have to work for a different team. Naturally, this point might not be a subject for discussion on day one. Further, in some agencies, the organization culture does not let career officials duck politics. In places like the Navy, which have considerable unit cohesion, and in places like the U.S. Forest Service, where even relatively low-level officials must negotiate with state and local politicians, careerists are expected to fight political battles.

Ninth, disagree without being disagreeable

Survey research demonstrates that when confronted with implementing policies they disagree with, as often happens, most career officials feel free to tell their political superiors—nine of ten report taking this course.[79] For example, in an anonymous survey one Health and Human Services (HHS) career executive reported requesting different duties when detailed to develop regulations he/she strongly opposed. Political appointees respected the request and did not retaliate. "I was not detailed, and this is the way these matters usually are resolved," the respondent said. Again, negotiation over duties is more accepted in some organizations than in others. In defense organizations, such boldness might be seen as disloyalty and have serious consequences.[80]

Sometimes invoking the law to officials who genuinely may not know it can head off possible conflicts. For example, a careerist who blocked a personnel move he thought illegal recalled:

> When this individual came back to me to say the super two levels above supported him, I said there must be some misunderstanding because what he said was contrary to our legal obligations, so I suggested a meeting with my superior and his superior, and for all the politicals to be there just to make sure we were all on the same page, and then he backed down and said he would just go with what I said. . . . There was no price for doing that.[81]

To the degree possible, career officials should try to limit disagreements until they have established trusting relationships with appointees. Dissent can use up political capital, so it should not be used too casually or too often. For good guidance on the tools of ethical dissent, political appointees and career officials would do well to read John H. Johns's Guidelines for loyal dissent in government (see Box 1.7).[82]

Tenth, mobility is a possibility

Sometimes career officials disagree with a boss or a whole administration's entire agenda regarding their agency or simply cannot work with a particular political leader. In this situation, it might not make sense to wait them out. Most studies suggest appointees serve an average of about two years in their positions, but my own data from the Reagan administration suggest that in two-term administrations, political appointees serve an average of 2.6 years in their position and 3.7 years in their agencies—a long time to wait. More recent empirical work suggests that this has not changed much.[83] Given that the average government executive will serve twenty-five years or so, this could mean spending 10 percent of one's government career in administrative purgatory—more than enough time to develop ulcers. Life is too short to suffer; rather than persevere, it might make more sense to seek a soft landing elsewhere, especially if the boss is a career executive. Most career executives are terrific, but a few seem to have studied the leadership secrets of Saddam Hussein, and there is precious little we can do about them. Emigration in the face of oppression makes even more sense if a toxic boss is a careerist than a political because the career boss may be firmly entrenched.

Eleventh, careerists should show respect to lame-duck appointees

"Holdovers" from one administration to the next, like Bush/Obama Defense Secretary Robert Gates, are rare. "Blanketing in," political appointees switching to career civil service positions, is equally rare—only twelve known cases occurred in the 1992–1993 period. Thus, sooner or later, for better or worse, any political appointee will be gone. But they may not be gone forever. Often appointees go on to Congress or to interest groups, so they continue to influence agency affairs. Many will return to government at higher levels in later administrations. Someday, in the not too distant future that General Schedule (GS)-12 Schedule C may return as undersecretary. For entirely practical reasons, they should be treated as humanely as possible. In Washington it's nice to be smart, but it's also smart to be nice.

Unfortunately, in most cases the incoming crew will be less than respectful of the outgoing, "loser" administration, particularly at lower levels, where new politicals tend to be more passionate and less experienced. Older folks know that they too will someday be on the losing end of an election. For that reason, it may be up to the career service to buck up the outgoing (and perhaps future) politicals.

Finally, career officials must keep perspective

In our constitutional democracy, the worst ideas of political appointees seldom last long. They are blocked by other appointees, Congress, the *Washington Post*, or the mere thought of the *Washington Post*. Constitutional blocking of bad (and good) ideas is even more likely under divided party government—indeed, one career SES I interviewed longed for the days of divided government when "you could play your mother against your father or your father against your mother. Bad things could come up on the Hill and you could turn to the administration, or bad things from the administration could be stopped on the Hill." But even under united party government, gridlock happens.

In the long run, the best ideas of political appointees, including some regarded skeptically by career bureaucrats, may live on after appointees are long gone from government. As Wilcox admits, the soft approach to military shipyards taken by political appointees in the 1970s and 1980s was not the defense policy the career executives wanted, but perhaps turned out to be what was needed to end the Cold War.[84] Policies that seem questionable in the short term may produce long-term rewards. And when all else fails, career and political officials might, as the Serenity Prayer puts it, have the strength and wisdom to change what they can and accept what they cannot because constitutional governance involves endless patience, constant struggle, and periodic change.

A final word

Rather than curse the political system in general and the political appointee system in particular, presidents, political appointees, and career leaders should seek opportunities to manage the system to produce more rather than less social capital across the career and political sectors, to get more out of the dynamic career-noncareer nexus. After all, measurements suggest that the American government is relatively innovative, efficient, representative, and open compared to foreign governments, and in part these characteristics reflect the impact of outsider political appointees keeping bureaucracies accountable.[85] In a time of challenges—terrorism, environmental degradation, and natural disasters—that cut across organizational lines, it is more vital than ever to have politically skilled outsiders able to work with career experts to find and then politically sell feasible solutions. After all, that is what democracy should be all about.

Tips for leadership success

- Avoid stereotypes.
- Do reconnaissance.
- Put yourself in their shoes.

- Be proactive.
- Forgive them their trespasses.
- Respect enthusiasm.
- Disagree without being disagreeable.
- Mobility is a possibility.
- Show respect to lame ducks.
- Keep perspective.

Resources for further learning

Mark A. Abramson and Paul R. Lawrence, eds., *Learning the Ropes* (2005). This book offer great insights for both career and political public servants.

Ed DeSeve, *Speeding Up the Learning Curve: Observations from a Survey of Seasoned Political Appointees* (2009). This recent report offers sound advice for new appointees.

Robert Maranto, *Beyond a Government of Strangers: How Career Executives and Political Appointees Can Turn Conflict to Cooperation* (2005). My own book offers advice to career executives dealing with political officials. Before and during a presidential transition, the Senior Executives Association, at http://seniorexecs.org/index.php?id=117, often issues useful pamphlets advising members on some of the finer points of political-career etiquette.

Richard P. Nathan, *So You Want to Be in Government?* (2000). This is another very useful book for political appointees.

Anne Joseph O'Connell, *Waiting for Leadership: President Obama's Record in Staffing Key Agency Positions and How to Improve the Appointment Process*, recently published by the Center for American Progress (2010). The author provides ideas on how to improve the appointee system, and a good update on where the Obama administration stands in comparison to recent presidencies.

James P. Pfiffner, *The Strategic Presidency: Hitting the Ground Running* (1996). Bringing together a variety of insights, this is the best and most readable work on how to manage presidential transitions.

John H. Trattner, *The Prune Book* (2005). This offers perhaps the best advice for political appointees about how to conduct themselves while in office, particularly in relations with their career partners. The title parodies the "Plum Book" of government jobs.

Notes

1. Quoted in Maranto (1993), 96.
2. Quoted in Maranto (2005), 49.
3. See, for example, Murray and Wamsley (2007); Cohen (1998); Editors (2005). For responses, see Maranto (2005); Maranto (1993). See also Maranto (2002a); Bearfield (2007, 2009).
4. Niskanen (1971); Peters and Nelson (1978); Savas (1982); Moe (1985). For responses, see Goodsell (2003).
5. "Quotes about Change" (2006).
6. Bunker (1996).
7. Van Riper (1958).
8. Hofstadter (1964).
9. Maranto (1993), 31–60.
10. See essays in Nye, Zelikow, and King (1997).
11. These failures are often state and local responsibilities. For example, I have found that on an annual basis trust in government correlates closely with the homicide rate: Americans seem to blame their national government for state and local government failures to fight crime. Notably, New York City has reduced its homicide rate by roughly 80 percent in the past two decades. Yet other cities have refused to copy what works in crime prevention, as former NYPD chief William Bratton laments in *Turnaround* (1998). Despite these horrid failures, mayors still win reelection, and police chiefs keep their jobs.
12. Anechiarico and Jacobs (1996); Mackenzie (2001). See also Mackenzie (2002).
13. Lewis (2011).
14. For two rather different, but essentially concordant views on (mis)education, see Ravitch (2003); Zimmerman (2002).
15. Kettl and Fesler (2005), 32–33.
16. Goodsell (2003), 84–94.
17. Ibid., 27–34.
18. Ibid., 35–41.
19. Maranto (in press).
20. Wood and Waterman (1994); Meier and O'Toole (2006).
21. Aberbach and Rockman (2000), 164.
22. Newcomer (1988).
23. Maranto (1993), 85–87.
24. Aberbach and Rockman (2000), 123.
25. Michaels (2005), 13.
26. DeSeve (2009).
27. Durant (1992).
28. Bowman (2010).
29. Bearfield (2007), 101–120; quote, 102.
30. Maranto (2002b), 175–178; Maranto (2005), 42; Maranto (1993).
31. Ferrara and Ross (2005), 42.
32. Sniderman and Piazza (1993).
33. Maranto (2005), 53.
34. Ibid., 7–8.
35. Ibid., 32. In fairness, political appointees themselves often hold negative stereotypes about career bureaucrats, a topic I have treated. See Maranto (1993).
36. Maranto (1993); Maranto (1991), 247–266.

37. Maranto (1993), 127–137; Maranto (1991).

38. Pfiffner (1996); Lorentzin (1985). Overcoming stereotypes is the main theme of Maranto (2005).

39. Brewer and Maranto (2000).

40. Maranto (2005), 20.

41. Maranto (2005); Mackenzie (2001).

42. Personal interview, March 20, 2000.

43. Michaels (1997), 198–212.

44. Maranto (2005), 31.

45. Ibid., 32.

46. Aberbach and Rockman (2000), 123.

47. Maranto (2005), 26–29, 33–36.

48. For good comparative data on how long it takes presidents to get their teams on board, see O'Connell (2010). O'Connell also notes that some of the failings of the fledgling Obama administration, including the Toyota brakes problems and the near success of "underwear bomber" Umar Farouk Abdulmutallab may have been caused or exacerbated by vacant leadership positions at the NHTSA and the Transportation Security Administration.

49. Ferrara and Ross (2005), 63.

50. Khademian (2002), 108–121.

51. Krepinevich (1986).

52. Ouchi (1981).

53. Kelman (2005), 83–85; Maranto (2005), 55–58.

54. Harris and Milkis (1989), 201.

55. Ferrara and Ross (2005), 68.

56. Maranto (2005), 51.

57. Herspring (2005), 406.

58. Kelman (2005); Abramson and Lawrence (2001).

59. Maranto (1993), 103–115.

60. Maranto (2005), 54.

61. These lessons are included in a number of books, including Maranto (2005); Abramson and Lawrence (2005); Kelman (2005); Haass (1999); Nathan (2000); Trattner (2005).

62. Hofstadter (1964).

63. Devine (1972).

64. Maranto (2005), 99–102.

65. Maranto (2002a).

66. Maranto (2010a, 2010b).

67. Wilcox (2005).

68. Lewis (2008). For information on where the Obama administration put its patronage appointments, see Burge and Lewis (2010); Horton and Lewis (2010).

69. Wilcox (2005).

70. Maranto (1993), 87–88; Lewis 2008.

71. Maranto (2005), 53.

72. Wilcox (2005). Wilcox reports that the appointee-to-appointee exchange of information regarding career public servants is particularly well developed in the Defense Department, perhaps because defense policy remains less partisan than domestic policy. It is notable in this regard that President Obama retained Bush Defense Secretary Robert Gates.

73. Ibid., 66.

74. Ibid., 68.

75. Kelman (2005).
76. Maranto (2005), 46–47.
77. Powell (1995).
78. Maranto (1993).
79. Maranto (2005), 104–107.
80. Wilcox (2005); Herspring (2005).
81. Maranto (2005), 107.
82. Ibid., 133–134.
83. O'Connell (2010).
84. Wilcox (2005), 74–75.
85. Maranto (2002a); see also Goodsell (2003).

10 Working with Congress: Building relationships across the constitutional divide

GRACE CUMMINGS, FOUNDER, WORKING WITH CONGRESS

Career civil servants must work with Congress, even though the Constitution creates tensions between the two. In bridging the legislative and executive branch divide, civil servants have to negotiate among issues of policy, politics, and personality. Doing so requires an understanding of how Congress works—especially the role of committees, hearings, and oversight—and the responsibilities of different types of Capitol Hill staff. Even more, success with Congress demands an ability to build trust through effective communication and strong one-on-one relationships. Though never easy, all of these tasks have been further complicated by the hyper-partisanship and declines in Congressional comity in recent years.

ON MARCH 7, 2002, THE *WASHINGTON POST* REPORTED, "Michael Parker, the recently appointed leader of the Army Corps of Engineers, was abruptly forced to resign yesterday for failing to defend President Bush's proposed budget cuts."

The article continued: "Parker, a former House member from Mississippi who was confirmed as assistant army secretary for civil works five months ago, was the first major administration official ousted since Bush took office. He had made no secret of his disdain for the Office of Management and Budget's efforts to rein in the corps, and recently told a sympathetic House committee that he had requested $2 billion more than the OMB proposed in the president's budget. At a Senate hearing, he questioned the administration's decision to fund no new corps projects, adding that he did not have a 'warm and fuzzy feeling' for OMB officials."[1]

As a role model for bridging the constitutional divide between the legislative and executive branches, Parker is an interesting case study. Although he was able to span the divide by establishing trust and maintaining relationships with legislators—in large part due to his tenure as a member of Congress—he ultimately failed as an effective federal manager. In bridging the chasm between these two competing branches of government, he did two things very well and one thing very wrong.

First, Parker knew that information is an important commodity on Capitol Hill. By providing pertinent and concise information about corps activities in members' states and districts—information that was helpful to the political interests of those members—he was able to serve members' needs and establish trust while simultaneously furthering the corps' mission.

Second, Parker recognized the importance of stakeholder relationships when working with Congress. Over the years, Parker had developed strong personal and professional bonds with his congressional colleagues and continued to nurture those relationships after his departure from the Hill. More important, in his role as the civilian head of the Corps of Engineers, he identified the members who had great interest in corps projects—especially those benefiting from corps dollars spent in their states and districts. He worked closely with the committees with jurisdiction over corps programs and funding. In addition, he identified other stakeholders—business interests, local officials, military supporters—who could reach out to members of Congress and reinforce the message he wished to project for the corps.

So far, he was a model for effectively bridging the constitutional divide.

His downfall, however, came in bucking the executive branch chain of command and not appropriately representing the president's policy choices before Congress. As a federal executive within President George W. Bush's administration, Parker had the responsibility of "carrying the water" up on the Hill, even if he disagreed with the president on policy matters. In bridging the constitutional divide, federal executives must not lose sight of their role as executive branch representatives, and they must respect the separation of powers the United States has observed for more than two centuries.

The Founders envisioned a working relationship between the legislative and executive branches, but knew tension between the branches helped keep them in check. More important, this balance is the foundation for trust among the American public. Former representative Lee Hamilton stresses this point by asserting, "The American people, despite their criticism of politics and politicians, have an unshakeable faith in the Constitution and in the American system and its power sharing arrangements. The performance of government may disappoint them, but they firmly support the basic structure of our government set up by the founders."[2]

In order to effectively bridge the constitutional divide, government executives need to utilize pertinent information and supportive stakeholders to build relationships and trust among key members of the legislative branch. In doing so, they must also respect this constitutional divide by supporting the policy choices of the president and the administration.

Challenges for federal executives when working with Congress

Federal managers face the reality that they serve two masters within our constitutional structure. As executive branch employees, they serve under the auspices of the president in his capacity of chief executive as spelled out in Article II of the Constitution.

Article I establishes Congress as the "first branch" of government vested with the power to establish laws, appropriate funds, and maintain oversight authority to monitor how federal executives carry out their duties. The Senate has advice and consent power over presidential appointees, and senators use it to block appointees they deem not fit for the task.

Federal executives, therefore, must be responsive to the president as the chief executive and to members of Congress as those who establish, fund, and oversee what they do. As many managers can attest, although they are ultimately responsible for running efficient and effective programs, the legislators who drafted the authorizing or appropriations language have specific ideas about the ways they want these programs administered or the money spent.

Increasing this challenge is the highly charged relationship between the president's Office of Management and Budget (OMB) and members of Congress. OMB's current mission "is to assist the President in overseeing the preparation of the federal budget and to supervise its administration in executive branch agencies. In helping to formulate the president's spending plans, OMB evaluates the effectiveness of agency programs, policies, and procedures, assesses competing funding demands among agencies, and sets funding priorities."[3] As such, OMB officials have enormous power over executive branch managers and in recent years have extended their reach beyond financial management and into performance aspects of program delivery.

The problem, however, is that members of Congress and congressional staff members often pay no attention to the hoops federal managers must jump through to satisfy their OMB examiners. Moreover, members of Congress can be openly hostile to OMB officials, as witnessed in 2002 when then-OMB director Mitch Daniels went before the House Appropriations Committee. This hearing included Rep. David Obey lecturing Daniels and waving a copy of the Constitution. "This little book is not very impressive to look at, but it runs the show," he said.[4] As described in the *Washington Post*, "members were especially fond of quoting from Article 1, Section 9 which states that 'no money shall be drawn from the treasury, but in consequence of appropriations made by law.' The subtext was that unelected executive branch budget officials should butt out."[5] During the Parker hearing on the Corps of Engineers budget, Rep. Peter DeFazio referred to OMB officials as "idiots" and "thugs."[6] It is clear that federal managers are stuck between competing powers—OMB officials representing the president and members of Congress who perceive the "unelected budget officials" as trampling upon their constitutional jurisdiction.

Finally, there is the challenge of working in an environment driven by partisan politics. Working in a nonpartisan fashion with an institution that uses partisan identification as a decision axis can be extremely difficult. Federal executives can become the congressional whipping boy for the presidential initiative that the majority or minority party in Congress opposes. These executives must represent the administration's policies in a nonpartisan fashion while bombs are lobbed at them by partisan members of the House and Senate.

In recent years the political polarization in the House and Senate has become more extreme, making this challenge even greater. Citing the 1994 electoral takeover of the House of Representatives by the Republicans, Thomas Mann and Norman Ornstein, in their book *The Broken Branch*, mark it as a pivotal election that spurred the rapid rise of extreme partisanship in Congress and its corrosive effects on the chambers. More recently, George Packer, writing in the August 9, 2010, issue of the *New Yorker*, details the causes of heightened political rancor within the Senate and refers to that chamber as a "broken chamber."[7] In her book, *Fight Club Politics*, author Juliet Eilperin traces the causes of the rising tide of partisanship and incivility in contemporary politics and its effects on the House. Kathleen Hall Jamieson, Director of the Annenberg Public Policy Center, speaking at an April 2010 conference noted current incivility does not rise to the level experienced during much of the nineteenth century, but today's media, by prominent displays of name calling and by program formats designed for rude and uncivil discourse, are promoting such behavior in politicians. In addition, the relatively new phenomenon of political blogs is a format tailor-made for partisan harangue.

From an insider's perspective, the most important factor giving rise to rancor, incivility, or hard partisanship can be summed up in one word—competition. It is easy to forget the rancor within the Congress during the cycles of 1986 through 1996. The rhetoric over Social Security, Welfare, contras, taxes, health care, and impeachment was, at times, extremely personal and highly partisan. During that ten-year stretch, the Senate changed hands twice and the House went Republican for the first time in more than forty years. Within the next ten years, both chambers switched again and as a result of the 2010 elections, the Republicans once again gained control of the House of Representatives. This much volatility in the political marketplace leads to brutal battles for control of the chambers.

In addition, computer-enhanced redistricting dating back to 2001 has allowed most districts to be made safe for one party or the other, eliminating swing districts that were often occupied by moderate or centrist members. It was these centrist members, now a very rare breed in either chamber, who were the force behind many of the bipartisan discussions and decisions in previous congresses. The elimination of "the middle," combined with the constant threat of loss of control, or the real prospect of gaining control, keeps partisanship front and center in both chambers.

The result for federal executives is a highly charged partisan arena where factual arguments are often trumped by political strategies and tactics focused on political wins rather than policy advancement. In such an environment, the challenge of bridging the constitutional divide is heightened and building relationships and trust among key congressional contacts is even more important.

Building trust through communication

David Gergen, former White House communications director and well-known political analyst, says, "Trust is the coin of the realm," in Washington. For many federal managers, however, the concept of trust as a commodity on Capitol Hill seems to be an oxymoron. Legislative politics at its worst can be a treacherous business where veracity may be set aside with victorious ends justifying unscrupulous means. For congressional members and their staffs, however, information is highly valued and the ability to trust the individuals providing this information is essential. As Washington lawyer Donald deKieffer notes in his book, *The Citizen's Guide to Lobbying Congress*, "Accuracy and thoroughness are hallmarks of successful lobbying campaigns."[8]

Providing concise, pertinent, and reliable information to members of Congress and their staff members is the primary building block for developing trust and building relationships on the Hill. For federal managers, establishing channels of communication and developing trusted relationships with the relevant congressional offices can set the foundation for fruitful partnerships with lawmakers.

The good news for executives is they have lots of useful information for legislators (see Box 10.1). Departments and agencies can build relationships with senators and representatives by providing information that affects the economies of their states or districts and ultimately touches the lives of their constituents. Workforce plus-ups (increases), environmental superfund dollars, new soldiers transferred to military facilities, and disaster preparedness spending are all examples of opportunities for federal executives to communicate with legislative offices. Moreover, the dialogue may go beyond the economy—numbers of veterans served, new hurricane warning systems, gang eradication measures, and port security enhancements are all examples of federal activities relevant to congressional offices.

Beware of misinformation. When incorrect information is discovered by legislators, it can be the death knell for any organization trying to gain support on the Hill. Legislators judge mistakes harshly, often assuming someone provided the material intentionally to mislead or gain political advantage. Capitol Hill is a small community, and rarely is the source of bad information kept quiet. If staff members have been "burned" by bad information, they tend to share the identity of the perpetrator with their colleagues so other offices will not become victims. And a damaged reputation on the Hill is very hard to repair.

Lessons can be learned by examining the tactics of effective Washington lobbyists. Many lobbyists build trust with members of Congress by providing both the pro and con of the issue they are raising. Lobbyists know members and their staffs are smart enough to realize there are always two sides to an issue. Although lobbyists will always put the best possible spin on their side of the argument, by providing their opponents'

During my tenure as chief of staff for Rep. Jack Kingston, R-Ga., one of the best working relationships I developed was with John Hankinson, regional director for the EPA in Atlanta.

Our friendship hinged on periodic calls to share information. I would call John to let him know when my boss was going to criticize the EPA publicly, and John would call me when the EPA was going to do something in our district my boss was not going to like.

In most cases, one of us was not happy after the call, but we both agreed it was better than being surprised. Communicating, even under tense circumstances, was important.

argument, they help these offices avoid unwanted surprises. They know garnering trust within the office is essential if they are to make headway—and being upfront with all the information helps to establish that trust.

Strengthening relationships by building stakeholder support

As a representational body, the legislative branch is driven by political interests. On any given day, a member of Congress or senator may have meetings on many different issues: agriculture subsidies, high-tech weaponry, wetlands protection, local transit projects, stem cell research, educational testing, and on and on and on. The number of issues Congress deals with on an annual basis is enormous, and the multiplicity of constituencies represented continues to grow.

Members must therefore make policy decisions based on their own beliefs and the needs of the constituents they represent. Facts and evidence matter, but in the legislative environment, substance may not always carry the day. When approaching Congress, many federal executives make the mistake of believing that if they can make a good factual and statistical argument for a program's efficacy, Congress simply cannot reject it. This way of thinking is especially true for managers representing agencies where the scientific method rules, statistical information provides evidence, and black and white results are prized. The Hill, however, is full of gray.

Facts, evidence, and statistics all matter in the legislative process, but if executives are not cognizant of how many stakeholders are weighing in on

Box 10.2 Cultivating local stakeholders

The Federal Law Enforcement Training Center (FLETC) is located near Brunswick, Ga., an area represented in Congress by Republican Jack Kingston. During my service in Kingston's office, I would periodically get updates from the executive staff at FLETC. More often than not, however, I would get most of my information about FLETC from our constituents. Whether it was the president of the Brunswick Chamber of Commerce, the mayor of Brunswick, or the head of the economic development authority for Glynn County, they all cared about the facility and made sure I knew it.

Ralph Basham, FLETC director at that time, and his executive staff did an excellent job creating local stakeholder support. Our congressional office, in turn, made certain we paid special attention to the health and well-being of the facility.

any given issue, they are missing an important ingredient in the congressional decision-making process. To strengthen their hand it therefore is important that executives look beyond the substance of their programs and develop relationships with constituencies that value their work.

By identifying vested stakeholders, executives build political support for their work and make themselves less vulnerable to legislative intervention or funding cuts. If a member of Congress receives multiple points of input about a project or program (especially if these contacts are coming from their home district or state), it becomes much more difficult for him or her to arbitrarily cut or criticize the program (see Box 10.2). Political pressure from a wide variety of district or state interests creates an effective political buffer.

In addition, building stakeholder support for programs and projects gives executives a real reason for dialogue with legislative offices and the ability to develop working relationships that may not have existed before. By building relationships with stakeholders in districts and states, federal executives are then working with the individuals most important to members of Congress—their constituents. Congressional staff members pay particular attention to activities affecting their member's district or state and regard the federal agents who can provide such information as allies.

Stakeholder information is valuable to committee staff members because they must build political support for their bosses' policy agenda. By identifying stakeholder support for given programs or projects, executives are providing important information to the committee staff and can build valuable relationships with those who have oversight and budget authority over their programs.

Successful lobbyists know all about the importance of stakeholder support and use it to their advantage when working issues on Capitol Hill. A common misperception about lobbyists is that they cozy up to members, slide campaign contributions over, and then use their personal relationships with these members to have them cast a vote for or against a piece of legislation. There is no doubt that contributions are a factor in elective politics and that many lobbyists utilize giving as a means to garner member attention. Furthermore, with the 2010 Supreme Court ruling allowing groups such as corporations and labor unions to directly spend on campaigns, the pressure that can be brought to bear has increased tremendously. Yet, in my experience, members of Congress (with rare exception) do not vote one way or the other on an issue because they have received one or more contributions.

Lobbyists do utilize fund-raising opportunities to get known by members and staff so that when an issue comes up, they are not making a "cold" sales call. Yet, their persuasiveness with a member hinges on the political stakeholders they can bring to bear in favor of their issue. Prior to approaching a member, effective lobbyists bring together a coalition of individuals who can have maximum impact on the targeted representative. They utilize the collective force of these individuals to champion their cause and convince a member of Congress that relies on support within his or her electorate. Likewise, executive branch managers should be investing time building relationships and coalitions among public, private, and nonprofit entities in support of their programs or projects. Although federal managers do not have the luxury of getting known through "political giving," they can utilize these coalitions to build support for their work within Congress.

The intersection of politics, policy, and personality

Understanding the legislative environment is a little like learning how to play three-dimensional chess. In this strategic board game, players must watch each level of the playing surface and know that all three levels are interconnected. When one piece moves, it can affect any of the pieces on all three levels. Consequently, a player's strategy needs constant reevaluation with each successive move.

Working with Congress is also a multidimensional endeavor, but in this case, the three levels at play are policy, politics, and personalities. To navigate effectively in the legislative environment, executives must watch all three "P's" all the time. Moreover, as many executive branch employees can attest, personality and political factors often trump policy substance when dealing in the legislative environment.

Members of Congress are very reactive to current political situations, and executives are best able to connect with them when their substantive presentations have "real-time" relevancy. When approaching legislators, executives need to take the political temperature of the moment and judge how the current climate might influence or affect the issue at hand. Items to consider include: What are the "hot button" issues currently before Congress? Is it an election year? How high (or low) are the president's poll ratings? What is the current state of the economy? Is a particular crisis driving policy development?

President Barack Obama's July 2010 signing of the Dodd-Frank Wall Street Reform and Consumer Protection Act is an example of how political pressure can make all the difference. For years, some members of Congress pushed for greater regulatory oversight of Wall Street. With a relatively prosperous economy and a wide pool of happy investors, however, the political will of the majority to do so was not in evidence. In addition, the investment and banking industries spent lots of time and money lobbying Congress against such changes and were effective in persuading enough members to thwart such legislation.

With the massive financial crisis kicking off in 2008 and continuing through 2009, the political winds shifted and many citizens and commentators began clamoring for increased oversight on an industry that they felt recklessly brought about "The Great Recession" and sent the economy into a tailspin. As is often the case, the House—the people's chamber—was the first to act and passed its version of the bill, HR 4173, in December 2009.

The Senate, the much more deliberative body and the chamber most prone to obstructionist tactics by the minority, was far slower in coming to terms on a bill. Nevertheless, between anger with the bank bailouts, outrage over continued executive bonuses being given at investment firms, and the general angst around the continued recession, the political moment was right and Senator Christopher Dodd was able to get passage of his legislation in May 2010. Although only four Senate Republicans supported the Dodd bill, it was enough to hand the president and congressional Democrats a major legislative victory.

On Capitol Hill, policy and politics always are intertwined. All members can come up with an idea for a bill, have their legislative assistants, in conjunction with the legislative counsel's office, draft the proper language and then introduce it for consideration in their respective chambers. Influences that guide the formulation of this legislation might include, but are not limited to, members' ideological beliefs, their personal interests, the regional orientation of their district, or their coalitional alliances or pressures exerted by their constituents. Members, however, often introduce bills without the intention of ever having them enacted into law—in fact, in proportion to the number of bills introduced in each session of Congress, very few pass and become law. Rather, the intent of introducing the legislation may be to help the members build momentum as they run for higher office, appease a constituent group, garner press attention during a critical political moment in time or set a future agenda.[9]

When members wish to influence policy, drafting legislation is not the only tool in their arsenal. Congressional oversight is another path that allows members to assert policy power over executive branch organizations. Members see themselves as the principals and executive branch employees as their agents carrying out the programs and policies passed by the House and Senate. By asserting oversight pressure on an agency or department, members can have significant impact on the conduct of programs or projects.

It is also essential to understand that political timing greatly influences policy development. If the chorus "location, location, location" is true for real estate, the refrain "timing, timing, timing" is appropriate for the policy process. There are times when political pressure builds up on a given issue and Congress determines that it must act.[10]

Other times, no matter how much the president or a member of Congress wishes to push policy forward, the timing may just not be right. Even though President Obama and congressional Democrats were able to claim credit for passing two massive pieces of legislation in 2010—health care reform and regulatory oversight of the financial industry—the timing was not right to achieve a third important goal—a bill to address climate change by capping emissions.

In 2009 Democrats in the House of Representatives passed landmark climate change legislation. Feeling the momentum from that victory, many within the environmental community and President Obama himself pushed the Senate to act. Yet the legislation stalled. Recognizing that by July 2010 he still did not have the votes to advance the long-awaited measure capping greenhouse gases, Senate Majority Leader Harry Reid instead moved forward an energy bill that responded to the Gulf of Mexico oil spill earlier that year. Leading up to the November elections, this was a much more attractive and achievable piece of legislation given outrage over the BP oil disaster. Climate change legislation would have to wait for a more advantageous political moment.

Congress is an institution built on personal relationships, and the force of personalities cannot be overestimated. In an interview, the late Jack Valenti, former president of the Motion Picture Association and longtime political adviser and confidant to President Lyndon Johnson, said that one of Johnson's greatest strengths, as Senate majority leader, was his understanding of human nature. According to Valenti, Johnson was extremely smart, studied issues inside and out, and devoted his full energies to his political success. His effectiveness, however, was in large part derived from knowing every member of the Senate well and using that knowledge in leading the chamber. He not only knew all the senators' political leanings but also studied their personal likes and dislikes, their families, their political ambitions, their goals. He paid great attention to how they related to other members of the chamber. With this knowledge, he was able to influence policy decisions by playing to each member's needs, weaknesses, strengths, and political agendas. If stroking a senator's ego was in order, Johnson knew which buttons to push. If the situation called for a subtle threat, Johnson knew the personal vulnerabilities. It was through such personality-driven forces that Johnson was able to control the Senate chamber like no one before him and no one since.[11]

When working the Hill, effective lobbyists build portfolios containing personal information about each member. These portfolios include the member's legislative interests, personal interests, educational background, business and political history, family history, hobbies, and anything else they can garner. As an integral part of these profiles, the files include information on each member's political ambitions. Lobbyists then use the information to tailor their arguments to each member of Congress.

Personalities can also determine how offices function. Some offices are known to be very efficient and others frenetic and inefficient. Some offices engage in long-term planning, while others are reactive. Some offices require lengthy briefing packages, while others want nothing more than an executive brief. Most often, the member's personality dictates these peculiarities. To work effectively with an office, the lobbyist must have this information.

The bicameral body

By nature and history, the Senate and House are two very different institutions. Senators serve six-year terms with a third of the chamber up for election every two years, while the entire House goes before the voters every two years. The House debates legislation on the floor under strict rules of order, while Senate debates are freewheeling with few restrictions. House members represent a narrower constituency, while senators represent a much broader constituency. The House has a leader chosen by a vote of the whole chamber—the Speaker of the House—who has the ability to dictate activities in the chamber. The Senate has no such leader; consequently, it is harder for the majority and minority "leadership" to impose their will. In the House, coalitions matter. In the Senate, through a little-known maneuver called the legislative hold, every senator has the ability to stall legislation, so each person matters.

Although the House and Senate ultimately must work in unison to produce legislation for presidential consideration, they are often at odds with each other. The consequence for executives can be devastating if they are not aware of the friction that can exist between the two chambers and the need to formulate relationships on both sides of the Hill.

When working on an issue with one side of the Hill, it is always judicious to ascertain what action is (or is not) being taken in the other chamber. Sometimes members of the House and Senate agree on an issue, but discord is common. Jurisdictional rivalries can exist between the committee chairs of the two chambers, and unsuspecting executives can become ensnarled in a bicameral conflict. During the annual budget process, the House and Senate appropriators must come up with their respective appropriation bills—and rarely are the corresponding bills the same. It is altogether possible for an agency program to receive full funding in one chamber's appropriation bill and be zeroed out in the other chamber's bill. Knowing that senators and representatives are not obligated to work together and often do not, federal executives should cultivate relationships in both bodies.

Understanding committees, hearings, and oversight

The Constitution provides federal managers with the best reason for building relationships and establishing trust with the legislative branch—in doing so, they ensure the integrity of America's system of government. The desire to limit the authority of the executive and provide direct representation for the citizenry led the Framers to make Congress the most powerful branch of government. But leery of unchecked representational government, the Framers also put into place a system of checks and balances so that the legislative branch could not act rashly or solely upon the political will of the moment. To serve as good stewards of the Constitution, legislative and executive branch employees have the responsibility to work together to ensure good governance.

Referencing James Madison and *Federalist Paper* No. 47, Walter Oleszek, a senior specialist in American national government at the Congressional Research Service, points out, "The Constitution creates a system not of separate institutions performing separate functions, but of separate institutions sharing functions (and even competing for predominant influence in exercising them). Indeed, the overlap of powers is fundamental to national decision making."[12]

On the Hill this observation plays out most directly in the work done by committees, and it is here where federal executives can develop the most important relationships. Eventually, both chambers may debate and vote on the legislation developed by committees. It is within the committee system, however, where the details of programs, projects, and funding take shape, and it is here where executive branch input is most crucial.

Committees and subcommittees do the hard work of formulating legislation. As mentioned previously, all members of Congress can come up with an idea for a bill, have it drafted into legislative language, and introduce the bill in their respective chamber. Once introduced, however, the legislation is referred to the correct committee of jurisdiction and in most cases passed on to the subcommittee that handles the issue. For a piece of legislation to come to the House or Senate floor for consideration, it must usually be discussed and "marked-up" (revised and put into final draft form) within a committee and then reported out for consideration. If at the end of a congressional session (measured in two-year increments) both chambers have not passed the bill, it dies. For further consideration, it must be reintroduced during the next session of Congress, and the process begins again.

The implication for federal executives is that contact—whether directly or through their legislative affairs office—with the committees overseeing their programs and funding is extremely important. To be at the table as initial concepts are being developed within the committee process allows federal executives to supply the statistical information pertaining to the proposed program, discuss potential pitfalls in design, and bring a "real world" workability evaluation to the discussion. Granted, federal executives cannot lobby for or against specific pieces of legislation. They do, however, have the information base that is essential material for committee staff members to evaluate as they work with their members of Congress to develop, alter, or revise current programs and funding priorities. The Founders, in establishing the balance of powers, envisioned and deemed necessary an active interchange between the executive and legislative branches for our government to function well.

Members of Congress also use the power of their committees to advance their policy objectives, and in some cases, bend the executive branch to their legislative will. Congressional hearings are an example of how legislators can use the power of their committees to bring public attention and pressure to bear on a policy they wish to advance or defeat. Although proffered as information-gathering events—witnesses are called to provide testimony—these hearings are rarely held to obtain information. Instead, hearings are called to get material on the public record—and in the media—and put a positive spin on the chair's policy objectives or a negative spin on someone else's policy objectives or programmatic performance (be it the executive branch, private sector, or nonprofit community under scrutiny).

When Michael Brown, former head of the Federal Emergency Management Agency (FEMA), testified before the House Government Reform Committee in late 2005, new information about the Katrina disaster was not the objective. The hearing was called for members to publicly vent their outrage at what they perceived to be Brown's ineptitude, criticize the Bush administration's mismanagement of the disaster, register their criticism with the voters, and call for new policies to strengthen federal disaster assistance and reform FEMA. It was a public show to gain political capital with the American people and policy momentum for reform legislation.

Likewise, in June 2010 when Ed Markey, Chairman of the House Energy and Environment Subcommittee, called CEOs of the largest oil companies to testify before his committee, his intent was not to gather information about the BP disaster in the Gulf of Mexico. Rather, his intent was to publicly lambaste these companies, highlight how unprepared they were for a similar disaster, and ultimately throw down the gauntlet for congressional action to further regulate the oil industry.

In his opening remarks at the hearing, Chairman Markey stated:

> The oil companies may think it is fine to produce carbon copies of their safety plans, but the American people expect and deserve more. It is time to expect more from the oil industry. And that needs to start today. First, Congress must ensure that there is unlimited liability for oil spills by oil companies. While we try to cap this well, we must lift the cap on oil industry liability. Second, Congress must also enact wide-ranging safety reforms for offshore drilling. If oil companies are going to pursue ultra-deep drilling, we must ensure that it is ultra-safe and that companies can respond ultra-fast. Third, the free ride is over. Oil companies need to pay their fair share to drill on public land. Right now every single one of the companies here today and dozens of others are drilling for free in the Gulf of Mexico on leases that will cost American taxpayers more than $50 billion dollars in lost royalties. Fourth, we must ensure that new technologies are developed for capping wells, boosting safety and cleaning up spills. I will soon introduce the Oil SOS Act to ensure that we have 21st century technologies in place for 21st century drilling risks.[13]

Although these are high-profile and extreme examples, executive branch employees routinely deal with the same hearing dynamics on a smaller scale. By understanding that hearings are rarely for substantive input, but are a legislative and political tool, executives can better prepare themselves for such hearings. The key to understanding the hearing process is realizing that 90 percent of what will happen in the hearing is determined before a single witness testifies.

Building relationships with committee staffers can also help protect executives from being ambushed at congressional hearings—or at least allows for some defensive preparation if the hearing is going to be hostile. Contacting a staffer prior to the hearing is an opportunity to ask some questions: What are the politics behind this particular hearing? What is the significance of calling the hearing at this particular time? What specific committee members are interested and apt to attend? Who else will be testifying at the hearing, and should we expect any surprises?

By understanding the nature of these gatherings, executives can discuss the hearings for what they are—political theater. Instead of getting angry that the committee is paying no attention to the substance, executives can work with the staff members to best position themselves in these public forums.

Legislators work in concepts, and their final output is paper. Executive branch employees are the implementers. The process works best when legislators and administrators are in dialogue about the development of legislative language and resulting programs. Without such dialogue, legislators can lose sight of the "real world" consequences of their decisions, and federal managers are stuck with administering untenable mandates.

Although law prohibits executive branch employees from lobbying on legislation, they have abundant technical, statistical, and operational material to share with their legislative counterparts. Executives and legislators may butt heads when it comes to decisions on programs and projects, but dialogue—even if it is in conflict—is far better than having committees create legislation in an information vacuum or legislation based only on information from outside forces not charged with administering these programs.

The Constitution also vests legislators with oversight responsibility to ensure federal executives do not overstep their bounds. This oversight can be a burden to executives, and in some cases administered in a heavy-handed fashion by congressional members and staff, but it is important to our system of checks and balances. Unfortunately, in recent years, due to the heightened partisanship in both chambers of Congress, oversight has been used as a political tool to do damage to the opposing party. Federal managers can't do anything about this.

When dealing with congressional oversight, however, it is important to recognize that members of Congress oftentimes see it as the "principal" and the executive branch as their "agents" in carrying out the legislation they have passed. Although this may be a misnomer, federal managers can nonetheless build positive relationships with legislators and their staff— those who deal in paper and concepts—by helping them understand how programs actually work in real life. The legislators may not always agree with the administrators, but it is far better to be in dialogue around task, rather than being a target for political purpose. Federal managers can provide critical input at all stages of the policy process, but it is within the realm of congressional oversight that they can help legislators understand how their concepts become real and either work or need to be adjusted. Legislators want to see their ideas succeed and federal managers can be the ones to make this happen.

Working with congressional staff

Without question, ultimate power in Congress resides with the elected members of the House and Senate. They are the only individuals who can officially introduce legislation, serve on committees, and vote on legislation brought before their respective chambers. The vast majority of the day-to-day work on Capitol Hill, however, is done not by members of Congress but by the legions of congressional staff that populate the legislative branch. The reliance of members of Congress on their staff should not be underestimated, nor should the enormous influence these staff members can have on executive branch activities. Two distinct types of legislative staff members work on the Hill: those employed in members' personal offices and those who serve on committees.

Personal office staff

Personal office staffers serve at the pleasure of an individual representative or senator. Once elected, new members of Congress receive a budget and are able to hire a staff that serves their office needs in Washington, D.C., and in their district or state. Other than limits on the number of staff employed, members of Congress have no set standards for how they configure their offices. The General Schedule (GS) ranking system for employees does not apply on Capitol Hill; members have sole discretion over hiring and firing their teams. The rules of the House and Senate prohibit staff members from engaging in political campaign activities during their official working hours, but they can participate in partisan political activities after hours, including attending and participating in fund-raising activities. Although there are no written rules, most members of Congress hire personal office staffers that share their political affiliation, and the offices are consequently very partisan in nature.

A typical Hill office employs a chief of staff and a support staff to handle all matters related to the member's legislative responsibilities. Members' offices also employ press operatives to coordinate media outreach, receptionists for front office duties, and an office manager who covers administrative duties and may serve as executive secretary/assistant to the member.

In a congressional office, federal executives will most likely deal with legislative directors and legislative assistants. These staffers are charged with briefing their members on all pending legislation, preparing members for upcoming committee hearings and mark-ups, attending meetings with constituent groups, and responding to all district or state inquiries (by phone, fax, mail, or e-mail) pertaining to legislation. Federal executives will encounter this staff whenever they are dealing with programs, projects, or legislation that affect a member's district or are of special interest to that member.

Personal office staff members are extremely focused on their member's district or state; their principal concerns are the needs of their boss and the interests of his or her constituents. Although these staffers deal with national issues, the lens by which they evaluate any issue is the interest of their respective members and the interests of the district or state. These staffers tend to be legislative generalists on most issues and legislative specialists only on those matters that pertain to their member's specific policy initiatives or affect their state or district (see Box 10.3).

When a federal executive briefs staff, more information is not always better, and technical details will often elude them. An effective briefing will

Box 10.3   Building relationships

In 1998 the Navy's congressional liaison office invited me and several other congressional staff members to Kings Bay Naval Base to spend a day and a night on a nuclear submarine. For me, it was important to learn more about the base because it was one of the largest employers in our congressional district. Plus, the chance to spend a night in a submarine was just too cool to pass up.

During the trip, I learned a lot about the technology on the sub, the challenges for the crew, the mission of the base, and the base's economic impact in our district. More important, I spent thirty-six hours building relationships with the liaison officer, the base commander, and the submarine captain.

After the voyage, when one of those men called, I always answered. We had built a working relationship around mutual interests.

include material related to their member's constituent base or touch on their member's particular policy interests; otherwise it is good information falling on deaf ears. A two-page executive brief on the most important elements of a program (wisely pointing out district or state impacts within the first two paragraphs) is far better than a 150-page report on the program. When these staff members send inquiries to government agencies, they are usually not seeking to write a thesis on the issue at hand; rather, they are responding to a constituent request—many times on an issue they know nothing about.

To build trust with personal office staff members, it is essential to remember their focus is their member and their district or state. Good material is good for them only if it relates to their boss's needs or the needs of their boss's constituents. It is an enormous relief for legislative staff members when public- or private-sector executives come into their office understanding that time is limited and get to the point quickly—what is the issue and why should their boss care?

Be aware that many of these staff members are in their early twenties and look even younger. It is typical for a senior federal executive to brief a twenty-three-year-old legislative assistant. Although this scenario can be disconcerting, it is, in fact, the norm on Capitol Hill. Bright young staff members populate the Hill, and their bosses rely on them heavily. Senior executives are wise to understand this reality and endeavor to treat the "kids" with respect. Some of these staff members will be impressive, some will not. Often, however, they are the only conduit for communicating with a member of Congress and can turn into valuable allies if treated with professional courtesy.

Personal offices also include staff in members' home districts or states. District or state directors oversee the local staff, monitor current events, and most important, work for the economic well-being of the local area. They consider anything the federal government does in their district or state within their purview and are most interested in information pertaining to jobs and dollars entering or exiting their member's jurisdiction. These directors see an Army base not just as a military installation but also as a huge economic engine in the district. They see a government research laboratory not just as a scientific facility but also as an employer of professionals who earn good salaries. Grants to universities, employment in regional offices, federal highway projects, crop insurance subsidies, and disaster preparedness are just a few of the areas that provide executives a reason for discourse with these directors. Federal executives cannot lobby for a given program or project, but sharing pertinent and timely information on items affecting a state or district is a terrific way to begin building trust within these offices.

District or state caseworkers are the staff members charged with working directly with constituents who have encountered problems with the federal government. Whether constituents have missed a Social Security check, need a passport expedited, have been denied service at the local veterans' hospital, or are having problems with their Medicare prescription drug plan, they can turn to caseworkers for help. Caseworkers tend to have long tenures, and their knowledge of how the government works and where to go to solve a problem is a valuable commodity for any member of the House and Senate. It is through these problem-solving relationships that many federal managers find their easiest and most trusted avenue into congressional offices.

Committee staff

Committee staff members, also known on the Hill as professional staff members, are a completely different type of employee with an entirely different focus. Committee staff members are broken down along partisan lines; those in the majority offices serve at the pleasure of their chairs, and those in the minority offices serve at the pleasure of their ranking minority members.

The core staff for most House and Senate committees and subcommittees includes majority and minority staff directors and majority and minority professional staff (also referred to as legislative analysts). Administrative staff members also work in these offices and handle functional issues such as records management, scheduling, and office administration.

Unlike their legislative counterparts in personal offices, the professional staff members are usually older, longer tenured, and better paid. Many of them hold advanced degrees or come to the job with a legal background. More important, where the personal office staff members tend to be generalists, the professional committee staff members are experts in their field. Many are hired for their subject knowledge expertise and completely master the issues they cover for the committee. These staffers often serve for ten, fifteen, or even twenty years with a committee and consequently become leading experts in the nation on their issues. Committee staffs deal with formulating the legislation, making detailed policy recommendations to the members, and sometimes inserting legislative language into pending legislation.

In 2004, a furor arose when a staffer inserted language into a spending bill that allowed certain congressional staff broad access to Americans' tax returns. According to the *Washington Post*, "Richard Efford, a 19-year veteran of the House Appropriations Committee, said he did not inform any elected official before inserting the provision and advised his immediate boss, Rep. Ernest Istook, only after it was too late to make changes. 'I would guess we all thought it was a housekeeping thing that would help our bosses but did not need to be elevated up to them,' said Efford, who described himself as 'dumbfounded' by the uproar."[14] Congress eventually stripped the language from the bill, but not before "irate lawmakers in both parties denounced it as a sinister encroachment on Americans' privacy."[15]

When briefing committee staff members, be aware they may feel they know more about a program than the executives who administer the program. In many cases, these staff members helped draft the original legislative language creating the programs and projects they oversee. Where a one-page executive brief is appropriate for a meeting with personal office staff members, expect to provide committee staff members with detailed technical briefings.

As a rule, committee staffers enjoy the legislative process and understand the give and take that must go on with the executive branch in order for our system of government to function. Consequently, executives have statistical, programmatic, and evaluative information to share with them and a constitutional rationale to engage on this level. These staff members seek information, and providing good, concise, pertinent input about programs and projects builds trusted relationships over time.

Conclusion

As a former member of Congress, Mike Parker knew all about how Capitol Hill worked. As an executive branch manager, Parker had been effective in communicating with his former colleagues, gaining their trust, and building stakeholder support for the Corps of Engineers. His dismissal prompted outrage on Capitol Hill, yet at the end of the day, the Bush administration had both the right and responsibility to oust Parker from his position—and members of Congress knew it. As an executive branch representative, Mike

Parker was obligated to represent the president's policies and, by failing to do so, he was undermining executive branch authority.

To serve as proper stewards of the Constitution, government executives have the responsibility to play their appointed roles well. A good performance requires building relationships that bridge the constitutional divide, but it also requires a respect for the divide itself.

Building relationships and providing pertinent, accurate information to legislators is an effective way for executive branch managers to bridge the constitutional divide with the legislative branch. In bridging the divide, executives and legislators must also understand that the Founders intended tension as a means of keeping power in check and respect their wisdom. To maintain the integrity of our constitutional system, and the trust of the American people, executives and legislators must work as equals to maintain the separation of powers.

Tips for leadership success

1. Provide concise, pertinent, and correct information:

   - Make it constituent-oriented whenever possible.
   - Make it relevant to the member or committee you are addressing.
   - Provide an executive summary.
   - Double-check facts and numbers, and immediately correct any errors.
   - Use the interchange to build relationships.

2. Network with stakeholders:

   - Build a support base for agency or department activities.
   - Search for political landmines.
   - Provide political cover.
   - Share relevant information with legislative offices.

3. Be aware of the political climate:

   - Periodically check your priorities against the changing environment.
   - Keep tabs on the political circumstances of key legislators for your department or agency.
   - Avoid partisan entanglements.
   - Build bipartisan relationships to mitigate against abrupt changes in the legislative power structure.

4. Respect the constitutional framework:

- Represent the policies of the administration you serve.
- Seek to have substantive input with committees holding jurisdiction over your agency or department.
- Recognize legislative oversight as a necessary check on executive authority.
- Build relationships with legislators as coequal stewards of the nation's democracy.

Resources for further learning

Books

Roger Davidson, Walter Oleszek, and Frances Lee, *Congress and Its Members* (2009). This is a fundamental text, which includes many current examples and anecdotes, for understanding how Congress really works.

Lawrence Dodd and Bruce Oppenheimer, *Congress Reconsidered* (2008). Though geared for undergraduates, this book provides an accurate portrait of how the House and Senate currently function.

Juliet Eilperin, *Fight Club Politics* (2007). An investigation into the causes of growing polarization and incivility in today's politics and how it has changed the House of Representatives.

John Kingdon, *Agendas, Alternatives, and Public Policies* (1995). A classic statement of the dynamics of policy formation, establishing the notion of "policy windows" and the importance of timing.

Thomas E. Mann and Norman J. Ornstein, *The Broken Branch: How Congress Is Failing America and How to Get it Back on Track* (2008). A powerful review and critique of Congress's recent practices, along with a prescription for change.

David Mayhew, *Congress: The Electoral Connection* (2004). A classic, succinct essay on congressional structure and behavior, viewing Congress through the lens of the pursuit of reelection.

Costas Panagopoulous and Joshua Shank, *All Roads Lead to Congress* (2007). A first-hand, behind-the-scenes look at the process of crafting congressional legislation utilizing a recent transportation bill as their vehicle.

David E. Price, *The Congressional Experience: Transforming American Politics*, 3rd ed. (2004). A first-person account of recent congressional dynamics from the perspective of a member of Congress who is a former political science professor.

Web Resources

The following are official government websites related to Congress that can provide a wealth of useful information.

www.senate.gov. Official Senate website with links to committees and members.

www.house.gov. Official House of Representatives website with links to committees and members.

www.loc.thomas.gov. Library of Congress legislative database.

Notes

1. Grunwald and Allan (2002).
2. Hamilton (2004), 8.
3. See the OMB website at www.whitehouse.gov/omb.
4. Kessler (2002).
5. Ibid.
6. Grunwald (2002).
7. Packer (2010).
8. deKieffer (1997), 177.
9. See Mayhew (1974) for further information on legislative behavior and electoral politics.
10. See Kingdon (1995) for further information on the timing and influences around policy development in Congress.
11. Material based on personal interview by the author with Jack Valenti, March 18, 2005.
12. Oleszek (2007), 4. Also see *Federalist Papers*, No. 47.
13. Congressional testimony before the House Energy and Environment Subcommittee, June 15, 2010.
14. Morgan (2004).
15. Ibid.

11 Engineering experiences that build trust in government

LOU CARBONE, FOUNDER AND CEO, EXPERIENCE ENGINEERING, INC.

People—whether citizens or government employees themselves— trust government if they have a good experience with it. Yet most government agencies lack the concepts and tools to think carefully about and engineer positive citizen and employee experiences. Such experiences depend on addressing the emotional, not just the cognitive, needs of customers. Customers filter and make sense out of experience clues—those sensory inputs in their environment that are provided by government. Exceptional customer experiences with government thus require attention to three types of sensory clues. Leaders must orchestrate functional clues: Do their programs, processes, forms, and systems work (that is, function) as intended? But the true emotional payoff comes when they get mechanic clues (the physical or virtual setting in which service is provided) and humanic clues (the people who serve citizens and how they act) right.

IN 1994 THE U.S. MINT WAS 202 YEARS OLD and acted like it. Although it produced 20 billion circulating coins a year for the Federal Reserve system, it was an old-line manufacturing outfit with terrible labor relations and, for its commemorative coins, equally poor customer service. If you called the Mint, it took on average two minutes before anyone answered, and if you sent a letter, you could wait forty-two days for an answer. If you actually ordered something, you could wait eight weeks or more to get it. Needless to say, the Mint engendered little loyalty or trust from its customers.[1]

After becoming director of the Mint, Philip Diehl changed all that. By 1999 the buyers of its numismatic and commemorative coins gave the Mint a higher score than any other government agency measured by the American Customer Satisfaction Index. Calls were answered on average in 17.5 seconds, letters in three days, and orders were filled in less than two weeks. More important, the Mint rediscovered the magic in its product, turning its customers on to the fact that buying its new fifty state quarters was a way to emotionally connect parents and grandparents with children through the nation's history. The Mint discovered the Internet, exciting and enabling the public to participate actively in designing the Sacagawea dollar and inviting children to play games on its H.I.P. (History in Your Pocket) Pocket Change™ site. These changes became possible because Diehl listened to customers. The customer experience improved dramatically, and along with that came financial success. Diehl found new support in Congress as well. In short, by changing the customer's experience, one of the oldest manufacturing companies in the United States rebuilt trust, strengthened loyalty, and emerged as a government success story.

As Diehl recognized, the way we as citizens experience government services and leadership today has changed dramatically since the Founders established our democratic form of government. The changes are due in great part to instantaneous communications and the complex global, political, and economic frameworks that have evolved. As we discuss throughout this chapter, managing how citizens experience government in this environment presents a major opportunity to build trust and value in government and its leaders.

How people feel about the experiences they have with government services and leadership greatly influences their value assessment. A systematic and holistic framework for managing experiences that build trust and commitment should be foundational to every government leader's vision and the keystone of the execution of their duties.

Experience and trust

In both the private and public sectors it is clear that consumer and citizen trust is earned or revoked based on our experiences.[2] The private sector, for its part, has become increasingly aware that trust built by a good customer experience correlates positively with business success.

- Dr. Leonard Berry of Texas A&M University states that the basic components of trust are rooted in behaviors that foster feelings of reliability, competence, and fairness.[3]
- A 2004 Yankelovich State of Consumer Trust report states that a large majority of consumers will shop at companies that have earned their trust even if they charge more.[4] If trust is violated,

however, 96 percent spend less, 76 percent tell family and friends, and 49 percent increase business with competitors.

- Research by the Gallup organization demonstrates that the financial payoff to organizations that are high in both customer and employee "engagement" is 3.4 times that of organizations that have low scores on this measure of the customer and employee experience.[5]
- A Harvard Mind of the Market case study ("Companies that have Consumer's Best Interest at Heart, a ZMET[(r)] Study") directly linked trust to honesty, dependability, and continued patronage.[6] It concluded that to build trust, companies must consistently send cues that the consumer can interpret as "caring," which leads to trust, which leads to loyalty.

Customers behave like detectives in the way they unconsciously organize "clues" embedded in their experiences into a set of feelings. They recall these feelings when deciding whether to use, not use, recommend, or reuse a product or service. Where those feelings are positive, trust is developed. The more important, complex, and personal the service, the more deeply rooted the feelings. The more deeply rooted the feelings, the more important the experience clues are, and the more the bond of trust can be built.

The same process correlates to citizens' experiences with government. For example, dealing with the Internal Revenue Service (IRS) could leave someone with a feeling of vulnerability, injustice, and insensitivity or with a sense of fairness, openness, and empathy. The signals or clues that exist in the experience with the agency range all the way from language used in correspondence to the demeanor of a telephone representative. An experience with the Veterans Administration, the Social Security Administration, or an agency of the Department of Homeland Security has the potential to emit a set of "favorable" feelings or "negative" feelings that profoundly impact perception. Considering how to manage the customer experiences of government services may seem overwhelming, but we can bring it into focus by first understanding what feelings customers want an experience to evoke.

In some of his earliest work involving how customers think and process the experiences they have, Gerald Zaltman, professor emeritus at Harvard Business School, stated that "the tangible attributes of a product or service have far less influence on consumers than the unconscious sensory and emotional elements derived from the total experience."[7] After standing in two different lines for nearly an hour and a half at the Department of

Motor Vehicles, your driver's license may have been renewed, but chances are the experience will have left you irritated and angry as well as bored and tired. Your memory of this government office and more generally your trust in government will have been negatively affected. In other words, loyalty and trust are more a result of how customers feel in the overall experience they have, rather than the rational functional service they receive. Feelings shape how customers think about and behave with regard to an organization's products or services, and this point is equally true in government and the private sector. An experience with the IRS might be efficient yet not engender any positive feelings that would cause a taxpayer to feel the agency is trustworthy or reflects any value the citizens derive.

This gulf between the government's service and the customer's feelings about it underscores the need for a monumental shift in the focus of thinking in many government agencies, where the focus has traditionally been on efficiency (doing more with less). Leaders in government, for the most part, have not seen themselves in the customer experience business, but as Table 11.1 on the following page suggests, all government agencies are serving customers for whom the emotional part of the experience matters.

Whether serving citizens directly on a fee-for-service basis (a common occurrence as government struggles to earn the revenue it needs), in a franchise operation that sells services to other government agencies, in a regulatory or law enforcement mode, or even in just the effort to recruit and retain employees in a competitive labor market, government agencies can reap significant benefits if they pay attention to what customers feel in their encounters with them.

This point may not always be obvious. Consider services where cooperation is essential, such as law enforcement, judicial proceedings, corrections, and immigration. Positive feelings among those served make such agencies function more smoothly. For example, jurists who experience inadequacy and inefficiencies in the legal system consequently view this duty of citizenship as an inconvenience or waste of time rather than an honor and obligation to others in a democratic society. Leaders in correctional facilities can attest to the dramatic difference that the cooperation (as opposed to the resistance) of incarcerated felons can make in achieving the objectives of their organizations at reasonable cost, not to mention the impact on the experience (and therefore morale and retention) of their employees.

Government agencies have the opportunity to create value for their constituents, leaders, and the organizations themselves by understanding,

Table 11.1 Government services and their customers

Type of service	Agency examples	Customers
Direct service	Social Security (SSA) IRS Transportation Security (TSA)	Pensioners Taxpayers Travelers
Fee-for-service	U.S. Postal Service National Park Service Agricultural Marketing Service	Postal patrons Vacationers Produce shippers/receivers
Interagency franchising	Financial Management Service (Treasury)	Agency financial managers
Technical assistance	General Services Administration	Users of the federal supply service
Law enforcement	Inspectors General (IG) Bureau of Prisons FBI	Agency managers Incarcerated felons State/local law enforcement, citizens, and suspects
Regulatory	Federal Aviation Administration	Commercial airlines and pilots
Employee recruitment	All agencies	Potential hires
Employee retention	All agencies	Existing employees

designing, and managing their agencies' value propositions around the total experience they deliver rather than simply the efficiency of the service or function they perform. Many leaders may find themselves solely focusing on achieving the fundamental goal of the efficient delivery of government services, when greater attention to experience management on both an emotional and rational level can increase effectiveness, help maintain funding, improve customer satisfaction, and decrease oversight.

Most importantly, enhancing the customer experience builds trust. As we saw in the Introduction (Figure I.4 and repeated as Figure 11.1 here), while individual government agencies may be able to do little to affect the level of trust in government overall, they can do a lot to affect trust in their own agency, as shown by data from the American Customer Satisfaction Index. Improved satisfaction leads to improved trust.

Figure 11.1   Strong link between satisfaction and trust

Percentage

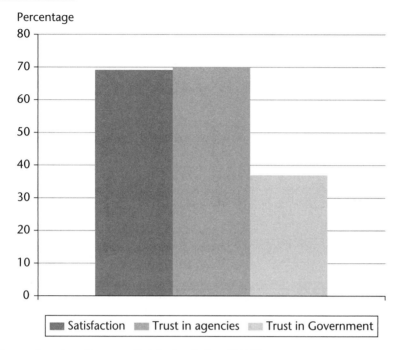

Satisfaction   Trust in agencies   Trust in Government

Source: American Customer Satisfaction Index, 2007 Data.

Perceptions of government agencies

How well do government agencies currently address the emotional needs of their customers? This is not an easy question to answer. The data most often collected about government services focus on broad measures of trust, satisfaction, or how efficiently government agencies serve the public, not on how well the emotional needs of citizens are met. Indeed, many government agencies have long followed the way of most private-sector businesses and focus on efficiencies rather than the experiential emotional equity being built (or diminished) for customers.

If an organization focuses on efficiency to the exclusion of effectiveness (on behalf of customer needs), it will always fall short in building long-term advocacy, value, and loyalty. How leaders in government manage experiences will impact how leadership and government services are valued. Experiences can be purposefully managed to create emotional connections that build powerful relationships and trust. How people feel in an experience is unconsciously the basis for how they feel about an agency, and by extension, the leadership of the agency and of government.

A 2010 national survey by the Center for American Progress found that only 21 percent of Americans rate the federal government as being "excellent or good" at "being customer-friendly and providing quality services,"[8] yet at present, the American Customer Satisfaction Index (ACSI) is the best tool we have to gauge the emotional perceptions of customers to the services they receive from government. The ACSI is a sophisticated customer survey conducted quarterly by the University of Michigan for private- and public-sector agencies that pay to be included. The ACSI measure of customer satisfaction, on a scale of 0 to 100 (100 is the highest possible score), includes measures of the perceived quality of government services (including customization and reliability), the extent to which customer expectations are met, a comparison of services provided to the customer's ideal for those services, the extent of customer complaints, and the customer's perception of the service outcomes.

Table 11.2 provides a sample of 2010 data for selected federal agencies. The overall average for all government agencies included in the ACSI was 68.7 (by comparison, the private-sector average was 75.9).

As the data demonstrate, the customer experience with government differs dramatically across and even within agencies. Not surprisingly, the two services shown in the table that have the lowest scores are also associated with some of the most emotionally frustrating experiences citizens currently have with government—applying for a business loan to help recover from a natural disaster and filling out and seeking personal help with the maze of paper tax forms. In the latter case, as the 23-point spread between the experience of paper and electronic filers demonstrates, it is not surprising that the IRS is encouraging more people to file their taxes electronically.

Despite these striking results, the ACSI does not give us a full picture of the emotional reaction of citizens to government. Indeed, customer satisfaction is a proxy and incomplete measure. Current studies and writings in the private sector by business consultants such as Frederick F. Reichheld and Thomas Teal, authors of *The Loyalty Effect* and Frederick F. Reichheld author of *The Ultimate Question*, counter the idea that customer satisfaction measures are viable in accurately determining an organization's customer advocacy or ability to create loyalty and growth. In the private sector at least, many customers who respond on surveys that they are "satisfied" or "very

Table 11.2 ACSI data for selected federal agencies, 2010

Service area/agency	Recipients	ACSI score
Individual benefits		
Pension Benefit Guaranty Corporation	Retirees	87
Corporation for National and Community Service	Grantees	71
Information providers/ technical assistance/supply		
Federal Citizen Information Center (GSA)	Citizens who ordered materials via mail or Internet	85
Defense Technical Information Center (DOD)	Information users	75
Financial services		
Office of Disaster Assistance, Small Business Administration	Renter loan recipients	85
	Business loan recipients	68
Tax collection		
Internal Revenue Service– Treasury	Individual electronic tax filers	77
	Individual paper tax filers	54

Source: American Customer Satisfaction Index, www.theacsi.org/index.php?option=
com_content&view=article&id=238:acsi-scores-for-us-federal-government-2010&
catid=14&Itemid=298.

satisfied" defect to other providers. "Satisfaction" does not ensure loyalty. In the public sector, there may not be another organization to which one can turn to meet a need, but citizens who want to express their displeasure do have other places to turn—535 other places on Capitol Hill to be exact.

> Satisfaction surveys are a far less accurate test of satisfaction than behavior. In business after business, our research has shown that 60 to 80 percent of customers who defected had said on a survey just prior to defecting that they were satisfied or very satisfied.
>
> — *Frederick F. Reichheld and Thomas Teal,*
> *The Loyalty Effect*[9]

So there is an apparent opportunity, just as the private sector discovered, to enhance the value that constituents sense they receive from government. Government agencies need to focus on the experiences they deliver, and to succeed at this they must understand how customers think about and process the experiences they have.

Customers filter experience clues

Basic to managing experiences is the premise that customers consciously and unconsciously filter experience clues when they interact with an organization. They organize the clues into a set of impressions, some rational and calculative, and others more emotional.

Passengers going through a Transportation Security Administration (TSA) airport screening will encounter a barrage of clues, including the orderliness or confusion of the surroundings, the way their privacy is respected, and the speed and quality of the screening itself. They will have an emotional as well as a cognitive reaction to the screening experience and draw conclusions that, collectively, have a profound affect on TSA.

What exactly is an experience clue? It is anything present in the experience that the customer can see, hear, taste, touch, or smell. Each clue carries a message, and added together the clues help create the customer's total experience. Clues tell a story in the most powerful of ways. It is far more beneficial to weave a consistent, cohesive, and compelling story than an inconsistent, disjointed one that does not engage individuals. Even the absence of clues is part of an experience. Private-sector organizations such as Starbucks, the Mayo Clinic, Federal Express, and Target have long realized the value of developing their stories and creating supporting evidence through purposeful, systematic clue management. Some federal agencies have also mastered clue management. One outstanding example is the Veterans Health Administration, which has generated a highly regarded patient experience through improved care, an innovative electronic medical records system, and is one of the (unintentionally) best kept secrets of government excellence.[10]

Customers unconsciously work out the "clue math." They add up the clues and unconsciously compute intricate calculations that will affect their decisions, opinions, and preferences as a result of their assessment of a service. They decide whether clues are emotionally positive (differentiate the service in a memorable way), negative (are destructive of loyalty and trust), or neutral (fail to differentiate the service provided in any helpful way)

Figure 11.2 Experience preference model™

A tool to visualize how clues in an experience add up
to a positive, negative, or neutral feeling

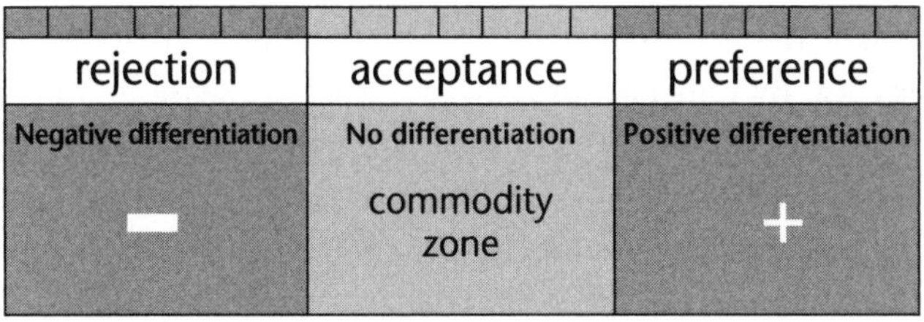

rejection	acceptance	preference
Negative differentiation	No differentiation	Positive differentiation
—	commodity zone	+

Source: Experience Engineering Inc.

(see Figure 11.2). Although an organization may or may not understand that this process is happening, the reality is that experience delivery can range from very purposeful to haphazard. Thinking about experiences in this way helps an organization take a more systemic and focused approach to the management of clues in the experience.

Building a new competency

As never before, today's environment requires government leaders to recalibrate their perspectives on how they create value for the people they serve. A systematic focus on experience can provide the framework to influence the creation of feelings of trust and value. To fully leverage experience, organizations must manage the emotional components with the same rigor they bring to the management of product and service functionality and efficiency.

How do you design, create, and manage the appropriate clues in a customer experience to make it more valuable and sustainable? How do you structure efforts to optimize the value their experiences can create for customers? Leaders and managers must develop new perspectives and skills, with associated tools that are rooted in the following fundamental experience management principles:

Understand customers on a deeper level. Critical to optimizing experiences is to first understand the emotional needs and desires that drive your customers' preferences and advocacy. Invest in learning what customers want to feel in the experience, what will engage them

cognitively and emotionally in a manner that creates strong preference and loyalty. Success requires a commitment to research.

Be clue conscious. Cultivate a sensibility about the experiences you deliver.
Understand what customers see, hear, touch, smell, and taste. Most
important, develop a sensitivity for what they are feeling throughout the
experience. By understanding what customers sense in an experience,
you will understand the story that stringing clues together creates. By
comparing what customers feel in an experience to what they want to
feel, you will begin to identify how to modify current clues and add new
ones to deliver the desired experience in a predictable, powerful way.

Understanding customers at a deeper emotional level—the experience motif

The results of identifying customers' deeper needs, along with consideration of an organization's overall market strategy, form the basis for the
creation of an "experience motif." The experience motif is ideally a three-
word expression of the customers' desired feelings in an experience. The
reason for choosing three words rather than a longer phrase or a sentence is
to keep the expression simple and focused so that it can be an effective tool
for the assessment, design, development, and management of experience
clues. Otherwise, the motif may resemble a conventional mission statement
and make the interpretation considerably less focused and more diffuse.

Consider the case of Doylestown Hospital's Health and Wellness Center in Warrington, PA, which developed an experience motif of "understood, strengthened, and renewed." This motif clearly articulates what
patients want to feel, and it offers a concise directive to staff for the design,
development, and management of each subexperience to get people to feel
understood, strengthened, and renewed. Compared to a mission statement
such as "The Center will provide a world-class healthcare experience that
provides for the health and well-being of the community," Doylestown's
motif is far more actionable and focused.

Clue management

The experience motif becomes the North Star—the foundation for integrating and reconciling all elements of the experience. It is the unifying

element for every clue in an experience. It becomes the filter that facilitates alignment of what would otherwise be a collection of random clues into a well thought-out, purposefully designed set of clues orchestrated to create certain feelings and tell a certain story.

Clues generally fall into three main categories:

1. *Functional* clues concern the technical quality of the offering. Functional clues are the "what" of the experience and reveal reliability and competence. Anything that indicates or suggests the technical quality—its presence or absence—is a functional clue. Does the key issued at the front desk open the hotel room door? Does the television set work? Was the wake-up call made as promised? Is the room service order correct? In a government agency, is the application for assistance clear and easy to understand? Is all the needed information—and only the needed information—collected on one form? Does the agency website enable you to drill down to get needed information quickly and easily?

2. *Mechanic* clues come from the sensory presentation of the service. Whereas functional clues concern reliability, mechanic clues concern the sights, smells, sounds, tastes, and textures of the surroundings. The wide aisles, signature red color scheme, and numerous check-out counters serve as mechanic clues in Target stores. Consider the sign shown below, which appeared on the door of a state government's highway welcome center. In this case, the mechanic clue counteracts the very purpose of a welcome center, which is to encourage people to visit and spend their dollars in the state.

3. *Humanic* clues come from the behavior and appearance of service providers—choice of words, tone of voice, level of enthusiasm, body language, neatness, and appropriate dress. Southwest Airlines flight attendants' typically friendly manner as they interact with passengers on a flight and their distinctive polo shirt and khaki slacks uniform illustrate humanic clues. The way you are greeted on entering a national park or the tone of voice you hear on an 800-helpline are humanic clues in

NO SMOKING

NO FOOD OR DRINKS ALLOWED INSIDE

SHOES AND SHIRTS REQUIRED

NO PETS

Welcome center sign

government settings, and they contribute to citizen loyalty or disaffection. Humanic and mechanic clues, the "how" of the service experience, reveal much about an organization's commitment to understanding and satisfying customers' needs and wants.

The distinction among functional, mechanic, and humanic clues can be subtle. For example, a retail salesperson who answers a customer's question about when an out-of-stock item will be available is producing both functional and humanic clues. The accuracy of the information is a functional clue. The salesperson's choice of words and body language are humanic clues. One salesperson may answer the question disinterestedly— "Sorry, we're out of that"—and another may answer enthusiastically—"We expect a shipment next week. Would you like me to hold the item for you?" A customer's emotional response to these humanic clues is likely to be quite different even if the information is accurate in both cases.

The power of different humanic clues to produce different customer feelings among competent professional service providers showed up dramatically in a study of patients who filed and did not file malpractice claims against fifty-nine primary care physicians in Oregon and Colorado. When audiotapes of routine office visits were analyzed, the no-claims physicians (compared with those with two or more lifetime malpractice claims) used more statements of orientation (educating patients about what to expect and the flow of the visit), laughed and used humor more often, and used more behaviors that invited patients' opinions, checked for understanding, and encouraged patients to talk. No-claims physicians also spent longer in routine visits. Although the difference in time was small (18.3 minutes versus 15.0 minutes), it represented greater communication with patients and made a real difference in the patient experience.[11]

Subtleties aside, managers who wish to improve their customers' service experience must effectively manage the clues that make up the experience. The different clues play different roles and can vary in importance. It is a rare organization, however, that can deliver truly excellent service and be deficient in any of the clue categories: functional, mechanic, and humanic.

Conducting an experience audit

Organizations and leaders embracing experience management typically make a commitment to research by conducting a customer experience audit. This process is a thorough analysis of the current customer experience that can reveal customers' emotional needs as well as an understanding of their response to specific experience clues.

Videotape and digital photography may be used to document actual customer experiences. Managers might accompany and observe customers as they go through an experience. In-depth interviews may be held with customers and employees to learn their feelings about different aspects of an experience.

Doylestown Hospital conducted an extensive experience audit and came to understand that their customers unconsciously evaluate the experience they create based on how understood, strengthened, and renewed they feel, and the hospital made these values into its experience motif. The audit allows the organization to set an emotional compass upon which it can evaluate existing clues in the experience or create new clues that engender those feelings and emotions.

The Federal Executive Institute (FEI) in Charlottesville, Virginia, is a residential executive education campus for senior career leaders in government. FEI's staff sought to understand the current experience from the customer's vantage point, especially during the first (and critical) twenty-four hours an executive lives on campus. FEI's experience audit included interviews with executives; "clue scanning," in which staff used digital photography and guided observation techniques to see the experience as the executives might see it, and a thorough analysis of all printed and online material executives received prior to the start of the program. At the same time, a contractor conducted a metaphor analysis with potential customers to see what they expected to feel during the FEI experience. The combination of these techniques yielded an experience motif and the kind of audit data illustrated in Figure 11.3.

When the actual clues in the audit (organized by whether each clue was positive, neutral, or negative in the feelings produced) were held up against the desired feelings in the motif, the gaps became evident. As Figure 11.3 shows, the positive feelings produced by a warm greeting and registration process had to struggle to overcome the anxiety and confusion created for executives who had trouble locating the facility and finding a parking space, and then noticing facility maintenance problems that should have been corrected before they arrived.

This combined picture has enabled the institute to redesign many of the experience clues and create new clues more likely to produce arriving participants who feel, as FEI's experience motif puts it, valued, strengthened, and inspired.

Figure 11.3 Federal Executive Institute: Experience audit – partial results

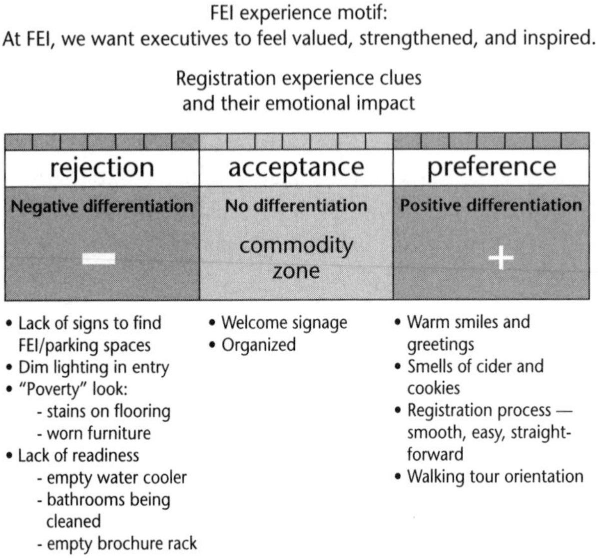

FEI experience motif:
At FEI, we want executives to feel valued, strengthened, and inspired.

Registration experience clues
and their emotional impact

rejection	acceptance	preference
Negative differentiation	No differentiation	Positive differentiation
–	commodity zone	**+**

• Lack of signs to find FEI/parking spaces
• Dim lighting in entry
• "Poverty" look:
  - stains on flooring
  - worn furniture
• Lack of readiness
  - empty water cooler
  - bathrooms being cleaned
  - empty brochure rack
	• Welcome signage
	• Organized
		• Warm smiles and greetings
		• Smells of cider and cookies
		• Registration process — smooth, easy, straight-forward
		• Walking tour orientation

Source: Experience Engineering Inc.

Designing experiences

The audit process leads to designing experiences from the customer's perspective ("customer-back" or "citizen-back") versus the agency's perspective ("agency-out") and involves paying closer attention to what customers are sensing and feeling—much of which will be at an unconscious level. If you are not thinking of the experience from inside the customer's mind, you can easily miss not just minor nuances but also important pieces of the experience that shape customer perception.

Avis Car Rental learned that the way they store and handle infant car seats at the rental facility has a greater impact on customers' perceptions of the cleanliness of the rental car than anything they could do to clean the inside or outside of the vehicle. By looking at the experience customer-back through an experience audit, they discovered that the Avis locations that put infant seats in poly bags and placed them neatly on shelves within customer view (previously they had been piled on an oil-stained floor) found themselves being rated higher for the cleanliness of their cars.[12] This nuance would never have been revealed without the benefit of a customer experience audit.

The FEI audit indicated that many executives felt their arrival was like checking into a hotel, whereas the staff wanted them to feel they were being welcomed to a home. This information led to changes in everything from how visitors are greeted at the security gate to how they are guided to parking spaces, welcomed into the building, and escorted to their rooms.

A commitment to experience management affects all levels of an organization. It is important to understand the roles and responsibilities in carrying out experience initiatives, and even more important for leadership to foster and manage those roles and responsibilities. As summarized in Table 11.3, all levels of the organization play vital roles in extracting the most value from managing experience clues.[13] Senior leadership must set the tone and focus attention on the importance of experience management. Middle managers must be clue conscious: they must incorporate clue language into daily discussion, become personally involved in improving the company's clue presentation, support direct reports who are invited to serve on cross-functional clue management project teams, and, in general, empower, encourage, and facilitate systematic clue management. Middle managers must also select, orient, teach, encourage, assess, and reward employees who perform the service and provide the clues that play such a dominant role for many services.

Frontline employees are powerful generators of experience clues and need to be clue conscious as well. It is critical for leaders to share with these employees relevant market research that distills what customers value in the service experience—their emotional needs, not just their functional needs. To provide the humanic clues that support the organization's strategy, service providers need to know their customers, and they need to be armed with a customer experience "emotional compass" that clearly and concisely articulates customers' desired feelings. In addition, employees need ongoing training, education, and reinforcement to present the right clues effectively.

Benefits to leaders in democracy

The ultimate measure of success is how people feel in the experiences they have and how they associate those feelings with the experience. If people feel insignificant or undervalued in a government experience, they are

Table 11.3 Clue management in the organization

Organizational level	Role	Action
Senior leadership	Create and support imperative for clue management	Demonstrate a strong commitment to understanding the role of managing clues and its importance to customers' preference and loyalty. Establish and stay focused on a mandate for systematic experience clue management.
Middle management	Understand and empower clue management	Demonstrate understanding of the role of managing clues and establish it as a high priority. Support the development of clue management proficiency within the organization.
Frontline workers	Sense and respond to clue management	Become sensitive to the presence and absence of clues with a bias for action in the management of clues. Be aware of customers' emotional and functional needs in an experience and respond to customers accordingly.

more likely to develop negative perceptions—and share them with others—that shape the reality of the reputation of an agency. Whether leaders put this all together—or not—customers and constituents do. They work out the "clue math" in every interaction they have. They add up the clues that shape their assessment of government agencies and services. Experience management presents the opportunity to positively imprint with constituents on a deeper and more lasting level and create greater advocacy and loyalty.

As government leaders continue to face higher costs, increased oversight, and the need for new ways to maintain funding, they will benefit by focusing with greater rigor on the experience created for all their constituents. They can accomplish this by assessing what systems they have in place to learn how customers feel in the current experience and understand how customers want to feel on a deep, unconscious level, and then design and consistently manage clues that could close any gap between the two.

Leaders embracing experience management as a competency in their organization are far more likely to connect with their constituents, foster emotional engagement, and create a deeper sense of value and commitment from them. They will also reap the benefits of greater trust and loyalty that so many leading companies in the private sector are beginning to realize through experience management initiatives.

Leaders in government may think experience management applies solely to enhancing the experience of outside customers and constituents, but an exceptional experience is needed for those who work in government, its own employees. Research suggests that it is very hard to produce customer value if you do not also produce employee value.[14] Employees who feel ill-treated and not respected at work are less likely to provide an engaging, positive experience for external customers. So, we end with the story of Michael Abrashoff, former commanding officer of USS *Benfold*, a $1 billion advanced Navy warship with a crew of more than 300 that in the late 1990s was assigned to duty near Iraq. The ship won the Spokane Trophy for having the best combat readiness in the fleet—the first time in at least ten years that a ship of its class had received that honor.[15] The *Benfold* became known not only for its operational and financial success (in fiscal year 1998 it returned $600,000 of its $2.4 million maintenance budget and $800,000 of its $3 million repair budget to the government), but also for its innovative practices that created a culture of excellence.

From finding pumpkins for a pumpkin-carving contest while deployed in the Middle East to ditching traditional and costly Navy food for tastier commercially available menu items (the savings sent five of the ship's cooks to culinary school), the *Benfold* was able to create a crew experience unparalleled in the fleet. Listen to its creative commander talk about how he fashioned an unparalleled experience for all newly arriving crew members and for those new recruits whose first on-ship experience he was charged with creating:

> Within two days of when new crew members arrive, I sit down with them face-to-face. I try to learn something about each of them: Why did they join the navy? What's their family situation like? What are their goals while they're in the navy—and beyond? How can I help them chart a course through life? Ultimately, I consider it my job to improve my little 300-person piece of society. And that's as much a part of the bottom line as operational readiness is.

I looked at what usually happens when new 18- or 19-year-old recruits check in: They fly in from boot camp on a Friday night. They feel intimidated and friendless. They stow their gear in their berths and immediately get lost in San Diego. To change all of that, we've created a welcoming plan: Now, when new recruits come on board, their bunks are assigned, their linen and blankets are there, and we match them with a hand-picked sponsor who shows them the ropes. They can even call home—on my nickel—to tell Mom and Dad that they've made it.[16]

Michael Abrashoff may not have talked about enhancing the employee experience, but it was in his work and in his heart, and it produced a ship of loyal sailors that cut the time needed for redeployment training from twenty-two days to five days in port and from thirty days to fourteen days at sea. The experience of employees is vital to earning their trust and loyalty, just as the experience of customers is important for achieving the same gains. When employee trust and loyalty are matched with customer trust and loyalty through the power of exceptional experiences, government works.

Tips for leadership success

How citizens experience government presents a major opportunity to build trust and value. Leaders may find the following framework valuable for embarking on an experience management strategy.

- Assess the experience: identify and prioritize the various potential experience audiences in your agency or department.
- Audit the experience: understand customer needs and desires. Research the experiences you are currently delivering through customer interviews and mystery shopping. From these insights generate an experience motif that guides clue creation.
- Design the experience: identify and create preferential clues in your environment, processes, and behaviors that reflect the experience motif.
- Implement the experience design: plan and execute implementation of specific experience clues into business operation; set metrics.
- Steward the experience: monitor the experience design through feedback and metrics; adjust clues as needed.

Resources for further learning

Books and Articles

Leonard L. Berry, *Discovering the Soul of Service* (1999). Berry offers a systematic way to think about great customer service. His nine core drivers of exceptional service are illustrated with examples from the real world. The drivers include: leading with values, strategic focus, executional excellence, control of destiny, trust-based relationships, investment in employee success, acting small, brand cultivation, and generosity.

Leonard L. Berry, Eileen Wall, and Lewis P. Carbone, "Service Clues and Customer Assessment of the Service Experience" (2006). This article focuses on the power of functional, mechanic and humanic clues to shape the customer experience.

Lewis P. Carbone, "What Makes Customers Tick" (2003); and *Clued In: How to Keep Customers Coming Back Again and Again* (2004). Carbone focuses on why the customer experience matters so much in the modern economy and how to craft experiences that build customer loyalty. Meeting the deeper emotional needs of the customer takes center stage along with the management of sensory clues (sights, sounds, smells, taste, texture) delivered by the functional aspects of the product or service, the setting in which it is offered, and the people who provide it. This book also offers an approach to customer experience management over time and descriptions of tools for use at various stages of the experience management process.

John H. Fleming and Jim Asplund, *Human Sigma: Managing the Employee-Customer Encounter* (2007). Seen as a companion to the widely known process improvement approach to quality known as Six Sigma, Human Sigma addresses the people side of improving the customer experience. Human Sigma is based on five core principles: (1) employee and customer experiences must be managed together—not as separate entities; (2) emotions drive and shape the employee-customer encounter; (3) the employee-customer encounter must be measured and managed at the local level; (4) employee and customer engagement interact to drive enhanced financial performance. This interaction can be quantified and summarized with a single performance metric; and (5) sustainable improvement in the employee-customer encounter requires disciplined local action coupled with a company-wide commitment to changing how employees are recruited, positioned in roles, rewarded, recognized, and managed.

Frederick F. Riechheld with Thomas Teal, *The Loyalty Effect: The Hidden Force Behind Growth, Profits and Lasting Value* (2001). Business success depends on customer loyalty. The lifetime value of a loyal customer is immense and often slighted by firms that focus on getting new customers and not enough on keeping the old ones. Loyal employees are essential to keeping loyal customers. As with customers, the lifetime value to the firm from a loyal employee is huge, especially when one considers both the cost of replacing good workers and the impact losing them has on the customer loyalty these employees have built.

Gerald Zaltman, *How Customers Think* (2004). Zaltman runs a market research lab at Harvard built on the notion that 95 percent of what customers think is below the level of their own conscious recall. The implication is that you cannot get into the mind of the customer by simply asking. Using traditional means such as surveys and focus groups is not adequate. Instead, you need to penetrate the subconscious through techniques such as using metaphors to probe for the customer's deeper feelings by bypassing rational thought processes. The Zaltman Metaphor Technique plays a major role in helping organizations identify what matters most when they decide to focus on the customer experience.

Web Resources

The following websites offer helpful information:

www.expeng.com/. This is the homepage for Experience Engineering Inc., the author's website.

www.opm.gov/surveys/services/Customer.asp. This site describes a Customer Satisfaction Survey developed by the U.S. Office of Personnel Management and available for agency use.

www.theacsi.org/. This is the homepage for the American Customer Satisfaction Index. From this page, users can navigate to see both government and private-sector ACSI scores as well as the model used for deriving scores in government.

www.usa.gov/webcontent/improving/evaluating/types/satisfaction.shtml. This website focuses on how to measure and improve customer satisfaction with government websites.

Notes

1. Muoio (1999).
2. The terms citizen, constituent, and customer are used interchangeably in this chapter. We believe that experience management applies at all levels of government, in all branches of government, and in all interactions of government workers with their colleagues, other agencies, citizens, and elected and appointed officials they serve.
3. Berry (1999).
4. Wood (2004).
5. Fleming and Asplund (2007)
6. Braun and Zaltman (undated).
7. Zaltman (2003).
8. Molyneux, Teixeira, and Whaley (2010), 22.
9. Reichheld and Teal (2001), 237.
10. Longman (2010).
11. Levinson et al. (1997).
12. Carbone (2004).
13. Berry, Wall, and Carbone (2006).
14. Reichheld and Teal (2001); Fleming and Asplund (2007).
15. LaBarre (1999).
16. Ibid.

12 From e-government to e-governance: Harnessing technology to strengthen democracy

GEORGE E. MITCHELL, DEPARTMENT OF POLITICAL SCIENCE, MAXWELL
SCHOOL OF CITIZENSHIP AND PUBLIC AFFAIRS, SYRACUSE UNIVERSITY
GRANT REEHER, CAMPBELL PUBLIC AFFAIRS INSTITUTE AND DEPARTMENT OF
POLITICAL SCIENCE, MAXWELL SCHOOL OF CITIZENSHIP AND PUBLIC
AFFAIRS, SYRACUSE UNIVERSITY

*One of the best ways to demonstrate trust in people—and also
improve government—is to engage the public in governing.
Electronic communications technology offers a unique opportunity
to involve citizens, but using it well requires that leaders adopt an
e-governance rather than an e-government approach to their
Internet-based outreach efforts. In e-governance, citizens are
actively included in the governing dialogue and encouraged to
work together, with the agency serving as facilitator. Despite a
recent emphasis on "Government 2.0," there is much work still to
do in this area. Effective approaches to engaging citizens can be
drawn from electoral politics, commerce, and the experiences of
selected U.S. and international government agencies.*

LIKE MANY OTHER STATES IN 2004, Maine and its first-term governor, John
Baldacci, faced a budget problem. To maintain a balanced budget, difficult
trade-offs would be necessary. In accord with the standard process, the governor proposed a budget to the state's legislature, but accompanying it was
something new: on the governor's official website was an interactive exercise called "The Budget Balancing Education Tool."

The site invited citizens to figure out how to close the state's deficit by
raising various taxes or cutting various kinds of spending. A box at the bottom of the page provided a running tally of one's progress toward a balanced budget. The exercise used Internet technology to serve at least two
important democratic functions. The first was the more obvious of the two:

when citizens were finished adjusting the figures, the site allowed them to register their taxing and spending preferences with the governor's office by clicking a button. But the second function was arguably more important: participating in the exercise also allowed citizens actually to experience—and therefore better appreciate—the difficult trade-offs that the state budget process requires. The exercise was so successful that the governor decided to use it in future budget cycles.

In spring 2006 French budget minister Jean-François Cope used a similar device as his nation faced a similar problem: how to respond to an apparent national consensus to cut taxes while staying within the European Union's mandated deficit ceiling of 3 percent of a nation's gross domestic product (GDP). His office launched a budget balancing game called "Cyberbudget" on a site that could handle up to 10,000 players at a time and included a simulation for presenting a citizen's preferred budget to parliament.

These budget-balancing tools are innovative examples of e-government—the use of electronic technology, most notably the Internet, to improve the work of government offices and agencies. E-government's potential is unlocked by increasing citizens' sense of ownership in what government does. To create this sense of ownership, government executives can learn a great deal from their counterparts in the political and commercial realms. But to fully unleash the Internet's power, agency leaders need to think in terms of e-governance, rather than simply e-government—and toward this end there is much more yet to be done.

Our idea of e-governance draws on more general writings about governance, which emphasize not only government institutions but the linkages between those institutions (and their personnel) and the social and political realms that surround them. Political scientist Donald Kettl has written widely on governance, and among his ten core principles for effectively building those linkages, e-governance is intimately tied to at least four: (1) the importance of networks; (2) emphasis on interpersonal processes rather than strict authority; (3) transparency; and (4) popular participation in what government does.[1] But our notion of e-governance extends beyond that literature to a more proactive and deeper involvement of the public in the central activities of government. That civic involvement can in turn generate stronger senses of investment, trust, and efficacy regarding government. Fostering greater involvement is also integral to what, in Chapter 1 of this volume, Terry Newell termed values-based leadership on the public stage.

Steven Clift, the former manager of Minnesota's state government web portal, founder of E-Democracy.org, and recipient of the prestigious Ashoka Fellowship for social entrepreneurship, has set his hopes on the private sector to deepen online citizenship: "With our governments and representatives ill-equipped to 'e-listen,' *civil society* needs to fill a void and create places and experiences online that allow people to learn from one another, build respect, influence agendas and over time impact decision making, and most importantly meet public challenges."[2] But we believe that government must not abandon that challenge either, and this chapter aims to provide agency executives with a framework for thinking more creatively about how to meet it.

Federal initiatives to harness technology

Early "Government 1.0" efforts to leverage Internet technology to improve government service and public awareness largely employed "static" web pages that displayed basic information published by government agencies. Throughout the 2000s, public managers began experimenting with "dynamic" content such as blogs, social networking tools, and Real Simple Syndication (RSS) feeds that encourage greater civic interaction and engagement by providing the public with more timely information while inviting their feedback. This "Government 2.0" model represents an evolution from the e-government of the late 1990s and early 2000s into an emerging model of e-governance. Ines Mergel, a scholar who writes extensively about the intersection of technology and public management, suggests that governments are gradually transitioning into "Participation 2.0," in which technologies are increasingly used to "engage citizens in the identification, organization, prioritization, and solving of pressing issues."[3] In the future, citizens will find opportunities not only to respond to government initiatives online, but also to help author them. The next two sections summarize some of the most important federal initiatives in recent years to improve governance through technology.

George W. Bush's management agenda

E-government has come a long way in a short time. Government has made use of electronic technology to make citizens' lives more convenient, in terms of obtaining useful public information, paying user fees, and filing important forms. These efforts have included online tax forms, tax filing, DMV services, and information and payment of fees for national parks. It has also made available to citizens a wider and richer array of information related to what government does. As more government-generated and government-related information has become available online, greater numbers of citizens have genuine opportunities to be better informed. And by placing important political information online—for example, records of campaign donations—government can inform the public and increase the transparency of the democratic process. Running through all these advantages is the tantalizing possibility that the technology can help cut administrative costs and improve service delivery at the same time.

The general acceptance of the importance of e-government initiatives was reflected in the fact that e-government was made a centerpiece of President George W. Bush's Management Agenda in his first term of office. The main goals of e-government, the agenda stated, were to cut government spending, reduce the paperwork burden on citizens and businesses, and to improve the government's performance—primarily by easing access to information and services. The White House established an office of e-government and appointed an e-government director at the Office of Management and Budget (OMB). At the same time, states and counties were also establishing similar offices and pursuing similar initiatives.

In many respects, the initiatives have been successful. By 2004, for example, 97 million Americans had made contact with government through the Internet for reasons other than filing tax forms. The use of the Internet to contact government grew by 50 percent between 2002 and 2003.[4] Indeed, since 1998, making use of e-government has been one of the fastest-growing Internet activities.

Government executives quickly found the Internet to be a handy tool. As early as 2000 they were reporting that the Internet had helped them in important ways with internal administration, public relations, and coordination with other agencies.[5] And citizens apparently agreed; based on traditional customer satisfaction measures, electronic encounters with government have rated comparably to other forms of interaction.[6] (See Box 12.1 for another way citizens and government interact via the Internet.)

There are many success stories about how government has effectively employed Internet technology to improve its operations. In collaboration with the Council for Excellence in Government, Harvard University's Ash

Institute has assembled examples of these successes, which can be found on its website.[7] But most early e-government efforts, especially at the national level, left the basic relations between government and its citizens intact, and it is this relationship that must change for citizens to be fully energized by technology. In an overview of e-government, political scientist Darrell West, a long-time student of technology, politics, and government, offered the following conclusion about Government 1.0 websites:

> From a technical standpoint, there is no reason why government agencies have not incorporated more interactive features into their sites. The technology exists and has been well tested. Interactive technologies are common on some sites and have been used to serve customer needs. The failure to incorporate these advances is not a problem of technology as much as it represents a problem of political will and vision. . . .
>
> Public officials must recognize that government websites can do more than merely deliver information and services. They represent a powerful tool for transforming democracy and reaching out to the general public. . . . The Internet has the power to revolutionize the relationship between citizens and leaders, but realization of this hope takes more vision and political will than have thus far been established in the public sector.[8]

And, indeed, if one reads the OMB's reports on President Bush's Management Agenda, it becomes clear that the emphasis was on government to citizen (G2C), government to government (G2G), and government to business (G2B) connections, as well as internal efficiency and effectiveness (IEE).[9] Little emphasis was placed on citizen to government (C2G) and citizen to citizen (C2C) connections, where the Internet can do the most to change the way government functions and to increase trust among citizens.

Informed by a market orientation and the "reinventing government" vein of what has come to be known as the "new public management" literature, the dominant view government has of its citizens is as customers. The resulting aim is to provide them with efficiencies in information access and service delivery, and to save them tax dollars in the process—all laudable goals. But that view does not equally emphasize citizens as active participants in a process of decision making and governance. Citizens must be seen as significant partners in what government agencies are trying to accomplish.

Barack Obama's open government initiative

Upon taking office, President Barack Obama issued a memorandum calling for an Open Government Directive to promote transparency, participation, and collaboration through technology.[10] The President's Open Government Initiative established guidelines and deadlines for improving the quantity and quality of government information available to the general public, for providing citizens with meaningful opportunities to provide input and feedback, and for implementing tools to foster better collaboration and coordination. This initiative has catalyzed a veritable explosion of new and revamped "dot-gov" websites across federal agencies. Despite some criticisms, prominent transparency advocates recently presented Obama with an award in recognition of his initiative and "deep commitment to an open and transparent government—of, by, and for the people."[11]

The Open Government Directive itself was a product of an extensive online listening exercise in which citizens were invited to help craft the substance of the initiative and even draft its language using a "wiki."[12] A wiki allows individual participants to change the product that is being created collectively, either by adding or editing. Probably the best-known example is the online encyclopedia, Wikipedia, which is remarkably accurate and useful on the whole.[13] As a result of this "crowd-sourcing" process, the administration was able to distill practical suggestions about how to improve government websites. One need contributors stressed was the importance of releasing government data in machine-readable formats that allow developers to create applications that make government data more accessible. One of the administration's new flagship websites, Data.gov, thus offers a massive repository of data from government agencies freely accessible to developers. The site also encourages visitors to provide suggestions and feedback on their blog, where users offer practical suggestions such as how to improve searching and data labeling, reduce duplication, and report errors.[14]

Making relatively obscure data available in a machine-readable format has unleashed the creative potential of thousands of web-savvy developers who are creating value with government data in new ways. Drawing on Department of Transportation statistics available through Data.gov, for example, FlyOnTime.us provides airline travelers with estimated flight delays between U.S. cities through an easy-to-use website. Users simply search for their airports and receive detailed predictions about delays

Box 12.1   E-rulemaking

An area of e-government of particular note concerns the comment process prior to government regulatory action, often called "e-rulemaking." The use of e-rulemaking points toward some of the more genuinely interactive possibilities provided by the Internet, as well some of the pitfalls lurking in the use of the technology. Under the traditional off-line process of soliciting comments from an invited list of interested parties and through announcements via standard public notice channels, those who participate in the public comment process usually represent a narrow sliver of the nation, limited for the most part to representatives of large commercial institutions.

Using electronic technology to open up the process of submitting comments on proposed U.S. government regulations has, on the one hand, been shown to solicit a broader set of participants and a more diverse set of comments, including comments from individuals and organizations not originally appearing on the initial invitation list. It has also solicited a different kind of comment, more personal and individual in its approach, versus the more formal style of communication typical of a large organization affected by the proposed regulation. In these ways, the process has been made more democratic, and the quality of the information gathered by government through the process has been improved.[1] The government of Virginia, to take a state-level example, has also received high praise for what it has accomplished in these realms by moving most aspects of its rulemaking process online.[2] In a similar vein, the West Virginia Departments of Education and Health and Human Resources employed a web portal to effectively open up the information flows related to the rulemaking process for the establishment of a universal prekindergarten program.[3]

On the other hand, large organizations and interest groups—both private and public—quickly caught up to the practice and adjusted their tactics accordingly. Now, electronic public commenting procedures often generate hundreds of thousands of duplicative, at times even "canned" comments, in much the same way that multiple political messages are e-mailed, phoned in, and sent by postcard to the White House and Congress. Such instances of public action that at first appear to be spontaneous, but that in fact are orchestrated by large or wealthy organizations—"Astroturf" rather than true grassroots

caused by weather and holidays, as well as helpful guidance about which flights and days are the best and worst for traveling.

While Data.gov is geared more toward researchers and developers, other dot-gov websites are explicitly designed to present data to the general public using visualizations that promote financial accountability and lobbying—can clog the system with information not especially useful to the process or genuinely reflective of public moods. And in terms of interactivity this use of e-government is still quite limited. With e-rulemaking, the relationship between government and citizens remains essentially unchanged, as does the process, except that it has been moved online.

Stuart Shulman, an assistant professor at the University of Massachusetts Amherst, has studied e-rulemaking for more than ten years. Although he remains optimistic about the future of e-rulemaking, he finds that current practices often fall short of their potential. "Some companies are asking employees to submit form letters or talking points on their behalf," while within government agencies the process is sometimes "perceived not necessarily as a bad thing, but as just another requirement to meet with limited time and resources." However, there are plenty of government agencies that do use the process very effectively. For example, the U.S. Access Board, which services the disabled community, successfully solicited more than 500 comments through Regulations.gov from "real stakeholders with substantive, germane comments." With crowd-sourcing initiatives, it's important to remember that more is not always better. A few hundred high quality comments can be much more valuable than thousands of canned responses. "You don't need 10,000 people to make a point," Shulman explains, "eventually you hit a saturation point where you just keep getting more of the same."

It's also critical that agencies have a strategy in place to analyze the comments they receive. "You can't just calculate word counts," Shulman advises, "you need to have a way of identifying the good comments and understanding them in context." Shulman is currently working with several federal agencies to help them put their data to good use. You can read more about his work on his group's website http://people.umass.edu/stu/eRulemaking/.

---

1. For these findings and arguments, see among others Stanley and Weare (2004); Coglianese (2004a), (2004b); and Shulman's writings on http://people.umass.edu/stu/eRulemaking/.

2. See Holzer et al. (2004); and the Virginia portal itself at www.townhall.virginia.gov.

3. Bushouse (2006).

encourage visitors to reflect on government priorities. One major dot-gov site, USAspending.gov, provides interactive graphs and maps that show federal spending trends over time and across states.[15] Users can easily identify federal agencies' most expensive programs and even create custom figures using intuitive online tools. Another popular site, Recovery.gov, tracks how funds awarded and received under the American Recovery and Reinvestment Act of 2009 have been distributed around the country using interactive maps.[16]

The Obama administration's emphasis on increasing government transparency and public participation has set a high bar, one that could potentially backfire if the White House's efforts fail to meet expectations.[17] Assessing Obama's Open Government Initiative after its first year, Carolyn Lukensmeyer of AmericaSpeaks and Patrice McDermott of OpenTheGovernment.org concluded that "agencies have made significant progress . . . but there was still a long road ahead."[18] Similarly, Donald F. Norris observed that "e-government began and remains principally information and service oriented," involving mostly "static information and downloadable forms, a limited number of transactions, limited interactivity, and not much else."[19] And Lisa Blomgren Bingham argues that although the Open Government Initiative is "a major step toward making government more transparent, there remains much work to make it more participatory and collaborative."[20]

In addition, unpredictable outcomes can result from relinquishing control of online content to the general public. When the Obama administration experimentally launched "Open for Questions" (whitehouse.gov/openforquestions), a public crowd-sourcing initiative in which visitors could suggest and vote on questions for President Obama to answer, the marijuana legalization movement flooded the site in nearly every category by voting up one another's pot-related questions.[21] The onslaught illustrates a major risk of Participation 2.0's vulnerability to co-optation by particular interest groups or social movements. Since its launch, the website reports that almost 100,000 users have submitted more than 100,000 questions that have been voted on almost 2 million times. As of this writing, questions for the president now cover a wide variety of topics, but the legalization movement still maintains an unusually strong presence.

An important responsibility with this form of citizen engagement is the imperative for government to actually respond to the public's concerns. Visible neglect of the public's input can breed cynicism, not trust, if contributors believe that their voices are being ignored. We still need to broaden our consideration of the values and purposes of e-governance, and doing so will yield constructive engagement with the problem of trust. Research on trust in government has suggested that trust may not have a close connection with government performance, as indicated by objective measures, nor with the ideological fit between specific government policies and the beliefs of respondents.[22] Instead, e-governance may be best able to engender trust by inviting citizens to become more active in the work of government agencies and, through that process, instill a sense of ownership in government.

And though it is not our focus here, it is worth noting that similar approaches might be employed within a government agency and between government agencies or offices to improve levels of involvement, investment, and trust among employees. Toward that end, after reading this chapter the reader would be well-served to review Chapter 8, Russ Linden's discussion of collaborative leadership, and consider the possible linkages.

Also important to note are concerns about a digital divide, which could cause the increased use of the Internet to be undemocratic in its ultimate effect. Those concerns are real, but based on the available evidence we believe that in terms of basic access, the divide is closing, and that in any event recent developments in the online world compare favorably with those in the off-line world.[23]

E-politics: What agency managers can learn from campaigns

If government's greatest potential to invigorate agency-citizen relations and generate trust through new technology remains still largely untapped, clues to unlocking that potential might be found in electoral politics and political advocacy as well as business. These realms have shown much innovation, which has mirrored the rapidly changing landscape of the technology itself. Because we are political scientists who study the political uses of the Internet, we focus our attention on politics, but comment on commerce along the way.

Here is the clear lesson from observing a decade's worth of innovations: the central need to generate authentic two-way interactions between citizens and the organizations working with and for them (C2G), and to facilitate more horizontal, multiway communications among citizens, which are centered on the mission of the organization (C2C).[24] In pondering how to get the most out of e-governance, federal executives should recognize that in politics and commerce, a learning curve had to be traveled before the lesson was internalized. An initial impulse to approach the Internet as another vehicle to deliver the same services and messages yielded limited success; it was only as the Internet began to be viewed in distinctive terms, with the potential to help change the very nature of the approach taken toward citizens and customers, that it realized its potential.

Granted, there are limits on the kinds of techniques from politics and commerce that a government agency can adopt wholesale—limits generated by legal-liability concerns, the need to maintain control over the integrity of both the content and the presentation of the agency's central mission, as well as the more general need for greater top-down control over what an agency does. While we are sensitive to these limitations, we nevertheless believe the basic insight can be imported to good use. And we believe that more can be done to invite the participation of citizens.

What has the Internet realized so far? The following sketch of its use is primarily modeled on the election cycles of 2000, 2004, and 2008. While Internet-based and Internet-facilitated political participation obviously exists between elections and extends beyond them—indeed, one of the Internet's principal values is its ability to sustain civic activity and create alternative forms of political engagement—elections mobilize and concentrate a great deal of political activity. For that reason, we have chosen to anchor our discussion in the people and events surrounding those years. Our discussion of election 2000 relies in particular on *Click on Democracy*.[25]

First steps: The Internet in election 2000

We begin our account in 2000, when the Internet's impact was first readily seen.[26] Just two years earlier, Reform Party candidate Jesse Ventura had ridden the Internet to victory in the Minnesota governor's race. The Internet was credited with helping Ventura raise money, organize volunteers, and respond to the opposition. In the following year, Steve Forbes announced his presidential candidacy online, and Bill Bradley became the first candidate to raise $1 million online. More and more people were going online, and applications of the technology for political uses were expanding rapidly. Consequently, expectations that the Internet would have a dramatic impact on the 2000 election reached a high point going into the cycle's final year.

And from one perspective, the 2000 election did indeed look like a watershed moment. Sen. John McCain gathered more than $2 million online in one week; Arizona conducted a binding online primary; and presidential candidate George W. Bush posted his campaign contributors online. Interest groups such as MoveOn.org, which started in 1998 to oppose the impeachment of President Bill Clinton and then morphed into a broad-based liberal organization, were getting real political traction through the Internet. More political information with greater depth and variety was available online, and many citizens were making good use of it.

But in the end, particularly when we look at how large political institutions and the media used the Internet, the reality fell so far short of the hype that a chapter of *Click on Democracy* was titled "Election.dud."[27] Perhaps the best metaphor for the Internet's trajectory in the election was the contrast between the Republican and Democratic conventions, held just two weeks apart in the summer. The Republicans went first, staking their claim to the presidency in Philadelphia. Soon after the start-up dot-com Pseudopolitics arrived on the scene, it became the media darling of the festivities. Its skybox was the trendiest place for politicos to be seen. Fifty-five other Internet outlets were there, too, housed in a media pavilion dubbed "Internet Alley." Online chats, instant polls, web cams mounted to roving reporters' heads, and interviews that included questions fed to anchors through chat rooms were some of the innovative and at times irreverent features they added to the traditional mix of excerpted speeches and media commentary.

But the initial buzz created by the web's presence at the convention did not translate into anything more significant among citizens or advertisers, and the politics-cum-business ventures failed to generate expected revenues. Two weeks later, when the Democrats convened in Los Angeles, the Internet-based coverage had been dramatically scaled back. Pseudopolitics dropped its live, interactive features, and its skybox appeared placid. The buzz evaporated, and many of the people involved in the different Internet operations there used the convention to network for new jobs.

That was not the whole story, however. A deeper look beyond the traditional campaign events and institutions revealed something quite hopeful: groups of individuals, some loosely organized and others more formally organized, were using the Internet in more genuinely interactive ways to form political communities and pursue collective action. These groups included one called 80-20, a national-level group of Asian Americans trying to raise their political clout; the People's Campaign, a local group trying to contest elections in New Brunswick, NJ; and loosely linked sets of groups trying to protest the Republican convention. After surveying the entire political field during the election cycle, we discovered the central conclusion of the book: the importance of interactivity and horizontal connections, which in turn helped to create and foster political communities.

Like their present-day e-government counterparts, the political and media institutions had approached the Internet largely as a new version of the older, one-to-many TV, radio, and print media, and they were in fact able to achieve some notable innovations in political communication and collective action. But they failed to change political life in the dramatic ways many Internet and political observers had hoped to see. Neither the media nor the candidates used the Internet effectively for interacting with voters, essentially short-circuiting any chance they had of truly connecting with the online electorate. Their notions of the Internet's political role were limited for the most part to a few narrowly defined, traditional uses.[28] In their mind's eye, a campaign's website or a political news story sat at the hub of the political wheel, and individual citizens logged on as spokes, received the broadcast information, and sent back financial contributions through cyberspace.

All the while, the Internet's most profound and positive political impact was the way informal groups and individuals used it to create and enhance political communities. The Internet made its most effective contribution to politics—and held its greatest future promise—as a facilitator of political community building and multiple-way communication, rather than as a one-to-many broadcast device employed to capture viewers, money, and votes. Furthermore, the Internet was more useful in achieving even those more mercenary purposes if it was used in ways that challenged the command-and-control model and encouraged people to connect with each other under the aegis of the organization's ultimate aims.

Commercial enterprises certainly understood, as a *BusinessWeek* article called it, "The Power of Us."[29] "User-generated content," "peer-production," "co-production," and "architectures of participation" were some of the buzzwords hinting at the new approach. Consider, for example, the way Amazon and Travelocity employ (with minimal cost) their customers to review their products, or the way Google uses the accumulated decision making of web page designers to organize its search output. Despite being vulnerable to sabotage by political partisans, the citizen-crafted Wikipedia is remarkably useful and accurate. (Wikipedia is nonprofit, but it illustrates the point.) Mostly free Craigslist has captured a lot of the classified advertising business in large cities, from help-wanted to personal ads, and made the information deeper, the process more interactive, and the experience better. It has also fostered spin-off communities of shared interest and action, both online and off-line.

Writers, pundits, and activists who understood the importance of the difference in approach encouraged the candidates and the political institutions to appreciate the value of a more inclusive and participatory framework, pointing out the few interactive glimmers of hope supplied during the 2000 election. They also encouraged the candidates and institutions to open up back channels and relax top-down control. And indeed, many of them made these changes in the 2004 election cycle, which is one reason that 2004 looked more like a genuine breakout year for the Internet.

But most of them also struggled, and continue to struggle to this day, with the tension between facilitating the co-creation of the political efforts on the part of their would-be supporters—which requires giving up some control and authority—and the desire to control the messages coming out of the organization and manage the activities occurring under its umbrella.[30] That tension is something that government executives attempting to employ the Internet more creatively will feel with a vengeance, a topic we return to below.

It walks and talks: The Internet in election 2004

By all measures, the political force of the Internet could not be ignored in 2004. The largest, most established political institutions turned to interactive, horizontally focused grassroots models with great success. To list just a few of the Internet's biggest steps: it supplied the organizational glue and logistical resources for Howard Dean's volunteers; facilitated much of Dean's financing, allowing him to smash Clinton's record for Democratic fundraising in the twelve months before an election year and propel himself from dark horse to frontrunner; gave John Kerry a similar fundraising boost and in particular helped him to make up ground on President Bush's huge early-money lead in the critical later months of the campaign; underwrote the grassroots movement to draft Wesley Clark into the race; supplied the primary organizing and fundraising device for myriad 527 organizations, such as Moveon, America Coming Together (ACT), Democracy for America (formerly Dean for America), and Swift Boat Veterans for Truth; got millions of people to talk politics and organize local political efforts through Meetups and other similar venues; and enhanced Bush-Cheney '04's massive ground-level volunteer effort, a critical component in an election that turned on approximately 120,000 voters in Ohio.[31]

Larger numbers of informal groups and individuals turned to the Internet for political information, communication, and organization, including heretofore nonpolitical individuals making their first real foray into political activity, people organizing carpools and chartering buses to register voters in swing states, and those starting their own interest and activist groups.

At the same time, blogging became an Internet phenomenon of its own. Millions of blogs emerged, and a few, such as DailyKos, Talking Points Memo, Power Line, InstaPundit, and Little Green Footballs, worked their way into political discussions at elite levels. Perhaps their greatest influence was that many reporters and editors in the traditional media canvassed the blogs, which then became, according to Internet observer Michael Cornfield, "the agenda setters for the agenda setters."[32] But the blogs were also drawing many ordinary people into active discussions, and the cross-posting and cross-linking among the blogs generated a sense of community among large subsets of them. Smaller, locally oriented blogs helped to stimulate meaningful political dialogues. Individual blogs, even those read by just a handful of friends and family, unleashed the personal political expression of countless citizens.[33]

A few aggregate-level statistics suggest the positive effect of the Internet on political life. In 2004, 37 percent of all adults, 75 million people, used the Internet to get political news and information, discuss candidates, donate money, or otherwise volunteer their political services. A Pew Research Center survey of those making election-related uses of the Internet in 2004 found that half believed that the Internet had supplied them with important information that made a difference in their vote, and a quarter of them said that what they found on the Internet made the difference in their vote.[34] A quarter of the respondents also reported that their use of the Internet encouraged them to vote. More than half thought that the quality of the political debate was raised by the information available on the Internet, and that the Internet supplied them with information they could not get through the print media or television. Additional evidence from a separate Pew survey suggested that the people using the Internet to get political information were not just seeking out items with which they agreed; in fact, they were exposed to a greater diversity of views than off-line citizens.[35]

Arguably more important, the available evidence also suggested that the Internet was instrumental in bringing new people into the political system. A study by the Institute for Politics, Democracy, and the Internet

(IPDI) of online political activity during the primary season found that almost half of those who were the most active politically through online means had not been previously involved in politics.[36] Additional research on presidential campaign Meetups during the early months of 2004 suggested that the Internet-organized get-togethers brought new people into the system.[37] Another study found that the Meetups were important in fundraising efforts.[38] It is also worth noting that in the major conferences on Internet politics held after the election, the political professionals—left, right, and center—all agreed that the Internet contributed significantly and independently to the rise in political interest and participation.

Perhaps the most telling aggregate-level evidence concerns campaign finance. Between 2000 and 2004 the number of people who contributed to campaigns online doubled.[39] An IPDI study of small donors and online donors to the presidential campaigns contained a number of intriguing and hopeful findings about how this change affected the pool of donors.[40] First, the percentage of large donations accounted for by the extremely wealthy appeared to drop. Second, although all groups of donors were still wealthier than nondonors, smaller donors were relatively much closer in income to the average citizen. Third, the numbers of small and large donors both increased between 2000 and 2004, but the increase in the number of small donors was approximately four-fold, and much of that increase came from online donations—high percentages of first-time donors gave online. Most important, however, was the finding that small, online donors were just as politically active as large donors—they were more likely than other small donors to solicit others to give and to attend political events. Based on those findings, the study's authors argued that:

> The Internet is leveling the playing field. Small donors lack the resources and social networks that large donors have, but the Internet in 2004 helped connect them in ways that made up for fewer resources. Online small donors are just as likely as large donors to try to convince someone to support their candidate, and soliciting others to donate seems particularly spurred by being online.[41]

And, after reviewing all the evidence they had gathered about the demographic changes in donors and the Internet's role in the influx of new and small donations, the authors concluded their study with the hope "that [the Internet] can help bring to campaign fundraising a richer social and political diversity that marks the American political system at its best."[42]

Obamamania: The Internet in election 2008

Obama's campaign manager, David Plouffe, recognized the mobilizing potential of Participation 2.0 and empowered his new media team to great effect during the 2008 presidential race.[43] The Obama campaign built a national movement of supporters not simply by issuing top-down directives from campaign headquarters, but by making available a vast infrastructure of social networking websites, community-based organizations, and other support structures to facilitate self-organization. Their strategy empowered local volunteers to become a major driving force behind the Obama campaign. By encouraging authenticity, dialogue, and participation, the campaign was able to build the trust and enthusiasm necessary to motivate supporters to take action. To be sure, traditional media and outreach still played a critical role, but a pragmatic willingness to experiment with new media was also a key to the campaign's ultimate victory.

Messaging is an important component of any political campaign, and in the age of Participation 2.0, citizens expect to actively engage with political messages beyond just the passive reception of tried and true sound bites. In many respects, such interactive, on-demand platforms like YouTube came to be even more important during the 2008 race than traditional media like television and radio. Obama announced his decision to form an exploratory committee with a YouTube video that could be instantly streamed anytime, anywhere by anyone. When a scandal later emerged over controversial remarks made by Obama's pastor, Jeremiah Wright, Obama responded through a mix of new and traditional media. Versions of Obama's widely praised speech on race, which helped diffuse the crisis, have together been viewed more than 8 million times on YouTube, nearly as many times as Martin Luther King's landmark "I have a dream" speech. According to Plouffe, most people did not watch Obama's speech on TV, but on YouTube:

> This marked a fundamental change in political coverage and message consumption, and one that will only continue as technology rolls forward: big moments, political or otherwise, will no longer be remembered by people as times when everyone gathered around TVs to watch a speech, press conference, or other event. Increasingly, most of us will recall firing up the computer, searching for a video, and watching it at home or at the office—or even on our cell phones.[44]

The public is not only consuming but also producing and sharing huge amounts of political content using new media like YouTube and Facebook. Although Obama's speech on race remains popular, it is dwarfed by user-created content championing or lampooning the Obama campaign. Videos on YouTube include a surprising number of computer-edited "dance-offs" between Obama and his Republican rival John McCain, various love ballads by "Obama Girl," and a professionally produced, rather risqué music video featuring intimately engaged Obama and Hillary Clinton lookalikes called "Umbrella," which alone has been viewed more than 84 million times.

And online campaign messages and user-generated content are increasingly available on millions of smart phones capable of streaming audio and video in real time and notifying users with a ding or a buzz when, for example, a political campaign, federal agency, or a friend posts a new message or comment. The growing popularity of smart devices like the iPhone in the pockets of millions of citizens empowers users to generate and pass along information among hundreds of their friends instantly and almost effortlessly.

Another component of the Obama campaign's strategy involved the creation of the social networking site my.barackobama.com or "MyBO." On MyBO users volunteered their contact information, searched for events, joined local organizing groups, and even got training on community organizing. Spaces like MyBO helped connect people to one another in addition to providing a venue for pushing out campaign messages and collecting information about supporters like postal codes and e-mail addresses.

In one clever move the Obama campaign collected more than 2 million cell phone numbers—a fifteen-fold increase at the time—by allowing users to sign up for a text message announcing Obama's pick for vice president. This offered subscribers an energizing feeling of "being the first to know" while gathering a veritable treasure trove of data. New technologies like social networking sites and smart phone applications also allow for sophisticated tracking and data analysis that can improve the effectiveness of communications and fundraising. In the case of the Obama campaign, their new media tactics gathered not just names and addresses but also many active volunteers.

The Internet has long been seen as a potential game-changer for political fundraising, and in 2008 this came into stark relief. The Obama campaign's average contribution was under $100 throughout the primary, but

Box 12.2   Participation 2.0? There's an app for that*

Apple's first iPhone was released in January 2007 and heralded as a revolutionary Internet-enabled device with the potential to fundamentally alter the way people interact with technology. In July 2008 Apple launched its "app store," an online store offering programs specifically designed for the iPhone. Since its introduction, billions of apps have been downloaded by iPhone users and the app store now offers more than 200,000 apps, many of them free, that help users do anything from checking the weather and finding local restaurants to posting updates to Facebook or Twitter. The innovation of the iPhone and many similar devices has introduced new possibilities for public management and e-governance that simply didn't exist on a meaningful scale until 2008.

Recognizing this potential, in October 2008 the Obama campaign released a free iPhone app to help volunteers get out the vote. One of the app's features, called "Call Friends," encouraged users to phone their friends to garner support for Obama. It ranked users' contacts by telephone prefix, placing contacts from battleground states at the top of the list. Other features called "Get Involved" and "Local Events" used GPS location information to connect users with local campaign offices and events, and a link at the bottom of the screen allowed users to donate directly to the campaign.

In the 2010 midterm elections, the Democratic Party was back with an app called "Barack Obama | Organizing for America." Users could search for local events, review party "discussion points," call their local congresspersons, receive and respond to alerts and current updates, and, of course,

its ability to reach millions of potential contributors at low cost using new technologies quickly became an important asset. In January 2008 the campaign was able to raise $28 million of $32 million online and in September $100 million of $150 million was raised online, at times at a rate approaching $500,000 per hour.[45] Studies and anecdotal evidence suggest that citizens who cross the giving threshold, even with small amounts, are more likely to feel vested in their candidates and participate and volunteer in other ways.[46] At a broader level, small givers also may tend to be more moderate and libertarian in their political views, with potentially transformative effects for the future of American politics.[47]

The use of technology in political campaigns has evolved dramatically from 2000 to 2008, largely mirroring the evolution from Government 1.0 to Participation 2.0 (see Box 12.2). The Obama 2008 campaign example shows donate. The app was also available on Apple's iPad, a popular Internet-enabled tablet.

And the White House was not to be outdone. In January 2010 White House Press Secretary Robert Gibbs released a short YouTube video announcing their new "White House App" that allows users to stream live video events over their iPhones, among other features. "If you want to see me set the White House press corps straight every day, live—now there's an app for that," said Gibbs, as his iPhone displayed a live feed of an empty podium in the White House press room. As Gibbs placed the phone on a desk and walked into the actual press room, the phone screen showed him approaching the podium in real time.

It is hard to predict how smart phone technology will continue to evolve as more users acquire devices, Internet connections become faster and more reliable, and developers continue to develop ever-more finely tuned applications. But certainly the opportunities for advancing civic participation through mobile technology are impressive. Current hardware technology can enable users to coordinate phone call and door-knocking campaigns in real time with other volunteers, record and post videos of speeches and rallies using built-in video recording hardware and social networking applications, and even report the location of potholes to their municipal governments using GPS information. Unlike other media, smart phone users generally keep their phones with them at all times, always connected and ready to create, receive, and share information with their friends, colleagues, and the general public.

*Source: Stephen Shankland. "Obama Releases iPhone Recruiting, Campaign Tool." CNET, October 2, 2008 at www.whitehouse.gov/blog/2010/01/25/your-entertainment-and-information-robert-gibbs-white-house-iphone-app.

that the successful use of Internet technology within the sphere of governance requires a willingness to experiment and take risks, and that if well managed, technology can be effectively harnessed to facilitate grassroots organization on a national scale. Successful campaigners and managers today do not view the Internet simply as another medium for advertising and fundraising, but as a communal space in which anyone with something to say has a voice and great rewards accrue to those ready to listen and able to act.

Applying the insights in a government agency context

Government agencies have different kinds of missions and therefore different needs for control over what they make available to citizens. Executives at the CIA necessarily work within a set of constraints different from those at the National Park Service, but even the CIA has jazzed up its website with an interactive personality quiz designed to invite applicants (also see Russ Linden's discussion of the CIA's "Intellipedia" in Chapter 8). Not all the possibilities suggested here will be viable in all agencies; nevertheless, we believe that some core principles are widely applicable. Government agencies have one advantage over the other areas we are citing as examples: the citizens' needs for government services and information.

How to realize these ideas on the ground? Web page design is obviously important—the sites must be inviting, easy to navigate, and supply smooth paths leading to greater activity. But that is just the beginning. The agency must be committed to interaction and horizontal activity and be ready both to respond and instigate.

To start, it is essential to *reach out to citizens where they already are*—and then encourage them to join the agency in going further. This principle operates at three levels. The first level is quite literal. Agencies must be proactive in reaching out to potentially interested citizens in the places they already visit online. Although many agencies in fact have captive audiences for their online efforts, they cannot rely solely on them. There is no reason why agency employees could not frequent Internet crossroads related to the agency's mission, and alert the people congregating there to the agency, its work, and the possibilities for their involvement.[48] These efforts could be as simple as posting agency-approved video archives to YouTube.com or having employees contribute relevant entries on Wikipedia (see above) that invite a visit to an agency's website.

The second level is the way citizens are engaged once they arrive. To illustrate this point, in a Federal Executive Institute seminar Reeher once asked his government executive participants to adopt a fictional identity, with accompanying interests or concerns, and then spend an evening accessing the federal government's online presence as if they had those identities.[49] Many of the executives reported back the next day that they were appalled at how technical and uninviting the available information seemed to their fictional characters—ordinary citizens with specific concerns. It is imperative that citizens find easily understandable language in the government's Internet space. Speaking clearly is necessary for all governments in all mediums; in the United States, Washington State has led the way with its "plain talk" principles.[50] But such plain talk is especially critical in creating an Internet environment that citizens will want to join.

The third level is what efforts citizens are asked to join. The citizens' prior interests and concerns must overlap with the projects for which the agency is soliciting their help. As a first step, the Internet can be employed to discover what those interests and concerns are. The agency must then offer citizens activities and information that provide multiple connections between agency and citizen, facilitate horizontal connections among citizens, and encourage them to undertake related but new activities. Accomplishing that transition leads us to our second set of core principles.

Agencies must *keep the back channel genuinely open*. Again, this principle has several dimensions. Citizens must have ways to communicate their views back to government, and the government must establish ways to acknowledge, respond to, and use this feedback, beyond an automated response. Citizens must also have the option of making their views known to others; it is important to them that other citizens can know what they think and respond if they wish. As we have stressed before, citizens need to be encouraged and provided with the means to establish horizontal connections and communication networks around shared interests or concerns. And for all these methods to work, another core principle must be followed: *The experiences created must be authentic* for the individual citizen.

Many kinds of material can be put online that invite response or participation. Podcasts, videos, and blogs related to the work of the agency can be posted for viewing and comment. Some of these items can be informal and personal, communicating the sense of the agency mission that brought public servants to their work in the first place. Elected officials, including President George W. Bush, have enjoyed great success posting informal and human interest-focused communications on their websites. Such material can both inform and help to generate empathy for the agency and its employees, as citizens are invited to virtually walk in someone else's shoes.[51]

And in most agencies there is plenty of additional room for digital public discussions coordinated by agency representatives, from lightly moderated informal discussions to actively led forums in a more formal question-and-answer format, if that is more appropriate for the topic.[52] These spaces can be divided up into areas of specific interest, which correspond to different divisions of the agency or the branch. Other possibilities include simulations similar to the Maine budget exercise described at the beginning of this chapter and kindred "TurboTax" approaches, in which a software package or simulation available on the agency's website demonstrates to individual citizens or businesses how a particular set of rules, regulations, or benefit eligibilities would affect them in terms of an outcome, rather than just describing through text how the provisions work.[53] Citizens could also sign up with an agency for automatic updates and alerts to any changes or proposed changes that might affect their interests. Virginia already uses a version of this with its e-rulemaking process. Abroad, Seoul, South Korea, provides reports to the online forums it sponsors regarding actions the government takes that are related to the discussions generated there.[54]

With genuine feedback, critical thoughts about what an agency is doing will get voiced, and not all of them will be benign or even fair. That is the cost of complete transparency. But if the experience so far in other realms on the Internet is any indication, an agency having both the courage and confidence to let these views stand and be seen by others visiting the site will earn more respect than enmity.

For government executives the greatest power of the Internet lies in drawing citizens into the work of agencies as coproducers of value, which can be done by further opening up the space created for agency-oriented discussions, providing tools for individuals to do things, and then actually using what they do. The core principle to unlock this last stage is: *Remember that citizens already want to help.*

By allowing others to respond to and evaluate comments posted on their websites, and then employing metrics to accumulate these reactions, agencies can enlist citizens to highlight the most useful comments, and to place ideas on the agency's agenda for further consideration. Consider, for example, how Travelocity employs its customers to rate the accommodations it lists, or how Amazon asks customers not only to review its books, but also to rate the usefulness of the posted customer reviews.

An agency might also provide a space for citizens and groups to post information about nonagency events that are related to the agency's mission, in much the same way as politically related event-sharing sites currently do. The agency could go a step further and invite those who signed up for an event through the site to evaluate that event after the fact, and then post on the site a cumulative rating for that event or an entire organization's events. Working Assets did something similar on its "Volunteer for Change" site. As activist and writer Greg Bloom points out, asking for feedback causes the sponsoring organization to take greater care with the quality of the events it is posting to the site.[55]

But such approaches can be taken even further, to ask individual citizens to help with the central aspects of an agency's mission. An off-beat (but spot-on) example of this potential can be found in Australia, created by the government's "National Continence Management Strategy," part of the Department of Health and Ageing. The program offers an interactive online map of all public restrooms in the nation.[56] Citizens planning a trip can generate a customized toilet map for their travel route. It is an extremely handy device when one pauses to consider it—very practical, very British.

But now imagine adding to that map a system for individual travelers to report on the quality and cleanliness of the facilities, and feed their reports back into an Amazon-type automatically updating rating system, which was in turn integrated into the map. Note that when Reeher posed this possibility to the executives in his Federal Executive Institute seminar, they looked at him like he was in the loo. The prototype of such a system exists, but it is found in the private sector, in the form of a site called "The Bathroom Diaries," which rates more than 8,000 public bathrooms in more than 100 countries around the world.[57]

Another imaginative potential use emerged in Texas in summer 2006, when Gov. Rick Perry proposed making available online live video streams from cameras installed along remote stretches of private land bordering Mexico.[58] The specific placement of individual cameras would not be made public. Citizens viewing the videos could report suspicious activity, presumably by a camera identification number, by dialing a toll-free telephone number. The governor presented the idea as a way to respond to cuts in federal homeland security funding and increases in border violence; he characterized it as a broader, virtual equivalent of a neighborhood watch program. What would have made the idea even more intriguing from an Internet networking standpoint would have been to provide a way for the citizens watching the site at any given time to communicate with each other, should they choose to do so. That way, they could alert each other to activity that they saw and get second and third opinions on whether the activity was indeed suspicious.

To be sure, the politics surrounding the proposal and its possible effects made it controversial—it was dubbed the "virtual posse," and denounced as crazy, half-baked, race-baiting, even illegal. In addition to legitimate concerns about the political message that such a system of monitoring might convey and how some individuals and organizations might use it, what also appears to be embedded in the critiques is an assumption that the general public cannot be trusted to help the state do its job. And this leads to another core principle: at some meaningful level, agencies must *trust the people*. Trust, after all, is not unidirectional; it is a mutual relationship, and that aspect of it must be taken seriously.

Agencies can choose less controversial actions. Individuals expressing kindred views or sharing kindred problems or concerns could be encouraged to join together, and agencies could supply them with the networking tools to sustain those initial connections. Agencies could also, after obtaining the permission of the individuals, share information about them with others who might want to join them, and in that way actively facilitate the creation of networks. Citizens coming together through these means could share their experiences with each other and, for example, discuss practices they have learned for coping with whatever problem or concern brought them to interact with government in the first place. These practices are already primary features of the most effective online party-based and campaign-oriented organizing efforts.

Agencies can also provide tools for individuals to create and carry out activities on their own. Howard Dean's presidential campaign did this with its legions of online volunteers in 2003 and 2004, when it latched on to the gatherings in support of Dean—and against the Iraq war—that were already happening through Meetup.com. Bush-Cheney '04 took a more coordinated and planned approach to the same strategy by supplying willing e-volunteers whom it had been cultivating since before 2000 with walk lists of registered Republicans in their own neighborhoods, contact information for other volunteers in their area to join in, and contact information for other potential supporters across the country with shared occupations or interests.

Agencies could take such efforts even further, into the realm of "wikis," for example. But here is a more suggestive example of how an agency might use the wiki approach: in the aftermath of Hurricane Katrina, John Scalzi, a writer and blogger, posted on his website a poetic essay, "Being Poor," intended to counter criticisms of those who did not evacuate New Orleans.[59] Others began to add to his essay, wiki-style. The result was a moving and insightful tapestry of reflections on poverty and the tragedy in the Gulf Coast.

For all the important civic reasons discussed throughout this chapter, government agencies should be among the leaders in supplying interactive outlets for our citizens. And agencies are uniquely situated to act as effective instruments for civic bridging. But there is another reason for them to do this, and that reason is our final core principle and the conclusion of our argument.

Agencies need to move forward on e-governance because they have to. Citizens who use electronic technology as a primary way of communicating expect and demand this kind of interactivity. As the worlds of politics and commerce have illustrated, interactivity is an essential part of the new digital culture. Government agencies—and the executives who manage them—simply cannot afford to be left behind.

Tips for leadership success

- Experiment with new technology and be prepared for the unexpected.
- Try engaging with user-created content on the Internet on sites like YouTube.
- Have a strategy in place for how you're going to analyze and react to comments solicited through e-rulemaking or crowd-sourcing.
- Reach out to citizens where they already are.
- Keep the back channel genuinely open.
- Instead of telling stakeholders what to do, empower them with tools that foster authentic participation.
- Remember that citizens already want to help.
- Citizens increasingly demand and expect e-governance. Move forward!
- Be mindful of the 'digital divide.' Not all citizens are able to participate in e-governance effectively.

Resources for further learning

Books

For a thorough overview of the state of e-government, see Darrell West, *Digital Government: Technology and Public Sector Performance* (2005), but note that works such as this, despite anyone's best efforts, become somewhat dated fairly rapidly. For overviews of the uses of the Internet in politics, see Andrew Chadwick, *Internet Politics: States, Citizens, and New Communication Technologies* (2006); and Andrew Chadwick and Philip

Howard, eds., *Routledge Handbook of Internet Politics* (2008)—but note again the caveat just stated.

Books that might help stimulate some big-think ideas about innovations include Steve Davis, Larry Elin, and Grant Reeher, *Click on Democracy* (2002); Allison Fine, *Momentum* (2006); Malcolm Gladwell, *The Tipping Point* (2002); Howard Rheingold, *The Virtual Community* (2000) and *Smart Mobs* (2003). But what is probably better is to wade into the deep and see what is actually being done by others.

Web Resources

Try some of the many websites referenced in the text and in the endnotes for this chapter.

For case studies of innovative e-governance initiatives, see Steven Clift's Democracies Online website, www.dowire.org. Also see his organization's website facilitating online public discussion forums, www.e-democracy. org. In addition, Carolyn Lukensmeyer and Lars Hasselblad Torres, "Public Deliberation: A Manager's Guide to Citizen Engagement," is a report on public deliberation from a government agency perspective. It includes a rich discussion of online deliberation, with several useful examples, and is available at www.businessofgovernment.org/pdfs/LukensmeyerReport.pdf.

For ongoing updates, feature essays, and informed discussions of how the Internet is affecting the conduct of electoral politics and political advocacy, check out the "techPresident" site of Personal Democracy Forum, at techpresident.com.

The nonprofit Sunlight Foundation is pushing the boundaries of transparency when it comes to elected representatives, particularly Congress. Its website is worth exploring and could generate specific ideas. See www.sunlightfoundation.com.

The IBM Center for the Business of Government, at www.businessofgovernment.org, offers many insightful reports to introduce government managers to important topics such as online deliberation, Web 2.0, the digital divide and virtual worlds.

For more "traditional" forms of innovation in government administration, including e-government efforts, see the Ash Institute at Harvard University, at www.innovations.harvard.edu.

Regarding blogs, to get a sense of their culture and framework, the best thing to do is to read some of them. We could list thousands, but our recommendation is to follow your own political inclinations and interests and pay attention to what draws you in and prompts you to share your own comments, and then think of that in terms of your own agency's work.

Online organizer and activist Alan Rosenblatt has assembled his favorite blogs that deal with politics and the Internet. Rosenblatt's blog is at www .drdigipol.com. Here is his list, minus repeats from above, and without annotation:

www.bivingsreport.com

http://congressonlineproject.org

www.internationaldemoblog.blogspot.com

www2.democracyinaction.org/blog

http://digitalpolitics.blogspot.com

http://digitalstreetjournal.com

www.epolitics.com

http://engagism.blogspot.com

www.frogloop.com/care2blog

www.idealware.org/blog

www.internetadvocacycenter.com/thinktank/library.html

http://mopocket.com

www.pewinternet.org

www.politicalgastronomica.com

www.politicalwarez.com

www.politicsonline.com

http://rkcsi.indiana.edu

www.apsanet.org

Notes

1. See Kettl (2002).
2. Clift (2006), emphasis added.
3. Nabatchi and Mergel (2010), 2.
4. See Horrigan (2004) for these and other figures on Internet use.
5. Council for Excellence in Government (2001).
6. See Horrigan (2004); Stowers (2004).
7. See the website at www.innovations.harvard.edu.
8. West (2005), 113.
9. See, for example, Willemssen (2003).
10. Orszag (2009).
11. O'Keefe (2011).
12. Orszag (2009).
13. Wikipedia can be found at www.wikipedia.org.
14. See www.datagov.ideascale.com/.
15. See www.usaspending.gov/.
16. See www.recovery.gov/Pages/default.aspx.
17 Coglianese (2009).
18. Lukensmeyer and McDermott (2010).
19. Norris (2010), S180–S181.
20. Bingham (2010), 1.
21. Thompson (2009).
22. See the discussion of trust appearing in the introduction to this volume; and Tolbert and Mossberger (2006).
23. This argument is made at greater length in the first edition of this book, and in Davis, Elin, and Reeher (2002).
24. See, for example, Davis, Elin, and Reeher (2002); Reeher and Davis (2004); Armstrong and Moulitsas Zuniga (2006); Fine (2006); Trippi (2004).
25. Davis, Elin, and Reeher (2002). Material similar to some of what follows can be found in that work.
26. In selecting many of these signposts, we were guided by "The First Digital Decade" (2004). More generally on the Internet in 2000, and for more detail on some of the stories that follow, see Davis, Elin, and Reeher (2002).
27. Much of this and what follows is taken from Davis, Elin, and Reeher (2002); and Reeher and Davis (2004).
28. The observation extends to the way scholars have tended to study Internet politics. Their principal focus has been on the Internet as an effective, efficient, flexible, and low-cost substitute for traditional one-to-many activities. This assumption has restricted the consideration of the role of the Internet in many different aspects of political life. In electoral politics, the Internet has been viewed primarily as another vehicle for broadcasting information, raising money, and publicizing a highly focused message. In public administration, the attention has centered on analogous efforts by government, such as communicating agency information and regulations or enrolling clients online. Typical academic studies of the Internet's political use have followed from these assumptions and have tended to focus on content analyses of candidate and government agency websites, studies of user-friendliness and participation rates for candidate sites and for online government forms and applications, or qualitative evaluations of online services. While useful to other researchers and some political practitioners, these works have been rather dry affairs, which fail to capture much of the

Internet's true political value and are unlikely to inspire readers to greater civic engagement. Beginning in 2004, and in particular with studies of the Dean campaign, this began to change, but there is still a focus on these kinds of efforts.

29. Hof (2005).

30. Greg Bloom (2006) reports on his experiences attending the New Organizing Institute's three-day training seminar and nicely reveals these tensions.

31. To get a sense of Meetup, see its website at www.meetup.com.

32. Brooks (2006).

33. The seemingly endless discussions at conferences and in the media about whether blogs are an alternative form of "legitimate" journalism, while an important topic, largely miss their political and social significance. Millions are writing them, billions are reading them, and billions are talking about them. On June 27, 2006, for example, Technorati.com, the well-known tracker of blogs, was keeping tabs on 46.1 million blog sites and 2.6 billion links on those sites. On the same day, a Google search of the word blog recorded 2,100,000,000 sites containing that word. Now podcasts and uploaded video are adding to the richness of blogs and other sites. The blogs provide interactive hubs for participation, in the form of political expression in a variety of forms. More important than the people running the blogs and the content of the main pieces they write on them are the many others who contribute and post to them.

34. Rainie, Cornfield, and Horrigan (2005). Subsequent data reported in this paragraph are also taken from this report, unless otherwise noted.

35. Horrigan, Garrett, and Resnick (2004).

36. Graf and Darr (2004).

37. Williams, Weinberg, and Gordon (2004).

38. Graf et al. (2006).

39. Rainie, Cornfield, and Horrigan (2005).

40. Graf et al. (2006). The study places the line between "small donors" and "large donors" at $200.

41. Ibid., 32.

42. Ibid., 44.

43. This section draws substantially from Plouffe's account. See Plouffe (2009).

44. Ibid., 214.

45. Ibid.

46. Wilcox (2008); Plouffe (2009).

47. Wilcox (2008).

48. See similar advice for political organizers in Levy (2006).

49. The identities ranged from "the mother of a 5-year-old child diagnosed with autism, wanting to find out what kinds of federal programs apply to them, and what kinds of support are available," to "a 70-year-old widow with a Medigap insurance plan who is concerned about the new Medicare drug benefit plan—how the benefit plan will affect her insurance, and what its advantages are." Other identities were persons interested in space travel, the environment and national parks, and policies in Africa, among others.

50. La Corte (2006).

51. Among the most frequently viewed and downloaded sets of materials from the Bush White House were the "Barney" videos that, although at first viewing appeared to be light-hearted treatments of the West Wing as seen through the eyes of the family dog, were in fact savvy, effective communications of some of the central political themes of its occupants.

52. For an intriguing model of an EPA discussion, along with some best practices for leading these discussions, see Holzer et al. (2004). See also a broader discussion of electronic

public deliberation, including deliberations sponsored by government, in Lukensmeyer and Torres (2006).

53. See, among others, Coglianese (2004a, 2004b).

54. Clift (2006).

55. Bloom (2006). The website was http://volunteerforchange.org. Working Assets has since taken this website in a different direction.

56. For the map, see www.toiletmap.gov.au/default.aspx.

57. See www.thebathroomdiaries.com.

58. Caldwell (2006).

59. The essay, with comments, links, and additions, can be found at www.scalzi.com/whatever/003704.html.

13 Global leadership: Strengthening a skeptical world's trust in America

PETER RONAYNE, SENIOR FACULTY, FEDERAL EXECUTIVE INSTITUTE*

The United States enjoys a dominant and potent combination of military, economic, cultural, and political power, but that power is relatively ineffective if the world does not trust the nation and its leaders. In recent years, that trust has been questioned and the nation has struggled to rebuild it. Building trust requires government officials who have a sense of American history and how it has shaped the American worldview. Government leaders also need to appreciate how other nations view the United States and the constellation of forces shaping global interactions and issues. In addition, leaders must possess the skills and knowledge to be effective internationally. The evidence suggests, however, that too many government leaders lack this critical understanding and these skills. Identifying the knowledge and skills civil servants need, and developing programs to instill them, is critical work for the global context of the twenty-first century.

There is nothing we need to build here except relationships.

—*Col. Thomas Wilhelm, U.S. defense attaché, Mongolia*[1]

IN A NONDESCRIPT WHITE TRAILER at the Marine Corps Training and Education Command in Quantico, VA, innovation in global leadership is under way. Marines have reflected on their experience in Iraq, Afghanistan, and elsewhere and have acted to significantly enhance the cultural capabilities of their forces. At the Center for Advanced Operational Culture Learning (CAOCL), training is focused on getting marines to view cultural understanding as a tool that can help them in conflict, in nation building, in

---

* The views expressed here are the author's and do not necessarily reflect those of the Federal Executive Institute or the U.S. Office of Personnel Management.

whatever high stress, high threat international environments they face. Whether dealing with Islamic allies in Iraq, training indigenous military forces in Africa, or collaborating with local leaders in Mongolia, the twenty-first century marine will be able to use cultural knowledge "to establish rapport and build relationships, a key aspect of successful counterinsurgency operation," and a major component of trust. As Barak A. Salmoni, the center's deputy director, explains, "Three plus years ago the moniker was 'cultural sensitivity.' But being sensitive is not the same as being aware, and being aware is not the same thing as being capable—being able to apply your knowledge so as to have any effect on the people with or against whom you're operating."[2]

Indeed, this is not sensitivity for sensitivity's sake. As the CAOCL's goal statement lays out, it "does not teach culture for its own sake, or for a nondirected appreciation of or sensitivity towards foreign peoples. CAOCL executes operationally focused training and education in individual training, PME [professional military education], and pre-deployment phases, reflecting current and likely contingencies and functions, to ensure Marines and leaders deploy a grasp of culture and indigenous dynamics for use as a force multiplier."[3] The effort is now under way to build this "operational cultural learning" into all levels of the vast Marine Corps professional education system and embed it as one of their "bread and butter skills."[4] This is the new frontier of global leadership in the public sector—and the time is now for such perspectives and programs to permeate every corner of American government.

As its practitioners know, there is no more demanding context for leadership than in the public sector. A dizzying array of issues, actors, and interests challenge even the most savvy leader in ways not likely imagined or envisioned even half a century ago. As best-selling business and leadership writer Jim Collins observes in his monograph, *Good to Great and the Social Sectors*, "Social sector leaders are not less decisive than business leaders as a general rule; they only appear that way to those who fail to grasp the complex governance and diffuse power structures common to social sectors."[5] An era of succession planning, knowledge management, emotional intelligence, and network government is rendered exponentially more complex and perilous (and interesting) by the ever-accelerating pace of globalization and our deepening awareness of its impact.

The concept of trust in government, the core idea behind this book, also resides at the center of the global leadership issue. At this macro level—the world stage—in which the United States seeks to promote its interests and create a foundation of security and prosperity, trust is precious, fragile, and absolutely imperative. Global military reach and an economic preponderance of power are indispensable tools in the promotion of U.S. national security abroad. Yet, without a strong measure of trust, an important part of what we might call America's "soft power," the elements of hard power will have limited impact and fall short of their vast potential. Indeed, mistrust of American intentions, goals, and purposes on the world stage is like a viral insurgency, slowly but surely eroding the nation's ability to lead collective action against security threats such as terrorism, nuclear proliferation, and transnational diseases. These and other threats and opportunities combine to create what the late Richard Holbrooke described as the most "difficult set of international challenges since World War II."[6]

The equation is, in fact, a simple one: today's most pressing national security priorities are global issues; global issues demand global leadership; and successful global leadership requires global trust. Early in the new century, the worldwide reservoir of trust in the United States had sunk to an alarming low for a number of reasons. After the 2008 election, that decline was at least temporarily arrested. A government tuned into these issues and capable of deploying a cadre of public servants with a heightened level of global perspective and savvy can help sustain the revival of trust. With enhanced trust and improved global relationships, the United States and its partners can play a stronger hand and maximize the opportunities for significant progress on the pressing issues of the day.

> The United States, working with the governments of the other major powers, can still shape the course of the twenty-first century and bring about a world that is to a striking degree characterized by peace, prosperity, and freedom for most of the globe's countries and peoples. Opportunity, though, is just that. It represents possibility, not inevitability.
>
> —*Richard Haass,* The Opportunity

This opportunity cannot be emphasized enough. Perhaps never before in the history of the world has a nation enjoyed such a dominant combination of military, economic, cultural, and political power. Shorn of trust, however, the United States is hobbled in some areas, impotent in others.

Like fish in water, Americans can be remarkably oblivious to the nation's power. A quick survey of the scale and scope of American power provides an important element of the self-awareness and global perspective that today's leaders must possess. The United States has:

- More than 750 military installations in 130 countries.
- A military budget equal to the combined military budgets of the next 15 nations.
- Nearly 5,000 nuclear weapons (to fall to 1,550 with the New START Treaty ratified in 2010).
- Close to one-third of the world's economic output.
- The world's third-largest population (but less than 5 percent of the total global population).
- Nearly half of the world's top 500 global businesses.
- More than 60 of the world's top 100 brands.
- The world lead in exporting film and television.

How should we label this power? Empire? Hegemony? Sole superpower? Semantics aside, the simple fact remains that the United States is a world power on a scale not seen since Rome. But, paradoxically, as Kennedy School of Government professor Joseph Nye and others point out, the United States on its own cannot solve the most pressing and challenging national security issues facing it.[7]

> Yet what word but "empire" describes the awesome thing that America is becoming? It is the only nation that polices the world through five global military commands; maintains more than a million men and women at arms on four continents; deploys carrier battle groups on watch in every ocean; guarantees the survival of countries from Israel to South Korea; drives the wheels of global trade and commerce; and fills the hearts and minds of an entire planet with its dreams and desires.
>
> —*Michael Ignatieff,* New York Times, *January 10, 2003*

America in the mirror

> We have it in our power to begin the world over again.
>
> —*Thomas Paine*

Americans have a nearly unwavering trust in America on the world stage. While seemingly obvious to the point of silliness, probing that statement and understanding its origins and enduring nature are critical to the trust enterprise in America's global leadership. Furthermore, meaningful attempts by presidents, policymakers, and public servants to enhance trust in the United States on the world stage require an understanding of the nature and size of the gap between America's sense of self and international perceptions. If we are oblivious to the extent of the nation's power, we are equally oblivious as to how other countries feel about us. As Terry Newell argues in compelling fashion in Chapter 1, effective leadership requires an understanding of and connection to one's core moral values. His point applies equally to a nation acting and attempting to lead on the world stage. And as Beverly Fletcher and Alfred Cooke describe in Chapter 2, "know thyself" is the first step on the path to leading others.

As noted in Chapter 1, a foundational piece of that understanding for America at home and abroad comes from John Winthrop and his 1630 "A Model of Christian Charity" sermon delivered to his Puritan congregation. Known widely as the "City on a Hill" speech and based on the New Testament's Sermon on the Mount, the oration urged the fledging Massachusetts Bay Colony to see their colonial enterprise within the broader trajectory of history. Declared Winthrop:

> For we must consider that we shall be as a city upon a hill. The eyes of all people are upon us. So that if we shall deal falsely with our God in this work we have undertaken . . . we shall be made a story and a by-word throughout the world. We shall open the mouths of enemies to speak evil of the ways of God. . . . We shall shame the faces of many of God's worthy servants, and cause their prayers to be turned into curses upon us til we be consumed out of the good land whither we are going.

From that stridently religious and teleological origin has come a more secularized and powerfully enduring concept: American exceptionalism.[8] The vision of the City on a Hill/American exceptionalism has resonated through the ages, from the founding period and "Manifest Destiny" through to present-day America, and emerging with particular prominence in the political rhetoric of Presidents John F. Kennedy and Ronald Reagan. Colin Powell referenced the concept at the 2000 Republican National Convention. The Clinton administration coined their own synonym, referring to the United States as "the indispensable nation." American exceptionalism in part underscored the doctrine of "pre-emptive" military action during the presidency of George W. Bush, and President Barack Obama openly addressed the concept during an April 2009 press conference.

Thus, from Puritan origins came a powerful and resonant core belief in, first, the American experiment as unique, as world-historical, as qualitatively different from other attempts at government, and, finally, as having great power. Coupled with exceptionalism comes a proselytizing element in which the United States believes that the basket of democratic values (or "constitutional values" as *Newsweek's* international affairs editor Fareed Zakaria would emphasize[9]) it holds dear—freedom, equality, self-determination, rule of law—are not only American or Western values but instead have universal applicability and desirability.[10]

> These are American principles, American policies. We could stand for no other. And they are also the principles and policies of forward-looking men and women everywhere, of every modern nation, of every enlightened community. They are the principles of mankind and must prevail.
>
> — *Woodrow Wilson*

This merging of the American and the universal and the accompanying champion's role strikes some as a proud, enlightened commitment to principles larger than one's parochial interest; others see it as prideful, narrow, a symptom of hubris, or blatant self-interest clothed in hypocritical self-righteousness.

How to put into practice this American exceptionalism or this peculiar "American mission" has caused much debate since the nation's founding.[11] Early incarnations argued that the City on a Hill concept best promoted its values and vision by serving as a model, as an example for the world to observe and emulate. This "exemplarist" school of thought has a distinguished pedigree and enjoyed decades of ascendancy following President George Washington's Farewell Address.[12] In that precedent-setting speech, Washington put pragmatic borders around the City on a Hill: "The great rule of conduct for us in regard to foreign nations is, in extending our commercial relations to have with them as little *political* connection as possible. . . . It is our true policy to steer clear of permanent alliances with any portion of the foreign world." Thought leaders and political actors such as Thomas Jefferson and John Quincy Adams followed suit, anchoring American exceptionalism solidly at home. Indeed, one recent observer of the philosophy of American foreign policy labeled this exemplarist tendency the Jeffersonian School.[13]

Rising globalism

Modern American global leadership has, however, been shaped and characterized by the other vision, the opposing pole, the competing model for the United States in the world: internationalism. This more active, some would say aggressive, approach blends the language of duty, responsibility, and leadership. The exemplarist's fraternal twin is active rather than passive, external instead of internal, bold where the other is retiring. Because of its conviction, the internationalist variant of exceptionalism, together with the emergence of America's quasi-imperial power, poses a significant challenge to building and maintaining trust on the world stage. Here we see the most striking clash of perceptions between self (America) and others (much of the rest of the world).

America's precipitous and nearly unbroken rise to globalism began after the Spanish-American War in 1898 and led to a concomitant rise in internationalist outlook, bedazzled in the language of duty, responsibility, and mission. Sen. Albert Beveridge's speech on American responsibility in the Philippines in 1900 captured perfectly that ascendant sentiment (complete with period ethnocentrism). Urged Beveridge, "God has not been preparing the English-speaking and Teutonic peoples for a thousand years for nothing but vain and idle self-contemplation and self-admiration. He has given us the spirit of progress to overwhelm the forces of reaction throughout the earth. . . . We are the trustees of the world's progress, guardians of its righteous peace."

What Walter Russell Mead of the Council on Foreign Relations calls the "Wilsonian" school of thought inched toward newfound primacy first with the onset of Cold War in 1947 and today finds expression in the so-called "neo-conservative" and "liberal internationalist" movements. Echoing Winthrop's mantra but in a secularized and sanitized version, this variant of exceptionalism urges the United States to embrace activist, impassioned global leadership. Proponents call for an enlightened, almost benevolent empire to pursue its interests, which by their nature simultaneously champion the cause of democracy, open markets, and rule of law everywhere.

Today's Americans might not be powerfully interventionist (particularly when chastened by lengthy conflicts in Iraq and Afghanistan). They nevertheless maintain a reservoir of internationalism coupled with pride and the conviction that American ideas and beliefs are good for the rest of the world. A December 2010 *USA Today*/Gallup poll found, 80 percent of respondents believing that "America's history and Constitution make it unique and the greatest country in the world." While more than 65 percent believe that the United States has "a special leadership responsibility in world affairs."[14] Earlier polling by the Pew Research Center further illustrates this exceptionalist core:

- Sixty percent of Americans agree with the statement "Our people are not perfect, but our culture is superior to others."
- Seventy-nine percent of Americans believe it is a good thing that U.S. ideas and customs are spreading around the world.
- Seventy percent of Americans think it is a good idea to promote "American style" democracy in the world.[15]

Data from the Pew Global Attitudes Survey and similar outlets also confirm that despite such attitudes, the American public is not imperial or expansionist in their mindset or goals and prefers multilateral action and shared leadership when possible. Still, empire is in the eye of the beholder. Amercia's preponderance of power and confidence wielding it can make trusting the United States a tricky proposition.

Trust: Contemporary global context

> America defines itself as the leader of the free world, and there is much truth in that idea. But leadership requires having followers who are prepared to move in the same general direction. And walking a path without followers, allies or partners can quickly become self-isolation—even for the sole superpower.
>
> —*Paul Saunders*, National Interest Online, *March 1, 2007*

Effective leadership at any level requires understanding the context in which you are trying to lead. That context includes the way the leader is perceived, viewed by those around him or her. In the end, one might disagree with or have relevant variables that explain or illuminate some of the more negative perceptions. Still, perceptions matter; image isn't everything but it is something of importance. And understanding how (and perhaps why) others view you is a major element in designing a leadership style and strategy that allows for the steady accumulation of trust.

One cannot fully understand the issue of trust and global leadership without briefly surveying the landscape of global perceptions and attitudes—namely, how sizable portions of the rest of the world view the United States and its claim to leadership. The point here is not partisan or unnecessarily provocative. Widespread in the field of leadership development today is the well-researched and supported concept that feedback is critical to leadership success. Individual leaders in organizations can benefit tremendously from receiving candid, honest feedback from those around them—360 degree feedback, as it is described in the field of leadership development and in Chapter 2. So, too, is 360 degree feedback required for American leaders, including the dedicated public servants implementing the myriad U.S. policies that extend to and influence every corner of the globe. This element of national self-knowledge is even more critical because the story of the United States and trust on the world stage is experiencing a troubling chapter.

The view from abroad

Anti-Americanism (for lack of a better phrase) is nothing new and at a certain level should not generate surprise. With great power comes not only great responsibility, but also a potent mix of jealousy, admiration, fear, and emulation. As survey data show, much of America's self-image and sense of its historic role on the world stage clashes with or contradicts how others see the so-called last remaining superpower. It is also important to note that some of the world's misgivings spring both from specific U.S. policies—particularly in the Middle East—and more deeply from America's sense of self and perceived missionary zeal.

Recent findings from the Pew Global Attitudes Project provide remarkable and compelling insight into turbulent and evolving worldviews—and shifting trust levels—of the United States. In Europe, ambivalence about America, its perceived inexperienced arrogance, and its rise to power have roiled for decades. From 2000 to 2005, U.S. favorability dropped by as many as ten, even twenty, percentage points in Britain, France, and Germany, traditional allies and North Atlantic Treaty Organization (NATO) colleagues since the end of World War II. Non-Western attitudes toward the United States also turned sour early in the decade. As Pew director Andy Kohut highlights in his book *America Against the World*, "In Brazil, for example, where 52 percent of the public expressed a favorable opinion of the United States in 2002, the pro-American portion of the population had dropped to 34 percent. In Russia, there was a 25-percentage-point decline in the U.S. favorability rating, from 61 percent to 36 percent, in the course of less than a year."[16]

In any organization, it is difficult to trust a boss, a manager, or a leader who one believes does not take into consideration the interests, concerns, and perspectives of others. When it fails to communicate this concern, the United States suffers in world esteem in this regard as well, with other nations viewing American leadership as unilateral, even imperial, with little regard for the rest of the world community, even its allies. During the recent low ebb of trust in America, sizable majorities in Britain, Germany, Spain, and Russia, and eight in ten French respondents, believed that American leaders did not take their interests into account when making policy decisions. This perception diminished trust. As part of a dangerous disconnect, simultaneously two-thirds of Americans believed that the U.S. government, at least to a fair amount, did concern itself with the interests of other nations before acting.[17]

> No one would expect Finland, Australia and Botswana to have identical foreign policies simply because each enjoys a representative form of government. And even when democracies share both values and interests, they often have different priorities. Without understanding these realities and developing strategies to manage them, the United States cannot maintain a position of real leadership, even within the "free world."
>
> —*Paul Saunders,* National Interest Online, *March 2007*

Fair or not, partisan or apolitical, the prospects for an enhanced trusted leader role for the United States improved with Barack Obama's election in 2008. In an intriguing—and puzzling in many corners—development, the freshman president was awarded the Nobel Peace Prize in October 2009. In language redolent of trust, the Norwegian Nobel Committee explained the award based on the president's "extraordinary efforts to strengthen international diplomacy and cooperation between peoples. . . . His diplomacy is founded in the concept that those who are to lead the world must do so on the basis of values and attitudes that are shared by the majority of the world's population."

While critics then and now question Obama's level and depth of accomplishment, the change in tone—and its trust-building capacity—has undoubtedly resonated with much of the world, even as the president's job approval at home has declined markedly since he first took office. European views of America moved significantly by mid-2010, for example, with approval at 73 percent in France, 63 percent in Germany, and 61 percent in Spain. From 2009 to mid-2010 the United States saw its ratings in Brazil rebound by 28 percent to 62 percent, in Russia by 13 points to 57 percent, in China by 11 points to 58 percent.

Meanwhile, with the Iraq and Afghanistan conflicts still looming large and tensions with Iran perpetually fluctuating, largely Muslim countries continue to hold overwhelmingly negative views of the United States. Even allied states like Turkey and Pakistan hold the United States (whether Bush America or Obama America) in low esteem—both giving the United States an approval rating under 20 percent.[18] For all the global star power of President Obama significant work remains—and the current trust "bounce" can little be taken for granted. The embarrassing WikiLeaks exposures of American diplomatic cables remind us of the tenuous nature of trust on the global stage and how easily it can be punctured if not severely deflated.

Furthering the mistrust and concern about American power is that, for many around the globe, the phenomenon known as "globalization" has come to mean "Americanization" or to be seen as predominantly associated with American values and American economic reach.[19] In short, the most recent wave of globalization involves highly interdependent economic activity around the world; revolutions in information technology and communication making the world more of a global village than ever before; intense cultural merges and clashes; and a sharp spike in transnational issues, communities, and interests.[20]

Globalization is not Americanization, even though the core assumptions behind the economic side of the phenomenon do represent core U.S. interests and values. The fact remains that in many corners of the world, the exponential growth of cross-border economic integration and tremendous technological advances that facilitate the transmission of Western (often American) culture, lead to heightened levels of anxiety about weakness, the decline of one's own nation-state, and the Borg-like march of American-led globalization.[21]

Americans do not appear to waltz along, oblivious to their nation's ongoing public relations challenge. Exceptionalism and world-historic mission aside, Americans generally believe that any decline in the image of the United States on the world stage is a major problem.[22] For his part, so, too, does President Obama. In an intriguing 2009 NATO press conference statement, he addressed both American exceptionalism and global concern about American arrogance and parochialism. Commented Obama,

> I believe in American exceptionalism, just as I suspect that the Brits believe in British exceptionalism and the Greeks believe in Greek exceptionalism. I'm enormously proud of my country and its role and history in the world. . . . And so I see no contradiction between believing that America has a continued extraordinary role in leading the world towards peace and prosperity and recognizing that that leadership is incumbent, depends on, our ability to create partnerships because we create partnerships because we can't solve these problems alone.[23]

Perhaps partly because of such rhetorical attempts to bridge the gap between exceptionalism and multilateralism, America's "approval rating" is (for now) on an upward track. To build on that momentum and strengthen the foundation for global trust will require multitiered and multiyear action. And part of the solution rests in developing globally aware, savvy public servants to represent the United States in its myriad international dealings.

The transnational agenda

It's nice to say we can do it unilaterally, except you can't.

Former secretary of state Colin Powell[24]

Synonymous with Americanization or not, globalization has a major impact on even its most ardent proponent and symbol. The United States and therefore the public sector find themselves in an unprecedented maelstrom of globalization. Name an issue, really any issue, and it likely has a relevant global component. Trade policy. Drug interdiction. The AIDS pandemic. Labor practices and protections. Biological diversity. Clean air standards. Food and drug safety. Transportation security. Nation building. Disaster relief. At least eight of twelve critical issues in the GAO's report on challenges facing the federal government have significant global content, as do a preponderance of forces shaping the world.[25] Whether it's columnist Thomas Friedman's "flatism" or the new map drawn up for the Pentagon by analyst Thomas Barnett or Fareed Zakaria's "post-American world," the combined and accelerating forces of economic integration, networking across national borders, an exponential communications revolution, massive proliferation of nongovernmental organizations (NGOs) and international organizations, and the rise of transnational issues are dramatically reshaping the contours of world politics and the issues facing governments everywhere.[26]

The work and responsibilities of the federal sector are clearly a sprawling microcosm of these trends, even in traditionally domestic agencies and organizations (the Social Security Administration, after all, manages more than thirty bilateral agreements). With each passing day the traditional division between the domestic and the foreign is more of a fiction, a concept that helps us mentally map and order our world but describes it less and less accurately. The long-standing, knee-jerk presumption that "global leadership" and related issues are limited to the foreign affairs and defense agencies alone is invalid and dangerous. Indeed, the new face of "national security" reflects truly transnational issues and challenges. Energy, environment, economic growth, population, science and technology, AIDS and other pandemics, and terror networks are all national security priorities, and none of them can or will be solved solely through the application of American power, however dominant.

For all its merits, globalization comes with significant demerits, too. Moises Naim, editor of *Foreign Policy* magazine, chronicles this downside of our global society in his succinctly titled book *Illicit*. What emerges is a compelling, if troubling, vision of the future of American foreign policy and the challenges facing America's public servants as global leaders. To the list above, Naim highlights:

- Human trafficking—4 million people smuggled or sold (500,000 into the United States) a year for a value of $7 to $10 billion.
- Money laundering—estimated between $800 billion and $2 trillion annually.
- Violating intellectual property rights, which cost the United States almost $10 billion in 2001.
- Arms trafficking—more than $1 billion a year in small arms with potentially devastating consequences in stolen weapons of mass destruction technology.
- Drug trafficking—more than $400 billion a year (larger than the Spanish economy).[27]

For too long, the domestic and foreign policy arenas have been viewed as mostly separate and distinct spheres of action. Government leaders who worked in domestic agencies felt they needed to know little about world affairs or other countries and had little, if any, international interaction. But the combined and accelerating forces of globalization and technology have forged an interconnected world in which change—and the need to anticipate and respond to it—are both faster and more complex, the international and the domestic are inextricably linked, and trust is in short supply.

The imperative of global leaders(hip)

The leadership development agenda for today's public servants must now include the international, intercultural, and strategic perspectives essential for success in this rapidly changing, globalized world. Patricia McGinnis, past president and CEO of the Council for Excellence in Government underscores this point: "The Council believes that career federal executives must be able to lead for results in all aspects of their work. Today, an increasing number of career public servants outside the federal government's traditional foreign affairs community have responsibilities with an international dimension. Improving their ability as leaders in a global context has therefore become a very important goal."[28] Similarly, in a forward-looking report on human capital in the federal workforce, the GAO states, "Government organizations must undergo a cultural transformation allowing them to work better with other governmental organizations, non-governmental organizations, and the private sector, both domestically and internationally, to achieve results."[29]

Despite awareness of the need for change, most federal civil servants—particularly in "domestic" agencies—have received little preparation for their global roles and have minimal understanding of critical global trends shaping the world. America faces unique leadership demands and possibilities, which in turn require that we invest time and resources to ensure that every federal public servant is the best and brightest global leader possible, whether one of more than 90,000 civilian government employees stationed overseas or one of the legions stateside working on issues with vast and expanding international implications.

The global leadership gap

So far the United States has not placed anything close to a premium on overcoming its parochial tendencies and developing globally savvy leaders. According to a RAND report on developing global leaders, "The nation is producing too few future leaders who combine substantive depth with international experience and outlook. So, too, managers with a broad strategic vision in a rapidly changing world are in short supply."[30] In research by the Federal Executive Institute (FEI), more than two-thirds of federal leaders surveyed rated their own proficiency for international work below the midpoint of a five-point scale. According to the U.S. Advisory Commission on Public Diplomacy, training is an essential yet underutilized pillar of public diplomacy, as the United States tries to make itself and its policies understood and works to project a positive and respectful image in the world. In its September 2004 report, the commission faulted the current state of training to foster U.S. international goals in several areas, including media skills and cross-cultural communication skills.[31]

America's well-known language limitations have deep, early roots and may prove insurmountable given the country's relative geographic isolation and the emergence of English as the modern world's *lingua franca*. For now, only one-third of the nation's seventh through twelfth graders study a foreign language; that drops to fewer than one-in-ten students at the college level—with the vast majority studying Spanish. Interest in Arabic is growing but still accounts for just 0.8 percent of foreign language enrollments in postsecondary institutions. Study abroad numbers are on the rise, with greater percentages of students going to India and China than ever before—but a mere 1 percent of undergraduates study abroad.[32] The National Security Language Initiative launched in early 2006 to increase the number of Americans with advanced proficiency in critical languages is an important step forward. And building language skills is important not just for intelligence and national security. It signals engagement with and respect for other nations, and fluency adds immeasurably to one's ability to interact with, understand, and ultimately influence international counterparts. As a former dean of the School of Language Studies at the State Department's Foreign Service Institute put it: "Part of the reason for our difficulty is that we simply don't have enough competent speakers of Arabic with credible policy context and an ability to connect with the intended audience so they will at least listen to what we are trying to say and give us a hearing."[33]

But fluency in a foreign language is only one of the necessary global leadership skills. In the past decade, a significant body of literature has examined, defined, and refined the competencies leaders need for success in international activities. In their study, "Accelerating International Growth," Philip Rosensweig and his colleagues outline five global leadership capabilities worth noting:

1. Strategic capability. Develop and implement strategy in a global context, not just national or regional.

2. Partnership capability. Work effectively with cross-border partners dealing with similar issues. Partners include global alliances; bilateral, multilateral, and international organizations, where cultural sensitivity and perspectives are important.

3. Staffing capability. Develop global teams where employees and contractors from different countries and cultures can work together without one dominating the other.

4. Learning capability. Hardwire international learning as part of development, so as not to be blindfolded by or exclusively wedded to one's national perspective and biases or force international experiences into one's national lens.

5. Organizational capability. Arrange organizations in a way that facilitates and capitalizes on leadership, not through host country dominance but through a true global network of executives.[34]

All five of these capabilities translate well in a public-sector context.

In FEI research, government executives cited the following five elements as critical in developing their global perspective:

1. Content learning on topics such as the global economy, national security issues, protection of intellectual property, export control, and global environmental issues.

2. Cultural awareness and regional/country-specific overviews along with information on government structures, the economy, and the regulatory framework in which a host country operates.

3. Protocol and suggested success strategies for dealing with and doing business with foreign governments and corporations.

4. Overviews of the ever-growing international governance networks— international agreements between the United States and other nations;

international institutions—and their impact on U.S. global policies and efforts.

5. Skill building in areas such as negotiation strategies and communication to international audiences (public diplomacy).[35]

Armed with leadership enhanced by these capabilities and competencies, our local, state, and national public servants can be better agents of what Nye refers to as "soft power." As Nye perceptively explains, "A country may obtain the outcomes it wants in world politics because other countries want to follow it, admiring its values, emulating its example, aspiring to its level of prosperity and openness. In this sense, it is just as important to set the agenda in world politics and attract others as it is to force them to change through the threat of military or economic weapons. This aspect of power—getting others to do want what you want—I call soft power."[36]

Developing global leaders

The private sector is more than a decade into its global leadership epiphany. A 1998 survey by the Conference Board of senior managers and executives pointed to the importance of developing global leaders for business success.[37] Research a year later involving 108 Fortune 500 companies also highlighted competent global managers as "the factor most critical to achieving international success."[38] Signaling this evolving mindset, the August 2003 *Harvard Business Review* focused entirely on global perspectives and leadership for a changed world. Following suit, a myriad of business schools now offer internationally-focused "Global MBAs". For the public sector, the massive and multiplying effect of globalization, the 9/11 attacks, and America's waning image abroad, and the Iraq conflict should combine to create a Sputnik moment for global leadership development. Thomas Friedman sounds the clarion call when he says that meeting the challenges of globalization "requires as comprehensive, energetic, and focused a response as meeting the challenge of Communism."[39]

Within the federal sector, outposts of global perspective have slowly emerged. At the National Aeronautics and Space Administration (NASA), the agency's managerial and executive leadership models include international competency and cross-cultural competencies. (see Figure 11.1). At FEI, the flagship *Leadership for a Democratic Society* program includes global perspectives as a core curriculum theme for its interagency audience. To chart its future in this area, the institute in September 2001 convened public, private, and nongovernmental thought leaders to explore the issue of developing global leaders. FEI's growing Center for Global Leadership now offers the week-long *Leadership for a Global Society* program, which challenges participants to assess America's role in the world, better understand contemporary world affairs, and explore global leadership best practices like negotiation, geographically dispersed teamwork, and cross-cultural skills. In 2010 FEI launched *The U.S.-China Executive Program*. Based in Beijing, this weeklong experience allows American public-sector leaders to exchange perspectives and information with peers from the government of China. Participants gain newfound insight into Chinese party politics and governance and engage in off-the-record discussions with their Chinese counterparts in diverse areas such as military, energy, environmental, space, and agricultural policies.

The military's firm commitment to growing leaders often pushes it to the forefront in certain areas of professional development. The defense community has shown forward thinking on international skills. According to the Defense Language Transformation Roadmap, "Language skill and regional expertise have not been regarded as war-fighting skills, and are not sufficiently incorporated into operational or contingency planning. Language skill and regional expertise are not valued as Defense core competencies, yet they are as important as critical weapon systems."[40] Now, efforts to overcome past deficits in language skills are under way across the Department of Defense.

Commenting on his early experiences in Iraq with the 101st Airborne Division, Gen. David Petraeus, commander of Multinational Force Iraq, revealed, "We had terrific situational awareness; what we lacked was cultural awareness." To improve that situation, the U.S. Army has used a small cadre of specialists known as foreign-area officers. Equipped with language skills and cultural knowledge, they support the combat troops in various missions. Although debate continues in the Pentagon over the long-term role of the foreign-area officers, many believe it represents the future of development for all officers.[41] At Fort Leavenworth American and Allied soldiers engage in true post–Cold War programs developed to learn lessons from experiences in places such as Bosnia and Iraq. The programs emphasize the complex cultural conditions surrounding policing and nation-building efforts.[42] As mentioned at the beginning of the chapter, the Marine Corp's Center for Advanced Operational Culture Learning is another fine example—perhaps even a best practice—of such efforts.

Figure 13.1 NASA leadership model executive level

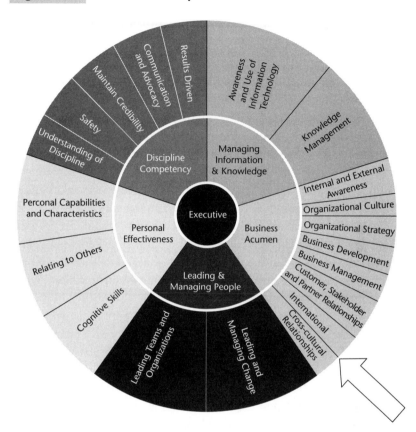

Competency

International: Familiar with policies that regulate or dictate how to work with an international partner.

Cross-Cultural Relationships: Understands the important aspects of language, behaviors, beliefs, and environment that comprise the culture of international partners.

Skills

Policy/ Partnering/Alliances • Understands the rules and policies that relate to import and export of materials, technology and information (ITAR). • Understands how Agency policy relates to working with international partners.

Cross-Cultural Leadership • Understands how cultures differ in approaches to time, authority, physical space, friendship, and individualism, and how these differences impact work behavior. • Applies knowledge relating to national culture to increase the effectiveness of relationships. • Addresses the special challenges and adjustments of employees living abroad.

Source: http://leadership.nasa.gov/Model/Executive.htm

The private sector, too, offers innovative and replicable models. To help its emerging leaders develop a broader international view and earn valuable global experience, PricewaterhouseCoopers (PWC) founded the Ulysses program in 2001. Young partners participate on cross-cultural teams drawn from PWC firms spread around 139 countries. The action learning teams travel abroad for up to three months to help tackle challenges faced by various developing nations, including Belize, Moldova, Namibia, and Zambia. Ralf Schneider, PWC's head of global talent development, says that learning in the Ulysses program takes place at the individual, team, and organizational levels, and includes a new appreciation for collaboration and for cultural differences as a spark to innovation.[43]

Similarly, the Boeing company starting in 2001 re-energized its efforts to create a truly global cadre of leaders. Based on the philosophy that with increased global activity must also come a new human resources approach, Boeing launched the Global Leadership Program, an experiential course that sends managers to Europe, Asia, or South America to learn about Boeing suppliers, customers, and competitors in their own surroundings. While learning the business side of Boeing, executives are also steeped in the history, politics, culture, and traditions of a specific region. To widen the global knowledge circle within the company, the senior vice president for international relations, Thomas Pickering (former U.S. ambassador to the United Nations), and his staff pick up their pens. The team "regularly writes articles and analysis pieces about the world's political and economic situation. These are forwarded to members of Boeing's Executive Council, providing timely information on world business prospects and political changes that could affect business units and Boeing markets."[44] Boeing subsequently expanded the Global Leadership program and created an International Consortium Program to convene like-minded international companies committed to developing the "global brain" of their leaders.

The way forward

The fact remains that despite some innovation and true strategic thinking, too few public-sector leaders receive any globally oriented leadership development or formal preparation for international assignments. The public sector has not yet developed a comprehensive approach or system to prepare leaders for success in their critical global work. Until there is such a system, global leadership competence remains a promise not a program, and public servants will not fulfill their potential as significant factors in enhancing the nation's trust profile. In the meantime, individual leaders and federal organizations must take responsibility for incorporating the "global" into their values, vision, and vital strategies. Without it, public-sector leaders will continue to cling to the comfortable yet fictional notion of a line delineating the foreign and the domestic, the national and the international. And in an ongoing embrace of that fiction, they will limit now and in the future their ability to successfully implement their agency's efforts to advance the interests of the American people. Indeed, U.S. relationships, enhanced trust, and effective leadership in the world demand public-sector leaders prepared for the dynamic global context in which they operate. We can imagine no greater leadership development priority.

Tips for global leadership success

The following ideas and principles are worth considering by individuals and organizations seeking to become truly "world class" by developing global leadership skills:

- Use cultural awareness inventories to gauge needs and design professional development opportunities.
- Structure all management and leadership development programs to include global content and awareness building.
- If possible, require even short-term global assignments, exchanges, and action learning for high potential leaders. Similarly, invite international peers to join leadership development programs and for short-term work assignments in your organization.
- Subscribe to an international newspaper or journal such as *The Economist* or even the *International Herald Tribune* as a relatively easy and inexpensive way to grow global perspective.

Resources for further learning

Books and Articles

Maxine Dalton et al., *Success for the New Global Manager* (2002). A useful and basic "global leadership handbook" by a team from the Center for Creative Leadership. Dalton and her colleagues combine qualitative and quantitative research to craft a practitioner-oriented book with several tools and recommendations for emerging global leaders and those working to develop them.

Francis Fukuyama, "Nation-Building 101" (January/February 2004). In his article for the *Atlantic Monthly*, Fukuyama builds on the Earthlights/Liotta/Miskel thesis (see below) and stresses that the future of America's global leadership will in fact involve helping other nations find stability and then sustainable political and economic institutions. To do so, Fukuyama argues, will require involvement from a wide range of the federal sector.

P. H. Liotta and James F. Miskel, "Redrawing the Map of the Future" (2004). In this *World Policy Journal* article, Liotta and Miskel—both faculty at the U.S. Naval War College—provide compelling insight into the future of American foreign policy. They argue that the NASA "earthlights" map (a composite of images of the world's city lights) provides striking visual evidence of the growing divide between light and dark, developed and underdeveloped, north and south—and it is in these dark regions and zones where failed states and feral cities take shape and threaten stability and ultimately U.S. interests. "Earthlights" can be seen at www.cojoweb.com/earthlights.html.

Joseph Nye, *Soft Power* (2004). A book-length exposition on the term he coined. Nye explores in a coherent and convincing way the necessity of multilateral and multinational cooperation by the United States as it grapples with increasingly difficult and complex transnational security threats.

James Q. Wilson and Peter H. Schuck, eds., *Understanding America: The Anatomy of an Exceptional Nation* (2008). For a stark study in contrasts on the emotional and ever-resonant issue of American exceptionalism, see the "pros" in this work. For the "cons," see Donald Pease, *The New American Exceptionalism* (2009).

Fareed Zakaria, *The Post American World* (2008). Readable and full of relevant facts and informational tidbits, Zakaria paints a compelling portrait not of American decline or collapse but instead of a still strong America surrounded by stronger potential partners. In this somewhat "re-leveled" international system, the need for nimble, savvy, and collaborative American leadership is even more paramount.

Web Resources

Foreign Policy magazine, www.foreignpolicy.com. The online version of the journal provides a thoughtful and engaging analysis of contemporary international politics, with a consistent focus on globalization and American foreign affairs. Of particular interest are the "Think Again" articles that challenge conventional wisdom about contemporary global affairs and their eclectic mix of bloggers.

Pew Research Center/Pew Global Attitudes Project, http://pewglobal.org. This is a good place for those who want to explore in more detail America's sense of itself and how the world sees America.

STRATFOR, www.stratfor.com. This website offers a more strategic analysis approach and understanding of global affairs, with plenty of free content for casual visitors.

Watching America, http://watchingamerica.com. This site contains English language versions of foreign press articles and editorials about the United States.

Notes

1. Kaplan (2005), 129.
2. Peters (2007), 14. For more specifics on the work of the CAOCL and underlying replicable principles, see Salmoni's book *Operational Culture for the Warfighter* (2009).
3. United States Marine Corps (2007).
4. Peters (2007), 15.
5. Collins (2005).
6. Holbrooke (2008).
7. Nye (2003).
8. Most analysts credit Alexis de Tocqueville with first coining the term in his classic *Democracy in America.*
9. Zakaria (2003). In both this book and in a 1997 article for *Foreign Affairs*, Zakaria stresses the importance of "constitutional liberalism" versus "democracy."
10. It is interesting to note that Winthrop was powerfully antidemocratic. His vision of the City on a Hill did not include such values. Winthrop stated, for example, "If we should change from a mixed aristocracy to mere democracy, first we should have no warrant in scripture for it: for there was no such government in Israel. . . . A democracy is, amongst civil nations, accounted the meanest and worst of all forms of government. To allow it would be a manifest breach of the 5th Commandment."
11. The 2012 presidential election has been shaping up as the latest battleground for this discussion. Former House speaker Newt Gingrich predicted that the debate over American exceptionalism will be "one of the two or three deciding issues of 2012." See www.usatoday .com/news/washington/2010-12-21-1Aexceptional21_CV_N.htm?csp=34news.

12. Brands (1998). Brands suggests that the term exemplar is more appropriate to American foreign policy than isolationist and explores the tension between this approach and what he calls the "vindicator" tradition in American foreign policy.

13. Mead (2002).

14. Page (2010).

15. Kohut and Stokes (2006), 44, 46, 71; Pew (2002–2005).

16. Kohut and Stokes (2006), 25–26.

17. Ibid., 169.

18. Pew (2010)

19. For some elaboration on globalization and the mental/political/identity divisions it might be fostering, see Barber (2003) and Friedman (2000), the writer's first book-length foray into the topic.

20. Countless descriptions and definitions of globalization exist, but all tend to revolve around the main issues listed here and drawn from Huddleston (2000).

21. The Borg are a cyborg race featured in the *Star Trek: The Next Generation* television series. Characterized by cold and constant pursuit of other cultures for assimilation and an ability to surmount almost any defense, they have become a pop culture synonym for any homogenizing juggernaut against which "resistance is futile"—their robotic catchphrase. For insight into rising optimism about globalization see "The Redistribution of Hope" in *The Economist*, December 16, 2010.

22. Pew (2004).

23. The White House, Office of the Press Secretary, News Conference by President Obama, Strasbourg, France, April 4, 2009.

24. Secretary of State Powell speaking to President George W. Bush, August 5, 2002, as reported by Woodward (2002), 333.

25. Walker (2002).

26. Friedman (2006); Barnett (2004); Zakaria (2008).

27. Naim (2006).

28. Brower et al. (2002).

29. Walker (2002).

30. Bikson et al. (2003).

31. U.S. Department of State (2004).

32. Committee for Economic Development (2006).

33. Lemmon (2004).

34. Lorange (2003).

35. Weiser (2003).

36. Nye (2003).

37. Conner (2000), 156.

38. Morrison et al. (1999), 45.

39. Friedman (2005), 37.

40. U.S. Department of Defense (2005).

41. Jaffe (2005).

42. Fichtner (2006).

43. Hempel (2004).

44. Beck (2002).

C onclusion

What, then, is the job of the government leader?

DAN FENN JR., ADJUNCT LECTURER IN EXECUTIVE PROGRAMS, KENNEDY SCHOOL OF GOVERNMENT, HARVARD UNIVERSITY

Government was not designed to be easy. Its leaders face intense pressure, conflicting demands, and a seemingly intractable set of hoops through which to jump. After all, the Framers decided that preserving freedom was more important than efficiency. So what can civil service leaders do? Turning in a solid professional performance is not enough. Leaders must build trust. To do so, they must engage citizens in their own government, however messy that may get. Engagement allows citizens a voice in decision making, and as they gain a voice, trust can build. Government leaders must also help the public understand how government works and how to affect the governing process. Government is not a private-sector business designed to make a profit. It is a set of countervailing pressures designed to deliver service in a fair, equitable, accountable fashion—one in which a cacophony of voices must somehow be melded into viable public policy. Most Americans do not understand how their government functions, so one task of the public leader is to help them see how to have an impact. Will doing this earn the civil servant the public's admiration? Will the public conclude that government is as efficient as IBM? No. But making a difference where it really matters makes the civil servant's job worthwhile.

AS THE READER KNOWS BY NOW, this book opens a dialogue on a critical topic for government officials and, for that matter, for citizens generally: trust is important for public officials whatever the form of government. Even in authoritarian systems, leaders have to stay somewhere in range of public opinion, although, given repressive tools and a culture of compliance, that range may be extremely broad.[1] Shakespeare's Richard III paid close attention to the public's acceptance and cultivated it as he pursued the crown; Nicaraguan dictator Anastasio Somoza, until his ultimate downfall, was adept at managing the electoral process and keeping his constituency, in the words of the onetime Yale football coach referring to his alumni, "sullen, but not mutinous."

Thomas Jefferson told us in the Declaration of Independence that governments derive "their just powers from the consent of the governed." The Founders, who disagreed so deeply and often bitterly, even personally, on so much that was so important, came together in their commitment to creating a new kind of government, rooted solidly in the American ethos, based not on the divine right of the rulers to rule but on public accountability and participation. They sought new ways to effectuate the "consent of the governed." It was explicitly to implement that commitment to popular sovereignty that James Madison fashioned the U.S. Constitution.

But, as we have learned from living the great American experiment, if Jefferson's revolutionary idea is to work in practice, mutual trust is indispensible—and the more trust, the better it will work. Trust, of course, is not blind acceptance; rather, it is a basic, often unexpressed, assumption that not just me, but others are acting to an acceptable degree with the public interest in mind.[2]

All well and good. But, as with so much in the real world, the challenging dilemmas arise when the tires and the macadam meet. Viewed from the perspective of the public executive, the nagging question is "how?" Faced with a culturally and congenitally suspicious and skeptical public—another historical characteristic of Americans—what specifically can public executives do to create a level of understanding, acceptance, and trust so the tasks assigned and assumed can be carried out with a maximum of effectiveness and efficiency? To help respond to that question is the task of this book.

Every leader in every sector of the society—private, nonprofit, and public—knows full well that there is a degree of confidence that must be developed between herself (throughout this chapter, I use gender terms interchangeably) and her colleagues and especially her subordinates. "After all," as one Navy captain said to me, "They do the work!" A great deal has been written on this topic, some of it even useful.

We are concerned here with the peculiar set of relationships in a free society between the governing and the governed, between the citizen and public officials. We focus on this subject and, staying within the parameters of the book, we concern ourselves with the career executives—federal, state, and local—rather than elected or appointed officials, who are subject to the ultimate term limits: elections!

Unfortunately, it is not enough just to turn in a solid professional performance; we have to work consciously on building trust—which is hard to earn and easy to lose. That charge needs to be built into our job descriptions.

Participation and trust

One of the pillars of a structure of trust is participation in those decisions, which I believe impact on my life and well-being. When Maine's Department of Mental Retardation (DMR) tried to establish a halfway house for six of their clients in a suburb of Bangor, the officials went about it exactly the wrong way. Working through a nonprofit, the DMR bought the dwelling and then began to talk to the neighbors about the plan. The uproar was almost instantaneous, and the opponents seized every tool at hand to block the project, including the local zoning ordinances. We often airily dismiss this all-too-familiar community reaction to NIMBY (not in my backyard) or BANANA (build absolutely nothing anywhere near anybody), but in fact it is far more profound than that. When we disregard or disrespect the deeply held sense of the right of participation, we tap into a powerful American assumption about what we as government officials are supposed to be doing and how we are supposed to do it.

In some quarters, the feeling is that we should adopt the "moonless night" strategy: don't ask, don't tell, buy the house through a proxy, wait for dark, move the patients in, and then tell the community what you've done. Saves a lot of time and money to skip all that public relations stuff, right? But, in addition to the normative issues around the matter of how a government should behave in a free society ("consent of the governed"), there are the pragmatic ones. What is likely to happen? All of us who have been involved in or a witness to adverse community reactions to government action can testify that keeping citizens out of a decision is likely to stir up even more resentment than the substance of the decision itself. I often think that the action of the British redcoats who began to tear up the planks on the Old North Bridge in Concord on April 19, 1775, must have done as much as anything to arouse the colonials: "Who do you think you are, tearing up our bridge?"

I submit that as a society, we are more demanding today than ever before that we have a voice and a hand in government decisions. I remember a friend and constituent of mine who once asked me—perhaps in the late 1950s—why the water pressure in his house was so low. I went to the town engineer to check and found that the pipes were too small for all the development that had taken place in his community and that they were plugged up with accumulated rust and calcium. When I reported to him, my friend simply said: "Oh. Thanks." He had asked a question, and I had answered it. Today he would form a group, write chants, circulate petitions, and march on Town Hall complete with candles and battle cries. "I'm sick and tired of this and I'm not going to take it anymore," cried the character in the movie *Network*. Rosa Parks really started something.

Jefferson, who thought the New England town meeting, invented in the "plantation" in Dorchester, MA, by the first Puritans to establish themselves on these shores (1630), was the best form of government designed by mankind, would applaud our insistence on being players. Cicero told us, "Freedom is participation in power," so he would have liked it too. The decisions made at that first town meeting exist: If you don't keep up your fences, and your cattle drift into your neighbor's yard, they belong to him. Pretty clear what had happened. The elders, frustrated by the inaction of one of the company, came up with the idea of getting together and setting some rules for the community. Jefferson wanted to have what we came later to call "maximum feasible participation," with all male taxpayers getting together at the precinct level to decide the issues that concerned them. He wanted, in short, to establish the mechanisms for participation right from the start.

Alexander Hamilton's thinking was quite different. He could not see how national issues could be resolved on a precinct-by-precinct basis, nor did he see Jefferson's ideas as a viable prescription for building a nation. To make sure that the public interest, which, he said, "to my mind is sacred," could be accomplished, he believed it necessary to find those few men (in his time, it would be men) who had a sense of interests and concerns larger than their own and put them in charge. This kind of meritocracy was based on breadth of vision, not the accident of birth or the acquisition of wealth.

But President Harry S. Truman's Administrative Procedures Act and the Freedom of Information amendment thereto; President Richard Nixon's National Environmental Protection Act with its built-in public participation; all those local, state, and federal requirements and provisions for public hearings and publication of proposed regulations, and so many other laws reflect the Jeffersonian insistence of Americans to have a say in government.

I submit, however, that the formal requirements, useful as they are, have not proven to be sufficient. One of the frequent complaints from citizens is that government people are not open enough and do not seek out the opinions of the people.

The fact is, however, that in this country the sense of trust among the citizenry rises and falls with their sense of participation. Creating new mechanisms, experimenting (some ideas will work, some won't), opening and clearing channels, and using the new technologies—all of these activities, as we have seen in the preceding chapters, are part of our job descriptions, whether or not they are written down (they ought to be). The specifics of the techniques will vary with the issue, the constituency, the timing, the personalities of the players. The point is that we need to use our energy and imagination to find ways not just to communicate but to build structures of participation. In this regard, Jefferson was wiser than Hamilton. And we need to exchange views with one another on what works and what does not. Municipal associations, professional groups, as well as state and federal training programs need to focus on initiating such exchanges of experience. It is the way this society is supposed to function, and it helps us do our jobs by developing more trust in those we serve.

Since the 1980s, the Kettering Foundation has been paying attention to social capital, citizen action, and public opinion. The "Right Question Project" in Cambridge, MA, trains citizens in effective ways to approach public officials. Similarly, other organizations have helped groups of citizens mobilize and deal with problems. The War on Poverty put considerable emphasis on empowering and enabling people. Erwin Canham, the late editor of the *Christian Science Monitor,* wrote about what he called "The Authentic Revolution" in the 1940s, talking about the tradition of joint volunteer activity in America going back to the old New England barn-raisings; John Gardner, founder of Common Cause, also turned our attention to citizen action. I often wonder why those of us in government fail to devote attention to stimulating and helping and working with citizen organizations instead of either coping with them or dismissing them or even wondering what they are doing on our turf. Wouldn't positive behavior on our part serve to build trust?

Moreover, listening offers other obvious benefits. First, believe it or not, we can pick up some information that we may have missed before. And, second, if we listen—really listen—to what people are saying, we may well find ourselves reordering our priorities and thinking more deeply about what we are doing and why.

Helping the public understand how government works

Useful as all those approaches and the many more presented in this book may be, a massive obstacle looms up as we seek to cultivate a population that trusts us—or at least distrusts us less! Sargent Shriver, that great public servant who fashioned the Peace Corps and the War on Poverty, said to me at the time of Nixon's resignation: "You know, the Russian people understand what it was that Stalin did but our country does not understand what precisely Nixon did that was so bad. They knew he was doing things they didn't like, but they couldn't articulate just what they were and why they were wrong." What he was saying, I think, is that the American people, at a fundamental level, do not understand how their own government works or is supposed to work.

I am told that the civics courses that many of us had in school simply do not exist any more. That may be—but remember those textbooks that instructed us that we have (in most places) bicameral legislatures and that money bills start in the House and that most of the work is done in committees and that the president or the governor or the mayor is head of the executive branch and that there are two others known as the legislative and the judicial and that they are separate and that is called checks and balances and, like, who cares and how dull can you get? I am not convinced that phasing them out, if indeed it has happened, is such a great loss. I never learned what really happened in government, what those people did, and how and why; all that attention to the architecture, to the posts and beams of the structure, gave me no sense of the drama, of the *Sturm und Drang*, of the reality, of the people, of the actual play that was taking place within that structure. How can we expect people to trust us if they do not understand what we are doing and why we are doing it?

Superficially, the government of New York State looks like IBM. There is a CEO, the governor, and he has people working for him separated into different departments that are headed by bosses and local divisions that are subject to what headquarters wants. The whole thing is shaped like a pyramid with a place for everyone and everyone in his place and orders going down from the top and reports going up from the bottom. There are rules and regulations and policies and processes and budgets and tasks and inspections and evaluations, and products are supposed to be coming out of all this. No wonder they tell us government should be run like a business—why not?

But as anyone who has ever worked in a business knows, this picture is far more myth than reality. Businesses are run by people acting like people. There is pulling and hauling and conflict and cooperation and confusion and mistakes and success and near misses and good luck. It's called human behavior in organizations, and it provides us with a concept, caricature though it be, of a company.

We have no such image of government, so we naturally adopt the prevailing one we have of another big organization, namely a corporation. But the American government, hammered out during that summer in Philadelphia, was never designed to look like IBM—quite the contrary—nor was it conceived to function like IBM. Nor was it to serve the same purposes as a company.

The function of a business is primarily (though not exclusively) to generate profits for the shareholders, management, and employees. It accomplishes this end by producing goods and services that appeal to customers and potential customers. To maximize the income, it maximizes efficiency, producing as much output as possible with as little input as possible. The continuing search for ways to become more efficient, more cost effective, and more appealing to buyers is a demanding and intellectually stimulating endeavor. It calls for imagination, perception, clarity, creativity, and devotion to the bottom line. Business is critical to our well-being as a nation, as a society, and to our comfort as individuals.

But government, as Woodrow Wilson observed, is "not business. It is organic social life." And the ends of business are not those of government. The task of the public servant is to deliver service and to do that in a fair, equitable, accountable fashion. It is to seek out and implement the common good and to do so in a way that attracts and holds the support of the public. Part of the job of the government official, therefore, is to encourage public participation in her affairs so that "consent of the governed" can be ascertained and maintained. Government's role is to serve the common good and to deliver public value.

The fifty-five delegates—with shifting attendance, as we know—who gathered in Philadelphia that critical summer did not think they were starting up a new business, a new bank, canal company, or sawmill. They were well aware that they were drafting a formal document describing the way their new nation was to be governed. The Declaration of Independence had set forth the aspirations, the values, purposes of their new nation, won in what Washington called "The Glorious Cause." Their job was to raise the beams, the walls, the roof of this new government, indeed, a new *kind* of government. They set about replacing the Articles of Confederation with something more workable and serviceable and at the same time making operational the idea of popular sovereignty. Madison's two scholarly papers, one on the history of confederations and the other on the weaknesses of the existing American version, set the stage for their work.

However much they disagreed, however many different ways they interpreted the same words and phrases, however profound the conflicts between the small and the large states, they stood together in agreement on their conviction that the nation should be something new and different, above all that it should not be a monarchy.

But how, without a monarch, could all the ongoing differences be reconciled? They knew there was no such thing as "the public interest"; instead, as Madison was well aware, there were countless "factions," groups of citizens with roughly common views of just where the public interest lay—and they knew those views often directly contradicted each other. Similarly, there was no such phenomenon as "public opinion," but many different opinions about matters of great importance—economic, religious, political— and all were represented at Philadelphia. So when modern pundits talk glibly about the "intent of the Founders," I always wonder precisely which "Founders" they mean—Hamilton? Jefferson? Madison? Adams? Washington? Randolph? And at what stages of their careers, for their views changed with the changing times.

At any rate, Madison, "little Jemmy," seized the initiative in thinking specifically about what this Constitution should look like. Able to read Latin and Greek, backed by his library and the "cargo of books" Jefferson sent him from Paris, he sawed and hammered away at Montpelier, his estate in Virginia, and came up with a model. As shrewd a politician as he was profound as a thinker, he brought the Virginia delegation together at the same boardinghouse in Philadelphia two weeks before the first gavel sounded; they worked over his ideas and, ultimately, his formulation went before the convention as the Virginia Plan. The advantage still goes to the person who has something on paper at the start of the meeting to which the others will react!

And what was at the heart of Madison's grand plan? Not "separation of powers," to which they were all committed, given the British experience, rather it was "countervailing powers" (*Federalist* 10 and 51). Fearful that one or another of the "factions" could take over one or more of the branches, he mixed and matched, giving each some of the traditional powers of the others. In this way he set "ambition to counter ambition," meaning, I think, policy ambitions as well as personal ambitions.

Was this a recipe for business-like efficiency in an organization? Not hardly. It was a recipe for a cumbersome decision-making process. It was a recipe for "maximum feasible participation" of many players inside and outside the formal structure. It was a recipe for almost limitless accessibility to the decision makers and to the decision-making process from the governed. It is as though Bill Gates, Paul Allen, and Paul Balmer when they started Microsoft got together and said: "How can we make it as hard as possible to get decisions made? How can we bring as many people as possible into the decision-making process? How can we make our decisions as transparent as possible so as many folk as possible will know what we are doing?"

We all know this. We took civics or American history in school, and we all heard about checks and balances until we were sick of it. But we were not made aware of how these basic concepts have evolved and how they play out in the America of today.

But Bill Kelly, director of Job Corps under President Johnson and Sargent Shriver, head of the Office of Economic Opportunity (the so-called Poverty Program)—he knew all right. Of all the OEO programs, the Job Corps was in the most trouble in the 1960s. Its appropriation and authorization legislation were both coming up before Congress, and harsh criticism was heard everywhere, threatening its survival. The communities where the camps were located did not like it, wondered what all these African American kids were suddenly doing in their towns; Congress thought it was wasteful; the Office of Management and Budget was circulating memos against it throughout the government; the press was filled with stories about riots and high costs; the staff was demoralized, plagued by all this criticism and frequent turnover of leadership.

But Kelly, unfazed by all this as he sought to save the program, well understood the situation in which Madison's plan had placed him. He was in the middle of a wheel of power centers, each one of which could impact his program—perhaps terminally. His situation looked like Figure C.1.

Figure C.1 The power center wheel of Bill Kelly

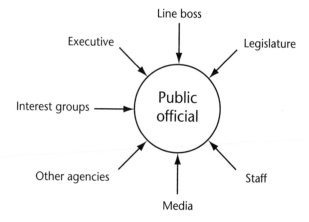

Source: Dan Fenn, "Making the Madisonian System Work: Case Studies in Contemporary American Government, Notes on Classroom Use," John F. Kennedy School of Government, 2004, 5.

In reality, things were not that simple because, with the exception of Kelly and his staff, all the other players had different sets of concerns and orders of priorities. It looked more like Figure C.2 on page 405.

But even that was not the whole story: there were all kinds combinations and networks and lash-ups among and between the players. So his world really looked like Figure C.3 on page 406.

Systematically, Bill Kelly went around the wheel, building relationships of trust in all the power centers. He met constantly with members of Congress and their staffs, stayed in close touch with his boss, worked with his staff to make sure they understood what was going on and what he was doing, courted the media and kept them informed, worked with the local communities on local projects and local purchases, was responsive to complaints, took action to improve the program. In short, he added to Speaker Tip O'Neill's famous dictum "all politics is local" his own: "all politics is personal."

The upshot of his work was that the Job Corps not only survived but also received an increase in its budget. And, despite many attempts over the years to do away with it, it exists today, larger and better funded than it was when Kelly left it.

Figure C.2 **The power center wheel of Bill Kelly — because others have their own concerns**

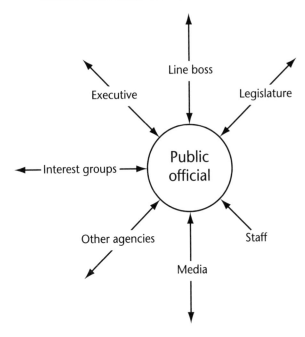

Source: Source: Dan Fenn, "Making the Madisonian System Work: Case Studies in Contemporary American Government, Notes on Classroom Use," John F. Kennedy School of Government, 2004, 6.

I find it interesting that a program director in another agency recently described to me just how he had managed not only to protect his project against the pressures of a hostile administration but also increased its scope and funding. Literally, I could almost have substituted his name for Bill Kelly's, so closely had he followed Bill's script—without ever having been aware of the Job Corps story.

Ah well, I can hear some say: That kind of interplay, the checks and balances system through which Kelly had to work himself, goes on way above me in the food chain.

So thought a supervisor in an agency when he was trying to deal with an employee with a great résumé but a poor record of performance. His story is a familiar one. Try as he would to help Neil Cooper become a productive member of his staff, Bob Morgenstern (not their real names) simply

Figure C.3 The power center wheel of Bill Kelly —with combinations and networks considered

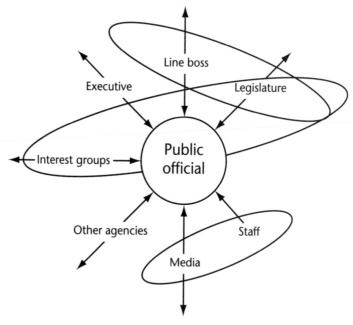

Source: Dan Fenn, "Making the Madisonian System Work: Case Studies in Contemporary American Government, Notes on Classroom Use," John F. Kennedy School of Government, 2004, 6.

could not make it work out. Finally, he started the termination process. To his shock and distress, he learned that Neil had just gone to the FBI complaining that he (Morgenstern) was covering up wrongdoing. Suddenly, what looked like, and was, a standard personnel supervisory matter had exploded into the whole Madisonian system. Or take the time the Nixon administration wanted to move the Veterans Administration (VA) administrator in Boston to Minneapolis because Nixon's people thought he was too political, too close to the Kennedy family. His bags were packed—when suddenly a line appeared in the VA appropriation bill saying that no part of these funds shall be used to move the regional administrator in Boston to Minneapolis.

In short, no one and no action of a public official is immune from the workings of Mr. Madison's system, because it provides so much leverage for so many people, inside and outside the government itself.

One public executive once told me: "In this country, to varying degrees, everyone wants to do their own thing, make things come out the way they want. Business is designed to channel that drive; government to empower it!"

Vice President Al Gore allegedly tells a story on himself. When he was first elected to the Senate, he held a dinner party for some of his closest friends. As they were having drinks in one corner of the room, he noticed a waiter putting down a pat of butter at each place. "Two pats," Gore commanded. The waiter kept putting down one pat. Gore said again, more forcefully: "Two pats." The waiter kept on as before. Gore, by this time quite irritated, said: "Do you know who I am?" "Yes," the waiter replied calmly. "And I know who I am. I'm the man in charge of the butter."

The American system of government was not put together with efficiency in mind, but with accountability and participation foremost. It was fashioned more than two centuries ago to protect the people against tyranny, arbitrary government people carrying out arbitrary policies. For there is no such thing as "the government"; that term is merely a convenient shorthand we commonly employ. Rather, there are thousands of men and women drawing a check from the U.S. Treasury or state or municipality taking certain actions. (It is strange how we have trapped ourselves by our own shorthand. If someone asks me whether I mind that "the government" may be reviewing my overseas calls, I would answer, "no, not particularly," because I have a more benign view of government in the abstract than most Americans. But if I am asked how I feel about some GS-9 working for some agency somewhere listening in on my calls, I can get very upset because I don't know this person, his abilities, his degree of discretion, his level of wisdom or his motives.)

Does all this mean that government officials aren't supposed to be concerned about being efficient, accomplishing their tasks in a timely and cost-effective manner? Of course not. The people have lent us their authority and provided us with their resources. It is incumbent on us to use them responsibly. It is thoroughly appropriate that we should be scrutinized to make sure that we are doing so.

It is only to say that for government people, efficiency is not the major goal and purpose. Responsiveness is.

Why has the U.S. Constitution stood fundamentally unchanged for all these decades? Because it was rooted in a set of values that are still dear to us: the values of John Locke, the Enlightenment, the social contract, self-reliance, freedom, liberty, and doing our own thing. And having a hand and a voice in matters that concern us. The traditions of congregational polity, expressed in that very first town meeting when the landholders came together to enact the rules for their new "plantation" and invented a new form of self-government, are alive and well.

As a matter of fact, as I said above, I would postulate that our generation is even more insistent on being a player than were our forebears. Woodrow Wilson in 1887 complained that the American public was all too involved in government and was often like a "clumsy rustic tinkering with delicate machinery." He should see us now! We are all children of Rosa Parks.

Attempts to change the fundamentals of decentralization and participation have taken place over the years, either formally or informally. Many of the so-called "management reforms" are basically attempts to shift power upward and remake our Madisonian system into a more pyramidal shape. During the Nixon years the President's Advisory Council on Executive Organization made recommendations to that end, but they foundered on Watergate. Calls for a "robust" executive today are part of that same effort. And the dilemma is indeed a taxing one—getting product out is hard in our government organization. It was meant to be. Hamilton is said to have complained to Madison: "You have created an organization to impede action, not to facilitate it." Madison is said to have smiled benignly and said something like "Yup."

Happily for the public servant, the American people understand all this, appreciate the fact that the jobs we do and the way we do them are directly traceable to Philadelphia in 1787, and so realize just how difficult it is for us to get things done.

Sure they do. "What's the matter with you government guys?" they ask. "In private industry we get things done while you screw around and screw around. Government should be run like a business."

And there goes the trust.

But if we adopt the Hamiltonian style, occupy ourselves with the task at hand, and do not stop to listen to their comments, complaints, chants, petitions, and songs, they say, "What's the matter with you, you pointy-headed bureaucrat? You work for me, remember?"

And there goes trust.

We are then, caught. If I am getting the job done, in response to their request, I am not being responsive. If I am listening to the public, I'm not getting the job done. So these two completely legitimate demands are irreconcilable, and either way I lose trust. That is the nature of the organization in which we find ourselves.

President Kennedy liked a stanza translated from the Spanish by Robert Graves:

> Bullfight critics, ranked in rows
>
> Crowd the vast arena full.
>
> But only one is there who knows.
>
> And that's the one who fights the bull.

What are those of us who fight the bull to do when the organization with which and through which we work, the very Constitution that we have sworn to uphold and defend, deprives us of the public trust because it often prevents us from acting with crispness and dispatch?

We need to see as part of our jobs the never-ending search for new and effective ways to build public participation into our decision-making processes. Naturally, we run some risk here. That little dog Toto really messed up the Wizard's operation when he pulled aside the curtain and we all saw the little man pulling the levers and manipulating the big awesome machine.

But I am convinced that the gains outweigh the hazards and the difficulties inherent in exposure because, as the curtain is pulled away, people will see how the system really works, not in junior high textbooks but in real life. They will see us struggling with many players, many interests, many viewpoints—as in fact the Constitution meant us to do. And, at some level, as they want us to do. We can, in short, transform an interface with a citizen or another player into a learning experience.

Suppose I am one of five people on an elected school board. Someone comes up to me at a party, as they often did in my hometown, and says: "I really think we should have four years of Latin in our high school curriculum." I recognize her all right—a friend. What do I say?

Recalling my own behavior, probably I would say something like "Interesting idea!" Going through my mind, however, would be: "Oh lord, I hope she doesn't pursue this. I have enough on my plate already, and I am not even sure it is a good idea, never mind a doable one."

Then suppose a week later she calls me and says: "You know, I have been talking with friends of mine and there is a group of ten of us parents who really think four years of Latin is important for these high school kids.

What do you think?" What I think is that I wish she'd forgotten it; what I think is, "How do I handle this?" But what I say is: "Okay, I'll look into it for you. Latin certainly is important, isn't it?"

I make the calculation that she isn't going away. I call the superintendent, who tells me we're short of classrooms and have no teachers capable of doing the job. Dutifully, I pass that along to my friend, hoping that will end it. But no. "Well, I'm sure there are logistical issues," she says. "But we think this is so important!"

Recalling my own public career, I would figure out some bob or weave—unfortunately. Probably ask her to put it all on paper so it could be considered carefully and blah blah blah.

What I could do is to sit down with her and say: "Let me walk through this process with you. First, as you know, I am only one of five members. There have to be three to move ahead with this. But then there is the superintendent. He actually runs the schools and, though formally he works for us, we wouldn't push something like this without his cooperation. Whatever the legal lines may be, the actual power to get things done is divided here between us and the professional staff. They implement, and furthermore, in virtually every situation, we confer and discuss and reach agreement with the superintendent and other school staff. And then he has the principal and the teachers' views to take into account. Beyond all that, we would have to displace another language to make room for the fourth year of Latin. Other parents may think Chinese is more important than Latin, or French, or Spanish. And there are teachers who feel that way, too. And they would fight this proposal very hard." And so on and so forth, trying to lay out the realities of the system for her. I could then guide her through the process.

I could have done that sort of thing in my career—but I didn't. I could have searched for chances to explain the realities to people. But I didn't.

What happens when we pull the curtain away like that? All of a sudden we don't look so all powerful. All of a sudden we are forced to admit that their priorities—a heart, a brain, courage—aren't necessarily our priorities. All of a sudden, instead of the big shot who gets things done, I am merely the AAA or MapQuest supplying them with the roadmap. Furthermore, that process is time-consuming and diverts me from all those other demands facing me.

But would it build understanding? Would it build trust? Would it mean that in future interactions with other public servants, my friend would be both more effective and more realistic? Would it be a better way to bring people to a recognition of just how our system works than all the talks to all the service club luncheons? I think so, and I wish I had done it.

In short, the problem for us public officials is that the community expects us to behave as they believe (fantasize?) IBM executives behave. But we cannot and we should not. So we are trapped. Consciously seizing opportunities to show our publics why and how, in fact, we do function can, gradually, incrementally, build a richer, deeper understanding and, with it, increased trust.

No one said this would be easy

"Building trust" in our relations with the public, our colleagues, other parts of the government, our staffs, and the press; adjusting to change; being change agents; doing the technical parts of our work well and effectively; working with a variety of bosses of varying abilities; finding new methods of public participation; being sensitive to our responsibility to the system itself, to its meaning and purpose as well as to its letter; and making sure that we, as the current stewards of the gift that Madison and his colleagues gave the nation, turn over to our successors a government even sturdier than it was when it was entrusted to us—that's the job description. And nobody promised us a walk in the park when we signed on.

We have, then, myriad responsibilities—many more even than I have listed above. That, in itself, is one reason our jobs are so tough—the most difficult managerial jobs that society has to offer, in fact.

Of course, all executive positions are hard. The facts, the scientific evidence, run in conflicting directions; judgment calls are often close ones; we never know all we need to know; and then there are all those pesky personnel matters—"time vampires" someone has dubbed them—which pervade all human organizations.

But our jobs in the public sector are especially taxing—and for several reasons. First, we are going where no one has gone before. How do you educate a widely diverse group of young people for a rapidly changing world? How do you provide decent health care at a reasonable cost? How do you clean the planet and halt global warming and not go broke in the process? How do you battle and defeat a shadowy and omnipresent enemy?

Second, there are so many players and potential players out there. Thank you, Mr. Madison, for making it possible for them to get into our business so much and so often!

Third, when you think of it, we are so often at the nexus of issues that deeply divide us as a nation, issues that may shift with changing circumstances. For example, the appropriate, acceptable, and working balance between our privacy, a freedom we cherish, and the security of the community as a whole needs constant rethinking and adjustment. I recall a customs chief at a busy airport who must give performance ratings to his people. One of his officers, remembering that he is supposed to knock and get a response before exercising a search warrant, dutifully does so; a second officer stations an agent at the back of the house who yells "come in" at the first knock, enabling his colleagues to come crashing into the building and preventing the inhabitants getting rid of dangerous or incriminating material. For this public official, the proper balance between individual and community rights is no mere topic for school debates or bull sessions; it is an ever-present reality.

It is unfortunate that those whom we serve, on whose trust we depend, not only fail to understand why we do what we do and how we do it, they do not think what we do is very important. I remember hearing of one woman, in a class of business and public executives, saying proudly that she had spent her life making lemon-scented furniture polish. Nothing intrinsically wrong with that—but where did the American people ever get the idea that figuring how many blue chips to put into laundry powder so it could be called "NEW Swish" and increasing point-of-sale purchases is more important than keeping the nation and our homes safe and mapping the oceans and managing the infrastructure of a free society and providing food and housing and caring for the most vulnerable among us—all the tasks to which public servants devote their minds and hearts?

The fact is that we work in a country whose citizens are basically opposed to government and, consequently, to government workers. Certainly one reason for this attitude is that, with the exception of most African Americans, our ancestors came over here precisely to get away from arbitrary government officials and government actions. So it is bred in our bones.

Finally, and perhaps most important, our jobs were explicitly designed to be tough. That is what those men in their powdered wigs and funny knickers, with their quill pens and parchments, set out to do.

Checks and balances and countervailing power indeed! Who, exactly, were they checking and balancing? Us, that's who. Whose powers were they trying to limit? Ours, naturally. What other executive in the society works in an organization specifically fashioned to make it hard for him to do his job?

How often do I wake up in the middle of the night, faced with three boxes: "In," "Out," and "Too Hard," and wonder why I'm not engaged in doing something sensible like selling shoes? Why did I choose this work? Because I figure that, one day, the lobby of my office building will feature my portrait or maybe a life size statue outside the door? Not likely. Or because the public will know and appreciate what I did and how hard it was? Equally unlikely. My spouse may have some ideas, but wonders why I was so preoccupied with the job that I never remembered to pick up the milk; my kids only know I couldn't often help them with homework; my father will know I did something but won't be quite clear what; and my mother always knew I would accomplish wonderful things, so I get no points there. And eventually—too soon—what I accomplished will be generally accepted as having always been there, my struggle to achieve it lost in the mists of history.

Discouraging? Maybe. But I recall a woman named Ramona Barth who, in the 1930s and 1940s, battled for the outrageous idea that women could be something other than housewives, teachers, and nurses, that they could be doctors and lawyers and Speakers of the U.S. House and business leaders. She was thought crazy and obnoxious in her time. In the last paragraph of her autobiography, she wrote: "What greater reward can a good worker desire than that the next generation should forget her, regarding as an obsolete truism work which her own generation called a visionary fanaticism?"

And then it could be the very fact that our work is so difficult and so important that gives it a special appeal to us. It is our full engagement—heart and mind—in matters that are at once extraordinarily difficult and vitally important to our generation and to our posterity that gives our lives purpose and meaning.

Over my desk I have a cartoon of two newly minted angels rising through the clouds with their wings and halos. One is saying wistfully to the other: "I spent my life making a difference—but in an area that didn't matter." The area where we spend our days and years does matter—it matters very much indeed, for today and for tomorrow.

Notes

1. Given new technologies, which make control of information to a populace so much more difficult to accomplish and communication between them so much easier, that range may be narrowing.

2. In modern America, people will cut their leaders a good bit of slack—but as the elections of 1994, 2006, and 2010 showed dramatically, their patience is not without limits.

References

Aberbach, Joel D., and Bert A. Rockman. 2000. *In the Web of Politics.* Washington, DC: Brookings Institution.

Abramson, Mark A., and Paul R. Lawrence. 2001. *Transforming Organizations.* Lanham, MD: Rowman and Littlefield.

———, eds. 2005. *Learning the Ropes: Insights for Political Appointees.* Lanham, MD: Rowman and Littlefield.

Anechiarico, Frank, and James B. Jacobs. 1996. *The Pursuit of Absolute Integrity.* Chicago: University of Chicago Press.

Arendt, Hannah. 1963. *Eichmann in Jerusalem.* New York: Viking Press.

Armstrong, Jerome, and Markos Moulitsas Zuniga. 2006. *Crashing the Gate: Netroots, Grassroots, and the Rise of People-Powered Politics.* White River Junction, VT: Chelsea Green.

Austin, James. 2000. *The Collaboration Challenge: How Nonprofits and Businesses Succeed Through Strategic Alliances.* San Francisco: Jossey-Bass.

Badaracco, Joseph, Jr. 2002. *Leading Quietly.* Cambridge: Harvard Business School Press.

Barber, Benjamin. 2003. *Jihad vs. McWorld.* New York: Ballantine.

Barger, Nancy J., and Linda K. Kirby. 1995. *The Challenge of Change in Organizations.* Boston: Intercultural Press.

Barnes, Cheryl, and Derek Gill. 2000. "Declining Government Performance? Why Citizens Don't Trust Government." Working Paper No. 9, State Service Commission, New Zealand (February).

Barnett, Thomas. 2004. *The Pentagon's New Map: War and Peace in the Twenty-First Century.* New York: G. P. Putnam's Sons.

Bass, Bernard. 1990. *Bass & Stogdill's Handbook of Leadership.* New York: Free Press.

Bearfield, Domonic A. 2007. "The Demonization of Patronage: Folk Devils and the Boston Globe's Coverage of the 9/11 Terrorist Attacks." In *American Public Service: Radical Reform and the Merit System.* J. S. Bowman and J. P. West, eds. Boca Raton, FL: Taylor and Francis Group, 101–120.

———. 2009. "Patronage: A Critical Reexamination." *Public Administration Review.* 69 (1): 64–76.

Beck, Katherine. 2002. "Going Global: How Boeing Is Changing the Way It Works Around the World." *Boeing Frontiers Online,* June 1. www.boeing.com/news/frontiers/archive/2002/june/cover.html.

Bendaly, Leslie. 1996. *Games Teams Play.* New York: McGraw.

Bennett, Janet. 2005. "Developing Intercultural Competencies," Presentation at the Federal Executive Institute, USAID Emerging Leader Program, Charlottesville, VA.

Bennis, Warren. 1989. *On Becoming a Leader.* Cambridge: Perseus Books.

Berry, Leonard. 1999. *Discovering the Soul of Service: The Nine Drivers of Sustainable Business Success.* New York: Free Press.

———, Eileen Wall, and Lewis P. Carbone. 2006. "Service Clues and Customer Assessment of the Service Experience." *Academy of Management Executive* 8 (May): 43–57.

Bikson, Tora, Gregory F. Treverton, Joy Moini, and Gustav Lindstrom. 2003. "New Challenges for International Leadership: Lessons from Organizations with Global Missions." Santa Monica, CA: RAND Monograph Report.

Bingham, Lisa Blomgren. 2010. "The Open Government Initiative." *SPEA Insights.* January, 1–5.

Block, Peter. 1991. *The Empowered Manager: Positive Political Skills at Work.* San Francisco: Jossey-Bass.

Bloom, Greg. 2006. "Meet the New Organizing—Same as the Old Organizing?" *Personal Democracy Forum,* September 8. www.personaldemocracy.com/node/1002.

Bok, Derek. 1997. "Measuring the Performance of Government." In *Why People Don't Trust Government.* J. Nye, P. D. Zelikow, and David C. King, eds. Cambridge: Harvard University Press.

Bok, Sissela. 1978. *Lying: Moral Choice in Public and Private Life.* New York: Vintage Books.

Bolino, Mark, William Turnley, and James Bloodgood. 2002. "Citizenship Behavior and the Creation of Social Capital in Organizations." *Academy of Management Review* 27 (4): 505–522.

Bolton, Robert. 1986. *How to Assert Yourself, Listen to Others and Resolve Conflicts.* New York: Touchstone.

Bossidy, Larry, and Ram Charan. 2002. *Execution—The Discipline of Getting Things Done.* New York: Crown Business Press.

Bowman, Tom. 2010. *Marines Would Prefer Gay Troops Not Tell.* National Public Radio, November 30. www.npr.org/2010/11/26/131610584/marine-leaders-would-prefer-gay-troops-not-tell.

Boyatzis, Richard, and Annie McKee. 2005. *Resonant Leadership: Renewing Yourself and Connecting with Others Through Mindfulness, Hope, and Compassion.* Cambridge: Harvard University Press.

Brands, H. W. 1998. *What America Owes the World: The Struggle for the Soul of Foreign Policy.* New York: Cambridge University Press.

Bratton, William. 1998. *Turnaround.* New York: Random House.

Braun, Kathyrn A., and Gerald Zaltman. Undated. "Companies That Have Consumers' Best Interest at Heart, a zMet Study." Mind of the Market Lab case study for classroom use. Boston: Harvard Business School. Originally accessed at: www.hbs.edu/mml/hide/MMLCBI/. For information on the zMet technique, go to: www.olsonzaltman.com/html/howzmet.html.

Brewer, Gene A., and Robert Maranto. 2000. "Comparing the Roles of Political Appointees and Career Executives in the U.S. Federal Executive Branch." *American Review of Public Administration* 30 (March): 69–86.

Bridges, William. 2004. *Managing Transitions: Making the Most of Change,* 2d ed. Reading, MA: Perseus Books.

Brooks, Jennifer. 2006. "Power of Blogs on Rise in Politics." *Detroit Free Press,* June 6.

Brothers, Chalmers. 2004. *Language and the Pursuit of Happiness.* Naples, FL: New Possibilities Press.

Brower, Dana, Terry Newell, and Peter Ronayne. 2002. "The Imperative of Developing Global Leaders." *The Business of Government* (Winter): 18–24.

Brown, Hutch, and Russ Linden. 2001–2002. "Daring to Be Citizen Centered." *The Public Manager* 30: 49–52.

Brown, Mark Graham. 2008. *Baldrige Award Winning Quality.* Milwaukee, WI: ASQ Quality Press.

———. 1996. *Keeping Score: Using the Right Metrics to Drive World-Class Performance.* New York: Quality Resources; distributed by AMACOM.

Bunker, Linda. 1996. *Winning Strategies for the Executive Playing Field.* Charlottesville, VA: Federal Executive Institute.

———. 2001. *The Johari Window [What Is It? Why Use It?]* A monograph written for use at the Federal Executive Institute, Charlottesville, VA.

Burge, Camille D., and David E. Lewis. 2010. "Campaigning for a Job: Obama for America, Patronage, and Presidential Appointments," Paper presented at the annual meeting of the Midwest Political Science Association Convention, Chicago.

Burns, James McGregor. 1978. *Leadership.* New York: HarperCollins.

Bushouse, Brenda. 2006. "West Virginia Collaboration for Creating Universal Prekindergarten." *Public Administration Review* 66 (Special Issue): 154–155.

Caldwell, Alicia A. 2006. "Texas May Stream Border Video on Web." *Syracuse Post-Standard,* June 9.

Canfield, Jack. 1989. *Self-Esteem and Peak Performance.* An audiocassette seminar. Boulder: CareerTrack Publications.

Carbone, Lewis P. 2003. "What Makes Customers Tick." *Marketing Management* (July/August).

———. 2004. *Clued In: How to Keep Customers Coming Back Again and Again.* Upper Saddle River, NJ: Financial Times Prentice Hall.

Chadwick, Andrew. 2006. *Internet Politics: States, Citizens, and New Communication Technologies.* New York: Oxford University Press.

———, and Philip Howard, eds. 2008. *Routledge Handbook of Internet Politics.* New York: Routledge Press.

Chapman, Alan. 2003. *The Johari Window.* Online presentation at: http://unpan1.un.org/intradoc/groups/public/documents/UNSSC/UNPAN022136.pdf.

Chrislip, David. 2000. "The New Civic Leadership." In *Cutting Edge: Leadership* 2000. B. Kellerman and L. R. Matusak, eds. James McGregor Burns Academy of Leadership, University of Maryland, College Park, 18–24.

Cleveland, Harlan. 2002. *Nobody in Charge: Essays on the Future of Leadership.* San Francisco: Jossey-Bass.

Clift, Steven. 2006. "Citizens 2.0 and Governance 2.0." *Personal Democracy Forum,* November 14. www.personaldemocracy.com/node/1096.

Coglianese, Cary. 2004a. "Information Technology and Regulatory Policy: New Directions for Digital Government Research." *Social Science Computer Review* 22 (1): 85–91.

———. 2004b. "E-Rulemaking: Information Technology and the Regulatory Process." *Administration Law Review* 56 (2): 353–402.

———. 2009. "The Transparency President? The Obama Administration and Open Government." *Governance: An International Journal of Policy, Administration and Institutions* 22 (4): 529–544.

Cohen, D. M. 1998. "Amateur Government." *Journal of Public Administration Research and Theory* 8 (4): 450–497.

Cohen, William A. 2010. *Drucker on Leadership.* San Francisco: Jossey-Bass.

Collins, James. 2001. *Good to Great: Why Some Companies Make the Leap and Others Don't.* New York: HarperCollins.

———. 2005. *Good to Great and the Social Sectors: A Monograph to Accompany Good to Great.* Self-published.

————, and Jerry Porras. 1994. *Built to Last: Successful Habits of Visionary Companies.* New York: HarperCollins.

Columbia Accident Investigation Board Final Report. 2003. Vol. 1, chap. 8, 201. For the full report, go to the board's website at http://caib.nasa.gov/.

Committee for Economic Development. 2006. *Education for Global Leadership.* Washington, DC: Committee for Economic Development.

Conner, Jill. 2000. "Developing the Global Leaders of Tomorrow." *Human Resource Management* 39 (August): 147–157.

Cooke, Alfred L. 1995. *The Individual and the Organization.* Unpublished monograph.

————, et al. 1999. *Reading Book on Human Relations Training,* 8th ed. Alexandria, VA: NTL Institute.

Cooper, Terry. 1998. *The Responsible Administrator: An Approach to Ethics for the Administrative Role,* 4th ed. San Francisco: Jossey-Bass.

Cooperrider, David L., and Diana Whitney. 2005. *Appreciative Inquiry: A Positive Revolution in Change.* San Francisco: Berrett-Koehler.

Council for Excellence in Government. 2001. *E-Government: The Next American Revolution.* Washington, DC: Council for Excellence in Government.

Covey, Stephen R. 1989. *The 7 Habits of Highly Effective People: Restoring the Character Ethic.* New York: Simon and Schuster.

————. 1997. Foreword to the twenty-fifth anniversary edition of Greenleaf's *Servant Leadership.* Mahwah, NJ: Paulist Press, 2.

————. 2006. *The Speed of Trust: The One Thing That Changes Everything.* New York: Free Press.

Crane, Thomas G. 2001. *The Heart of Coaching: Using Transformational Coaching to Create a High-Performance Culture.* San Diego, CA: FTA Press.

Dalton, Maxine, et al. 2002. *Success for the New Global Manager.* San Francisco: Jossey-Bass.

Davidson, Joe. "National Park Service Goes Back to College to Build Ranks, Diversity." *Washington Post,* August 11.

Davidson, Martin. Forthcoming. *The End of Diversity as We Know It: Why Diversity Efforts Fail and How Leveraging Difference Can Succeed.* San Francisco: Berrett-Koehler.

Davidson, Roger, Walter Oleszek, and Frances Lee. 2009. *Congress and Its Members.* Washington, DC: CQ Press.

Davis, Steve, Larry Elin, and Grant Reeher. 2002. *Click on Democracy: The Internet's Power to Change Political Apathy into Political Action.* Boulder: Westview Press.

De Drue, Carsten K. W., and Michael West. 2001. "Minority Dissent and Team Innovation: The Importance of Participation in Decision Making." *Journal of Applied Psychology* 86 (6): 1191–1201.

deKieffer, Donald E. 1997. *The Citizen's Guide to Lobbying Congress.* Chicago: Chicago Review Press.

Delmhorst, Frederic P. 2006. *Self-Awareness and Leadership Development.* Ph.D. diss., Columbia University.

DeLuca, Joel R. 1999. *Political Savvy: Systemic Approaches to Leadership Behind-The-Scenes.* Berwyn, PA: Evergreen Business Group.

Deming, W. Edwards. 1986. *Out of the Crisis.* Cambridge: MIT Center for Advanced Engineering Study.

Denhardt, Janet, and Robert Denhardt. 2003. *The New Public Service: Serving, Not Steering.* New York: M. E. Sharpe.

Dent, Stephen M. 1999. *Partnering Intelligence.* Palo Alto, CA: Davies-Black.

DePree, Max. 1992. *Leadership Jazz.* New York: Dell Publishing.

DeSeve, G. Edward. 2009. "Speeding Up the Learning Curve: Observations from a Survey of Seasoned Political Appointees." Washington, DC: IBM Center for the Business of Government. www.businessofgovernment.org/sites/default/files/Survey Politicals.pdf.

Devine, Donald J. 1972. *The Political Culture of the United States.* Boston: Little, Brown.

Deborah, Mackin, and Deborah, Harrington-Mackin. 2007. *The Team-Building Tool Kit: Tips and Tactics for Effective Workplace Teams.* New York: AMACOM.

Diamond, Jared. 1997. *Guns, Germs, and Steel.* New York: W. W. Norton.

Dodd, Lawrence, and Bruce Oppenheimer. 2008. *Congress Reconsidered.* Washington, DC: CQ Press.

Dukes, E. Franklin, et al. 2001. *Collaboration: A Guide for Environmental Advocates.* Charlottesville: University of Virginia, 2001.

Durant, Robert. 1992. *The Administrative Presidency Revisited.* Albany: State University of New York Press.

Eagly, Alice H., and Linda L. Carli. 2007. *Through the Labyrinth: The Truth About How Women Become Leaders.* Boston: Harvard Business School Press.

Editors. 2005. "Welcome to the Hackocracy." *New Republic,* October 17, 21–25.

Eilperin, Juliet. 2007. *Fight Club Politics: How Partisanship is Poisoning the House of Representatives.* Lanham, MD: Rowman and Littlefield.

Ekman, Paul. 2001. *Telling Lies: Clues to Deceit in the Marketplace, Politics and Marriage.* 3d ed. New York: W. W. Norton.

Ely, Robin, Debra Meyerson, and Martin Davidson. 2006. "Rethinking Political Correctness," *Harvard Business Review,* 84 (9):78–87.

Federal Executive Institute and Federal Consulting Group. 2002. *Guidelines for Federal Agencies Considering Executive Coaching.* Jointly developed document.

Fleming, John H., and Jim Asplund. 2007. *Human Sigma: Managing the Employee-Customer Encounter.* New York: Gallup Press.

Ferrara, Joseph A., and Lynn C. Ross. 2005. "Getting to Know You: Rules of Engagement for Political Appointees and Career Executives." In *Learning the Ropes: Insights for Political Appointees.* M. A. Abramson and P. R. Lawrence, eds. Lanham, MD: Rowman and Littlefield, 37–80.

Fesler, James W., and Donald F. Kettl. 2005. *The Politics of the Administrative Process,* 3d ed. Washington, DC: CQ Press.

Fichtner, Ullrich. 2006. "Civilized Warriors: The U.S. Army Learns from Its Mistakes in Iraq." *Spiegel Online,* December 18. www.spiegel.de/international/spiegel/0,1518, 455165,00.html.

Fine, Allison. 2006. *Momentum: Igniting Social Change in the Connected Age.* San Francisco: Jossey-Bass.

"First Digital Decade, The." 2004. *Washington, DC: Institute for Politics, Democracy, and the Internet,* George Washington University; and Rightclick Strategies.

Fleming, John H., and Jim Asplund. 2007. *Human Sigma: Managing the Employee-Customer Encounter.* New York: Gallup Press.

Friedman, Thomas L. 2000. *The Lexus and the Olive Tree.* New York: Anchor Books.

———. 2005a. *The World Is Flat.* New York: Farrar, Straus and Giroux.

———. 2005b. "It's a Flat World After All." *New York Times Magazine,* April 3.

Fukuyama, Francis. 1995. *Trust: The Social Virtues and the Creation of Prosperity.* New York: Free Press.

Gardner, Howard. 1983. *Frames of Mind: The Theory of Multiple Intelligences.* Cambridge, MA: Perseus Books.

———. 1999. *The Disciplined Mind: Beyond Facts and Standardized Tests.* New York: Simon and Schuster.

Gawthrop, Louis C. 1998. *Public Service and Democracy: Ethical Imperatives for the 21st Century.* New York: Chatham House.

Gilligan, Carol. 1982. *In a Different Voice.* Cambridge: Harvard University Press.

Gladwell, Malcolm. 2002. *The Tipping Point.* New York: Back Bay Books.

Goldfinger, Charles. 1994. *The Useful and the Futile: The Immaterial Economy.* Paris: Odile Jacob.

Goldsmith, Marshall, Beverly Kaye, and Ken Shelton, eds. 2000. *Learning Journeys: Top Management Experts Share Hard-Earned Lessons on Becoming Great Mentors and Leaders.* Mountain View, CA: Davies Black.

Goldsmith, Stephen, and William D. Eggers. 2004. *Governing by Network: The New Shape of the Public Sector.* Washington, DC: Brookings Institution.

Goldsmith, Stephen, and Donald F. Kettl, eds. 2009. *Unlocking the Power of Networks: Keys to High-Performance Government.* Washington, DC: Brookings Institution.

Goleman, Daniel. 1995. *Emotional Intelligence: Why It Can Matter More Than IQ.* New York: Bantam Books.

———. 2000a. *Working with Emotional Intelligence.* New York: Bantam Books.

———. 2000b. "Leadership That Gets Results." *Harvard Business Review* (March-April).

———, and Richard Boyatzis. "Social Intelligence and the Biology of Leadership," *Harvard Business Review* (September 2008): 74–81.

———, Richard Boyatzis, and Annie McKee. 2002. *Primal Leadership: Realizing the Power of Emotional Intelligence.* Cambridge: Harvard Business School Press.

Goodsell, Charles. 2003. *The Case for Bureaucracy: A Public Administration Polemic,* 4th ed. Washington, DC: CQ Press.

Graf, Joseph, and Carol Darr. 2004. *Political Influentials Online in the 2004 Presidential Campaign.* Washington, DC: Institute for Politics, Democracy, and the Internet, George Washington University.

Graf, Joseph, Grant Reeher, Michael J. Malbin, and Costas Panagopoulos. 2006. *Small Donors and Online Giving: A Study of Donors to the 2004 Presidential Campaigns.* Washington, DC: Institute for Politics, Democracy and the Internet, George Washington University.

Greenleaf, Robert. 1977. *Servant Leadership: A Journey into the Nature of Legitimate Power and Greatness.* Mahway, NJ: Paulist Press.

Grunwald, Michael. 2002. "Army Corps Chief's Ouster Prompts Outrage on Capitol Hill." *Washington Post,* web edition, March 7.

———, and Mike Allan. 2002. "Corps of Engineers Civilian Chief Ousted." *Washington Post,* March 7, A1.

Haass, Richard N. 1999. *The Bureaucratic Entrepreneur.* Washington, DC: Brookings Institution.

Halverson, Stefanie K., et al. 2002. *Self-Other Agreement on a 360-Degree Leadership Evaluation.* Paper presented at the seventeenth annual conference of the Society for Industrial and Organizational Psychology, Toronto, Canada. April.

Hamel, Gary. 1994. *Competing for the Future.* Boston: Harvard Business School Press.

Hamilton, Lee H. 2004. *How Congress Works and Why You Should Care.* Bloomington: Indiana University Press.

Hannam, Susan, and Bonni Yordi. 2010. "Engaging a Multi-Generational Workforce: Practical Advice for Government Managers." Washington, DC: IBM Center for the Business of Government.

Hargrove, Robert. 1995. *Masterful Coaching: Extraordinary Results by Impacting People and the Way They Think and Work Together.* San Francisco: Jossey-Bass.

Harkins, Phil. 1999. *Powerful Conversations: How High Impact Leaders Communicate.* New York: McGraw-Hill.

Harris, Richard A., and Sidney M. Milkis. 1989. *The Politics of Regulatory Change.* New York: Oxford University Press.

Hart Research Associates. 2006. "Partisanship Up, Confidence Down: Americans Want Compromise and Competition." Based on a survey in behalf of the Council for Excellence in Government, Washington, DC.

Heclo, Hugh. 1977. *A Government of Strangers.* Washington, DC: Brookings Institution.

Hegelson, Sally. 1995. *The Female Advantage: Women's Ways of Leadership.* New York: Doubleday Currency.

Heifetz, Ron. 1994. *Leadership Without Easy Answers.* Cambridge: Harvard University Press.

Heim, Pat. 1995. *The Power Dead-Even Rule (and Other Gender Differences in the Workplace).* Video. Libertyville, IL: CorVision Media.

Hempel, Jesse. 2004. "It Takes a Village—And a Consultant." *Business Week Online,* September 6. www.businessweek.com/magazine/content/04_36/b3898097_mz056 .htm.

Herspring, Dale R. 2005. *The Pentagon and the Presidency.* Lawrence: University Press of Kansas.

Hiatt, Jeffrey. 2006. *ADKAR: A Model for Change in Business, Government, and Our Community.* Loveland, CO: Prosci Learning Center Publications.

Hill-Stoks, Hattie, et al. 1990. *Women, Power, and Self-Esteem: Take Charge of Your Own Well-Being.* Audiocassette seminar. Boulder: CareerTrack Publications.

Hirsh, Elizabeth, Katherine W. Hirsh, and Sandra Krebs Hirsh. 2003. *Introduction to Type and Teams,* 2d ed. Palo Alto, CA: Consulting Psychologists' Press, 2003.

Hoagland, Jim. 2006. "A Change in Tone—and a Stumble on Iraq." *Washington Post,* September 3.

Hof, Robert D. 2005. "The Power of Us." *Business Week,* June 20.

Hofstadter, Richard. 1964. *Anti-Intellectualism in American Life.* New York: Vintage.

Holbrooke, Richard. 2008. "The Next President: Mastering a Daunting Agenda." *Foreign Affairs.* September/October.

Holzer, Marc, James Melitski, Seung-Yong Rho, and Richard Schwester. 2004. "Restoring Trust in Government: The Potential of Digital Citizen Participation." Washington, DC: IBM Center for the Business of Government.

Horrigan, John. 2004. *How Americans Get in Touch with Government.* Washington, DC: Pew Internet and American Life Project, May 24.

———, Kelly Garrett, and Paul Resnick. 2004. *The Internet and Democratic Debate.* Washington, DC: Pew Internet and American Life Project, October 27.

Horton, Gabriel, and David E. Lewis. 2010. "Presidents, Patronage, and Turkey Farms." Paper presented at the annual meeting of the Midwest Political Science Association Convention, Chicago.

Huddleston, Mark W. 2000. "Onto the Darkling Plain: Globalization and the American Public Service in the Twenty-First Century." *Journal of Public Administration Research and Theory* 10 (4): 665–684.

Hunt, James M., and Joseph R. Weintraub. 2002. *The Coaching Manager: Developing Top Talent in Business*. Thousand Oaks, CA: Sage Publications.

Isaacs, William. 1999. *Dialogue and the Art of Thinking Together*. New York: Doubleday.

Jackson, Phil. 1995. *Sacred Hoops*. New York: Hyperion Press.

Jaffe, Greg. 2005. "In Iraq, One Officer Uses Cultural Skills to Fight Insurgents." *Wall Street Journal*, November 15.

Janis, Irving. 1989. *Crucial Decisions: Leadership in Policymaking and Crisis Management*. New York: Free Press.

Jefferson, Thomas. 1801. *First Inaugural Address*. March 4. www.princeton.edu/~tjpapers/inaugural/infinal.html.

Jehn, Karen, et al. 2001. "The Dynamic Nature of Conflict: A Longitudinal Study of Intragroup Conflict and Group Performance." *Academy of Management Journal* 44: 238.

Johnson, Allan. 2005. *Privilege, Power, and Difference*. New York: McGraw-Hill.

Johnson, Spencer. 1999. *Who Moved My Cheese?* New York: G. P. Putnam and Sons.

Jones, Gareth, and Jennifer George. 1998. "The Experience and Evolution of Trust: Implications for Cooperation and Teamwork." *Academy of Management Review* 23: 531–547.

Juran, Joseph. 1988. *Quality Improvement: Service*. Wilton, CT: Juran Institute.

Kanter, Rosabeth Moss. 1994. "Collaborative Advantage: The Art of Alliances." *Harvard Business Review* (July-August): 96–108.

Kaplan, Robert. 2005. *Imperial Grunts*. New York: Vintage Books.

———, and David P. Norton. 1996. *The Balanced Scorecard: Translating Strategy into Action*. Boston: Harvard Business School Press.

Katzenbach, Jon R., and Douglas K. Smith. 2003. *The Wisdom of Team*. New York: Harper Collins.

Katzenbach, Jon R., David A. Garvin, and Etiene C. Wenger. 2004. *Harvard Business Review on Teams That Succeed*. Cambridge, MA: Harvard Business Press.

Kegan, Robert, and Lisa Laskow Lahey. 2002. *How the Way We Talk Can Change the Way We Work: 7 Languages for Transformation*. San Francisco: Jossey-Bass.

Kelman, Steven. 2005. *Unleashing Change*. Washington, DC: Brookings Institution.

Kessler, Glen. 2002. "Budget Director Lectured by House Appropriators." *Washington Post*, March 15, A21.

Kettl, Donald F. 2002. *The Transformation of Governance: Public Administration for the Twenty-First Century*. Baltimore: Johns Hopkins University Press.

———. 2006. "Managing Boundaries in American Administration: The Collaboration Imperative." *Public Administration Review* 66:6 (Supplement): 10–19.

———. 2009. *The Next Government of the United States: Why Our Institutions Fail Us and How to Fix Them*. New York: W. W. Norton.

———, and James W. Fesler. 2005. *The Politics of the Administrative Process*, 3d ed. Washington, DC: CQ Press.

Khademian, Anne M. 2002. *Working with Culture*. Washington, DC: CQ Press.

Khatiwada, Ishwar, Andrew Sum, and Tim Barnacle. 2006. "New Foreign Immigrant Workers and the Labor Market in the U.S.: The Contributions of New Immigrant Workers to Labor Force and Unemployment Growth and Their Impact on Native Born Workers, 2000 to 2005." National Center on Education and the Economy (NCEE). www.skillscommission.org/wp-content/uploads/2010/05/NewForeignImmigrant Workers.pdf.

Kidder, Rushworth. 1995. *How Good People Make Tough Choices: Resolving the Dilemmas of Ethical Living.* New York: Fireside Books.

———. 2005a. *Moral Courage.* New York: William Morrow.

———. 2005b. "Auschwitz at 60: The Lesson of Moral Perimeters." Camden, ME: Institute for Global Ethics. www.globalethics.org/newsline/2005/01/31/auschwitz-at-60-the-lesson-of-moral-perimeters/.

Kingdon, John W. 1995. *Agendas, Alternatives, and Public Policy.* New York: Harper Collins.

Klaus, Rudi., and Bernard M. Bass. 1982. *Interpersonal Communication in Organizations.* New York: Academic Press.

Kohut, Andrew, and Bruce Stokes. 2006. *America Against the World: How We Are Different and Why We Are Disliked.* New York: Times Books.

Kotter, John P. 1996. *Leading Change.* Boston: Harvard Business School Press.

Kouzes, Jim, and Barry Posner. 2002. *The Leadership Challenge,* 3d ed. San Francisco: Jossey-Bass.

Krepinevich, Andrew F. 1986. *The Army and Vietnam.* Baltimore: Johns Hopkins University Press.

LaBarre, Polly. 1999. "The Agenda: Grassroots Leadership." *Fast Company* (March).

La Corte, Rachel. 2006. "Washington State Personalizes Interfaces with Constituents." *Syracuse Post-Standard,* December 10.

Lash, Rick. 2002. "Top Leadership: Taking the Inner Journey." *Ivey Business Journal,* May.

Laszlo, Ervin. 2006. *The Chaos Point: The World at the Crossroads.* Charlottesville, VA: Hampton Roads.

Lemmon, Michael. 2004. "Meeting the Need for World Languages." Remarks Given at the States Institute on International Education in the Schools, November 16, 2004.

Lencioni, Patrick. 2002. *The Five Dysfunctions of a Team: A Leadership Fable.* San Francisco: Jossey-Bass.

———. 2005. *Overcoming the Five Dysfunctions of a Team: A Field Guide for Leaders, Managers and Facilitators.* San Francisco: Jossey-Bass.

Levinson, Wendy, et al. 1997. "Physician-Patient Communication: The Relationship with Malpractice Claims Among Primary Care Physicians and Surgeons." *Journal of the American Medical Association* 27 (7): 553–559.

Levy, Joshua. 2006. "Rules for Using MySpace in Politics." *Personal Democracy Forum,* December 4. www.personaldemocracy.com/node/1116.

Lewin, Kurt. 1943. "Defining the Field at a Given Time." *Psychological Review* 50: 292–310. Republished in *Resolving Social Conflicts & Field Theory in Social Science,* Washington, DC: American Psychological Association, 1997.

Lewis, Carol. 1991. *The Ethics Challenge in Public Service: A Problem-Solving Guide.* San Francisco: Jossey-Bass.

Lewis, David E. 2008. *The Politics of Presidential Appointments: Political Control and Bureaucratic Performance.* Princeton: Princeton University Press.

———. 2011. Presidential Appointments in the Obama Administration: An Early Evaluation." In *The Obama Presidency: Change and Continuity.* Andrew Dowdle, Dirk C. van Raemdonck, and Robert Maranto, eds. Philadelphia: Routledge.

Light, Paul C. 2002. *Government's Greatest Achievements: From Civil Rights to Homeland Security.* Washington, DC: Brookings Institution.

———. 2006. "The Tides of Reform Revisited: Patterns in Making Government Work, 1945–2002." *Public Administration Review* (January/February): 6–19.

Likert, Rensis. 1961. *New Patterns of Management.* New York: McGraw-Hill.

———. 1967. *The Human Organization: Its Management and Values.* New York: McGraw-Hill.

Linden, Russell. 2002. *Working Across Boundaries: Making Collaboration Work in Government and Nonprofit Organizations.* San Francisco: Jossey-Bass.

———. 2005. "The Quest to Become 'One': An Approach to Internal Collaboration." Washington, DC: IBM Center for the Business of Government.

———. 2010. *Leading Across Boundaries: Creating Collaborative Agencies in a Networked World.* San Francisco: Jossey-Bass.

Linney, Barbara J. 2010. *Turn Your Face.* Noida, India: AlBooks. www.a1books.co.in/turn-your-face-how-be/itemdetail/0982548206/.

Liotta, P. H., and James F. Miskel. 2004. "Redrawing the Map of the Future." *World Policy Journal* 21 (1): 15–21.

Lipnack, Jessica, and Jeffrey Stamps. 1997. *Virtual Teams: Reaching Across Space, Time, and Organizations with Technology.* New York: John Wiley and Sons.

Longman, Phillip. 2010. *Best Care Anywhere: Why VA Health Care Is Better Than Yours,* 2d ed. Sausalito, CA: PoliPoint Press.

Lorange, Peter. 2003. "Developing Global Leaders." *BizEd,* September/October. www.aacsb.edu/publications/Archives/SepOct03/p24–27.pdf.

Lorentzin, Paul. 1985. "Stress in Political-Career Executive Relations." *Public Administration Review* 45(3): 211–214.

Luft, Joseph. 1969. *Of Human Interaction.* Palo Alto, CA: National Press, 1, 41.

———, and Harry Ingham. 1955. *The Johari Window: A Graphic Model for Interpersonal Relations.* University of California, Los Angeles, Western Training Lab. http://sol.brunel.ac.uk/-jarvisibola/communications/Johari.html.

Lukensmeyer, Carolyn J., and Lars Hasselblad Torres. 2006. "Public Deliberation: A Manager's Guide to Citizen Engagement." Washington, DC: IBM Center for the Business of Government.

———, and Patrice McDermott. 2010. Viewpoint: "Happy Birthday, Open Government Directive." *Nextgov.* www.nextgov.com/nextgov/ng_20101208_2722.php?oref=search.

Luks, S. 2001. "Information and Complexity in Trust in Government." Princeton Conference on Trust in Government, November 30–December 1.

Mackenzie, G. Calvin, ed. 2001. *Innocent Until Nominated.* Washington, DC: Brookings Institution.

———, with Michael Hafken. 2002. *Scandal Proof.* Washington, DC: Brookings Institution.

Mackin, Deborah and Deborah Harrington-Mackin. 2007. *The Team-Building Tool Kit: Tips and Tactics for Effective Workplace Teams.* New York: AMACOM.

Mann, Thomas E., and Norman J. Ornstein. 2008. *The Broken Branch: How Congress Is Failing America and How to Get it Back on Track.* New York: Oxford University Press.

Maranto, Robert. 1991. "Does Familiarity Breed Acceptance? Trends in Career-Noncareer Relations in the Reagan Administration." *Administration and Society* 23 (2): 247–266.

———. 1993. *Politics and Bureaucracy in the Modern Presidency: Appointees and Careerists in the Reagan Administration.* Westport, CT: Greenwood Press.

———. 2002a. " 'Government Service Is a Noble Calling': President Bush and the U.S. Civil Service." In *Honor and Loyalty: Inside the Politics of the George H. W. Bush Presidency.* Leslie D. Feldman and Rosanna Perotti, eds. Westport, CT: Greenwood Press, 97–108.

———. 2002b. "Praising Civil Service but Not Bureaucracy: A Brief Against Tenure in the U.S. Civil Service." *Review of Public Personnel Administration* 22 (Fall): 175–192.

———. 2005. *Beyond a Government of Strangers: How Career Executives and Political Appointees Can Turn Conflict to Cooperation*. Lanham, MD: Lexington Books.

———. 2010a. "Obama vs. McCain: What's the difference?" *Baltimore Sun*, January 20. www.baltimoresun.com/news/opinion/oped/bal-op.obama0119,0,6895168.story.

———. 2010b. "The Perils of Big Doctor," *Philadelphia Daily News*, January 14.

———. In press. "From Reinventing to Reform to Routine: the Clinton Administration and the Bureaucracy."

Marquardt, Michael. 2005. *Leading with Questions*. San Francisco: Jossey-Bass.

Maslow, Abraham. 1943. "A Theory of Human Motivation." *Psychological Review* 50: 370–396.

Mayhew, David M. 2004. *Congress: The Electoral Connection*. New Haven: Yale University Press.

McGregor, Douglas. 1960. *The Human Side of Enterprise*. New York: McGraw-Hill.

McKay, Matthew, and Patrick Fanning. 2000. *Self-Esteem: A Proven Program of Cognitive Techniques for Assessing, Improving, and Maintaining Your Self-Esteem*, 8th ed. Oakland, CA.: New Harbinger.

McKee, Annie, Richard Boyatzis, and Fran Johnson. 2008. *Becoming a Resonant Leader: Develop Your Emotional Intelligence, Renew Your Relationships, Sustain Your Effectiveness*. Cambridge: Harvard University Press.

Mead, Walter Russell. 2002. *Special Providence: American Foreign Policy and How It Changed the World*. New York: Routledge.

Meier, Kenneth J., and Laurence J. O'Toole Jr. 2006. *Bureaucracy in a Democratic State*. Baltimore: Johns Hopkins University Press.

Michaels, Judith. E. 1997. *The President's Call*. Pittsburgh: University of Pittsburgh Press.

———. 2005. "Becoming an Effective Political Executive: 7 Lessons from Experienced Appointees." In *Learning the Ropes: Insights for Political Appointees*. Mark A. Abramson and Paul. R. Lawrence, eds. Lanham, MD: Rowman and Littlefield, 11–36.

Moe, Terry M. 1985. "The Politicized Presidency." In *The New Direction in American Politics*. John Chubb and Paul Peterson, eds. Washington, DC: Brookings Institution, 235–271.

Molyneux, Guy, Ruy Teixeira, with John Whaley. 2010. "Better, Not Smaller: What Americans Want from Their Federal Government." Center for American Progress, July, at www.americanprogress.org/issues/2010/07/what_americans_want.html.

Morgan, Dan. 2004. "Aide Takes Blame for Tax Return Provision." *Washington Post*, December 3, A1.

Morgan, Nick. 2002. "The Truth Behind The Smile and Other Myths—When Body Language Lies." in *Working Knowledge for Business Leaders Archive*, September 30. http://hbswk.hbs.edu/archive/3123.html.

Morrison, Allen J., Stewart Black, and Hal B. Gregersen. 1999. *Global Explorers: The Next Generation of Leaders*. New York: Routledge Press.

Moynihan, Donald. 2005. "Leveraging Collaborative Networks in Infrequent Emergency Situations." Washington, DC: IBM Center for the Business of Government.

Muoio, Anna. 1999. "Mint Condition." *Fast Company* (December).

Murray, William L., and Gary L. Wamsley. 2007. "A Modest Proposal Regarding Political Appointees." In *Strategic Public Personnel Administration*. Ali Farazmand, ed. Westport, CT: Praeger, 199–226.

Musselwhite, Chris. 2007. *Self-Awareness and the Effective Leader*. www.inc.com/resources/leadership/articles/20071001/musselwhite.html.

———, and Randall Jones. 2010. *Dangerous Opportunities: Making Change Work.* Bloomington, IN: XLibris Corporation.

Nabatchi, Tina, and Ines Mergel. 2010. "Participation 2.0: Using Internet and Social Media Technologies to Promote Distributed Democracy and Create Digital Neighborhoods." In *White Paper: Promoting Citizen Engagement and Community Building.* James H. Svara and Janet V. Denhardt, eds., Phoenix, AZ: Alliance for Innovation, 80–87.

Nahapiet, Janine, and Sumantra Ghoshal. 1998. "Social Capital, Intellectual Capital, and the Organizational Advantage." *Academy of Management Review* 23 (2): 242–267.

Naim, Moises. 2006. *Illicit: How Smugglers, Traffickers, and Copycats Are Hijacking the Global Economy.* New York: Anchor Books.

Nathan, Richard P. 2000. *So You Want to Be in Government?* Albany, NY: Rockefeller Institute Press.

Neill, Margaret James. 1999. "The Learning Journal." In *Reading Book for Human Relations Training,* Alfred Cooke et al., eds. Alexandria, VA: NTL Institute, 209.

Newcomer, Kathryn. 1988. "Public Versus Private Executives: A Competence Gap?" Paper presented at the annual conference of the Senior Executives Association, Washington, DC, July.

Newell, Terry. 2004. *The Ladder of Inference [What Is It? How to Use It].* A monograph written for use at the Federal Executive Institute, Charlottesville, VA.

Newman, R.G., M.A. Danziger, and M. Cohen, eds. 1987. *Communication in Business Today.* Washington, DC: Heath and Company.

Nichols, Michael P. 1995. *The Lost Art of Listening.* New York: Guilford Press.

Nierenberg, Gerard I. 1973. *Fundamentals of Negotiating.* New York: Hawthorn/Dutton.

Niskanen, William A. 1971. *Bureaucracy and Representative Government.* Chicago: Aldine-Alherton.

Norris, Donald F. 2010. "E-Government 2020: Plus ça change, plus c'est la même chose." *Public Administration Review.* December 2010 (Special Issue): S180–S181.

Nye, Joseph, Jr. 2003. *The Paradox of American Power: Why the World's Only Superpower Can't Go It Alone.* New York: Oxford University Press.

———. 2004. *Soft Power: The Means to Success in World Politics.* New York: Public Affairs.

———, Phillip Zelikow, and David King. 1997. *Why People Don't Trust Government.* Cambridge: Harvard University Press.

O'Connell, Anne Joseph. 2010. *Waiting for Leadership: President Obama's Record in Staffing Key Agency Positions and How to Improve the Appointment Process.* Washington, DC: Center for American Progress. www.americanprogress.org.

O'Keefe, Ed. 2011. "Obama Receiving Transparency Award (at a Later Date) Despite Criticism." *Washington Post,* March 16, at www.washingtonpost.com/blogs/federal-eye/post/obama-receiving-transparency-award-despite-criticism/2011/03/16/ABhEqCe_blog.html.

O'Leary, Rosemary. 2005. *The Ethics of Dissent: Managing Guerrilla Government.* Washington, DC: CQ Press.

Oleszek, Walter J. 2007. *Congressional Procedures and the Policy Process,* 7th ed. Washington, DC: CQ Press.

Orszag, Peter R. 2009. "Memorandum for the Heads of Executive Departments and Agencies Regarding the Open Government Directive." Washington, DC: Office of Management and Budget, December 8.

Osbourne, Larry. 2010. *Sticky Teams: Keeping Your Leadership Team and Staff on the Same Page.* Grand Rapids, MI: Zondervan.

Ouchi, William G. 1981. *Theory Z.* New York: Avon.

Packer, George. 2010. "The Empty Chamber. Just How Broken Is the Senate?" *The New Yorker*, August 9.

Page, Susan. 2010. "America's Place in the World Could Play Part in 2012 Elections," *USA Today*, December 20.

Panagopoulous, Costas, and Joshua Shank. 2007. *All Roads Lead to Congress: The $300 Billion Fight Over Highway Funding.* Washington, DC: CQ Press.

Patterson, Kerry, Joseph Grenny, Ron McMillan, and Al Switzler. 2002. *Crucial Conversations: Tools for Talking When Stakes Are High.* New York: McGraw-Hill.

Patterson, Thomas. 2000. "Doing Well and Doing Good: How Soft News and Critical Journalism Are Shrinking the News Audience and Weakening Democracy—and What News Outlets Can Do About It." *Typescript.* Cambridge: Harvard University.

Pease, Donald. 2009. *The New American Exceptionalism.* Minneapolis: University of Minnesota Press.

Peters, Charles, and Michael Nelson, eds. 1978. *The Culture of Bureaucracy.* New York: Holt, Rinehart, and Winston.

Peters, Katherine McIntire. 2007. "Culture Club: The Marine Corps Aims to Add Cultural Knowledge to Its Arsenal." *Government Executive*, April 1.

Peters, Thomas, and Robert Waterman Jr. 1983. *In Search of Excellence.* New York: Harper and Row.

Pew Global Attitudes Survey, 2002–2005. www.pewglobal.org.

Pew Research Center, Global Attitudes Project. 2010. "Obama More Popular Abroad Than At Home, Global Image of U.S. Continues to Benefit." http://pewglobal.org/2010/06/17/obama-more-popular-abroad-than-at-home/.

Pew Research Center for the People and the Press. 2004. "Foreign Policy Attitudes Now Driven by 9/11 and Iraq." http://people-press.org/2004/08/18/foreign-policy-attitudes-now-driven-by-911-and-iraq/.

Pfiffner, James P. 1996. *The Strategic Presidency: Hitting the Ground Running,* 2d ed., rev. Lawrence: University Press of Kansas.

Phillips, Donald T., and James M. Loy. 2003. *Character in Action: The U.S. Coast Guard on Leadership.* Annapolis, MD: Naval Institute Press.

Pink, Daniel. 2009. *Drive: The Surprising Truth About What Motivates Us.* New York: Riverhead Books.

Plouffe, David. 2009. *The Audacity to Win.* New York: Viking.

Porter, Lawrence. 1999. "The Learning Journal: Some Mechanics." In *Reading Book for Human Relations Training.* Alfred Cooke et al., eds. Alexandria, VA: NTL Institute. Page 217.

Porter, Margaret. 2000. *Definition of Mentoring.* Developed for the Federal Executive Institute's Coaching Program, Charlottesville, VA.

Powell, Colin L., with Joseph C. Persico. 1995. *My American Journey.* New York: Random House.

Price, David E. 2004. *The Congressional Experience: Transforming American Politics,* 3d ed. Boulder: Westview Press.

"Quotes About Change." http://quotations.about.com/cs/inspirationquotes/a/Change7.htm?terms=matter+of+chance.

Rainie, Lee, Michael Cornfield, and John Horrigan. 2005. *The Internet and Campaign 2004.* Washington, DC: Pew Internet and American Life Project, March 6.

Ravitch, Diane. 2003. *The Language Police.* New York: Knopf.

Reeher, Grant, and Steve Davis. 2004. "The Political Life of the Internet." *The Responsive Community* 14 (2/3): 26–31.

Reichheld, Frederick F., with Thomas Teal. 2001. *The Loyalty Effect: The Hidden Force Behind Growth, Profits, and Lasting Value.* Boston: Harvard Business School Press.

Remland, M. 1981. "Developing Leadership Skills in Nonverbal Communication: A Situational Perspective." *Journal of Business Communication,* 18 (3): 17–29.

Rheingold, Howard. 2000. *The Virtual Community.* Cambridge: MIT Press.

———. 2003. *Smart Mobs: The Next Social Revolution.* New York: Basic Books.

Roberto, Michael A. 2005. *Why Great Leaders Don't Take Yes for an Answer: Managing for Conflict and Consensus.* Upper Saddle River, NJ: Wharton School Publishing.

Roet, Brian. 2001. *The Confidence to Be Yourself.* London: Piatkus.

Rogers, Carl R., and Richard E. Farson. 1987 [1957]. "Active Listening." In *Communication in Business Today.* R. G. Newman, M. A. Daniziger, and M. Cohen, eds. Washington, DC: Heath and Company.

Rohr, John. 1998. *Public Service, Ethics, and Constitutional Practice.* Lawrence: University Press of Kansas.

Salmoni, Barak A., and Paula Holmes-Eber. 2009. *Operational Culture for the Warfighter: Principles and Applications.* Quantico, VA: Marine Corps University Press.

Savas, E. X. 1982. *Privatizing the Public Sector.* London: Chatham House.

Schwartz, Shalom. 1994. "Are There Universal Aspects in the Structure and Contents of Human Values?" *Journal of Social Issues* 50 (4): 19–45.

Schwenk, Charles R. 1989. "Devil's Advocacy and the Board: A Modest Proposal." *Business Horizons* 32 (4): 22–27.

———, and Richard Cosier. 1986. "Effects of the Expert Devil's Advocate and Dialectical Inquiry Methods on Prediction Performance." *Organizational Behavior and Human Performance* 26 (3): 409–424.

Scire, Mathew J./US Government Accountability Office. 2007. "2010 Census: Diversity in Human Capital, Outreach Efforts Can Benefit the 2010 Census," U.S. Government Accountability Office—Testimony Before the Subcommittee on Information Policy, Census, and National Archives, House Committee on Oversight and Government Reform. 105th Cong., 1st sess. GAO-07–1132T.

Scott, Susan. 2004. *Fierce Conversations: Achieving Success at Work and in Life One Conversation at a Time.* New York: Berkley.

Seligman, Martin. 1998. *Learned Optimism: How to Change Your Mind and Your Life.* New York: Pocket Books.

Senge, Peter M. 2006. *The Fifth Discipline: The Art and Practice of the Learning Organization.* New York: Crown Business.

———, et al. 1994. *The Fifth Discipline Fieldbook.* New York: Doubleday.

Shackleton, Ernest. 1998. *South.* New York: Carroll and Graf.

Shrage, Michael. 1990. *Shared Minds: The New Technologies of Collaboration.* New York: Random House.

Silsbee, Doug. 2008. *Presence-Based Coaching.* San Francisco: Jossey-Bass.

Sniderman, Paul P., and Thomas Piazza. 1993. *The Scar of Race.* Cambridge: Belknap Press.

Sosik, John J., and Lara E. Megerian. 1999. "Understanding Leader Emotional Intelligence and Performance." *Group & Organization Management* 24 (3): 367–390.

Stanley, J. Woody, and Christopher Weare. 2004. "The Effects of Internet Use on Political Participation: Evidence from an Online Discussion Forum." *Administration & Society* 36 (5): 503–527.

Stone, Douglas, Bruce Patton, and Sheila Heen. 1999. *Difficult Conversations: How to Discuss What Matters Most.* New York: Penguin Books.

Stowers, Genie N. L. 2004. "Measuring the Performance of E-Government." Washington, DC: IBM Center for the Business of Government.

Strozzi-Heckler, Richard. 2007. *The Leadership Dojo: Build Your Foundation as an Exemplary Leader.* Berkeley, CA: Frog Books.

Sum, A., et al. 2002. *Immigrant Workers and the Great American Job Machine: The Contributions of New Foreign Immigration.* Boston: Northeastern University, Center for Labor Market Studies.

Sunstein, Cass. 2003. *Why Societies Need Dissent.* Cambridge: Harvard University Press.

Surowiecki, James. 2004. *The Wisdom of Crowds.* New York: Doubleday.

Tannenbaum, Robert. 1999. "Self-Awareness: An Essential Element Underlying Leadership Effectiveness." In *Reading Book for Human Relations Training.* Alfred Cooke et al., eds. Alexandria, VA: NTL Institute, 221.

Thompson, Nicholas. 2009. "Thumbs Up for Obama's 'Open for Questions.'" *Wired,* March 25.

Tichy, Noel. 1999. "The Teachable Point of View: A Primer." *Harvard Business Review* 77 (2): 82–83.

———, with Eli Cohen. 1997. *The Leadership Engine: How Winning Companies Build Leaders at Every Level.* New York: HarperBusiness.

Titan Systems Corporation. 2001. "After Action Report on the Response to the September 11 Terrorist Attack on the Pentagon." Arlington, VA.

Toffler, Alvin. 1980. *The Third Wave.* New York: William Morrow.

Tolbert, Caroline J., and Karen Mossberger. 2006. "The Effects of E-Government on Trust and Confidence in Government." *Public Administration Review* (May/June): 354–369.

Tolle, Eckhart. 1999. *The Power of Now.* Novato, CA.: New World Library.

Trattner, John H., with Patricia McGinnis. 2005. *The Prune Book: Top Management Challenges for Political Appointees.* Washington, DC: Brookings Institution.

Trippi, Joe. 2004. *The Revolution Will Not Be Televised: Democracy, the Internet, and the Overthrow of Everything.* New York: HarperCollins.

Uldrich, Jack. 2005. *Soldier, Statesman, Peacemaker: Leadership Lessons from George C. Marshall.* New York: American Management Association.

Ulrich, David. 1998. "A New Mandate for Human Resources." *Harvard Business Review* (January-February).

United States Marine Corps Center for Advanced Operational Culture Learning. 2007. www.tecom.usmc.mil/caocl.

U.S. Department of Defense. 2005. *Defense Language Training Roadmap.* Washington, DC: U.S. Government Printing Office.

U.S. Department of State. 2004. *2004 Report of the United States Advisory Commission on Public Diplomacy.* Washington, DC: U.S. Government Printing Office.

Vaill, Peter. 1989. *Managing as a Performing Art.* San Francisco: Jossey-Bass.

Van de Walle, Steven, and Geert Bouckaert. 2003. "Public Service Performance and Trust in Government: The Problem of Causality." *International Journal of Public Administration* 26 (8/9): 891–913.

Van de Walle, Steven, Jaal Kampden, Geert Bouckaert, and Bart Maddens. 2002. "Service Delivery Satisfaction and Trust in Government: The Micro-Performance Hypothesis." Paper presented at the 63rd national conference of the American Society for Public Administration, Phoenix, March 23–26.

Van Riper, Paul P. 1958. *History of the U.S. Civil Service*. Evanston, IL: Row, Peterson.

Waldo, Dwight. 1988. *The Enterprise of Public Administration*. Novato, CA: Chandler and Sharp.

Walker, David M. 2002. "Maximizing Human Capital in the Government Workforce." Washington, DC: Government Accountability Office.

Walters, Jonathan. 2005. "Contention Over Catastrophes." *Government Executive* (December): 51–57.

Washington, Harriett. 2008. *Medical Apartheid: The Dark History of Medical Experimentation on Black Americans from Colonial Times to the Present*. New York: Anchor.

Waterman, Richard W., and B. Dan Wood, 1994. *Bureaucratic Dynamics*. Boulder: Westview Press.

Weisbord, Marvin. 1976. "Six Places to Look for Trouble With or Without a Theory." *Group & Organization Studies* 1 (4): 430–477.

———. 1978. *Organizational Diagnosis: A Workbook of Theory and Practice*. Reading, MA: Perseus Books.

———. 1988. *Productive Workplaces*. San Francisco: Jossey-Bass.

Weiser, Carl. 2003. "Report Lists Public Diplomacy Failures." *USA Today*, September 16.

Weisinger, Hendrie. 1998. *Emotional Intelligence at Work*. San Francisco: Jossey-Bass.

Werhane, Patricia. 1999. *Moral Imagination and Management Decision Making*. New York: Oxford University Press.

West, Cornell. 2001. *Race Matters*. Boston: Beacon Press.

West, Darrell M. 2005. *Digital Government: Technology and Public Sector Performance*. Princeton: Princeton University Press.

White House. 2009. "Open Government: A Progress Report to the American People." Washington, DC: U.S. Government Printing Office.

Whitworth, Laura, Henry Kimsey-House, and Phil Standahl. 2007. *Co-Active Coaching: New Skills for Coaching People for Success in Work and Life*. Mountain View, CA: Davies Black.

Wilcox, Clyde. 2008. "Internet Fundraising in 2008: A New Model?" *The Forum* 6 (1).

Wilcox, Harvey. 2005. "A Careerist's Perspective: Keeping Bad Ideas from Becoming Presidential Policy." In *Beyond a Government of Strangers*. Robert Maranto, ed. Lanham, MD: Lexington Books, 63–79.

Willemssen, Joel C. 2003. "Electronic Government: Success of the Office of Management and Budget's 25 Initiatives Depends on Effective Management and Oversight." Testimony before the Subcommittee on Technology, Information Policy, Intergovernmental Relations, Census, Committee on Government Reform, House of Representatives. Washington, DC: Government Accounting Office, GAO-03–495T.

Williams, Christine B., Bruce D. Weinberg, and Jesse A. Gordon. 2004. "When Online and Offline Politics 'Meet Up': An Examination of the Phenomenon, Presidential Campaign and Its Citizen Activists." Paper presented at the annual meeting of the American Political Science Association, Chicago.

Wilson, James Q., and Peter H. Schuck, eds. 2008. *Understanding America: The Anatomy of an Exceptional Nation*. New York: Public Affairs.

Winthrop, John. 1630. "A Model of Christian Charity." http://history.hanover.edu/texts/winthmod.html.

Wood, B. Dan, and Richard W. Waterman. 1994. *Bureaucratic Dynamics*. Boulder: Westview Press.

Wood, Craig. 2004. "State of Consumer Trust: A Crisis of Confidence—Rebuilding the Bonds of Trust." Presented to the 10th annual Fred Newell Customer Relationship Management Conference, June 2–4, 2004, Chicago.

Wooden, John R., and Steve Jamison. 1997. *A Lifetime of Observations and Reflections on and off the Court.* Lincolnwood, IL: Contemporary Books.

Woodward, Bob. 2002. *Bush at War.* New York: Simon and Schuster.

Yankelovich, Daniel. 1999. *The Magic of Dialogue: Transforming Conflict into Cooperation.* New York: Simon & Schuster.

Zakaria, Fareed. 2003. *The Future of Freedom: Illiberal Democracy at Home and Abroad.* New York: W. W. Norton.

———. 2008. *The Post-American World.* New York: W. W. Norton.

Zaltman, Gerald. 2003. *How Customers Think: Essential Insights into the Mind of the Market.* Boston: Harvard Business School Press.

Zander, Benjamin, and Rosamund Stone Zander. 2000. *The Art of Possibility.* Boston: Harvard Business School Press.

Zenger, John H., Ed Musselwhite, Kathleen Hurson, and Craig Perrin. 1993. *Leading Teams: Mastering the New Role.* New York: McGraw-Hill.

Zimmerman, Jonathan. 2002. *Whose America? Culture Wars in the Public Schools.* Cambridge: Harvard University Press.

Index

Note: page numbers followed by *f, t, b,* and *n* indicate figures, tables, boxes, and notes, respectively.

A

Aberbach, Joel D., 269, 273–274
Abramson, Mark A., 289
Abrashoff, Michael, 335–336
Action planning, 189
Active listening. *See* Listening
Adams, Abigail, 26, 125
Adams, John Quincy, 26, 376
ADKAR (Hiatt), 199
Administrative behaviors in teams, 156
Administrative Procedures Act (APA), 36, 398
Affirmative action (AA), 216*t*, 217
Affirmative feedback, 104–105
Age, 209
Agencies. *See specific topics, such as* teams
Agendas, Alternatives, and Public Policies
     (Kingdon), 316
Alignment, 126, 148
Allen, Paul, 403
All Roads Lead to Congress (Panagopoulous &
     Shank), 316
Ambassadors, 279
Ambiguity, 124
America Against the World (Kohut), 379–380
American Arbitration Association, 158
American Customer Satisfaction Index (ACSI),
     6, 11, 20*n*25, 318, 324, 325*t*, 338
American exceptionalism, 374–376, 382
American Recovery and Reinvestment Act
     (2009), 348
American Society for Public Administration
     code of ethics, 29, 29*b*
Annenberg, Walter, 279
Apple iPhone, 358*b*–359*b*
Applied Change Levers, 172
Appointees. *See* Political appointees
Appreciative Inquiry (AI), 122–123
Arab population in U.S., 208
Arendt, Hannah, 22, 51*n*4
Argumentative responses, 98
Argyris, Chris, 67

Army Corps of Engineers, 293–294
Ash Institute (Harvard), 343–344
Asplund, Jim, 337
Assessment, 159, 185–186
Assumptions
     feedback and, 73
     ladder of inference, 67–69, 68*f*
     Theory X and Theory Y, 119–120
Attention, faked, 98–99
Austin, James E., 263
Australia, 363
Authentic self-presentation, 69, 71
Autobiography, 61–63, 64*f*
Avis Car Rental, 332–333

B

Badaracco, Joseph, Jr., 48
Bahrami, Ali, 40–41
The Balanced Scorecard (Kaplan & Norton), 199
Baldacci, John, 340
Balmer, Paul, 403
Barger, Nancy J., 165
Barnett, Thomas, 382
Barth, Ramona, 413
Basham, Ralph, 300*b*
Bass, Bernard M., 88*b*
"Be All You Can Be" slogan, 113
Bearfield, Domonic, 270
Becoming a Resonant Leader (McKee, Boyatzis,
     & Johnson), 79
Behavioral values, 191, 194–195
Bendaly, Leslie, 165
Bennet, Janet, 95–96
Bennis, Warren, 53, 54
Bernstein, Jarrod, 248
Berry, Leonard L., 319, 337
*Best Places to Work in Federal Government,
     2010* (Partnership for Public Service), 218
Beveridge, Albert, 377
Beyond a Government of Strangers
     (Maranto), 289

Bill of Rights, 205
Bingham, Lisa Blomgren, 348
Bissell, Ben, 169n34
Blame, 85
"Blanketing in," 287
Blind spots, 72
Block, Peter, 192–193
Blogs, 354, 369n33
Bloodgood, James, 15
Bloom, Greg, 362
Body language, 96–97, 98
Boeing company, 390
Bok, Derek, 3
Bok, Sissela, 16, 17, 30, 48, 51n13
Bolino, Mark, 15
Bolton, Robert, 109
Bork, Robert, 283
Bossidy, Larry, 126
Bouckaert, Geert, 10, 11f
Boyatzis, Richard, 78, 79, 109
BP oil spill, Gulf of Mexico, 1–2, 308
Bradley, Bill, 350
Bratton, William, 290n11
Bridges, William, 165
Briefs, executive, 311–312
Briggs, Kathryn, 167n6
Briggs-Myers, Isabel, 167n6
Brock-Smith, Cynthia, 271
The Broken Branch (Mann and Ornstein),
    296, 316
Brown, Mark Graham, 199
Brown, Michael, 307
Browner, Carol, 276
Budget balancing tools, 340–341
Budget cuts, 162, 293–294
Built to Last (Collins and Porras), 24
Bunker, Linda, 72, 266
Bureaucracy and bureaucrats
    change agents in, 276–277, 284
    cultures, 275–276
    distrust of, 267, 278
    ethical obligations, 37, 38f
    incompetency and, 272
    quality of, 268–270
    stereotypes of, 266–268
    values and, 22
Bureaucratic cycle, 193
The Bureaucratic Entrepreneur (Haass), 285
Bureau of Alcohol, Tobacco, and
    Firearms, 252b
Bureau of Land Management (BLM),
    256–257
Burford, Anne, 271
Burns, James McGregor, 24

Bush, George H. W., 278
Bush, George W.
    election campaigns, 350, 353
    government reinvention and, 268–269
    Management Agenda, 179, 342–344
    popularity of, 267
    pre-emptive military action and, 375
    website communication, 361
Business strategy/business model, 184

C
Campaigns. See Elections, campaigns, and
    e-politics
Canfield, Jack, 80
Canham, Erwin, 399
Capacity building, 189
Carbone, Lewis P., 337
Career civil servants. See Bureaucracy and
    bureaucrats; specific topics
Carli, Linda L., 151, 166
Carter, Jimmy, 10, 11, 267
The Case for Bureaucracy (Goodsell), 268
Caseworkers, 313
Catalano, Ellen, 90
Center for Advanced Operational Culture
    Learning (CAOCL), 371–372, 388
Center for Drug Evaluation and Research
    (CDER), 127
Center for Ethics and the Professions, 49
The Challenge of Change in Organizations
    (Barger & Kirby), 165
Chalmers Borthers, 133
Champions, in collaboration, 245–246
Change agents, 276–277, 284
Change Levers, 172, 172f, 184, 186–190,
    191–196
Change readiness, 278
Character in Action (Phillips & Loy), 49
Cherniss, Cary, 110
China, 388
Chrislip, David, 244, 252
Cicero, 398
The Citizen's Guide to Lobbying Congress, 298
Citizenship, 207, 342. See also Participation in
    government
"City upon a hill," 21, 23, 50nn1–2, 375–376,
    393n10
Civil unions, 212
Clarifying questions, 95
Clark, Wesley, 353
Cleveland, Harland, 252, 263
Click on Democracy (Davis, Elin, & Reecher),
    350, 351
Clift, Steven, 342

Climate change legislation, 303–304
Clinton, Bill, 51n4, 267, 350–351, 353
Clinton, Hillary, 357
Closed-ended questions, 107
Clues. *See* Experience and clue management
Coaching, 112–136
 overview, 112–113
 Bob and Lisa story, 114–119
 culture that supports, 125–128, 129b
 defined, 113–114
 as leadership imperative, 129–131
 mindset for, 119–125
 receiving executive coaching, 74–76, 167n2
 resources on, 133–135
 tips for success, 132–133
 in values spiral, 195
The Coaching Manager (Hunt & Weintraub), 134
Co-Active Coaching (Whitworth, Kimsey-
 House, & Standahl), 134
Code of Ethics for Government Service, 26
Codes of ethics, 26, 29, 29b
Cohen, William, 199
Collaboration (Dukes et al.), 263
The Collaboration Challenge (Austin), 263
Collaboration with other organizations,
 239–264
 overview, 239–242
 challenges to, 254–262
 constituency development, 251–252
 drivers, 243–249
 high stakes, demonstrating, 249–250, 251b
 leadership skills for, 252, 253b–254b
 paths to, 242–243
 resources on, 263–264
 tips for success, 262
 trusting relationships, 246–249, 247b
Collins, Jim, 24, 46, 174, 199, 372
Command and control style of leadership, 131
Committees, congressional, 306–307
Committee staff, 313–314
Communication
 Congress and, 297–299, 299b
 initiating, with political appointees,
 281–283
 misinformation, 298
 team strategies, 161
Communication technologies. *See* Technology
 and e-governance
Competing for the Future (Hamel), 126–127
Competition and partisanship, 297
Conceptual Change Levers, 172
The Confidence to Be Yourself (Roet), 79
Conflict management in teams, 158
Congress, U.S., 293–317

overview, 293–295
 as bicameral body, 305
 CDER and, 127
 challenges in working with, 295–297
 committee process, 306–307
 in Constitution, 295
 core values and, 26
 facts, evidence, and statistics in legislative
 process, 299
 hearings, 307–309
 oversight, 303, 309–310
 politics, policy, and personality, intersection
 of, 301–305
 resources on, 316–317
 staffers, working with, 308–309, 310–314
 stakeholder relationships and, 294, 299–301,
 300b
 tips for success, 315–316
 trust-building through communication,
 297–299, 299b
Congress and Its Members (Davidson, Oleszek,
 & Lee), 316
The Congressional Experience (Price), 317
Congress Reconsidered (Dodd &
 Oppenheimer), 316
Congress: The Electoral Connection
 (Mayhew), 316
Consensus and teams, 160
"Consent of the governed," 396, 397
Consortium for Research on Emotional Intel-
 ligence, 15, 16b, 110
Constituency development for collaboration,
 251–252
Constitution, U.S.
 Articles I and II, 295, 296
 Congress and, 295, 296, 306
 diversity and, 204–206
 1st and 14th Amendments, 236n2
 fragmented authority and distrust, 260–262
 Madisonian system, 402–403, 406–409
 organizational means vs. constitutional
 ends, 41
 Preamble to, 18, 27, 205
 values and, 23, 27, 27b, 39
Constitutional Convention, 205
Constructive feedback, 105–106
Contractors in teams, 155
Conversation, 82–111
 overview, 82–83
 dialogue, real, 86
 dialogue elements, 87–89
 dialogue vs. debate, 87
 on diversity, 223–227
 ECS Model overview, 90–92, 90f

ethical, 41–42
feedback and, 89–90, 91–92, 104–107, 105f
fundamental structures, 84–86
inquiry skill, 89, 91, 99–104, 100f, 101f
interpersonal competence, 88b
listening skill, 89, 91, 92–99, 93f, 94b
obstacles to, 83–84
resources on, 109–110
tips for success, 108–109
verbal vs. nonverbal communication and
    cultural diversity, 95–97
Cooke, Alfred, 78
Cooper, Terry, 48
Cooperrider, David, 123
Cope, Jean-François, 341
Core values
    Declaration of Independence and, 22–23
    ethical culture and, 42f
    of Marine Corps, 25b
    promoting, 40–41
    U.S. Constitution and, 23, 26–29, 27b
    worldwide, 28f
Corlett, John, 216
Cornfield, Michael, 354
Council for Excellence in Government,
    343–344, 384
"Countervailing powers," 403
Courage, moral, 45–46, 45f, 52n34
Covey, Stephen M. R., 263
Craigslist, 352
Crane, Thomas G., 134
Creative behaviors in teams, 156
Crisis and collaboration, 243, 248
Cross-representational teams, 155
Crucial Conversations (Patterson), 109
Culture, organizational
    coaching and, 125–128, 129b
    competitive vs. cooperative, 168n11
    independence vs. interdependence, 146
    political appointees and, 275–276
    teams and, 151
    unit-focused vs. agency-focused, 257–258
    of U.S. Coast Guard, 129b
Curiosity, 123–124
Customer, concept of, 180
Customer experience. See Experience and clue
    management
Customer value, 178, 181f

D

Dalton, Maxine, 391–392
Dangerous Opportunity (Musselwhite &
    Jones), 79
Daniels, Mitch, 296

Data Driven Approaches to Crime and Traffic
    Safety (DDACTS), 253b–254b
Data.gov, 345–346
Davidson, Martin, 224–225, 233
Davidson, Roger, 316
Davis, Phil, 240
Dean, Howard, 353, 364
Debate vs. dialogue, 87
Decision making
    ethics and, 43
    implications, considering, 37–38, 39f
    moral, 33–34
    teams and, 159–160, 169n34
    values trade-offs in, 37
Declaration of Independence, 22–23, 204–205,
    396, 402
DeFazio, Peter, 296
Defense Language Transformation Roadmap, 388
DeKieffer, Donald, 298
DeLuca, Joel, 263
Deming, W. Edwards, 177
Democracy
    distrust as danger to, 7–10, 8f
    experience management and, 333–336
    values-based leadership and, 25–26
Democratic National Convention (2000), 351
"The Demonization of Patronage"
    (Bearfield), 270
Dempsey, Joan, 240, 246
Denhardt, Janet, 48
Denhardt, Robert, 48
Dent, Stephen, 263
Department of Commerce, 223
Department of Defense (DOD)
    "Be All You Can Be" slogan, 113
    disability programs, 231–232
    Military Leadership Diversity
        Commission, 203
    teams, 144, 146, 168n13
Department of Education, 36b
Department of Justice, 253b
DePree, Max, 121
DeSeve, Ed, 270, 289
Devine, Donald, 278
Diagnostic questions. See High-Performance
    Organizations (HPO) Diagnostic/
    Change Model
Dialogos, 110
Dialogue. See Conversation
Dialogue and the Art of Thinking Together
    (Isaacs), 109, 133
Diehl, Philip, 318–319
Differing interests, encouraging expression
    of, 35–36

Difficult Conversations (Stone, Patton, and Heen), 84, 109
Digital divide, 349
Direction setting, 188–189
Disabilities, 210, 214, 215, 231–232
DISC, 142–144, 143*f*, 167*nn*6–7
Disclosure and teams, 141–142, 168*n*13
Discovering the Soul of Service (Berry), 337
Dissent
    encouraging, 206
    loyal, 43–45, 44*b*
    policies, disagreeing with, 285–286
    tolerating, 32–33
Distractions and listening, 97–98
Distrust. *See also* Trust
    across agencies, 8–9, 256–257
    anti-Americanism, 379–382
    bureaucracy and, 267, 278
    as danger to democratic governance, 7–10, 8*f*
Diversity, 201–238
    overview, 201–203
    in American population and workforce, 206–212
    best practices, 218–223, 219*b*
    Constitution and Declaration of Independence and, 204–206
    conversations on, 223–227
    cultural diversity and communication, 95–97
    definitions of, 203–204, 219*b*
    Diversity GPS, 227–231, 228*f*
    failure of diversity management efforts, 217–218
    high information diversity and low value diversity in teams, 52*n*29
    Key Results Areas, 220*b*–221*b*
    leadership questions for, 212–213, 214–215
    Leading Diversity Model as new paradigm, 215–217, 216*t*
    multiple intelligences and respect for, 120–121
    resources on, 233–235
    teams and, 153
    tips for success, 232–233
    toward *e pluribus unum*, 231–232
    workforce changes, 213–215, 213*t*
Dodd, Christopher, 302–303
Dodd, Lawrence, 316
Dodd-Frank Wall Street Reform and Consumer Protection Act, 302–303
"Don't Ask, Don't Tell" policy, 214
Doylestown Hospital, Warrington, PA, 328, 331
Drive (Pink), 199
Drucker on Leadership (Cohen), 199

Drug Enforcement Administration (DEA), 247–248, 248*b*
Dukes, E. Franklin, 263
Durant, Robert, 270

E
Eagly, Alice, 151, 166
Education, public, 37, 268
Efficiency vs. participation and accountability, 407
Efford, Richard, 314
Eggers, William D., 263
Ego needs in collaborative groups, 259
E-government and e-governance.
    See Technology and e-governance
Eilperin, Juliet, 296, 316
Einstein, Albert, 123, 130, 132
Eisenhower, Dwight, 266–267
Ekman, Paul, 96
Elections, campaigns, and e-politics
    overview, 349–350
    2000 election, 350–353
    2004 election, 353–355
    2008 election, 356–359
Electronic communication technologies.
    See Technology and e-governance
Ely, Robin, 224–225
Emerson, Ralph Waldo, 53
Emotional intelligence, 15–16, 16*b*, 110
Emotions and feelings. *See also* Experience and clue management
    empathy, 88, 122
    feelings conversations, 85
    government services and customers feelings, 321, 322*t*
    perceptions of agencies, emotional, 323–326
    reflection of, 93–94, 94*b*
Empathy, 88, 122
"Empire," 374
The End of Diversity as We Know It (Davidson), 233
Energy sources, 181–182
"Engaging a Multi-Generational Workforce" (Hannam & Yordi), 233
Enthusiasm, 254–255, 285
Entrepreneurial cycle, 193
Environmental Protection Agency (EPA), 36*b*, 183, 271, 276
E pluribus unum, 231–232
E-politics. *See* Elections, campaigns, and e-politics
Equal employment opportunity (EEO), 217
E-rulemaking, 346*b*–347*b*
Ethical culture, 41–42, 42*f*

Ethical obligations of public servants, 37, 38*f*
Ethics, codes of, 26, 29, 29*b*
Ethics laws and regulations, 267–268
Ethics Resource Center, 42, 50
Evaluative mindset, 98
Exceptionalism, American, 374–376, 382
Execution quality, 176–178
Executive briefs, 311–312
Executive Communications Skills (ECS)
    Model
    feedback, 104–107, 105*f*
    inquiry skill, 99–104, 100*f*, 101*f*
    listening skill, 92–99, 93*f*, 94*b*
    overall model, 90–92, 90*f*
Exemplarist school of thought, 376, 394*n*12
Experience and clue management, 318–339
    overview, 318–319
    benefits to leaders in democracy, 333–336
    designing experiences, 332–333
    e-governance and, 360–365
    emotional perceptions and satisfaction
        surveys, 323–326, 325*t*
    employee experience, 335
    experience audits, 330–331, 332*f*
    the experience motif, 328
    experience preference model, 327*t*
    filtering of experience clues, 326–327, 327*f*
    functional, mechanic, and humanic clues,
        329–330
    government services and customers feelings,
        321, 322*t*
    new competency, building, 327–328
    organizational levels and, 333, 334*t*
    resources on, 337–338
    tips for success, 336
    trust and, 319–322, 323*f*
The experience motif, 328
Extended DISC. *See* DISC

F

Facilitators, professional, 152, 152*f*, 259–260
Fanning, Patrick, 79
Farson, Richard, 92–93
Features quality, 176–178
Federal Acquisitions Regulations, 185
Federal Aviation Administration (FAA), 36*b*,
    40–41
Federal Emergency Management Agency
    (FEMA), 276, 277, 307
Federal Executive Institute (FEI)
    executive communications skills
        development, 90
    experience audit, 331, 332*f*
    on global leadership, 385, 386–387
    Henderson's leadership challenge, 50*n*3

"Leadership at the 'T'" model, 140, 140*f*
Leadership for a Democratic Society
    program, 139, 226, 387–388
Leadership for a Global Society
    program, 388
    oath of office and, 42
    seminar on citizen websites, 360, 363
    teams and, 139, 141
    U.S.-China Executive Program, 388
Federal Highway Administration, 169*n*27
Federalist Papers, 7, 205, 236*n*3, 306, 403
Federal Law Enforcement Training Center
    (FLETC), 300*b*
Federally Employed Women, 235
Federal Trade Commission (FTC), 275
Feedback
    affirmative vs. constructive, 104–106
    coaching and, 128
    as conversation skill, 89–90
    in ECS model, 91–92, 104–107, 105*f*
    self-knowledge and, 70–74, 70*f*, 71*f*
    in values spiral, 195, 196
Feelings. *See* Emotions and feelings
The Female Advantage (Hegelsen), 166
Ferrara, Joseph A., 270, 275–276
Fierce Conversations (Scott), 133–134
The Fifth Discipline (Senge), 234
Fight Club Politics (Eilperin), 296, 316
Financial Management Service (FMS), 257–258
Financial performance, sound, 178–180
First Amendment, 236*n*2
The Five Dysfunctions of a Team (Lencioni), 166
Fleming, John H., 337
FlyOnTime.us, 345–346
Forbes, Steve, 350
Force field analysis, 159, 160*f*
Foreign-born population, 207
Foreign Policy magazine, 393
Forgiving, 284
Fourteenth Amendment, 236*n*2
Fragmented authority, 260–261
Frames of Mind (Gardner), 78, 120*b*
France and budget balancing, 341
Friedman, Thomas, 263, 382, 387
Fukuyama, Francis, 392
Functional clues, 329
Fundamentals of Negotiating (Nierenberg), 102
Fundraising, 353, 357–358

G

Gallwey, Tim, 113–114
Games Teams Play (Bendaly), 165
Gandhi, Mohandas, 223
Gardner, Howard, 58, 59, 78, 120, 120*b*
Gardner, John, 399

Garvin, David C., 166
Gates, Bill, 403
Gates, Robert, 287
Gawthrop, Louis, 43, 48
Gay, lesbian, and bisexual Americans, 211–212, 213, 214, 215
Gender, 151, 209–210. *See also* Women
General Electric (GE), 126
Generational differences, 209
George, Jennifer, 15
Geraci, Mike, 252, 253*b*–254*b*
Gergen, David, 297
Ghoshal, Sumantra, 15
Gibbs, Robert, 359*b*
Gibran, Kahlil, 57
Gilligan, Carol, 151, 166
Gingrich, Newt, 393*n*11
Global leadership, 371–394
    overview, 371–374
    American exceptionalism, 374–376, 382
    anti-Americanism, 379–382
    internationalism and globalism, 377–378
    leadership development, 384, 387–390, 389*f*
    leadership gap, 385–387
    "relationships before work," 246
    resources on, 391–393
    tips for success, 391
    transnational agenda, 382–384
    trust and, 372–373, 378–379
    the way forward, 390–391
Goddard Space Flight Center, 218–219, 219*b*
Goethe, Johann Wolfgang von, 170
Goldin, Daniel, 277
Goldsmith, Marshall, 133
Goldsmith, Stephen, 263
Goleman, Daniel, 15–16, 20*n*34, 109, 110
Goodsell, Charles, 268
Good to Great (Collins), 46, 174, 199
Good to Great and the Social Sectors (Collins), 199, 372
Governance, 341. *See also* Technology and e-governance
Governing by Network (Goldsmith & Eggers), 263
Government. *See also specific topics, such as* Congress
    efficiency vs. participation, 407
    growth and performance of, 2–3
    local, 26, 247*b*, 250, 264, 290*n*11
    public understanding of, 400–411
    responsiveness, 407–411
    state, 26, 260–261, 264, 290*n*11
Government 1.0 vs. Government 2.0, 342. *See also* Technology and e-governance
Government Accountability Project, 50

Government Performance and Results Act (GPRA), 179
Graves, Robert, 409
Greenleaf, Robert, 23
Gregg, Dick, 257–258
Gregorius, Jay, 247–248, 248*b*
Gulf of Mexico BP oil spill, 1–2, 308

H
Haass, Richard, 285, 373
Hamel, Gary, 127
Hamilton, Alexander, 7, 11, 398–399, 408
Hamilton, Lee, 294–295
Hannam, Susan, 233
Hard, Allen, 246
Hard power, 23, 373
Hargrove, Robert, 134
Harkins, Phil, 109
Harriman, Pamela, 279
Harrington-Mackin, Deborah, 166
Harvard Business Review on Teams That Succeed (Katzenbach, Garvin, & Wenger), 166
Harvard University, 49, 343–344
Hautman, Jennifer, 74–75
Hawk, Jill, 222
Hearings, congressional, 307–309
The Heart of Coaching (Crane), 134
Heen, Sheila, 84, 109
Hegelsen, Sally, 166
Heim, Pat, 151
Henderson, Ursula, 22, 40, 50*n*3
Herspring, Dale R., 276
Hiatt, Jeffery M., 199
High-Performance Organizations (HPO) Diagnostic/Change Model, 170–200
    "according to whom?" (KDQ 3), 180, 181*f*
    "are we doing the right 'what'?" (KDQ 5), 182–183
    assumptions, 171
    defining (KDQ 1), 173–174
    "how are we going to treat each other?" (KDQ 7), 190–191
    "how good are we at delivering?" (KDQ 6), 183–186
    measurement (KDQ 2), 174–180, 177*f*
    model overview, 171–173, 172*f*
    resources on, 199–200
    tips for success, 196–199
    values change lever, 191–196, 192*f*
    vision change lever, 186–190, 187*f*
    "why do we need to?" (KDQ 4), 181–182
Hill-Stokes, Hattie, 80
Hirsh, Elizabeth, 166
Hirsh, Katherine W., 166

Hirsh, Sandra Krebs, 166
Hispanic/Latino population and workforce, 208, 214
Hoagland, Jim, 18
Holbrooke, Richard, 373
Holdovers, 287
Homicide rates, 290*n*11
Household living arrangements, 211–212
House of Representatives. *See* Congress, U.S.
How Customers Think (Zaltman), 338
How the Way We Talk Can Change the Way We Work (Kegan & Lahey), 234
How to Assert Yourself, Listen to Others and Resolve Conflicts (Bolton), 109
HPO model. *See* High-Performance Organizations (HPO) Diagnostic/ Change Model
Humanic clues, 329–330
Human Rights Campaign (HRC), 235
Human Sigma (Fleming & Asplund), 337
Humility, 46–47, 121–122
Hunt, James M., 134
Hurricane Katrina, 1–2, 243, 307, 364

I

IADS. *See* Integrated Air Defense System
"I" concepts (identity, intelligence, impact, and innovation), 227–231, 228*f*
Identity conversations, 85
Ignatieff, Michael, 374
Imagination, 123
In a Different Voice (Gilligan), 166
Incentives in teams, 148–149, 148*t*
Industrial model of work, 198
Inference, ladder of, 67–69, 68*f*
Informativeness, 92
Ingham, Harry, 70
The Inner Game of Tennis (Gallwey), 113–114
Input measures, 190
Inquiry
   as conversation skill, 89
   in ECS model, 91, 99–104, 100*f*, 101*f*
Institute for Global Ethics, 27, 50
"Intangible economy," 130
Integrated Air Defense System (IADS)
   drivers, 243–246
   formation and structure of, 240–241, 243
   stakes, demonstrating, 249
   success of, 241
Integrity, 30–32, 74–75
Intellipedia, 261–262
Intentions, 85, 86
Interdependent tasks, teams and, 146
Internal Revenue Service (IRS), 268, 320, 324, 325*t*

International Coaching Federation (ICF), 135
International leadership. *See* Global leadership
Internet. *See* Technology and e-governance
Introduction to Type and Teams (Hirsh, Hirsh, & Hirsh), 166
Involving others, as skill, 33
iPhone, 358*b*–359*b*
Iraq, 388
Isaacs, William, 86, 109, 133
Istook, Ernest, 314

J

Jackson, Andrew, 266
Jackson, Phil, 122
Jamieson, Kathleen Hall, 296
Jefferson, Thomas, 32–33, 376, 396, 398–399
JNET (justice information network)
   constituency development, 251–252
   drivers, 243–246
   formation of, 241–242, 243, 255–256, 264*n*2
   success of, 242
Job Corps, 403–404
Johari Window, 70–72, 71*f*
John, John H., 286
Johnny Got His Gun (movie), 22
Johns, John, 43
Johnson, Allan, 233–234
Johnson, Fran, 79
Johnson, Lyndon, 304
Johnson, Spencer, 78–79
Joint task forces, 257
Joint training, 257
Jones, Gareth, 15
Jones, Randell, 79
Jordan, Barbara, 201
Josephson Institute of Ethics, 50
Journal keeping, 65–67, 66*b*
Judgmental attitude, 98
Jung, Carl, 167*n*6
Juran, Joseph M., 177
Justice information network. *See* JNET

K

Kanter, Rosabeth Moss, 246
Kaplan, Robert S., 199
Katzenbach, Jon R., 137, 146, 166
Kaye, Beverly, 133
Keeping Score (Brown), 199
Keeping your house in order, 283–284
Kegan, Robert, 234
Kelly, Bill, 403–405
Kelman, Steven, 277, 284
Kennedy, John F., 50*n*1, 267, 375, 409
Kerry, John, 353
Kettering Foundation, 399

Kettl, Donald, 239, 260, 263, 341
Key Diagnostic Questions (KDQs). *See*
  High-Performance Organizations (HPO)
  Diagnostic/Change Model
Key products and services (KPS), 182–183
KEYS instrument, 196, 200*n*8
Khademian, Anne M., 275
Kidder, Rushworth, 43, 49
Kimsey-House, Henry, 134
King, Jim, 284
King, Martin Luther, Jr., 204, 356
King, Steven, 231
Kingdon, John, 316
Kings Bay Naval Base, 311*b*
Kingston, Jack, 299*b*, 300*b*
Kirby, Linda K., 165
Kizer, Kenneth W., 277
Knowledge economy, 24
Knowledge of self, 57–58
Kohut, Andy, 379–380
Krepinevich, Andrew, 275

L

Ladder of inference, 67–69, 68*f*
Lahey, Lisa, 234
Lame-duck appointees, 287
Language and the Pursuit of Happiness
  (Chalmers Brothers), 133
Languages other than English, 207, 385–386
Lao-Tzu, 57, 132
Lathrop, Phil, 240
Lawrence, Paul R., 289
Leadership. *See specific topics*
Leadership (Burns), 24
"Leadership at the 'T'" model (FEI), 140, 140*f*
The Leadership Dojo (Strozzi-Heckler), 134
Leadership philosophy, 191, 192–194
Leadership success model, 55–56, 55*f*
Leader to Leader Journal, 264
Leading Across Boundaries (Linden), 264
Leading Diversity Model, 215–217, 216*t*
Leading Quietly (Badaracco), 48
Leading Teams (Zenger et al.), 167
Leading with Questions (Marquardt), 133
Learned Optimism (Seligman), 80
Learning as priority, 126–128
Learning Journeys (Goldsmith, Kaye, &
  Shelton), 133
Learning the Ropes (Abramson & Lawrence), 289
Lee, Frances, 316
Legislative process. *See* Congress, U.S.
Lehman, John, 283, 284
Lencioni, Patrick, 166
Leveraging Differences website, 235
Lewis, David, 268, 274, 279

Lifeline Exercise, 63, 64*f*
Likert, Rensis, 171–172, 192–193, 196
Lincoln, Abraham, 18, 22, 31–32
Linden, Russ, 263–264
Linney, Barbara, 83
Liotta, P. H., 392
Lipnack, Jessica, 162, 166
Listening
  as conversation skill, 89
  in ECS model, 91, 92–99
  with empathy, 88
  identifying key words or ideas with active
    listening, 103
  impediments to, 97–99
  reflection of feelings, 93–94, 94*b*
  trust and openness in, 92–93, 93*f*
  values-based leadership and, 32
  verbal and nonverbal communication and,
    95–97
Lobbyists, 298–299, 301, 304
Local government, 26, 247*b*, 250, 264,
  290*n*11
Local stakeholders, 300*b*
Locke, John, 407
Lorentzin, Paul, 272
The Lost Art of Listening (Nichols), 109
Loy, James M., 41, 49, 129*b*
Loyal dissent, 43–45, 44*b*
Loyalties, tribal, 257
The Loyalty Effect (Reichheld and Teal),
  324, 325, 338
Luft, Joseph, 70
Lukensmeyer, Carolyn, 348
Lying, 30, 96
*Lying: Moral Choice in Public and Private
  Life* (Bok), 48

M

Mackin, Deborah, 166
Macro-level change, 11–12, 13*f*
Madison, James, 32–33, 205, 236*n*3, 306,
  402–403, 406–407, 408, 411–412
Magic of Dialogue (Yankelovich), 87–89
Mailer, Norman, 76
Maine, 340–341, 397
Management Agenda (Bush), 179, 342–344
Managing Transitions (Bridges), 165
Manhattan Project, 155
Mann, Thomas E., 296, 316
Maranto, Robert, 289
Marcus Aurelius, 59
Markey, Ed, 307–308
Marquardt, Michael, 133
Martin, Tom, 246
Martino, John, 277

Maslow, Abraham, 132, 166
Massachusetts Port Authority, 270
Masterful Coaching (Hargrove), 134
Maxwell Poll on Civic Engagement and
    Inequality, 7
May, Matthew, 124
Mayhew, David, 316
McCain, John, 350, 357
McDermott, Patrice, 348
McGinnis, Patricia, 384
McGregor, Douglas, 119–120, 192–193
McKay, Matthew, 79
McKee, Annie, 78, 79
Mead, Walter Russell, 377
Means values, 190–191
Mechanic clues, 329
Medical Apartheid (Washington), 234
Meetups, 355
Mental wandering and drifting, 99
Mentoring, 74–76. *See also* Coaching
Mergel, Ines, 342
Messaging, 356
Meyerson, Debra, 224–225
Michaels, Judith E., 269–270, 272–273
Micro-level change, 12–13, 13*f*
Military Leadership Diversity Commission
    (DOD), 203
Miller, Jim, 275, 284
Minorities. *See* Diversity
Miskel, James F., 392
Mission/niche thinking, 188
Mission statements, 36*b*
Mistakes, admitting, 40
Mistakes, forgiving, 284
Mobility, 286–287
Monitoring/recovery, 190
Monnet, Jean, 252
Moral courage, 45–46, 45*f*, 52*n*34
Moral Courage (Kidder), 49
Moral decision making, 33–34
Moral horizons, 39*f*
Moral imagination, 34*b*
*Moral Imagination and Management Decision
    Making* (Werhane), 49
Moral values. *See* Values; Values-based
    leadership
Morgan, Nick, 96
Multiple intelligences theory, 120, 120*b*.
    See also Emotional intelligence
Multitasking, 97–98
Musselwhite, Chris, 54, 79
MyBO (my.barackobama.com), 357
Myers-Briggs Type Indicator (MBTI), 57, 142,
    143–144, 167*nn*6–7

N
Nahapiet, Janine, 15
Naim, Moises, 383
Nathan, Richard P., 289
National Aeronautics and Space Administra-
    tion (NASA)
    Challenger and *Columbia* accidents, 32–33
    core purpose of, 35, 51*n*2
    global leadership and, 387, 389*f*
    Goddard Space Flight Center, 218–219,
        219*b*
    political appointees and, 277
    teams, 151
National Archives and Records Administration,
    226
National Association of Hispanic Federal
    Executives, 235
National Coalition for Dialogue and
    Deliberation, 110
National Coalition for Jail Reform, 158
National Continence Management Strategy
    (Australia), 363
National Environmental Protection
    Act, 398
National Highway Traffic Safety Administration
    (NHTSA), 253*b*–254*b*
National Park Service (NPS), 222
National Security Language Initiative, 385
"Nation-Building 101" (Fukuyama), 392
Neill, Margaret James, 65
Newcomer, Kathryn, 269
Newell, Terry, 69
The New Public Service (Denhardt &
    Denhardt), 48
New York City, 290*n*11
The Next Government of the United States
    (Kettl), 263
Nichols, Michael P., 109
Nierenberg, Gerard, 102
9/11 attacks, 1–2, 241, 243
Nine-dot exercise, 123, 127*b*
Nixon, Richard, 267, 398, 400, 406, 408
Nobody in Charge (Cleveland), 263
Nonverbal vs. verbal communication, 95–97
Norms
    collaboration and, 259
    for teams, 158, 159, 161
Norris, Donald F., 348
Norton, David P., 199
Note taking, overintensive, 99
NTL Institute, 235
Nuclear Regulatory Commission, 218
Nunes, Fred, 90
Nye, Joseph, 23, 374, 387, 392

O

Oaths of office, 26
Obama, Barack, and administration
on American exceptionalism, 382
Congress and, 303–304
diplomacy, 380–381
diversity and, 214
election campaign (2008), 356–359, 358*b*
Open Government Directive, 12, 345–349
policies, 270
popularity, 267–268
pre-emptive military action and, 375
transition, 278
Obey, David, 296
O'Brien, Bill, 132
O'Connell, Anne Joseph, 289
Office of Economic Opportunity, 403–404
Office of Government Ethics, 50
Office of Management and Budget (OMB)
Army Corps of Engineers and, 293
Congress and, 295–296
Office of Federal Procurement Policy, 277
Program Assessment Rating Tool (PART), 179, 274
Oil companies, 307–308
Oleszek, Walter, 306, 316
O'Neill, Tip, 404
Open-ended questions, 102
Open for Questions initiative, 348
Open Government Directive (Obama), 12, 345–349
Operating systems values, 191
Oppenheimer, Bruce, 316
Oppenheimer, Robert, 155, 168*n*22
Optimism, in coaching mindset, 122
Organizational Assessment Survey (OAS), 196, 200*n*8
Organizational culture. *See* Culture, organizational
Organizational development, 51*n*19
Organizational Diagnosis (Weisbord), 167
Organizational means vs. constitutional ends, 41
Organizational stage for values, 39–42
Organizational structure, 184–185
Organizational values, 39–42, 59, 60*b*, 63*b*
Orientation, 157–158, 282
Ornstein, Norman J., 296, 316
Osbourne, Larry, 166
Other awareness, 55*f*, 56
Other efficacy, 56
Ouchi, William, 275
Outside-in approach, 260
Oversight, congressional, 303, 309–310

P

Packer, George, 296
Paine, Thomas, 374
Panagopoulous, Costas, 316
Papaj, Ken, 258
Paradox, 124
Parker, Michael, 293–294, 296, 314–315
Parks, Rosa, 398, 408
Participation 2.0, 342, 348, 356, 358*b*
Participation in government. *See also* Technology and e-governance
involving others, 33
Jefferson and, 396
organizational development and, 51*n*19
responsiveness and, 407–411
trust and, 397–400
understanding how government works, 400–411
Partisanship, 296–297
Partnering Intelligence (Dent), 263
Patterson, Kerry, 109
Patton, Bruce, 84, 109
People Express Airlines, 184
Performance. *See also* High-Performance Organizations (HPO) Diagnostic/Change Model
financial, 178–180
of government, 2–3
vision to performance spiral, 186–190, 187*f*
Performance evaluations, teams and, 148–149, 168*n*17
"Permanent whitewater," 130
Perry, Rick, 363
Personality
Congress and, 304–305
self-awareness, 57–58
teams and, 142–144, 143*f*, 167*nn*6–7
Personal office staffers, 310–313, 311*b*
Personal values, 27, 59, 60*b*, 63*b*
Petraeus, David, 388
Pew Global Attitudes Project, 378, 379, 393
Pfiffner, James P., 272, 289
Phillips, Donald, 49
"Pick 3," 179
Pickering, Thomas, 390
Pink, Daniel, 199
Plouffe, David, 356
Poist, Betsy, 101
Political appointees, 265–292
overview, 265–266
agency cultures and, 275–276
bureaucracy, stereotypes of, 266–268
bureaucrats, quality of, 268–270

change agents and laggards in agencies and, 276–277
competencies, 273–274
forgiving, 284
initiating communication with, 281–283
lame-duck, 287
outside consultants hired by, 283
putting oneself in shoes of, 280–281
reorganizations by, 284
reputation and stereotypes, 270–274, 279–280
resources on, 289
tips for success with, 288–289
transitions, managing, 278–288
worst and best ideas of, 287–288
Political-industrial complex, 274
Political polarization, 296–297
Political Savvy (DeLuca), 263
The Politics of Presidential Appointments, 274
Porras, Jerry, 24
Porter, Lawrence, 65
Portfolios, 304
The Post American World (Zakaria), 392
Powell, Colin, 285, 375, 382
Power
dialogue and, 88
power center wheels, 403–404, 404*f*, 405*f*, 406*f*
soft and hard, 23, 373, 387
Powerful Conversations (Harkins), 109
Preamble to the Constitution, 18, 27
Presence-Based Coaching (Silsbee), 134–135
President's Advisory Council on Executive Organization, 408
Price, David E., 317
Pricewaterhouse Coopers (PWC), 390
Privacy vs. security, 412
Privilege, Power, and Difference (Johnson), 233–234
Problem solving, inquiry and, 100
Procurement Executives Association, 277
Productive and counterproductive behaviors, 195
Professional values, 28–29
Profile of Organizational Characteristics (Likert), 196
Program Assessment Rating Tool (PART), OMB, 179, 274
Project Management Institute, 199
ProRanger internship program, 222
Prosci, 200
Public, education of, 37
Public perceptions. *See also* Experience and clue management; Trust

of agencies, 10, 11*f*
bureaucracy, reputation of, 266–268
of government, 3–5, 5*f*
political appointees, reputation of, 270–274
Public purpose, 35, 36*b*
Public Service, Ethics, and Constitutional Practice (Rohr), 48
Public service, fostering sense of, 40
Public Service and Democracy (Gawthrop), 48
Public speaking, 114–115
Public stage for values, 35–39
Purpose
collaboration and, 243–244
dialogue and, 86
public, 35, 36*b*

Q

Quality, measurement of, 174–180, 177*f*
Questions
clarifying, 95
closed-ended, 107
for effective inquiry, 101–103, 101*f*
one at a time, 103
open-ended, 102
questing mindset, 114*b*
rhetorical, 102
Questions, diagnostic. *See* High-Performance Organizations (HPO) Diagnostic/ Change Model
The Quest to Become 'One' (Linden), 263–264

R

Race Matters (West), 234
Racial diversity, 208, 213*t*
Reading Book on Human Relations Training (Cooke et al.), 78
Reagan, Ronald, 50*n*1, 267, 271, 375
Recovery.gov, 347–348
Redistricting, 297
"Redrawing the Map of the Future" (Liotta & Miskel), 392
Reflection of feelings, 93–94, 94*b*
Regulations.gov, 347*b*
Reichheld, Frederick F., 324, 325, 338
Reid, Harry, 304
Relationship behaviors in teams, 156
Relationships
collaborative, 246–249, 247*b*
emotional intelligence and management of, 16*b*
power center wheels, 403–404, 404*f*, 405*f*, 406*f*
in teams, 146–147, 148–149, 148*t*
trust and, 13–15, 14*b*

Religious diversity, 211
Reorganizations by political appointees, 284
Republican National Convention (2000), 351
Resolution, in values spiral, 195–196
Resonant Leadership (Boyatzis & McKee), 78
Resource planning, 190
Respect and inquiry skills, 100
The Responsible Administrator (Cooper), 48
Responsiveness of government, 407–411
Rhetorical questions, 102
Ridge, Tom, 241, 243, 244, 246, 250
Right Question Project, 399
Rilke, Rainer Maria, 122
Risk and trust, 126
Rockman, Bert A., 269, 273–274
Roet, Brian, 79
Rogers, Carl, 92–93
Rohr, John, 48
Romer, Paul, 242, 248
Rosenblatt, Alan, 367
Rosensweig, Philip, 386
Ross, Lynn C., 270, 275–276
Rubin, Robert, 257
Rumsfeld, Donald, 276

S
Sacred Hoops (Jackson), 122
Saint-Exupéry, Antoine de, 119
Salmoni, Barak A., 372
Same-sex marriage, 212
Satisfaction. *See also* Experience and clue
    management
    emotional perceptions and satisfaction
        surveys, 323–326, 325*t*
    high marks given to agencies, 268
    trust and, 11, 12*f*, 323*f*
Saunders, Paul, 378, 380
Scaggs, Ben, 40
Scalzi, John, 364
Schneider, Ralf, 390
Schuck, Peter H., 392
Schwartz, Shalom, 51*n*11
Scott, Susan, 133–134
Seccia, Peter, 279
Security vs. privacy, 412
Seinfeld, Jerry, 114
Self as stage for values, 43–46
Self-awareness, 53–81
    overview, 53–55
    autobiography and Lifeline Exercise,
        61–63, 64*f*
    diversity and, 229
    emotional intelligence and, 16*b*
    feedback and, 70–74, 70*f*, 71*f*

finding time for, 76–77
journal keeping, 65–67, 66*b*
knowledge of self, 57–58
ladder of inference, 67–69, 68*f*
mentoring and executive coaching for,
    74–76
in model of leadership success, 55–56, 55*f*
resources on, 78–81
tips for success, 77–78
values exploration, 59–61, 60*b*, 62*b*–63*b*, 81
Self-Awareness and the Effective Leader
    (Musselwhite), 79
Self-disclosure, 69, 71
Self-efficacy, 56, 58
Self-Esteem (McKay & Fanning), 79
Self-management, emotional intelligence
    and, 16*b*
Self-oriented behaviors in teams, 156
Self-pride, 182
Self-reflection, 69
Seligman, Martin, 80
Senate. *See* Congress, U.S.
Senge, Peter, 234
Servant Leadership (Greenleaf), 23
"Service Clues and Customer Assessment of
    the Service Experience" (Berry &
    Carbone), 337
Service First initiative, 256–257
Sexual orientation, 211–212
Shackleton, Ernest, 144, 166, 168*n*9
Shakespeare, William, 74
Shank, Joshua, 316
Shaw, George Bernard, 82
Shelton, Ken, 133
Shrage, Michael, 258
Shriver, Sargent, 400, 403
Shulman, Stuart, 347*b*
Silence, effective use of, 103
Silsbee, Doug, 134–135
Six-Box Model, 147–151, 148*t*
Size of government, 2
Smart phone, 357, 358*b*–359*b*
Smith, Douglas K., 137, 166
Social awareness, 16*b*
Social capital, 15–16
"Social Intelligence and the Biology of
    Leadership" (Goleman & Boyatzis), 109
Social networking websites, 356–357
Soft power, 23, 373, 387
Soft Power (Nye), 392
Soldier, Statesman, Peacemaker (Uldrich), 49
Somoza, Anastasio, 396
South (Shackleton), 144, 166, 168*n*9
Southwest Airlines, 184

So You Want to Be in Government?
  (Nathan), 289
Speeding Up the Learning Curve (DeSeve), 289
The Speed of Trust (Covey), 263
Spending in government, growth of, 2
Staffers, congressional, 308–309, 310–314, 311*b*
Stakeholders
  collaboration and, 244–245, 244*f*
  Congress and, 294, 299–301, 300*b*
  high performance and, 180
Stalin, Joseph, 400
Stamps, Jeffrey, 162, 166
Standahl, Phil, 134
State government, 26, 260–261, 264, 290*n*11
State of the World Forum, 27–28
STATFOR, 393
Stereotypes
  of bureaucrats, 266–268
  of political appointees, 270–274
  transitions and, 279–280
Stewardship mindset, 197
Sticky Teams (Osbourne), 166
Stone, Douglas, 84, 109
StoryCorps, 235
Storytelling, 226
Strategic customer value analysis (SCVA),
  180, 181*f*
Strategy/business model, 184
Strong Vocational Interest Bank, 57
Strozzi-Heckler, Richard, 134
Success for the New Global Manager (Dalton
  et al.), 391–392
Supportive behaviors in teams, 156
Support systems, assessment of, 185
Swann, Brian, 252*b*
Systems 1, 2, 3, and 4 (Likert), 193
Systems thinking, 67
Szasz, Thomas, 77

T
Talmadge, Herman, 35
Tannenbaum, Robert, 55
Task behaviors in teams, 156
Task forces, joint, 257
Teal, Thomas, 324, 325, 338
The Team-Building Tool Kit (Mackin &
  Harrington-Mackin), 166
Teams, 137–169. *See also* Collaboration with
  other organizations
  overview, 137–138
  case for, 138–140
  complex environment and, 144–145
  cross-representational, 155
  facilitation, professional, 152, 152*f*

high information diversity and low value
  diversity, 52*n*29
interdependent tasks and, 146
inviting people to leave, 168*n*14
levels of collaboration, 154*t*, 156–157
membership, 153, 154–155, 154*t*
organizational environment and Six-Box
  Model, 147–153, 148*t*
personality and style concerns, 142–144,
  143*f*
processes, 154*t*, 157–161
purpose of, 145–146, 148, 148*t*
relationships in, 146–147, 148–149, 148*t*
resources on, 165–167
rewards and incentives, 148–149, 148*t*
roles, 154*t*, 155–156
short-term vs. long-term, 146
tips for success, 165
trust and, 141–142, 146–147, 169*n*29
virtual, 137–138, 161–164
Technology and e-governance, 340–370
  overview, 340–342
  blogs, 354, 369*n*33
  Bush's Management Agenda, 342–344
  digital divide, 349
  e-politics and election campaigns, 349–359
  e-rulemaking, 346*b*–347*b*
  Government 1.0 vs. 2.0 and Participation
    2.0, 342
  in government agency context, 359–365
  Obama's Open Government Initiative,
    345–349
  resources on, 365–367
  social networking websites, 356–357
  teams and technology, 138, 164
  tips for success, 365
  21st-century technological change, 130
Telling Lies (Ekman), 96
Texas, 363
The Art of Possibility (Zander & Zander), 134
Theory of business thinking, 188
"A Theory of Human Motivation"
  (Maslow), 166
Theory X and Theory Y, 119–120, 193
The Prune Book (Trattner), 289
The Strategic Presidency (Pfiffner), 289
360 degree assessments, 73–74
Throughput measures, 190
Through the Labyrinth (Eagly & Carli), 166
Tichy, Noel, 181
Timing, political, 303
Tocqueville, Alexis de, 393*n*8
Tolstoy, Leo, 266
Toyota, 124

Training, joint, 257
Transactional leadership, 24
Transformational leadership, 24
Transitions management, 278–288
Transparency, 283, 348, 362
Transportation Security Administration
    (TSA), 41, 326
Trattner, John H., 289
Tribal loyalties, 257
Truman, Harry S., 203, 398
Trust, 1–20
    in America on world stage, 374–375
    coaching and, 125–126
    collaboration and, 246–249, 247b
    communication and, 92
    Congress and, 297–299, 299b
    congressional staffers and, 312
    decline in, 3–4, 8f, 267–268
    defined, 13–14
    dialogue and, 88
    e-governance and, 364
    experience and, 319–322, 323f
    within federal government, 9–10, 9t, 14b
    global leadership and, 372–373, 378–379
    importance of, 395–396
    in institutions and career leaders, 5–7
    leadership role in building, 10–13
    participation and, 397–400
    political appointees and, 275
    in politics and political leaders, 3–5, 5f
    power centers and, 404
    public perceptions and, 10, 10f
    relationships and, 13–15, 14b
    risk and, 126
    satisfaction and, 11, 12f
    signaling willingness to trust, 125
    social capital and, 15–16
    teams and, 141–142, 146–147, 169n29
    values-based leadership and, 23–24
Truth, in conversation, 84–85
"The Truth Behind the Smile and Other
    Myths" (Morgan), 96
Truth-telling, 30–31, 31b
Turnley, William, 15
Turn Your Face (Linney), 83
Tuskegee Syphilis Study, 22, 51n4

U
Uldrich, Jack, 49
Ulysses program (PWC), 390
Understanding America (Wilson & Schuck),
    392
Unlocking the Power of Networks (Goldsmith &
    Kettl), 263

U.S. Access Board, 347b
U.S. Advisory Commission on Public
    Diplomacy, 385
U.S. Air Force, 42
U.S. Army, 188
USAspending.gov, 347
U.S. Census Bureau, 222–223
U.S. Coast Guard, 129b
U.S. Forest Service, 256–257
U.S. Marine Corps, 24, 25b, 371–372, 388
U.S. Mint, 277, 318–319
U.S. Navy, 186, 196, 311b, 335–336
USS Benfold, 335–336

V
Vaill, Peter, 130
Valenti, Jack, 304
Values
    behavioral, 191, 194–195
    conflicting, 60–61, 63b
    core, 22–23, 25b, 26–29, 27b, 28f,
        40–41, 42f
    diversity and, 206
    means, 190–191
    operating systems, 191, 194
    organizational, 39–42, 59, 60b, 63b
    personal, 27–28, 59, 60b, 63b
    professional, 28–29
    self-efficacy and, 58
Values-based leadership, 21–52
    overview, 21–22
    career leaders and, 25–26
    guiding values, 26–29
    humility and, 46–47
    importance of, 22–24
    on organizational stage, 39–42
    on public stage, 35–39
    resources on, 48–50
    self and, 43–46
    self-awareness and, 56
    skills for, 30–34
    tips for success, 47
Values exploration, 59–61, 60b, 62b–63b, 81
Values to work culture spiral, 191–196, 192f
Van de Walle, Steven, 10, 11f
Ventura, Jesse, 350
Verbal vs. nonverbal communication, 95–97
Veterans Administration (VA), 406
Veterans Health Administration, 52n27,
    277, 326
Virtual teams, 137–138, 161–164
Virtual Teams (Lipnack & Stamps), 166
Vision to performance spiral, 186–190, 187f
Vital Smarts, 110

W

Waiting for Leadership (O'Connell), 289
Waldo, Dwight, 37, 38*f*
Wall, Eileen, 337
Wall Street Reform and Consumer Protection
  Act, 302–303
War on Poverty, 399
Washington, George, 26, 46–47, 376, 402
Washington, Harriet, 234
Watching America, 393
Websites. *See* Technology and e-governance
Weintraub, Joseph R., 134
Weisbord, Marvin R., 147, 148*t*, 167, 172
Welch, Jack, 126
Wenger, Etiene C., 166
Werhane, Patricia, 49
West, Cornel, 234
West, Darrell, 344, 365
"What Makes Customers Tick" (Carbone), 337
Whitworth, Laura, 134
Who Moved My Cheese? (Johnson), 78–79
WIIFM question ("What's in it for me?"), 250,
  251*b*, 255
WikiLeaks, 381
Wikipedia, 345, 352
Wikis, 345, 364
Wilcox, Harvey, 279, 283, 284, 288
Wilhelm, Thomas, 371
Wilson, James Q., 392
Wilson, Woodrow, 376, 401, 408

Wilsonian school of thought, 377
Winthrop, John, 21, 375, 393*n*10
The Wisdom of Teams (Katzenbach &
  Smith), 166
Witt, James Lee, 276, 277, 284
Women
  changing roles and expectations, 209–210
  in federal workforce, 213*t*, 214
  Ramona Barth's campaign for, 413
  teams and, 151
Woodcock, Janet, 127
Wooden, John, 121
Workforce diversity, 208, 209, 213–215, 213*t*
Working Assets, 362
Work management and control processes, 186
Work processes, assessment of, 186
The World Is Flat (Friedman), 263
Wright, Jeremiah, 356

Y

Yankelovich, Daniel, 87–89
Yordi, Bonni, 233
YouTube, 356–357, 359*b*

Z

Zakaria, Fareed, 376, 382, 392
Zaltman, Gerald, 320, 338
Zander, Benjamin, 134
Zander, Rosamund, 134
Zenger, John H., 167